British Football and Social Change

Dedication

JW For Zelda Malak Fazaeli — a 'fan' who has *always* kept
my feet on the ground.

SW For my friend Tom Sullivan: socialist, supporter of Northampton Town and the man whom the players of
Kingsthorpe United Under 9's XI call 'Boss'.

British Football and Social Change:
Getting into Europe

Edited by
John Williams and Stephen Wagg

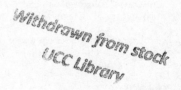

Leicester University Press
Leicester, London and New York

© Editors and Contributors 1991

First published in Great Britain in 1991 by Leicester University Press
(a division of Pinter Publishers)

Editorial offices
Fielding Johnson Building, University of Leicester, University Road,
Leicester, LE1 7RH, England

Trade and other enquiries
25 Floral Street, London, WC2E 9DS, England

British Library cataloguing in publication data
A CIP catalogue record for this book is available from the British Library.
ISBN 0 7185 1371 1 (hb)
     0 7185 1410 6 (pb)

For enquiries in North America please contact
PO Box 197, Irvington, NY 10533

Library of Congress Cataloging-in-Publication Data
British football and social change/edited by John Williams and Stephen Wagg.
    p. cm.
  Includes bibliographical references and index.
  1. Soccer—Social aspects—Great Britain. I. Williams, John
(John M.)   II. Wagg, Stephen.
GV944.G7B75   1991
796.334'0941—dc20   91-27553
                                                             CIP

Typeset by Witwell Ltd, Southport
Printed and bound in Great Britain by Biddles Ltd of Guildford and Kings Lynn

Contents

The contributors   vii
Introduction   ix

Part I: Politics and economics

1. English football in the 1990s: taking Hillsborough seriously?   3
   Ian Taylor

2. North and South: the rivalry of the Football League and the
   Football Association   25
   Alan Tomlinson

3. Rich man, poor man: economic arrangements in the Football
   League   48
   Tony Arnold

Part II: Playing

4. Putting on the style: aspects of recent English football   67
   Chas Critcher

5. Can play, will play? Women and football in Britain   85
John Williams and Jackie Woodhouse

Part III: Following

6. Walking alone together: football supporters and their
relationship with the game   111
Rogan Taylor

7. Playing at home: British football and a sense of place   130
John Bale

8. An era of the end, or the end of an era: Football and youth
culture in Britain   145
Steve Redhead

9. Having an away day: English football spectators and the
hooligan debate   160
John Williams

Part IV: Getting into Europe

10. The politics of football in the new Europe   187
Vic Duke

11. On the periphery: Scotland, Scottish football and the
new Europe   201
H. F. Moorhouse

12. Playing the past: the media and the England football team   220
Stephen Wagg

13. It's not a knockout: English football and globalisation   239
Adrian Goldberg and Stephen Wagg

Index   254

The contributors

Ian Taylor is professor of Sociology at the University of Salford. He is perhaps best known for being one of the co-authors of two seminal texts on criminology, *The New Criminology* and *Critical Criminology*, which were published by Routledge in the 1970s. His book *Law and Order: Arguments for Socialism* was published by Macmillan in 1981. He has written a number of articles on football and society since the late 1960s.

Alan Tomlinson is Reader in Sport and Leisure Studies at Brighton Polytechnic. He has edited a number of books in the fields of sport and leisure, the latest of which is *Consumption, Identity and Style* (Routledge, 1990).

Tony Arnold is Senior Lecturer in the Department of Accounting and Financial Management at Essex University and has written widely on the economics of football.

Chas Critcher is a Principal Lecturer in Communication Studies at Sheffield Polytechnic. He was co-author, with Stuart Hall and others, of *Policing the Crisis* (Macmillan, 1978) and, with John Clarke, of *The Devil Makes Work: Leisure in Capitalist Britain* (Macmillan, 1985). He has written several articles on sport.

John Williams works at the Sir Norman Chester Centre for Football Research and, with Eric Dunning and Patrick Murphy, wrote *Hooligans Abroad* (1984, second edition 1989), *The Roots of Football Hooliganism* (1988) and *Football on Trial* (1990), all published by Routledge.

Jackie Woodhouse is a researcher at the Sir Norman Chester Centre, where she is looking into aspects of women's relationship to football.

Rogan Taylor is a Research Associate of the Sir Norman Chester Centre and is researching the history of supporters' organisations. He also helped to found the Football Supporters' Association, and was its first chairperson.

John Bale is a geographer, teaching in the Department of Education at Keele University. He is the author of *Sport and Place* (Hurst, 1983).

Steve Redhead is Reader in Law at Manchester Polytechnic and Director of the Unit for Law and Popular Culture there. He has written two books: *Sing When You're Winning* (Pluto Press, 1987) and *The End-of-the-Century Party* (Manchester University Press, 1990). His third and fourth, *Football with Attitude* (Wordsmith, 1991) and *Unpopular Cultures* (Manchester University Press, 1992) are forthcoming.

Vic Duke is Senior Lecturer in Sociology at the University of Salford. He has published articles in political sociology and the sociology of sport and his book *A Measure of Thatcherism*, written with Stephen Edgell, was published in 1991 (Harper Collins). He is a member of the 92 Club of people who have watched matches on all of the 92 grounds of the Football League.

H. F. Moorhouse is Senior Lecturer in Sociology at Glasgow University. He edits *Work, Employment and Society*, a journal of the British Sociological Association. He has written widely on the social and cultural context of Scottish football.

Stephen Wagg is Lecturer in Sociology at East Warwickshire College, Rugby and Tutor in Sociology at the University of Leicester. His book, *The Football World: A Contemporary Social History*, was published by Harvester in 1984 and he has written a number of articles on the mass media.

Adrian Goldberg was a founder and co-editor of the football fanzine *Off The Ball* and, between 1989 and 1991, worked as a researcher in the Sir Norman Chester Centre. He is now a freelance journalist, based in Birmingham.

Introduction

The last twenty or so years have seen the emergence of a cogent, often — but not always — academic, discourse on football and British society. The main manifestations of this have been a growing body of 'serious' books and articles, the rise of the Football Supporters' Association, the growth of the fanzine movement and the establishment in 1987 of the Sir Norman Chester Centre for Football Research at Leicester University. All of the writers featured here have played some part in these developments and this book has, naturally, been conceived as a further collective contribution.

The book grew out of a conference called 'Football and Europe', held in Florence in the spring of 1990 and attended by many of the authors. There has been a shared resolve to take stock of changes in the British football world and to trace its history back past the turbulent 1980s — which brought more hooliganism, Bradford, Heysel, Hillsborough and the subsequent Taylor Report — while, at the same time, facing the future in the 'New Europe' after 1992. All the essays, with their various foci, attempt to do this.

The first three chapters look broadly at the *football world* itself. **Ian Taylor** offers an assessment of English League football in the wake of the Taylor Report on the Hillsborough disaster, and judges the political implications of that report; **Alan Tomlinson** deals historically with the rivalry between English football's main administrative bodies, the Football League and the Football Association, and examines its roots in class and region; and **Tony Arnold** offers a detailed analysis of the economics of the Football League clubs — an analysis which provides a base for a number of the later chapters.

The next two essays are about *playing* football. **Chas Critcher** looks at the history of tactics and interprets the English style of football in terms of ideas of masculinity, Englishness, and 'race'. **John Williams** and **Jackie Woodhouse** deal, similarly, with questions of gender in the context of the history of women's football and women as spectators and administrators in the professional game. The following four chapters are about *watching* football. **Rogan Taylor** recounts something of the history of supporters' clubs. **John Bale** discusses the relationship, now threatened in many instances, between the football supporter and his/her local ground. **Steve Redhead** links the world of the football fan to contemporary youth and pop culture and offers an optimistic view of the future of the English football crowd. **John Williams**, perhaps slightly less sanguine, weighs some recent contributions to the debate on hooliganism.

The final four essays are variously about Europe. **Vic Duke** details the repercussions in the football labour market of the break-up of the Eastern bloc and the onset of '1992'. **H. F. Moorhouse** outlines the place of football in Scottish culture and, in that context, discusses the tension between tradition, typified by Glasgow Celtic and others, and modernity, oriented toward Europe and represented by Glasgow Rangers.

Stephen Wagg explores the atavistic impulses in the English popular papers and argues that, in their coverage, the England football team has remained a metaphor for Britain itself and its decline. Finally, **Adrian Goldberg** and **Stephen Wagg** discuss football clubs in relation to globalisation and some of the many implications for football of the modern communications revolution.

Many thanks to Janet Tiernan and Ann Ketnor of the Sir Norman Chester Centre for typing much of the manuscript.

Part I:
Politics and economics

1
English football in the 1990s: taking Hillsborough seriously?

Ian Taylor

Discussion of the future of English soccer is obviously now impossible without reference to the disaster at Hillsborough on 15 April 1989 and the ensuing Reports of the Official Inquiry conducted by Mr Justice Taylor. The disaster itself was the 'end-point' — the logical conclusion — of those forms of political and journalistic discussion of football which had developed throughout the late 1960s, the 1970s, and the 1980s, articulated almost entirely around a 'law and order' theme and the identification of soccer's problems almost exclusively with the issue of hooliganism. Ninety-five Liverpool supporters died whilst penned into a human cage at the Leppings Lane end which had been reconstructed in the early 1970s as a response to 'crowd trouble'. The emergency itself, in its first fateful minutes, being understood not only by the police but also by the watching media and football authorities, as a further instance of ever-familiar 'trouble in the crowd'. In the aftermath of Hillsborough, nearly all commentators on English football now recognise the exhaustion of this kind of law and order talk, and practice, as a serious response to the problems and opportunities confronting English soccer.

But the Hillsborough disaster, for all of its catastrophic consequences for the ninety-five dead fans, their families and friends, was also vital for the kind of creative response which it provoked amongst 'ordinary' football fans and, indeed, amongst 'ordinary people' at large, including those who do not themselves go to football or even particularly like it. One of my key purposes in this chapter is to try to recall and to highlight some of these important 'cultural aspects' of the Hillsborough disaster.[1] No matter that the future of English football will crucially be shaped by the economic forces of a free market society, I would still argue that the present condition of football in England can only really be understood in terms of an exploration of football's relationship to working class culture and to popular culture in the past. It may also be the case that any attempt to reorganise English football which ignores the powerful and cultural specific significance of football to class and local identity may be quite fatally flawed. The popular response to Hillsborough constituted a powerful but momentary symbolic expression of those relationships.

The 'official response' to the Hillsborough disaster, in the shape of the Taylor Report,[2] constitutes an important moment in its own right in the history of English football — not simply because it is *the* official response to English football's worst-ever disaster, but specifically because the Report did turn out, against the expectations of many,[3] to be a sophisticated, sympathetic and creative intervention into the condition of the English Football League. Written from a position outside the 'law and order' rhetorics of previous inquiries,[4] the Taylor Report has been broadly understood as having offered 'a lifeline to English football', and in the afterword to this chapter, I will offer a series of observations on developments in English football since the publication of the Taylor Report. These observations will be 'realistic' enough to recognise that many of the problems of English soccer discussed in that Report are economic (in whose financial interest is it to invest in the wholesale reconstruction of the English football ground?), but they will hopefully also be historically and sociologically enough aware to remember the essential cultural and human lessons of Hillsborough.

Hillsborough

In this first part of the chapter, I want to 'retrieve' six different aspects of the disaster at the Hillsborough stadium on 15 April 1989 — the ground on which I watched my first soccer in the late 1940s.

1. The soccer ground as a shrine

I want first to recall the way in which the supporters of Liverpool — and, indeed, the supporters of Nottingham Forest (their semi-final rivals on that fateful day) and the fans of the host club, Sheffield Wednesday, and of Everton, Liverpool's Merseyside rivals — responded in the immediate aftermath of the disaster itself. The overnight decoration of the Leppings Lane entrance, and other accessible parts of the Hillsborough stadium, with flowers, wreaths and a vast range of football memorabilia (scarves, hats, rosettes, programmes, etc.) was a mass popular rite largely without parallel in Britain this century. Nothing similar had followed the Kings Cross Underground Station fire in 1987 or the Southern Region railway accidents of 1988 and 1989 (the month before Hillsborough), although there were reports of the traditional maritime ceremonials marking the sinking of the *Herald of Free Enterprise* — the throwing of wreaths on to the waters of Zeebrugge Harbour. The decoration of Anfield and Hillsborough had no such formal quality, however. Mourners carried with them to the ground, and left behind in the goals, the most basic, personal and apparently trivial of memorabilia. One television clip showed a quite elderly Sheffield Wednesday supporter depositing what was presumably his only personal copy of the 1966 FA Cup Final programme (played between Sheffield Wednesday and Everton) — the only close connection he could make 'affectively' with Liverpool. The only parallel to this simple offering of minimalist but intensely personal belongings that I have ever witnessed was the Shrine of Guadaloupe, in Mexico City. During my visit there in 1970, I saw poor peasants and others, all with desperate physical illnesses or crippling disabilities, crawl across the forecourt of the church to make humble offerings to their God. I was also reminded, when looking at the Anfield and Hillsborough shrines, of the much more formalised annual rituals in Derbyshire, the 'well-dressings', where flowers are fashioned into what are known as shrines, dedicated usually to particular saints, or, in some villages, to pagan godheads.

The pictures of the shrines shown on television, and, later, the repeated photographs carried in the daily press and in specialist soccer magazines, also reminded me how soccer stadia have historically for long periods been the objects of what we might call popular sanctification.[5] Certainly the description of Hillsborough used in the 1950s by my father as we got off the tram at Parkside Road, and walked along Penistone Road to spend a few minutes outside the Players' Entrance (hoping for a glimpse, perhaps, of Albert Quixall, the 'Golden Boy' of the Hillsborough faithful) was that we had come to 'the shrine'. When pitch invasions began, in 1962, and continued over subsequent years, I was insistently told, by both my father and my uncle, that this *never* happened 'in their day' because, in their day, they said, the pitch was *sacred*. In several newspaper reports written about Hillsborough, especially those emphasising the way in which the magnitude of the disaster had occasioned an enormous show of solidarity between soccer supporters and a suspension of the aggravation and enmity that has characterised football rivalry, there was a heartfelt sense that the creation of these shrines at Anfield and Hillsborough might mark the cleansing of a sport scarred since the early 1960s by divisiveness and violence. Such hopes were given further sustenance, and an ironic, symbolic significance, by the sight on television of Liverpool and Everton fans reverently parading around Goodison Park with ninety-five red and blue scarves knotted together in a continuous line, before the start of the Everton–Liverpool league game on 10 May, some twenty-five days after the disaster. When Liverpool went on to beat Everton 3–2 in the 1989 Cup Final at Wembley, press reports suggested that fans of both clubs were present during the traditional homecoming in almost equal numbers and that there was a 'roaring trade in Liverpool hats and badges' bought by Everton fans in tribute to the ninety-five dead of Hillsborough.[6]

2. The ground as an emblem of locality

The reconstruction of the ground as a shrine is a natural extension of existing relationships of the club to the fan: football grounds across the country have always had an almost religious hold on football fans and, indeed, on the families and kin on whom these, mainly male, fans have imposed their weekend and midweek-evening obsession. In different parts of the country, however, these shrines have taken on a particularly important additional significance as an *emblem of locality* (see Bale's essay in this volume), often quite widely shared, irrespective of gender position. Sheffield itself, unlike Liverpool (with its inimitable waterfront and its Victorian and Georgian arcades) or

Manchester (with its venerable Victorian insurance buildings and St. Peter's and Albert Squares), is a northern industrial city with no really outstanding architectural or other features (although lovers of the city, like myself, will always speak fondly of the Crucible Theatre, right in the city centre, and then fervently of the Peak District, on the city's doorstep, as unsurpassable features of the place). For many working Sheffielders, however, the symbol of the city's local pride (particularly since the closure of Bramall Lane as a Yorkshire cricket ground) has been Hillsborough itself, which has been remodelled and upgraded consistently over the years and, in the football community itself and beyond, is widely regarded as one of the best and most modern of stadiums for spectator sport in Britain. In the recently re-released and quite marvellous survey of *Football Grounds of Great Britain*, Simon Inglis observes about Hillsborough that:

[it] has proved that a club can provide all the facilities that a supporter wants, without robbing the surroundings of its intrinsic character. It is surely no coincidence that Wednesday men are always ready to talk about the club and about Hillsborough, and about the city of Sheffield that everyone seems to love . . . a visit to Hillsborough on a crisp, autumn afternoon remains one of the quintessential joys of English sport.[7]

In the local paper, the *Sheffield Star*, on the Monday after the disaster, a long-time local, Sheffield-born sports reporter, Paul Thompson, wrote in sorrow and in dismay: 'Oh no . . . not Hillsborough. Wednesday and their supporters are trying to come to terms with the fact that football's worse tragedy has occurred where anybody would have least expected it. . .'[8] He quotes Rita Nettleship, secretary of the Supporters' Club, as puzzling over the irony that 'If it had happened at any of the other grounds we have criticized . . . but at Hillsborough?' and he concludes: 'It is so sad that one of football's old clubs, run by decent men, is now synonymous not with sport, but with death on a grand scale . . . That is why the club and its followers can barely comprehend what has happened to them.'[9]

In Liverpool itself, the importance of the club to 'the people' was being displayed in ways which confounded even the most seasoned of footballers and football managers themselves. As Jeremy Seabrook so succinctly put it, this may be because football 'continues to reach' some aspects of the social being which cannot be fulfilled in private life or in ritualised public consumerism. That is to say, football continues, obstinately and insistently, to represent 'the passion of locality and of places once associated with something other than football teams'.[10] In the case of Liverpool, this has an unbearably tragic quality, since: '[in this] great maritime city, with its decayed function rooted in an archaic Imperial and industrial past, sport now has to bear a freight of symbolism that it can scarcely contain.'[11]

3. Hillsborough and the question of modernisation

Reactions to the Hillsborough disaster in the pages of the financial press in Britain as well as in the North American press as a whole placed an enormous emphasis on the issue of modernisation, or, more accurately, the total *lack of modernisation* of English soccer stadiums.[12] Particular attention was given to the fact that — with only a handful of exceptional cases — the vast majority of football clubs in England and Wales play in stadiums that were originally built before 1900. By implication, the argument which was being advanced in these reports was that this 'failure to modernise' was a key cause of British soccer's problems with both crowd safety and hooliganism.

The failure of English soccer clubs to modernise provision for spectators is legendary. At the majority of clubs, the only routine modernisation that seems to be contemplated, between seasons, is the repair of terraces and crash barriers and, during the 1970s, the introduction of perimeter fencing. The quality of seating, of toilets, of public address systems, and of first-aid facilities remains derisory. The standard half-time experience at the average English soccer club, in 1989, was of a ten-minute wait in line for a tepid and tasteless cup of tea in a polystyrene cup, for the English meat pie (a food item which would not be offered, in most countries in continental Europe, to a dog). What might have been taken for granted by a working-class soccer supporter in 1949 was unacceptable forty years later, in a society whose consciousness of the quality of food, and of consumer service generally, has significantly, if unevenly, expanded.

In the aftermath of the Hillsborough disaster, the blindness of football's Boards of Directors to the question of modernisation of spectator security and well-being, in particular, has quite properly become a part of football's agenda for change. The Taylor Report itself must be understood as a reprimand to Football League Clubs not only with regard to their failures in respect of crowd safety but also in respect of the general poverty of provision by clubs for paying spectators of comfort, entertainment, and refreshments, and, in general, of a worthwhile product or service to consumers.

I would like to suggest, however, that the response to Hillsborough which saw in it *only* the failure of soccer to modernise is a misleading and partial account of what happened at Hillsborough on 15 April 1989. (It also suppresses the fact that the disaster occurred, as we have already suggested, in a stadium in which very significant modernisation *had* taken place, notably in the mid-1960s, in preparation for the World Cup games of 1966.) The really definitive truth about Hillsborough, and the deaths of ninety-five people, was not 'the absence of modern provision', although this may have placed a really important role on the communication problems that were evident between the club and the police, in the mêlée developing outside the Leppings Lane end turnstiles before the kick-off; and it was certainly underlined by the appalling absence of first-aid provision and emergency preparedness in the aftermath of the disaster itself. The determining cause, if this is the appropriate word, of the Hillsborough disaster was the way in which the Leppings Lane terrace, like so many of the 'popular ends' at English soccer grounds, had been reconstructed over the years as a caged-in 'pen', from which there was no means of escape at a predictable moment of crisis of mass spectator excitement and anxiety. It is vital to understand that this process of caging-in a section of the soccer audience, identifiable with that portion of the underclass seen to be generally and universally capable of violent behaviour, is a social process – and a process that focuses, like the prison-building programmes of the 1980s, on 'secure containment'. It is a product or expression of a particular historical and *political* moment, originating in the late 1960s and early 1970s and evolving during the epoch of Thatcherism. So it is clear, for example, that the recommendations initially made by the Wheatley Report on Crowd Safety at Soccer Grounds in 1972 (see note 4 (iii)), in response to the Ibrox disaster and to a series of pitch invasions and other incidents of crowd trouble, concerning the safety of spectators at soccer grounds, were never really activated by Football League clubs during the following fifteen years, except at such times when new stands or terracing were being introduced. On such occasions, there is some evidence that architects were asked to take into account, and to design in, the 'egress time' of eight minutes which — the Report declared — spectators would require to escape from a major emergency. Nevertheless, the approach to crowd safety and provision at the popular ends, throughout the 1960s to the 1980s, continued to be determined by the question of containment and control of the terrace supporter. When I spent my very earliest years as a young Sheffield Wednesday supporter on the Leppings Lane end, often standing alongside supporters of the visiting teams, there were three means of entry on to the terrace itself and only a small ledge separating the terrace from the playing pitch. But by April 1989, this same terrace was divided into two cages, with a single tunnel entrance into one of these areas and absolutely no other means of 'egress'. It is *not* that the Leppings Lane end had not been 'modernised'; it is that it had been transformed for the purpose of physically containing 'an end' of the ground which had, in the meantime, become redefined as the section of the ground which was now dedicated (in respect of routine League games) to the exclusive use, and the effective containment and control, of supporters of visiting teams.

4. Hillsborough and the question of violence

In many of the first press reports of the Hillsborough disaster both in Britain and internationally, the events at the Lepping Lane end were interpreted as a further instance of the continuing problem of English soccer violence.

The Belgian newspaper, *La Dernière Heure*, offered a particular variant of the argument:

Don't tell us that here is no connection between what happened in Brussels on 29 May 1985 and the terrible catastrophe in Sheffield. This was not a question of hooliganism. The supporters of the Reds attacked no one. But the question must be asked about the attitude of people who, with or without a ticket, have deliberately risked triggering this drama.

The article by Martin Kettle which quoted this passage also reported a Professor George Vigarello of the Université de Paris as saying: 'It has always been the same. The English football fan is violent. He comes to the ground in groups, with his mates. He pushes and shouts.' [13] Undoubtedly the most notorious reaction from Europe to the disaster, however, was the set of comments made by M. Jacques Georges of the European Football Association, describing Liverpool supporters as 'beasts' and heavily implying that the

Hillsborough disaster ought to be understood, primarily, as an expression of that truth. These comments provoked great anger in Liverpool, and even evinced a direct admonitory response from Mr Hurd, the British Home Secretary,[14] who averred that there was no violence at Hillsborough, contrary to what M. Georges may have been told.

In Liverpool itself, any reference to misbehaviour, rowdiness or drink amongst the Liverpool fans at the fatal Hillsborough semi-final is seen as an intolerable slur: an informal boycott in Liverpool of the *Sun* newspaper, which had carried many reports along these lines in the aftermath of the disaster, made a significant dent in the sale of that 'newspaper' on Merseyside. The popular common sense seems to suggest that there is no connection between the disaster at Hillsborough (which continues to be interpreted by many Liverpool fans as an instance simply of incompetence and authoritarianism on the part of the South Yorkshire Police and bad planning by Sheffield Wednesday FC) and the tragic events at the Heysel Stadium in Brussels in 1985, where thirty-nine fans died as a direct result of a ritual 'taking of the ends' by drunken and rowdy supporters of the Liverpool club.

In Sheffield itself, a series of unpleasant stories continue to circulate about the behaviour of a minority of Liverpool fans after the disaster began to unfold. There is some scepticism about the reports, circulated nationally, that ambulancemen and police were assaulted during the disaster: many commentators observe that these 'assaults' may in fact have been the desperate attempts by fans who were trying to obtain help, sometimes in vain, to revive their stricken relatives. But there have been persistent reports of some snatching of wallets from the dead or the dying, and also of some obstructive action by drunken and aggressive fans *vis-à-vis* the attempts being made to mount rescues and revivals on the terrace and on the Hillsborough playing field itself.

Observations of this kind in no way detract from the extraordinary acts of heroism, and the display of fellow-feeling, which the majority of fans exhibited in the wake of the Hillsborough disaster. At the time these were subject to eloquent comment by several Liverpool players (John Aldridge,[15] Ian Rush,[16] Craig Johnston[17] and many others) and they have even been subject to praise by Mrs Thatcher herself, though it is barely conceivable that she could understand the sense of fellow-feeling that binds supporters of football clubs together in this way.

What I want to retrieve from the apparently confused reactions of British and European commentators to the violent deaths that took place at Hillsborough are two truths: first, the truth that the deaths of the ninety-five Liverpool fans must primarily be understood as a consequence of the architectural transformation of the Leppings Lane end into a human cage (a transformation born of the 'law-and-order' rhetoric applied to soccer over the previous twenty to twenty-five years); but, second, the truth that there *are* certain very rigid patterns of fan behaviour at English soccer matches (bound up with the consumption of drink,[18] masculinity[19] and an explosive mix of tribal solidarity amongst supporters of one team coupled with aggression towards the supporters of the other team)[20] which were all in evidence amongst the crowds attempting to enter Leppings Lane before the fatal semi-final (and which are

still all too obvious at many English League and Cup games). To recognise this
is not to say that all sections of the English soccer crowd conduct themselves
according to this particular, rigid set of 'codes', nor is it to say that there is a
direct, causal link between these codes of behaviour and hooligan behaviour in
all cases. Since its re-emergence as a major social problem in the early 1960s,
hooliganism has consistently been a minority phenomenon but it is nonetheless important to recognise that the reactions of spectators as a whole to police
activity against crowd trouble inside stadiums has remained quite noticeably
ambivalent, though there has tended to be more support for firm police action
with respect to drunken or threatening behaviour outside the stadiums. The
essentially class-based traditions of solidarity amongst supporters of individual
clubs and the accentuated masculinism of terrace culture have militated
against popular support from the crowd for police intervention. It has taken
the disasters at the Heysel, at Bradford and at Hillsborough to 'problematicise'
the patterns of drink and masculinity in football spectator behaviour in the
minds of football spectators themselves. This is an issue to which I shall return
in the second half of this chapter.

5. Hillsborough and the disaster theme

One vital aspect of the Hillsborough disaster (that was noted at the time by a
wide variety of social commentators) was the fact that it occurred in sequence
with a series of other disasters in public facilities in Britain. The truth was
captured most graphically on a poster which appeared on the walls of Britain's
city centres in April 1989, produced by the Socialist Workers Party, with the
now famous photograph of a Liverpool fan sitting alone and distraught among
the mangled perimeter fences at the front of Hillsborough's Leppings Lane
terrace. Underneath the photograph was the caption 'Thatcherism: Ten Years
of Disasters' (and, of course, a call to various political meetings). There is no
need, I think, to subscribe to the kind of simplistic causal theories associated
with the SWP to recognise the strength of the empirical claim which this
poster attempts to represent. This *is* a society which since 1979 has experienced a series of inner-city riots quite without precedent in their violence and
intensity, but which has also, perhaps more tellingly, experienced disastrous
breakdowns in public provision on the part of established institutions
purporting to provide for, or, indeed, to 'look after' the citizenry. The list of
such disasters now includes the Bradford City fire (57 deaths in May 1985), the
sinking of the *Herald of Free Enterprise* ferry in Zeebrugge Harbour in 1987
(188 British passengers drowned), the fire in King's Cross Underground
Station in November 1987 (31 deaths), the explosion of the Piper Alpha oil rig
in July 1988 (167 oil workers blown up or drowned), and the Southern Region
rail crashes at Clapham Junction in December 1988 (35 dead) and then at
Purley (2 dead, 52 injured) in March 1989. To this 'litany' of disasters, some
observers would add the deaths by fire of 55 holiday-makers in a British
Airways plane awaiting take-off at Manchester Airport in August 1985, the
Lockerbie disaster in December 1988, and the East Midlands Airport disaster
just three weeks later in January 1989. There has been nothing to approach
these disasters in Britain, either in scale or in public impact, since Aberfan, on

22 October 1966, when a landslide from a pitheap engulfed a local school and claimed the lives of 147, the vast majority of them infants.

Although some commentators have denied that there is a pattern to these disasters, this is certainly not how they are experienced in popular consciousness, nor how they are viewed by safety engineers and by informed commentators in the mass media. A report by the Toronto *Globe and Mail*, for example, quotes the Head of Safety Engineering at Cranford Institute of Technology as saying that 'what seems to be happening is that safety is judged by the amount of money that people want to spend [and] at this point in time, we are in an environment where money has become very, very important'.[21] This Canadian journalist, examining the record, concludes: 'Sifting through the public inquiries of tragedy after tragedy, common themes can be easily unearthed: rampant disregard for safety in private and public services; poor communications once disasters occur; inadequately trained and overworked staff and, especially, dilapidated public facilities.'

Public awareness of the declining condition of public space finds expression in a variety of ways, not least in the continuing high rates of the 'fear of crime'. They are also exhibited in a developing public concern about the extraordinary level of litter which besmirches British streets and public spaces generally. Implicit in this public consciousness of dilapidation and the potential for disaster in the public environment is a theoretical and socio-political connection which the immediate press coverage of Hillsborough did not even think to make, and which was certainly not obvious even in Lord Justice Taylor's Official Inquiry.

The 'litany' of disasters is, indeed, in the nature of a critique of a society which simply has not taken seriously the question of public safety and public provision. Even in the heyday of post-war reconstruction, social-democratic politicians attempting to build a New Jerusalem (for example, in the form of 'garden cities', or even council houses with space for growing families, shelves for reading matter, and materials adequate to prevent environmental deterioration) were seriously and consistently obstructed, most usually on grounds of cost (no council houses were ever built with shelving). So also was the establishment of the NHS vigorously obstructed by the medical profession and by other powerful private interests.

In more recent post-Keynesian times, 'public provision' in its most general sense has come to be equated, in political discourse, with the creation and/or elaboration of a 'nanny state', encouraging the growth of a 'state-dependent' mentality among the citizenry in general and the underclass in particular. But what none of these free market commentators ever discusses is the condition of public space (or, for that matter, of public life, whether in the form of interpersonal concern or conviviality) in a free market society. What possible guarantee is there, in a competitive free-market society, of safer public spaces, safer public transport and/or a sea change in the way that 'authority' treats, for example, the consumer, the sports fan or the traveller — that is, the citizen — in Britain?

The fires at Bradford City and at Kings Cross, like the routine vandalism and graffiti on nearly all British housing estates, were the product of a society in which the public's regard for disdainful, uncaring and inefficient public provision was expressed in a littering of the space so provided. The Piper Alpha disaster was a product of a society in which a sudden and continuing demand for oil vastly outstripped any serious concern for worker safety.[22] The Southern Region rail disasters of the late 1980s were a product of a society in which rail travel is increasingly underfunded (and whose equipment is therefore massively outdated and its staff callously overworked), and in which the Government is theologically committed, against nearly all environmental and economic evidence, to an expansion of the road system rather than of other public transport systems. The Zeebrugge disaster, in a more complicated way, seems to have stemmed from a disastrous individual oversight, but was clearly an expression of a kind of careless inefficiency and neglect for the public interest which characterises the British service industry in general. The Hillsborough disaster was the product of a quite consistent and ongoing lack of interest on the part of the owners and directors of English league clubs in the comfort, well-being and safety of their paying spectators: this particular failure within football that I am condemning is a generalised problem in English culture – the lack of regard by authority (and therefore by what we now call 'service providers') for the provision of well-being and security of others.

6. Official and popular discourses about Hillsborough

In my own earlier paper on the Hillsborough disaster (see note 1), written before the release of the Official Inquiry, I gave voice to certain misgivings and concerns about the appointment, and also the likely scope and rhetorical stance of an inquiry headed by a member of the senior judiciary. An appointment of this kind from Government was entirely predictable in Britain, since inquiries into breakdowns of the assumed routine practices of authority, both public and private, and their relations with the citizenry (or of what one might call the taken-for-granted custodianship of the citizenry by the state and other authorities) are nearly always conducted in this country by members of the judiciary. In the United States and in many European countries, by contrast, they might be conducted by senior officials within the state executive arm. In the Commisions of Inquiry completed within the United States into urban violence and crime, into pornography and sexuality, and a host of related areas, the process of collecting evidence and organising an analysis of the problem, in order to move strategically towards a solution, has routinely involved the participation of scholars and practitioners who are closely involved in the problem, or who have spent years in scholarly or applied research in the area. In Britain, however, such expertise and practical knowledge has always taken second place to the requirement that an 'independent' adjudication of a serious social probe of a disaster be exercised by a senior member of the High Court. The main qualification for the selection of such persons, in general terms, seems to be that they have developed, in the course of their occupational socialisation and upward mobility within the legal profession, a finely tuned understanding of what kinds of solutions and, indeed, analyses are acceptable — both in general and in more specific conjunctural terms — within the corridors of power. The domination of these inquiries by judges is a function of their refined understanding and practice of what Frank Burton and Pat Carlen, in reference to official inquiries into the Irish question, once called 'official discourse'.[23]

Certainly it is true that the three judicial inquiries conducted into the earlier post-war football disasters at Bolton in 1947, Ibrox Park in 1971 and Bradford in 1986 all tended 'in the final analysis' to reproduce, albeit in the measured and sometimes elegant tones of the senior judiciary, the political and common-sense assumptions that are dominant in powerful circles at the time.

The official inquiry into the Bolton disaster in 1947 spoke powerfully about the need to limit the size of crowds at a time of mass, popular interest in soccer: it said nothing about the modernisation of the conditions offered to spectators, whether seated or standing, in the light of the game's new-found post-war popularity. The Popplewell Inquiry, as already indicated, especially in its interim report, started out as an examination of fire risks and the relations of the safety inspectorate to private soccer clubs, but it finished up reading like a contribution to the debate, which was then current in England, on the Police and Criminal Evidence Bill and the extension of police powers of search.

My fears about Lord Justice Taylor's Official Inquiry, however, were mistaken and, in retrospect, what I had most crucially failed to grasp was the extent to which 'the common sense' of some sections of the senior judiciary had departed, by the mid- to late-1980s, from the sensibilities and policy preoccupations of the Thatcher Government.[24] The Taylor Report is not, of course, a detailed social scientific analysis of the broad framework of social relations (of social and regional inequality and working-class masculinism), and in that sense the limitations — and perhaps also the ideological or partial character — of Lord Justice Taylor's 'official discourse' are clear. But neither is this Report a further one-dimensional example of a law-and-order solution applied to football, a further neurotic twisting of the knife by something called 'the Authoritarian State'. In a Report which seems to be written *for* football and, in many ways, in the name of the football crowd as a whole, there is a firm insistence on the removal of the perimeter fences — the 'human cages' of Leppings Lane — from English League grounds; there is a clear rejection of the Thatcher Government's proposed Membership Scheme as a practicable solution to soccer violence and also as a meaningful intervention into football as a popular sport and entertainment; and there is also a powerful and entirely accurate denunciation of the squalid facilities which have routinely been provided for paying spectators over the years by football clubs the length and breadth of the country.[25]

There is, of course, quite vigorous controversy amongst football fans (and amongst football clubs themselves) with respect to the key recommendation in the Taylor Inquiry, namely, that all stadiums in the English First and Second Divisions, and all stadiums in the Scottish Premier Division, must become 'all-seater' by the end of the 1993–4 season. In the pages of the fanzines, in *When Saturday Comes*[26] and also in the press releases and other literature from the Football Supporters' Association, the proposal for all-seater stadiums is interpreted, in part, as an anti-hooliganism measure. Critics of the all-seater proposal have pointed, in effect, to the fallacies in what they see essentially as an architectural determinist argument, namely, that human social behaviour is a direct expression of the surrounding built environment.[27] They also make reference to the well-known truth amongst football fans — that incidents of hooliganism, so far as they are still occurring in the aftermath of the 1990 World Cup, tend to occur away from football stadia, in surrounding streets, on public transport or in public houses.

This kind of critique of the Taylor Report's all-seater proposal from representatives of existing circles of football fans may, however, be based on a misunderstanding of the Taylor Report's overall strategic agenda. A closer reading of the text of the Taylor Report suggests that the call for all-seater stadiums is one, important, element in an overall, insistent demand for the radical modernisation of spectator provision in British football. It is also quite clear that the demand made for the introduction of all-seater stadiums — discussed as if such seats might contribute to more orderly behaviour on the part of all fans — is one way in which the Taylor Report is able, strategically, to justify its call for the final removal of 'prison-like' perimeter fencing from English League grounds: it is the quid pro quo directed at the 'law and order' lobby's preoccupations with the effective 'containment of the crowd'.

One of the problems in the continuing defence of the standing terrace by the Football Supporters Association and other representatives of football fans as a whole is that it could be interpreted as a kind of acquiescence in the Football League clubs' stubborn refusal to modernise, justified as that resistance often is by reference to spectators' own preference for 'the traditional'. This is not of course the way to 'woo back' those erstwhile spectators at British soccer who have stopped coming to games because of the squalor of the stadiums, nor either is it a way to attract a new constituency of support. In the ongoing 'war of position' currently taking place over the future of football, I would argue that it is vitally important that the voice of football fans and spectators should clearly distinguish itself from the inert, reactionary nostalgia of Football League Boards of Directors and argue unambiguously for radical modernisation of provision, not only on behalf of existing spectators but also on behalf of the large body of potential support currently content to view their football on television from the comfort of their own homes.[28]

We are precisely in a situation (because of the Taylor Report), I would argue, where there is a possibility of radical modernisation and also transformation of the ways in which football is watched and supported in Britain. The Football Association, in April 1991, released its *Blueprint for Football*, proposing the introduction of an eighteen-club Premier League in season 1992-3,[29] whilst, in Europe, interest in the ideas of a continent-wide Super League continues to gather pace. In such a context it is very important to be careful and precise in one's evaluation of the essentially populist responses of existing football fan magazines and organisations to the Taylor Report and to other changes now proposed for the game. One of the responses to the Taylor Report's proposal for all-seater stadiums, for example, was to argue that the proposal constituted a kind of attack on traditional (sic) 'terrace culture' with its celebrated (or hypothesised) qualities of camaraderie, quick wit and collectivism. This image of terrace culture is, of course, very much the image which has been reactivated culturally by the fanzine movement during the 1980s, but it must be said that the experience of 'Kop End' terrace life during that same period at many clubs has actually been one of rampant racism, crudely sexist banter, and of aggravation conducted by groups of young white males of little education and even less wit.[30] There is a strong suspicion that the populist defence of terrace culture by those generally well-educated, largely good-humoured independent entrepreneurs producing the fanzines and the alternative football literature of the 1980s is a 'fantastic' representation of actual terrace culture in the same period.

In April 1991, two years after the Hillsborough disaster, when the jury at the official inquest before the South Yorkshire coroner, Dr Stefan Popper, finally returned a verdict of 'accidental death' on the ninety-five victims, there were heartfelt scenes of bitterness and anguish amongst relatives in attendance for the finding. Relatives had apparently been wanting a verdict of 'unlawful killing' and, in particular, affirmation that the opening of the gates at the Leppings Lane by police — an act which precipitated overcrowding on the terrace — should retrospectively be defined as a crime.

There is considerable room for debate between 'radical' and 'realist' critics over the finding of this inquest,[31] particularly in respect of what might have been the most instrumentally useful in encouraging action to prevent any recurrency of disasters like Hillsborough on other football grounds in the future. But I want to suggest here that the inquest was important also in the symbolic realm, not merely in providing for some vital means for dealing with the feelings of sorrow, loss and guilt of relatives, football authorities and police, but generally in providing a platform on which Hillsborough could be remembered in all its various important dimensions. I began this chapter by reference to redecoration of the Leppings Lane entrance at Hillsborough as a popular shrine and I then tried to retrieve a sense of the ground in a local people's 'sense of place' (their cultural geography of 'their' city). I also tried to recall how the magnitude of the disaster seemed to bring football and football supporters together in a collective sense of loss and also, for a time, in a new-found determination to rebuild football, especially the relationships of clubs to supporters, on a different, cooperative and collaborative basis. In the immediate aftermath of the disaster, Liverpool Football Club indicated that it was to suspend all its fixtures for the rest of the season, including its game in the FA Cup. Kenny Dalglish, the Liverpool Manager, was quoted as saying: 'Football is irrelevant when something like this happens' (*Observer*, 16 April 1989).

A memorial service was hurriedly arranged at Liverpool's Roman Catholic Cathedral on Sunday, 16 April (with five thousand in attendance and eight thousand other mourners outside). The Liverpool Manager and several of the Liverpool players (most notably, the Liverpool-born John Aldridge) were quoted as saying that they could not contemplate playing football in the immediate future, and that, minimally, the decision as to whether Liverpool Football Club should play out its remaining Cup and League games should be a decision of 'the people of Liverpool' and, particularly, those who had been bereaved. This sentiment seemed to be echoed by leaders of the Liverpool City Council, who themselves declared a week of mourning and indicated that no Hillsborough victims' families 'would go without'. 'This city will look after its own.'[32]

For a key period after Hillsborough, that is, there was a pressing sense that the Liverpool manager and players, along with the City Council and the local clergy, recognised, in a very fundamental sense, that 'Hillsborough' had in fact made impossible a continuation of the normal relations of the football club (and, behind it, the Football League, the FA and the familiar apparatus that is the professional football industry) with the community. The problem that was posed was not a problem of unmodernized stadiums or the absence of consumer-friendly, free market forces, but the problem of the contact which football has lost with its traditional constituency: 'the people'. In the week after 15 April, there was in insistent resurrection, in 'the talk about Hillsborough', of Arthur Hopcraft's idea of football as 'the people's game' *par excellence*: a form of passionate working-class poetry and a vital emblem of the distinctive qualities of one's own locality and identity.

Writing this chapter, two years (almost to the day) after Hillsborough, it is not clear that football has retained that urgent, powerful sense of the need to redraw its relations with its most important constituency: the people. During the last two years, the mass media have certainly given much greater coverage to issues of crowd safety and, to a lesser extent, crowd provision. Especially during 'Italia 90', representatives of the Football Supporters Association were given an access to television, radio and newspapers they might not have had in other circumstances. But there have also been unmistakeable signs of the Boards of Directors of some clubs 'dragging their feet' on the Taylor Report, not only because of the costs involved in the upgrading of stadiums but also on the grounds that modernisation of safety and provision was an unwanted and unjustified diversion from the 'true' purpose (*sic*) of a football club.[34] There has been a sense that the horror and meaning of Hillsborough has already been forgotten in some quarters and, in particular, that football's traditionally inattentive and ungenerous relations with its supporters, 'the people', reinstated. It is in the light of the pressure to normalise once again this kind of exploitative relationship between club and spectator that the angry populism that was awakened by the Hillsborough disaster is important and in need of constant reaffirmation.

Afterword

For all these last concerns, there are many positive aspects of the situation of English football in 1991, two years after the Taylor Report and some eight months after the English team's courageous performances in the 1990 World Cup. Not least of the changes is the sense that English League football is blessed once again with talented and exciting individuals (Paul Gascoigne, David Platt, Tony Daley, Lee Sharpe, Mark Hughes, Des Walker, Gary Lineker); that hooliganism, for reasons also connected with the World Cup initially and with the European idea, has become unfashionable; that football is gradually becoming more open to women spectators, women directors and women journalists; and, not least, that attendances are continuing to increase for the fourth consecutive season. Attendance at Football League games during 1989–90 was 19.4 million, an 18.3 per cent increase on the post-war low of 16.4 million in 1985–6.[35] The attitude of public authority to football, whilst not generous, is certainly more supportive and constructive than would have been possible in the dark days after the Heysel disaster.[36] There is also evidence, in the shape of a mushrooming football literature (in book as well as magazine form), of a renewed interest in football as a form of personal hobby interest (as a part of one's own cultural 'identity-kit').[37]

On any careful reflection, however, it is clear that this sense of possibility will depend for its eventual realisation, absolutely crucially, on football's ability to modernise its present material and social condition. The longstanding contribution of Mr Lord Justice Taylor's Report into Hillsborough will be to have placed the modernisation of stadiums and spectator provision at the centre of football's agenda. What is not directly addressed in the Taylor Report, however, are the economic and cultural contingencies which may obstruct or enable the new project of modernisation.

Discussion amongst television 'pundits' during the World Cup in Italy quite often strayed from events on the pitch to the quite extraordinary and beautiful stadiums which had been built, either from scratch or by ingenious renovation and extension of existing stadiums, to house the games. There was a remarkable consensus amongst these pundits that such stadiums could 'never' be built in Britain[38] — a consensus that seems on enquiry to be broadly shared amongst English football fans and television watchers alike. The acquiescence of the English on this issue clearly ought to be a matter for analysis in itself (are people indeed now accepting that England, the home of football, really is not so modern, efficient and creative a culture as Italy and therefore could not house its national game with a similar degree of artistry and financial commitment?). What does seem to be demanded, however, according to many surveys and according to all hearsay, is a radical upgrading of our squalid and outdated stadiums (see note 28).

In the summer of 1990, the Football League was estimating that a sum of £665 million would ideally be needed if clubs were to complete the ground improvements demanded by the Taylor Report by 1993–4. But they also indicated that, even with the support which was now forthcoming from the pools levies which were being channelled to clubs though the Football Trust, clubs still thought they would only be able to find a sum of £350 million to spend on these improvements.[39] Only a small proportion of this sum can be found from increased ticket sales, new sponsorship, increased TV rights or even from contributions from the Football League, football pools or the Football Trust. The recommendations of the Taylor Report had, of course, been given the support of Parliament precisely at the time that British economy has encountered its worst recession since the early 1980s. But it is also clear that — as in so many other areas of British life in the early 1990s — the fundamental problem remains the limited amount of capital investment in stadiums and infrastructure over the previous forty-five post-war years. Having never ever been run as profit-maximising businesses, and traditionally preoccupied with the glory of victories on the pitch, English League clubs are now confronted, along with a vast investment deficit, with no obvious set of solutions for the modernisation project demanded by the Taylor Report.[40] The recent modernisation of stadiums in Italy has been made possible primarily by the peculiar alliances of large capital and the state — the 'corporatist' deal in

Northern Italy (and also by the continuing personal commitment of major capitalist individuals like Signor Berlusconi or Signor Agnelli to AC Milan and Juventus). In the Netherlands and in France, on the other hand, the modernisation of stadiums appears to have been approached rather more steadily and systematically at local level, with close cooperation between local private interests and energetic, modernising local authorities. In 'free market' Britain, in the meantime, there has been a powerful feeling during the 1980s simply that football clubs have become another diversion for fast-moving entrepreneurs with no proven interest in, or commitment to, the medium- or long-term future of clubs. Manchester United, now in the final of the European Cup-Winners Cup, are still thought to be available for sale on the open market, though probably the price will now have climbed above a February 1991 quotation of £16 million.[41] In 1990, the Club was very nearly sold to property speculator Michael Knighton for slightly less. Sheffield United, in the meantime, were very nearly sold to an Iraqi businessman, Mr Sam Hashimi, who had absolutely no previous connection with the Club. Throughout the 1980s, Mr Robert Maxwell has been involved in attempts to buy Watford and Reading on top of Derby County and Oxford United, which he purchased in 1982 and where the chairman is now Mr Maxwell's son, Kevin. It is not at all clear how Mr Maxwell's direct or indirect ownership of these clubs has improved the performances of their teams or the quality of their stadiums. Nor is it clear how this activity helps Mr Maxwell's interest in the ownership of a British club that could compete in a European Super League.[42] What is apparent, however, is that these 'boardroom struggles' on the part of maverick property speculators and other capitalists for ownership of clubs are neither raising the kind of capital which clubs require for the project of stadium modernisation, nor guaranteeing the continuing integrity of clubs *vis-à-vis* the communities in which they have always been located. In this particular sense, the offering of these clubs for sale is a profound blow to the idea of the club as a specifically local and popular institution. The offering-out of shares in clubs via flotation on the Stock Exchange (as has happened at Millwall and, most notoriously, at Tottenham Hotspur) does not carry that particular danger; but it does now seem clear that football clubs — precisely because they are not profit-maximising institutions — are not providing very attractive 'opportunities' to the mass of investors.[43] There is a real sense in which the modernisation project of English football is encountering the limitations of the kind of free market individualism that was encouraged by Government throughout the 1980s. The only new modern sports stadium of any size and grandeur that is opening in the early 1990s in England is the Don Valley Stadium in Sheffield, built for the World Student Games in that city in the summer of 1991 on the initiative of a city council selling an idea to progressively and internationally minded capital.

So one of the pressing issues in the modernisation of English football after the Taylor Report is the source and the control of capital investment that is required. It now seems clear that this issue may require a return by clubs and the League to local authorities, for the creation of local or regional collaborations as a preamble to approaches to major international sponsors.

The second issue confronting football is even less open to effective action by football clubs themselves. The moves towards modernised and all-seater stadiums, towards a domestic Premier League and perhaps towards a European Super League are unlikely to occur without any kind of defensive–aggressive response from the popular ends themselves. Entry into a European League itself, as many journalistic commentators have observed, would institutio-nalise the practice of English fans travelling abroad 'on tour'. Though there seems to have been some reduction in the number of incidents of hooliganism in the first domestic season in England since the World Cup Finals in Italy, there are no grounds for believing that anything fundamental has changed in the 'conditions of existence' of hooliganism in the underclass of this country. These conditions of existence are not a product of social deprivation in any straightforward sense. Instead, as I have argued elsewhere,[44] the violence exhibited at the Heysel Stadium, and also routinely exhibited since the late 1960s by supporters of England and of English clubs abroad, is very much a product of the 'culture' of the upwardly mobile, individualistic fraction of the (male) British working class which has done relatively well out of the restructuring of British industry and business in the last twenty years. This fraction of the 'working class' (first sighted, perhaps, in the lump workers in the building industry and in London's Docklands) has done well because of its ability to master particular crafts and to move between work sites. It has a certain residual sense of solidarity, born of neighbourhood and gender, but it is generally individualistic, chauvinistic and racist. It is this particular fraction of the class that has exhibited what Raymond Williams summarised in *The Long Revolution* and, again, in *Towards 2000*, as 'mobile privatization',[45] and whose cultural and leisure preoccupations have more recently been pilloried quite mercilessly by commentators on the radical Right.[46] It is this particular fraction of the class, according to many different accounts, that is most deeply attached to its reading of the *Sun* newspaper (which, in October–November 1989, had achieved a daily circulation in Britain of 4,095,027) and the *Sunday Sport*, and which was most enthusiastically carried along by the jingoistic nationalism that accompanied the Falklands/Malvinas and Gulf wars.

At the very lowest end of the British working class, irretrievably caught in what Phil Cohen once described as an 'exploration' of 'downward mobility',[47] are cohorts of unemployed or underemployed young men, who have left school at 16, most with no qualifications or with a few largely irrelevant qualifi-cations. They are the most visible and, indeed, in large part because of their untutored, unchallenged 'masculinity', the most troublesome fraction of the vast population of young people who leave school at this age (some 70 per cent of all pupils in Britain, compared with only 30 per cent in Japan and 10 per cent in the United States). Glenwyn Benson and Stewart Lansley, analysing these figures, have shown that Britain has 'the lowest staying-on rates in Europe', the worst 'gap in attainment' between lowest and highest achievers of any comparable European or North American society and, most importantly for our purposes, the 'worst education' population of youth of a country that describes itself as being 'advanced'.[48]

The overwhelming point about figures of this kind is the way in which they underline the crucial, definitive 'conditions of existence' — the moral and cultural shallowness, and lack of alternative experience, which feeds into the tribal weekend rituals of the underclass soccer hooligan. A similarly narrow form of socialization underpins the nationalistic hostility exhibited by those workers who have escaped the trap of downward mobility, and, despite their lack of formal or non-technical education, could afford trips to the World Cup in Spain in 1982 or to the European Cup Final in Brussels in 1985. In the case of the downwardly mobile and much less affluent underclass, no doubt, this passionate preoccupation each weekend with 'the club' they support is exacerabated by the pressing sense of being excluded from any alternative 'symbolic' world of personal reward or recognition.

The working class in Britain and in other industrial societies can be observed as a class that is fractured into many quite distinct component parts. The respectable working class, gaining a sense of self-worth throughout labour and immersion in relatively integrated communities, may have gone forever; although it was a part of my earlier argument that this sense of fellow-feeling was 'magically' reinvented in the scenes of collaborative activity during the immediate aftermath of the Leppings Lane crush, and in the ensuing two weeks of 'abnormal' relations between the Liverpool Club and its supporters, as well as in the work done by working-class fans from different, often 'competing' teams across the country for the Hillsborough Disaster Fund. It is not at all clear whether this 'magical' moment can be sustained, in the absence of the industrial base and the social institutions which sustained that kind of neighbourhood and family-based culture of the working class in the first half of this century.

With less than eighteen months to go before full economic integration into the European Community, government educational policy in Britain seems to be focused almost entirely on the introduction of a core curriculum in schools, with a significantly increased component of science and technology and a greater attention to the basic skills of reading and writing. There is very little feeling that this culture is about to reposition itself as a full member of the multi-lingual, multi-cultural European Community, and very little preparation on the part of major national institutions, like the organised Football League itself, for a new, inter-national European reality. Discussions of the problems that may arise in international understanding within Europe, including the problems which might be posed in respect of the education given those 80 per cent of English school-leavers who do not go on to higher education, and many of whom are active fans of football, are non-existent. There is a depressing sense that England — confronting a moment of major cultural and national significance — has fallen asleep.

Readers of this chapter may feel that these are strange and rather speculative premonitions with which to conclude a series of reflections on a football disaster which occurred, after all, in the past, but to this I would immediately respond that the disaster at Hillsborough was a predictable outcome to the remorseless and unthinking application of law-and-order rhetoric to the problem of crowd control.[49] The real problem confronting English football, in the aftermath of the Taylor Report and Italia 90, I would argue, is a particular expression of the general cultural and political challenge confronting the English and their governmental representatives: do 'we' want to be a planned, cooperative and modernising society with new and efficient institutions and a range of relatively safe and accessible opportunities for sports and entertainment (available to all, regardless of gender, race or age), located internationally within the European market-place? Or do we, like football clubs throughout the last one hundred years, want to keep things as they are?

Notes

1. The discussion of Hillsborough in this chapter is a substantially reworked version of the paper I wrote in the immediate aftermath of that disaster: 'Hillsborough, 15 April 1989: Some Personal Contemplations', *New Left Review,* **177** (1989), pp. 89–110.
2. *The Hillsborough Stadium Disaster (15 April 1989) (Inquiry by the Rt. Hon. Lord Justice Taylor)*, Final Report, cm. 962, London: HMSO (1990).
3. I include my own misreading of the appointment of a senior judge to chair the Hillsborough Inquiry. cf. Taylor (1989), op. cit., pp. 98–100.
4. cf. (i) *The Moelwyn Hughes Report into the Disaster at Bolton Wanderers* (1946), Cmnd. 6846; (ii) *Report of the Working Party on Crowd Behaviour at Football Matches* (The Lang Report), London: HMSO (1969); (iii) *Report on Crowd Safety at Sports Crowds* (The Wheatley Report) (1972), Cmnd. 4952; (iv) *Committee of Inquiry into Crowd Safety and Control at Sports Grounds* (Chairman: Mr Justice Popplewell), Interim Report, July 1985, Cmnd. 9585, Final Report, January 1986, Cmnd. 9710.
5. Stephen Edgell has pointed out, in conversation, that soccer grounds have also been 'venerated', in part, as architectural icons: football supporters have retained strong affection for particular aspects of the stadia (the famous 'cottage' at Fulham, the grand entrance to Villa Park main stand, the Clock Stand at Highbury, the concourse at Old Trafford, etc.). It speaks volumes about the indifference of 'established opinion' that this form of popular interest in the football ground is never reflected in recognised literature or talk on the history of British architecture. For further discussion of the football ground itself as an arena of sociability, see Stephen Edgell and David Jary, 'Football: A Sociological Eulogy', in M. Smith, S. Parker and C. Smith (1973), *Leisure and Society in Britain*, London, Allen Lane.
6. Michael Morris, 'Liverpool's Cup Overflows', *The Guardian*, 22 May 1989.
7. Simon Inglis (1987), *The Football Grounds of Great Britain*, London: Willow Books.
8. Paul Thompson, 'Oh No, Not Hillsborough', *Sheffield Star*, 17 April 1989.
9. ibid.
10. Jeremy Seabrook, 'We Were Caged Like Animals in a Zoo', *The Guardian*, 17 April 1989.
11. ibid.
12. 'Football's Shame', *The Economist*, 22 April 1989, pp. 55–60.
13. Quoted in Martin Kettle, 'Feelings Abroad About the Soccer Disaster', *The Guardian*, 20 April 1989.
14. 'Hurd Slams the "Beast Fans" Tag', *Manchester Evening News*, 18 April 1989, p. 3.
15. Quote in the *Daily Mirror*, 17 May 1989.
16. Ian Rush, 'The Fans are Fantastic', *Shoot! Magazine*, 6 May 1989.
17. Craig Johnston, comments made in the half-time break during the televising of the Everton–Liverpool League game on 10 May 1989.
18. It is common knowledge amongst football fans that certain grounds (Anfield, St. James Park, Newcastle) can be relatively empty some ten minutes before kick-off

time and then fill up extremely rapidly as fans arrive in their masses from local public houses.

19. One of the witnesses to Lord Justice Taylor's Inquiry, Mrs Angela Hockenhull, who runs a carpentry workshop near Hillsborough, was quoted in later reports as saying that groups of twenty Liverpool fans came into her front garden to urinate, exposing themselves when requested to leave. She insisted that most of the fans 'thronging outside the ground' were drunk, *The Guardian*, 21 May 1989.

20. Some aspects of this tribalism, transferred on to the international scale in the 'tours' of fans of the England team abroad (prior to the World Cup of 1990) are discussed in John Williams, Eric Dunning and Patrick Murphy, *Hooligans Abroad*, London: Routledge, 1984. See also Ed Vulliramy, 'Live by Aggro, Die by Aggro', *New Statesman*, 7 June 1985, and Dave Hill, 'Football's Prisoners of War', *The Independent* (*Weekend*), 22 April 1989.

21. Edward Greenspon, 'Litany of UK Disasters Linked to Lack of Money', *Globe and Mail*, Toronto, 22 April 1989.

22. For exploration of this connection, see W. G. Carson (1981), *The Other Price of Britain's Oil*, London: Martin Robertson.

23. Frank Burton and Pat Carlen (1979), *Official Discourse*, London: Routledge and Kegan Paul.

24. One is reminded, now, of the precedent established for a reforming Judicial Inquiry, departing from the dominant thrust of government policy and thinking in the Thatcher era, by Lord Scarman in his Report into the riots in Brixton, Bristol, Toxteth and other urban centres in 1980 and 1981. cf. Lord Scarman, *The Brixton Disorders, 10–12 April 1981*, London: HMSO (1981), Cmnd. 8427.

25. For further commentary on the 'reformism' of the Taylor Report, see my column 'Here We Go', *New Statesman and Society*, 2 February 1990, and 'A New Standard for Football', *Leisure Management*, **10** (2) (1990), pp. 37–8. It is important to note how the Taylor Report takes seriously the critiques and denunication of British football made by the Conservative press in the aftermath of the disasters at the Heysel and Bradford (in the words of the *Sunday Times* on 19 May 1989, 'a slum sport played in slum stadiums increasingly watched by slum people') but then uses these truths as a rationale for a radical modernisation of British football, particularly in respect of what it provides for the committed fan and, indeed (to use the contemporary language of the market), 'the paying consumer'.

26. 'Are You Sitting Comfortably?' (Editorial), *When Saturday Comes*, **37** (March 1990), pp. 2–4.

27. Mancunian critics of the all-seater proposal in the Taylor Report point to the ways in which visiting fans at Manchester City's Maine Road ground consistently prefer to stand, rather than sit, on the new seats provided at the visitors' end.

28. One modest step in investigating fans' 'desires' with respect to stadium improvement was the survey commissioned by the Football League from MORI, released in February 1990 under the title 'The Missing Voice'. The findings of this very limited survey (of only 561 fans, 149 of whom watched their football on television) suggested that there is a widely felt interest in 'better refreshment and toilet facilities at grounds, more pre-match and half-time entertainment, a free Football League magazine and a voluntary membership scheme if it also covered free admission to local sports and leisure facilities' (David Lacey, 'Poll Shows Fans Want Less Than Taylor May Give Them', *The Guardian*, 15 February 1990.

29. The proposals for a new Premier League were approved 'overwhelmingly' at a meeting of the full council of the FA on 8 April 1991 whilst a set of proposals from the Football League (defending the existing ninety-two-club structure of the

League) was 'flatly' rejected. 'League Anger at FA "hijack" ', *The Guardian*, 9 April 1991.

30. 'Terrace culture' in the 1980s has been one of the reasons for many erstwhile fans and commentators actually deciding not to return to soccer. cf. the account given by Russell Davies as to why he was giving up his position as a football correspondent for a Sunday newspaper: 'Cockpits of Ignobility', *Sunday Times*, 28 August 1982. See also the powerful polemic of James Walvin, *Football and the Decline of Britain*, London: Macmillan, 1986.

31. Dr Phil Scraton, Director of the Hillsborough Project organised at Edge Hill College in Ormskirk, certainly was right in declaring that the inquest itself, focused as it was procedurally on the minute scrutiny of the death of individuals, is an inappropriate instrument for examination and analysis of a disaster on the scale of Hillsborough ('Anger Greets Hillsborough Verdict', *The Guardian*, 29 March 1991). What is more difficult from a radical perspective is the value of arguing for a verdict of unlawful killing (by South Yorkshire Police or Sheffield Wednesday FC).

32. Keva Coombes, leader of Liverpool City Council, quoted in a syndicated article by James Dalrymple, 'City in Mourning', *Ottawa Citizen*, 18 April 1989. The full, powerful statement read: 'Nobody will want for anything and certainly not money. We intend to get to every single family and make sure they get everything they need. This city will look after its own.'

33. Arthur Hopcraft (1968), *The Football Man*, London.

34. One unfortunate instance of this backtracking was the begrudging discussion of the cost of the Taylor recommendations on the part of Mr Derek Dooley and other Directors of Sheffield United FC, televised in the episode of the BBC-2 programme, *United!* on 19 April 1990. Another worrisome instance was the level of interest shown by clubs in the conference on 'Sports Stadia after Hillsborough' organised by the Sports Council and the Royal Institute of British Architects in March 1990: only 11 of the 92 League Clubs sent any representative (*The Guardian*, 31 March 1990).

35. *Rothman's Football Yearbook, 1990–91*, London: Queen Anne's Press (1990).

36. cf., for example, the Report of the House of Commons Home Affairs Committee of February 1991, recommending, *inter alia*, gradual desegregation of fans, scepticism about the importance of all-seater provision in the lower divisions, and the criminalisation of racial abuse and missile-throwing. The general thrust of this Report was that 'the national football authorities (must) start regarding (ordinary fans) as partners in the game, not as fodder for exploitation by those who cream off soccer's rich pickings'. ('MP's Delight Fans and League', *The Guardian*, 6 February 1991).

37. For another very balanced overview of the present circumstances of football in England, see Vic Duke 'The Sociology of Football: A Research Agenda for the 1990s', *Sociological Review* (forthcoming, 1991).

38. It is intriguing, as well, to remember the many reports by English sports journalists in 1989 which suggested that these stadiums were a pipedream. They would never be ready; the organisation would be chaotic and the technology could not possibly work. The convoluted 'Little England' sensibilities and prejudices of the average English football journalist are a problem which we do not have time to address in this essay.

39. 'Cost of Ground Plan Soars', *The Guardian*, 3 August 1990.

40. 1990 was not, of course, the first year in which British football confronted the spectre of its vast under-capitalisation. Dire warnings were widespread in the early 1980s about both the financial viability of the ninety-two clubs and the League as a

whole. cf. my discussion in 'Professional Sport and the Recession', *International Review for the Sociology of Sport*, **19** (1) (1984), pp. 7–30.

41. Henry Sutton, 'Overseas Float for Red Devils', *The European*, 15–17 February 1991.
42. Ian Ridley, 'Maxwell House Not So Easily Dissolved', *The Guardian*, 7 September 1990.
43. For detailed discussion of this issue, particularly in respect of the 'flotation' of Millwall FC, see Roger Cowe, 'Into the Lions' Den', *The Guardian*, 12 October 1989.
44. Ian Taylor, 'Putting the Boot into a Working Class Sport: British Football After Bradford and Brussels', *Sociology of Sport Journals*, **5** (1987), pp. 171–91.
45. Raymond Williams (1961), *The Long Revolution*, London: Penguin, and (1983), *Towards 2000*, London: Verso, pp. 188–9.
46. I have in mind, in particular, the acerbic comments of Auberon Waugh, subsequent to Heysel, proclaiming that 'the truth of Brussels . . . [was that] . . . none of these Merseyside animals were poor and few, apparently, were unemployed. They were quite simply our wonderful, overpaid "workers" on a spree and in a festive mood', *The Spectator*, 8 June 1986, p. 8.
47. Phil Cohen, 'Subcultural Conflict and Working Class Community', *Working Class in Cultural Studies*, **2** (1972), pp. 5–52.
48. Glenwyn Benson and Stewart Lansley, 'Failing the Masses, Passing the Buck', *New Statesman*, 11 September 1987, pp. 10–12.
49. I do sometimes rather painfully remember how I observed in a speech given to a conference on soccer hooliganism hosted by Glasgow Corporation in August 1972, one year after Ibrox, that '[whilst] I hesitate to raise the subject in this City, except out of a determination to contribute to its prevention, but there are grounds for suggesting that the fencing in of crowds in situations of high excitement . . . can have fatal consequences', 'Football Hooliganism', Conference, Glasgow, November 1972 (Proceedings), p. 19.

2
North and South: the rivalry of the Football League and the Football Association

Alan Tomlinson

The Football League was founded in 1888 and is the oldest professional soccer league in the world. In the spring of 1991 the Football Association, an older body by a quarter of a century, published plans to recruit the top eighteen clubs from the Barclays Football League and set up its own 'Super League'. Incensed — especially as the Chief Executive of the Football Association, the man behind this irreverent challenge to the League's 103-year-old authority, was a former Secretary of the League itself — many League representatives appealed to history, tradition and paternalism to justify the status quo of the League's structure. Tensions between the Football Association and the League were certainly nothing new, although at the beginning of the 1990s there had been increasing talk of fuller collaboration between, even the merger of, the two bodies. The source of these tensions over the last century will be the main focus of this chapter, followed by some comments upon contemporary case-studies of two types of club: the member of an embryonic European élite, Tottenham Hotspur; and two of the three most unsuccessful clubs in the season 1990-1, Aldershot and Halifax Town. Common themes explaining the crises in these two very different clubs/organisations will highlight the major shifts in the fortunes of football in the dawn of its second century of openly professionalised organisation.

A major interpretive strand to this chapter will be the traumas encountered by the League in its reluctant embrace of the new, its inelegant stumble towards modernity. In this, the League shares a dilemma with other cultural institutions which were born of the nineteenth-century industrial society, which have given pleasure to millions in traditional forms, but which have begun to look anachronistic in an age — which some would no doubt call post-modern — of cosmopolitan innovation, cultural experimentation and bland consumer sovereignty. In the same week in which news of the Football Association's initiative broke, the phased closure of London Zoo was leaked to the press. Sentimentalists called for the protection and retention of an institution dating from the 1820s; progressives pointed to the outdatedness of the London Zoo concept.

To progressive critics of the established cultural institution such as the football stadium and the zoological gardens, a different model of the future beckoned: the modern, purpose-built leisure environment, the consumer-freindly, multi-experience facility — the Disneyesque themepark. Big, big money would be needed for mega-complexes such as these, the need for and arrival of which would make the traditional nineteenth-century cultural facility less acceptable to a new, discriminating, McDonalds-fed public.

But traditions are not inventions or fictions. Traditional values might well stand for generations of stoutly defended beliefs, principles and practices. It is these principles and the influences upon them which this chapter sets out to examine and account for by looking at what key individuals in the making of the football culture have stood for, and at contemporary tensions over the future of football.

Football has always been characterised by a fascinating set of dynamics: North versus South; working class versus middle class and middle class versus upper class; new money versus old status. Professional players in the hundred years of the League's history have been predominantly working-class; administrators of the League have been predominantly first-generation middle-class; administrators on the level of the Football Association have been more upper-middle- and middle-class. This has led to many clashes of values, of a classically patrician–plebeian kind, in which the old amateur/professional tensions have been relived. To understand the source of such clashes it is necessary to look at the specific origins of the two rival organisations which have dominated English football.

The Football Association (FA)

The FA was formed in 1863. It was formed as an association of clubs, on the basis of an agreement between the representatives of a few clubs (mostly southern English ones) to play each other regularly according to a shared set of rules of play. By 1868 the FA had thirty member clubs; by 1870, thirty-nine clubs. Revealingly, though, only four of these thirty-nine clubs were still in existence by 1900. In the 1870s an increasing number of city- and county-based associations was established throughout England, but as Tony Mason has noted, 'after the speed of this expansion the other most important fact to notice was that all these associations looked to the FA itself and wished to affiliate with it' (Mason, 1980: 15). By the mid-1880s, then, the Football Association was a kind of umbrella body, an administrative catalyst for the county and district associations which were springing up throughout the country. The FA's most celebrated initiative — beyond the standardisation of the rules of the game — was the setting up of the FA Cup. This was first competed for in 1871–2, based on the public school competition at Harrow, and inspired by the youthful experiences of the Football Association's Secretary of the time, Charles Alcock. At the age of 22, he had been one of the influences upon the formation of the Wanderers FC, one of the fifteen teams first to contest the FA Cup in its inaugural season. The list of all fifteen of these entrants makes fascinating reading:

1. Wanderers	6. Hitchin	11. Royal Engineers
2. Harrow Chequers	7. Maidenhead	12. Reigate Priory
3. Clapham Rovers	8. Great Marlow	13. Hampstead Heathens
4. Upton Park	9. Queens Park (Glasgow)	14. Barnes
5. Crystal Palace	10. Donington School (Spalding)	15. Civil Service

The winner of this inaugural tournament was Wanderers, a team including 'four Harrow graduates, three Etonians, and one representative each from Westminster, Charterhouse, Oxford and Cambridge' (Tischler, 1981: 26). The Association itself had been founded by representatives of Harrow, Eton, Winchester, Rugby and Westminster Schools, and in its early days recruited exclusively from the upper classes and the public schools. Only Donington School (East Midlands/East Anglia) and Queens Park (Glasgow) represented any part of the United Kingdom outside Greater London and the Home Counties of South East England. It was not until 1882 that this essentially Southern and upper-class domination of the FA Cup was challenged, when Blackburn Rovers reached the Final, to be followed in 1883 by Blackburn Olympic's historic defeat of Old Etonians. Blackburn Rovers themselves then won the Cup in 1884 and 1885; after the 1884 victory a disapproving commentator in the capital wrote that London had witnessed:

an incursion of Northern barbarians on Saturday — hot-blooded Lancastrians, sharp of tongue, rough and ready, of uncouth garb and speech. A tribe of Sudanese Arabs let loose in the Strand would not excite more amusement and curiosity. (Pall Mall Gazette, 31 March 1884, cited in Tischler, 1981: 124)

If the followers of football were seen in this condescending light, the emergent professional was accepted as a necessary evil. It was 'veiled professionalism' to which the FA objected most vehemently, a form of professionalism which was in the words of C. W. Alcock, the FA's first Secretary, 'the evil to be repressed', and which needed therefore to be brought out into the open. As well as founding the FA Cup, Alcock was also the 'father of international matches' (Green, 1960: 61). The Cup's inauguration in 1871 had been followed by the first international match between England and Scotland, in Glasgow, in 1872, which led directly to the foundation of the Scottish, Welsh and Irish FAs in 1873, 1876 and 1880 respectively. Right at the beginning of the FA's existence, then, the two central concerns of the national knockout cup and the fielding of an international side were its clear priorities. Time and time again over the next 120 years, the FA would clash with the Football League over the implications of their discrete priorities.

Alcock held the post of Secretary to the FA from 1870 to 1895, and was succeeded by Frederick Wall (Secretary, 1895–1934) and Stanley Rous (Secretary, 1934–62) — an average of just over thirty years per incumbent. Wall had trained in the legal profession, and had himself been steeped in the upper-middle-class amateur ethic, shocked by the fact that bookmakers had quoted odds on the outcome of the first Cup Final: 'the austere, top-hatted Sir Frederick Wall, had been an arch-conservative who had longed for the days when football had been just a game and when he, as he often told people, had eaten a rump steak before playing Royal Engineers in the F.A. Cup, so careless had he been of the result' (Wagg, 1984: 32). Wall consistently offered the most reluctant of embraces to the embryonic world game, retaining a snooty distance in a response typical of the 'phlegmatic English upper-class: "The Council of the Football Association cannot see the advantages of such a Federation [FIFA], but on all such matters upon which joint action was desirable they would be prepared to confer" ' (Tomlinson, 1986: 85).

Wall kept the Association ticking over, but ran it as what Rous was later to call a 'quiet backwater'. Rous was to jerk the organisation more fully towards the modern age, with a twin strategy: to cultivate the world sporting bodies; and to reform the structure of the game on the home front by establishing a base at school and junior level. When Rous took up the post in the mid-1930s 'junior football was . . . controlled at the top by a form of middle-class gerontocracy' (Fishwick, 1989: 18). The FA's President from 1923 to his death in 1937, Charles Clegg, was also active at regional level, dominating the Sheffield and Hallamshire County Football Association (SHCFA) for more than forty years without the intrusion of 'debates or elections. Clegg was widely admired for pioneering the fifteen-minute AGM, and the SHCFA in the 1940s fought off an attempt by working-men's club teams, used to the more democratic procedures of the Club and Institute Union, to reform the system of contesting elections to the Committee' (Fishwick, 1989: 18). As well as such an oligarchy-cum-gerontocracy, Rous inherited a situation in which the insularity of the English game was seen as something to be proud of, and turned this round so effectively that by 1961 he left the post in order to take up the Presidency of the world ruling body, FIFA.

Rous was born into the lower-middle classes (his two elder sisters were schoolteachers) and studied at St. Luke's College, Exeter, before going on to teach at Watford Grammar School. He was a member of the developing service professions, socially mobile and inherited no established privileges. He played football at college, then in the army during the Great War, but his major impact on the game, initially, was as a top-class referee.

His sporting values were staunchly amateurist. In a broadcast documentary tribute on the occasion of his 90th birthday he recalled his own playing days:

We used to look upon it as a sport, as a recreation, we had little regard of points and league positions and cup competitions. We used to play friendly matches mostly. There was always such a sporting attitude and the winners always clapped the others off the field and so on . . . that's all changed of course. (BBC Radio 4, 22 April 1985)

Ironically, it was the schoolteacher/amateur himself who was to do so much to change it, modernising the English game in a number of important ways. He established a more efficient bureaucratic base for the FA; introduced teaching schemes at all levels of the game — coaching, playing and refereeing; encouraged players to qualify as coaches, and then sell their skills around the world; and firmly re-established the English game in soccer's global politics. In

spite of his commitment to such worldwide developments, as early as the 1962
World Cup in Chile he could mourn the loss of more innocent times such as
the 1930s when international matches were 'free and easy affairs'. Rous
straddled the old world and the new: he respected long-established values
whilst cultivating cosmopolitanism; he stood for archaic amateur values in
playing yet streamlined the professional side of the game's administration. He
could hob-nob with the Queen at Cup Finals, accept his peerage for services to
sport in 1949, the year after the London Olympics, and publicly rebuke the
Prime Minister Harold Wilson for posing with the victorious English team
after the 1966 World Cup victory. Charles Clegg had been knighted in 1927,
Frederick Wall in 1931. Sir Stanley Rous stood firmly in the same tradition —
honoured for his contribution on a national scale — and yet took the FA into
long-neglected spheres of influence.

Rous's successor in 1961 was Denis Follows, a professional administrator
with a background in the airline industry. After war service in the RAF he
served as Secretary of the British Airline Pilots Association until 1962, also
acting as Chairman of the National Joint Council for Civil Air Transport. He
had been Honorary Treasurer of the FA since 1956. He was schooled in
Lincoln before studying languages at Nottingham University and working in
the professional world of education in the 1930s, first as President of the
National Union of Students and then as a schoolteacher at Chiswick Grammar
School for Boys. On his appointment *The Times* called him 'an able speaker
with a clear mind' and a genuine love of football (*The Times*, 20 February
1962). He was succeeded in 1973 by Ted Croker, whose past experience of
modest playing success at professional level with Charlton Athletic and
Headington United (now Oxford United), combined with his proved dynamism
as a successful businessman, provided an appealing mix for a demanding set of
tasks. Croker too had been a flight lieutenant in the RAF, from the age of 18 in
1942. During his playing career Croker had, in his own words, 'always insisted
on having an outside job', and he moved smoothly into a career in sales and
then as self-made businessman, becoming chairman of a concrete manufacturing company. Some of his subsequent pronouncements, particularly on
hooliganism and women's fooball (see Williams and Woodhouse in this
volume) were typical of the self-made Conservative. *The Times*, described his
appointment as 'surprising', and Croker himself as however, 'trendy' (*The
Times*, 22 June 1973). He championed the concept of a smaller élite league, but
talked the language of cooperation: 'We must reduce the overload on our top
players. We are asking artists to be artisans. We are making the people with the
highest artistic skill play the most matches . . . There's no doubt we shall come
to a smaller premier league.' But despite this prophecy, Croker did not want
out-and-out conflict between the League and the FA: 'A battle is not the
answer. If the executive at the FA felt they were getting into a situation leading
to a battle there would be a ceasefire because we wouldn't pursue it. This
development [i.e. premier league] cannot be imposed on one side of football by
another' (*The Times*, 27 October 1973). Croker steered the FA precariously
through years of on-field, off-field and on-terrace crises, and when he retired as
General Secretary in 1989 it was to the Football League that the FA then
turned for a hardened administrative figure. With a new title of Chief

Executive, Graham Kelly moved South from Lytham to Lancaster Gate. In unison with FA Chairman Bert Millichip, Kelly embodied the shift that has characterised the FA's recent profile — a shift from the self-perpetuating upper- and middle-class oligarchy to a lower-middle-class meritocracy. And socially mobile meritocrats will often have little respect for history. It is intriguing that the moment of the most cataclysmic tension between the Football Association and the Football League is at precisely the time when they seemed to be developing a more genuinely integrated set of interests.

The Football League

Founded in 1888, the League was an inevitable outcome of the FA's legalisation of professionalism in the summer of 1885. Once professionalism was accepted, the expanding football industry needed to be put on a sound business footing, with regular fixtures, standardised procedures, rigorous monitoring of professional standards and enforcibility of accepted rules and regulations. The strongest teams which had moved towards a professional footing were in the industrial communities of the North of England and the Midlands. The founder members of the Football League were:

1. Preston North End	5. Bolton Wanderers	9. Burnley
2. Aston Villa	6. West Bromwich Albion	10. Derby County
3. Wolverhampton Wanderers	7. Accrington	11. Notts County
4. Blackburn Rovers	8. Everton	12. Stoke

Lancashire and the Midlands were the geographical strongholds of the pioneers of the League. William McGregor of Aston Villa was the prime mover, inspired, it is sometimes said, by the innovative new National Basketball League in the United States, but in his own expressed view modelling the League on the County Championship in cricket. McGregor himself was a self-employed, small-time shopkeeper selling linen. He also had a passion for football and a sense of its potential contribution to sport. Social conscience and municipal pride mingled with a passionate Liberal politics and a Methodist non-conformist conscience. McGregor was 'a dedicated Methodist, at a time when Christianity, combined with a concern for social welfare, often manifested itself in the promotion of sport' (Inglis, 1988: 2). Along with McGregor, six individuals met on the eve of the 1888 Cup Final. The Blackburn Rovers representative was a factory inspector. Burnley's representative was an auctioneer. The West Bromwich representative was a former player turned club secretary who had initially worked in a spring and scale manufacturing plant. Wolverhampton Wanderers were represented by a local boot- and shoe-maker. Stoke sent a local printer, soon to become the League's first secretary. Only one 'gentleman' attended that meeting, a solicitor and former Rugby schoolboy, representing Notts County.

So the socio-economic and cultural roots of the Football League are very clear: Northern and skilled working-class-cum-self-employed. The Football League was not a separatist initiative — McGregor was a faithful adherent to the FA as the ruling body — but it represented a very different set of sporting principles to those of the founding members of the FA itself. In the years immediately prior to the formation of the League, the commercial imperative had come more and more to the fore in the industrial areas where the game was flourishing. Clubs were recognising that players must be paid. A committee man at Burnley said in 1885: 'The fact of it is, the public will not go to see inferior players. During the first year we did not pay a single player, and nobody came to see us' (cited in Tischler, 1981: 47).

The FA's roots lie in the professional class's need for therapeutic exercise of a morally uplifting kind , and in certain circumstances in the patrician's zeal to convert the less civilised; whereas the Football League's roots lie in a vigorously assertive localized culture, and an alliance of the interests of the (often self-made) local élite and those of the predominantly working-class player and spectator.

In the rest of this section typical but key prominent figures in the history of the League are examined in more detail, following on from consideration of general patterns of regional influence in the League's history.

The Presidency of the Football League is a position which has remained dominated by representatives of Northern and Midland clubs, and delegates from Lancashire clubs in particular. Table 2.1 shows this, along with the occupational background of the incumbents. Of the thirteen Presidents of the Football League, six were from Lancashire clubs, one from Yorkshire, four from the Midlands/East Midlands, one from the North East and one from the East Coast of Central England. Early domination was in the hands of Lancashire men, and the troubled years of the late 1980s have seen the leadership back in the same hands. It is undeniable, then, that the leadership of the League has Northern roots, and that as an institution the League is founded on strong regional loyalties and identities. Although by its centenary year the League's eighty-six Committee men from forty-five different clubs did not exhibit an obvious bias to North West England — Everton, West Bromwich, Birmingham, Arsenal and Newcastle had provided most members of the Committee — the leadership had certainly had a Lancastrian brand. The location of the League's headquarters — up until 1946 in modest office accommodation rented by the League Secretary in Preston, then in an equally unprepossessing terraced house in the town bought by the League itself, and then from 1959 (and controversially) in a converted hotel in the retirement coastal resort of Lytham St. Annes — stubbornly reinforced this regional emphasis, in stark contrast to the ostentatious headquarters of the FA from 1929 onwards, around the corner from Marble Arch at 16 Lancaster Gate, in the country's capital.

Simon Inglis has claimed that two single individuals more than any others have affected the structure and character of the League in its 100-year history. These are the 'little lawyer from Lancashire', Charles Sutcliffe, and Alan Hardaker, the League's Secretary from 1957 for twenty-two critically stormy years.

The Lancashire legacy

Charles Sutcliffe did not assume the Presidency of the League until 1936, but he was a Committee man from 1898 through to 1939, the year of his death,

Table 2.1 Presidents of the Football League, 1892–1991

1892–94	W. McGregor	Aston Villa	Shopkeeper
1894–1910	J. J. Bentley	Bolton	Railway clerk
1910–36	J. McKenna	Liverpool	Grocer's boy, vaccination officer
1936–39	C. E. Sutcliffe	Burnley	Solicitor
1939–49	W. C. Cuff	Everton	Solicitor
1949–54	A. Drewry	Grimsby	Fish-processing business
1955–57	A. H. Oakley	Wolves	Coal merchant
1957–66	J. Richards	Barnsley	Pitboy/self-made manager/businessman
1966–74	L. T. Shipman	Leicester	Wholesale fruit/road haulage businessman
1974–81	Lord Westwood	Newcastle	Railway clerk/ manager/businessman
1981–86	J. J. Dunnett	Notts County	Solicitor/Labour Member of Parliament
1986–89	P. D. Carter	Everton	Managing director (Littlewoods Pools)
1989–(August)	W. Fox	Blackburn	Fruit/vegetable wholesaler, managing director (vehicle company)

with just one year of non-membership (1902–3). Sutcliffe was born in Burnley
in 1864, the son of a local well-established solicitor, and raised in a strictly
Methodist household which did not allow any games on Sunday, or even
newspapers in the house. As a young man he played rugby for Burnley Rovers,
a club which converted to soccer in 1882 and changed its name to Burnley FC.
Qualifying as a solicitor in 1886, around the time he actually stopped playing
for Burnley, he then became a nationally prominent referee and became one of
Burnley's directors in 1897. On giving up refereeing in 1898 Sutcliffe was
immediately elected on to the Management Committee of the League, and
joined a group of men steeped in non-conformist, respectable Liberal values. In
his politics and religion, Inglis observes, Sutcliffe continued to stand for the
core values of the League's founder, William McGregor. He was an active
Liberal, and a 'devout Methodist':

Sutcliffe . . . campaigned ardently for the Temperance Movement . . . as a youth
Charles was a leading member of the Curzon Street Mission's minstrel troupe in
Burnley. He taught in Sunday School, once gave evidence to a Royal Commission on
the problem of alcoholism, and . . . became a much sought after speaker on religion, the
Temperance Movement and, of course, football. (Inglis, 1988: 108)

Sutcliffe was the brains behind the four key phases of expansion of the League,
in 1898, 1905, 1919 and 1920–3, moves which increased the number of clubs
in the League from thirty-two to eighty-eight, and made it a truly national body
across England and Wales. He was also the spirit behind the League's survival,

indeed its strengthening, during the years of the First World War. He prosecuted corrupt players in the courts; organised refereeing appointments; and drew up League fixture lists. He also worked for the FA, on committees concerned with referees, international selection and the revision of rules; and sat on the International League Board and the Anglo-Irish League Board. He was President of the Lancashire FA and of the Northern Counties Amateur Championship; he served on Appeals Committees for twenty other leagues; and was Chairman and then Vice-President of Rossendale United — all of this on top of his devotion to Burnley Football Club and his work as a solicitor. In the world of football Sutcliffe was branded the 'football dictator' and acknowledged as the 'brains of football'. He had his failures in his lifetime of involvement, as well as his achievements. He failed to get approval for a two-referee system in 1935; and fought and lost the League's battles with the Pools companies in 1936, when details on League fixtures were withheld until the eve of some matches, as the League sought to establish a copyright for its fixture list, and in a confusion of mixed motives either to undermine the football pools gambling industry (the moral motive), or benefit commercially from the sale of the fixture-list (the business motive). But for forty years he cajoled, bullied, disciplined and developed the League towards the modern era. Indeed, Inglis identifies Sutcliffe's as the single most influential contribution to the development of the League in its entire history: 'His exhaustive mind took in fixtures, insurance schemes, wages, transfers, refereeing, the jubilee celebrations and the jubilee history' (Inglis, p. 163).

Sutcliffe also embodied an extremely important philosophy of mutual protection. For him the expanding League was like a prolifically multiplying extended family network. As he presided over its growth, he combined his adversarial skills with those of the compromising legalistic mind, and blended this with his patriarchal and paternalistic concern for the well-being of all the family. Two examples clearly illustrate how his specific skills could be put to work in defence of this philosophy.

First, in the 1890s when Charles Clegg of the FA was making a strong case for reform of the retain and transfer system, Sutcliffe defended the system on the basis of a League in which the better-off members would have shared interests with the less well-off members. At the League's 'Coming of Age Banquet' in 1909 Clegg reiterated his view that the FA was a magisterial body which presided, not always at all popularly, over the whole of the game; whereas the League was a body of entertainers. Clegg, after close to a quarter of a century haggling with the League over the hypocrisy of its financial arrangements concerning transfer fees, maximum wages, bonus payments and the like, observed that 'if this game cannot be carried on under honourable conditions, the sooner it goes to the wall the better for everybody' (Inglis, p. 72). Clegg, a Sheffield solicitor, Secretary to the FA and stout defender of amateurism, believed that there should be no imposed earning limits for players, and that they should also be free to choose where and for whom to play. The FA expressed its view with uncompromising succinctness:

In the opinion of (our) Committee, the practice of buying and selling players is unsportsmanlike and most objectionable in itself, and ought not to be entertained by those who desire to see the game played under proper conditions . . . During our enquiry it was stated that some clubs derived considerable pecuniary advantage from training young players and then selling them to the more prominent clubs. We think the practice in such cases, when applied to human beings, altogether discreditable to any system bearing the name of sport. (cited in Inglis, p. 46)

To Sutcliffe, though, and other prominent and principled League personnel, such economic realities were what retained the League's balance of rich/poor, powerful/weak. Sutcliffe and others stood up to Clegg's reformist interventions at key moments in the 1890s.

Similarly, in the Kingaby case in 1912 the same issue arose, with the same principle at stake. One of Aston Villa's former players — Kingaby — was supported by the Players' Union in a court case in which it was argued that an overvaluation of the player by Villa had restricted his work possibilities. Sutcliffe himself briefed the lawyer representing Aston Villa and convinced him that the retain and transfer system was legally watertight. Kingaby's case was not supported by the judge, and League controls were reasserted. The principle behind this was not just anti-unionism — though Sutcliffe is on record as saying that 'the League could not be dictated to by any organisation' — but, again, the power of all clubs to control their players equally. A free-for-all in the playing markets would no doubt strengthen the rich at the expense of the aspirations of the poorer clubs. Charles Sutcliffe ruled with a rod of tradition, but it was a protective rod. His anxieties were certainly prophetic. A freer movement of sporting talent in a commercially intensified climate would create an élite group of clubs.

The second example of Sutcliffe defending his central principle was in the immediate post-war years after the Great War. Players were demanding a doubling of expenses to £2 per week. Having ordered out the press and the players, the Management Committee handed over to Sutcliffe. He ordered an evaluation of the economic state of the clubs and then made a classically conciliatory proposal:

If every club paid each player £2, as . . . proposed, ten of the well supported clubs would have to subsidize seventeen of the others. The remaining thirteen would neither pay out nor receive help. It was the typical Sutcliffe formula: the rich helping the poor, to keep the family strong. (Inglis, p. 112)

Charles Sutcliffe's Lancastrian legacy has been a fascinating one: to argue for an authoritarian grip on the functioning of the League, in the interests of the minnows as well as the mighty.

In Sutcliffe's day the longest-serving Secretary of the League was Tom Charnley, who held the position from 1902 to 1933. He worked from four different rented offices in Preston during his thirty-one years in the job. Charnley was in the same Lancastrian mould as Sutcliffe — together they traversed the country with the ring of a respectable but unglamorous legal partnership. Sutcliffe saw him as the perfect Secretary, and he ruled the roost at the League headquarters until the age of 73, ensuring a succession, too, by bringing in as assistant in 1921, his son-in-law and next-door-neighbour, Fred

Howarth. Howarth himself became Secretary in 1933 and was to appoint
Charnley's grandson as Assistant Secretary in 1946. Fred Howarth had spent a
short spell as a teacher before serving in the First World War and then joining
what in retrospect would look like a seventy-one-year-long 'family business'.
Fred Howarth, Secretary himself until 1956, could not guarantee the succession, however: Charnley's grandson only lasted five years and Fred's nephew
Eric would stay with the League until 1973, but never in one of the big jobs.
Clearly, the world was changing. A young man called Alan Hardaker had been
standing in the wings since 1951, and was well aware of the need for
rationalisation, modernisation and the plethora of modernising initiatives
needed to usher the League into the contemporary world of communications
and cosmopolitanism.

But Tom Charnley supported Sutcliffe in the first three decades of the
century. They were similar types — both Liberals and committed Christians;
and no one remembers Charnley raising his voice or consuming alcohol,
whether at work or at play, his main relaxation being the game of bowls.
Retiring in 1933, he received from the League a £350 annual pension, and a
£200 cheque, along with an engraved silver tray. The following year, by
contrast, when retiring as Secretary of the FA, Sir Frederick Wall was given a
golden handshake of £10,000.

The metaphors of family and friendly society — lifelong obligation to shared
values, and support for the infirm or unfortunate when necessary; all steeped
in a rigidly paternalistic discipline defended with a zealousness akin to a moral
crusade — best describe the Lancashire legacy of the League.

Go West, young man: from Preston to Lytham

Alan Hardaker joined the Football League as Assistant Secretary when the
League felt compelled to advertise the post for the first time ever in 1951. After
a high-profile working life as a senior naval officer during the war and then as
Lord Mayor's Secretary in two big towns — Portsmouth and Hull — he arrived
at Preston to be greeted by a graceless resentment of his meritocratic
worldliness and potential. Fred Howarth would not even give this high-flying
39-year-old a desk; and Hardaker was snubbed extraordinarily in his first few
years, unconfirmed even in his post as Assistant Secretary until 1955. A day in
the life of the League was an unhurried day, and Hardaker began to diagnose
the condition of the organisation, 'a machine covered with rust and cobwebs':

Pressure was almost non-existent and a day at League headquarters was slow,
uncluttered, peaceful. It often reminded me of an endless patrol at sea — boredom
sometimes strangled you. Nobody really had enough to do, but Fred Howarth loved it
this way. He was against change of any sort, particularly if it meant more work for him
or threatened the familiar, traditional flow of life at headquarters . . .
I was a salaried outcast, I was given no responsibility. I was not allowed to talk to
anyone. I was told nothing. I was never asked for an opinion. I was not even allowed to
go to Inter-League matches and the only football I saw was at Preston — but even here I
knew nobody and nobody, apparently, wanted to know me. (cited in Inglis, p. 188)

Fred Howarth's endless patrol in a calm sea was ignoring meteorological forecasts, as Hardaker was well aware. Football could not keep cruising cosily into a secure future in an unchanging world. A post-war period of austerity ensured a period of peak popularity for the professional game, but many alternatives to the consumer gate-money were emerging, and the expectations of players themselves were certainly increasing. Hardaker sat in isolation but not idleness in his early years at the League, observing the consistently downward trend in the graphs of Football League attendances after the record-breaking figures of 1949.

Howarth had a style, that of the strict Methodist headmaster that he initially set out in life to become; he held strong views on the undesirability of betting, the sanctity of the maximum wage, and the absurdity, as he saw it, of player power or collective organisation by the players. He ambled through his administrative responsibilities, in Hardaker's eyes, doing only the bare minimum necessary. He also covered whatever tracks he might have left in his leisurely stride through League business by ignoring the Press; not filing material; cutting out selected minutes/items from Management Committee meetings, including Members' resolutions; collecting all written notes at meetings so that no personal notes could be taken away by members; and getting Committee members to sign blank cheques so that he could pay the bills. In the 1950s relatively low-profile and acquiescent Presidents had allowed Howarth to go on his own unchallenged and unchallenging way. 'If Fred Howarth did not like an idea it was never implemented — or even recorded,' recalled Hardaker. The new team of 1957 — Hardaker at the helm, and Joe Richards of Barnsley in the President's position — recognised the challenges of the day. Its response was to meet the challenge, but without sacrificing long-established core values.

Hardaker and Richards made up an ecumenical team. Hardaker himself was from a Hull family committed to Liberalism and Methodism; Richards was a Barnsley boy, a freemason, a practising Christian and an Independent politician. Both were born into white-collar 'management' worlds of work, where respectable careers in management, business and administration were promised as a reward for hard work. Both played football in their youth, Hardaker for Hull reserves, so becoming the first League Secretary ever to have been 'on the books' of a League club (as an amateur, as — ever pragmatic — he turned down the opportunity of signing up for an always precarious professional future). Richards suffered an industrial injury which curtailed his playing aspirations, but he was a fanatical Barnsley follower and at the age of 46 became Chairman of Barnsley Football Club, a position which he held for thirty-two years.

Richards was born in 1888, the year the League was founded. He stood down as President in 1966, the year England won the World Cup (with a team made up entirely of players from League clubs: five players from Lancashire clubs, four players from London clubs, one from the East Midlands and one from Yorkshire; that old Northern/Midlands combination had now conquered the world, Richards' beloved Yorkshire tipping the balance away from the South). And this was no ordinary Joe bowing out after a long and dedicated career in the game. It was Sir Joe — the 'Soccer Knight with the common touch', as the popular press gleefully labelled him — knighted the month before the World

Cup Final, ennobled by Harold Wilson, a Huddersfield Town fan and famous professional Yorkshireman who was then the country's Prime Minister.

Joe Richards was also a citizen with a conscience. He always showed a great interest in the welfare of young people, sat as a Governor of Barnsley Grammar School, chaired the juvenile court and spent twenty years sitting on the local probation committee. His sense of regional pride was legendary — he even stated that he got more pleasure out of Barnsley winning the Third Division than from England winning the World Cup.

Together Hardaker and Richards confronted the problems of the modern period. They introduced the League Cup in 1960, a tournament that was to emerge as a major one as soon as it was established as a gateway to Europe; though the metamorphoses of sponsorship from 1981 onwards might have confused them when the sponsorship meant that the trophy was known as the Milk Cup, then the Littlewoods Challenge Cup and the Rumbelows Cup. At the 1991 Final at Wembley the players were presented not to some member of an anachronistic royal clan, but to a person of the moment — Tracey Bateman from Edgbaston, Rumbelows Employee of the Year. Perhaps this was too much for the out-of-sorts aristocrats of the game, Manchester United, who were beaten by the Second Division Yorkshire side Sheffield Wednesday. Whether Sir Joe would have approved of the image of the moment is hard to tell. As for the League, in such a deal it gained a lot of money but lost its identity, bundled out of the limelight by Rumbelows: new generations of television-football fans in the late 1980s and the 1990s would not know what the League Cup was.

Joe Richards was also determined. In 1952, in his earlier years on the League Management Committee, he had proposed that the League establish a youth cup among its member clubs, but there was no support for his idea. He immediately took the idea to the FA, and within a few months the FA Youth Cup began. As this indifferent response by the League to one of its own stalwart members shows, the blinkered thinking of the League itself has on occasion pushed it towards forms of parochialism when it had the chance to pursue a policy of enlightened patronage. Episodes such as this show how a fuller remit for the good of the game generally might be more openly fostered in FA rather than League quarters.

Joe Richards and Alan Hardaker worked together to adapt an old dream to the demands of a new age. The philosophy behind their dream stressed continuity of core principles. This led them inexorably towards some very public defeats over issues which had gained an unstoppable momentum, and over which they lost much public credibility. The maximum wage had been a yoke around the talented individual player's neck for generations; the retain and transfer system had looked like an infringement of labour rights for the bulk of the League's history. They were principles fundamental to the formative values of the League's founders. Their survival in the age of affluence and a climate of the 'You've never had it so good' rhetoric looked almost ludicrous. A fluent, confident, irreverent figure emerged to speak for the players in the form of the bearded Fulham inside-forward, Jimmy Hill. With television and the popular press focusing in on the League's business in unprecedentedly intense and sustained ways there was an unanswerable case for overall reform of the League's structure and administration.

The maximum wage was abolished in January 1961, after the players' union was geared up to strike, backed publicly now even by iconic traditional figures such as Stanley Matthews (Wagg, 1984: ch. 8). Hardaker had sensed the need for reform, but when Richards asked the clubs to grant the Management Committee full powers with which to negotiate, this was refused. Hardaker showed a progressive pragmatism here, but was not empowered to act upon it. Two years later the famous George Eastham case in the High Court adjudged the rule in the 'retain and transfer' system which allowed clubs to retain a player to be 'an undue restraint of trade'. Some of the core principles which Charles Sutcliffe had stood for were now looking close to redundant, overtaken by history.

Hardaker had been fully aware of this, and drew upon his intimate knowledge of the inner workings of the 'machine covered with rust and cobwebs' to develop a radical plan for the modernizing and restructuring of the game. He did this as early as the 1960-1 season, early on in his partnership with Joe Richards. The League Cup proposal which surfaced in this plan was only one part of an overall package for the development of the game. The plan was called 'Pattern for Football', and proposed:

1. five divisions of twenty clubs (two of them making up an expanded regionally based fourth division);
2. four promoted, four relegated each year, to sustain public interest;
3. a League Cup competition, played at the beginning of the season, in regional groups.
4. automatic expulsion for a club seeking re-election two years in a row;
5. an amendment of the voting system at League meetings, scrapping the 75 per cent 'majority' rule.

Hardaker employed a market research consultancy to analyse the public–player relationship, and got the Management Committee to revive the debate on reconstruction. The clubs ignored most of the ideas first time round, backing just the League Cup, but the debate was sustained until a decisive vote in 1963 rejected all innovative plans and opted for an unreflecting adherence to the tried, tested and the familiar. The 'Pattern for Football' would have been adopted if at the Annual Meeting of June 1963 it had attracted thirty-seven votes, so securing the necessary three-quarters majority. The plan received only twenty-nine votes in favour. The twenty or so delegates who did not back this plan increased the resentment of non-League clubs who were looking for fairer means of winning entry into the League; and of the FA, which was interested in creating conditions more conducive to the cultivation of a national side (the World Cup was only three seasons away), and in creaming off an élite network of clubs into a Super League in preparation for a European League that the FA Secretary Stanley Rous believed to be inevitable.

Hardaker's plan was a beautiful balancing act, extending the concept of the League and opening it up more, but at the same time streamlining it. Under his proposals 100 League clubs would play 1900 League matches; at the time 92 League clubs were playing 2028 matches. The new League Cup would add more matches, excitement and revenue. Hardaker recalled that some club chairmen, though, had even refused to recognise the precision and correctness of this calculation. Hardaker has sometimes been depicted as a rigid battleaxe, an authoritarian dictator; but he was powerless in the face of the traditional obstinancies of the club chairmen:

We were wasting our time. It was defeated by selfishness and shallow thinking. It was rejected because, myopically, too many clubs could see no farther than their own little worlds. They were not interested in the future of the game as a whole. Their own concern was self-preservation. They closed their eyes and minds to anything which even remotely threatened their status and lifestyle. (cited in Inglis, p. 230)

So spoke St. Alan of St. Anne's, as he was cruelly called by critics of his style, in sad recollection of his doomed attempts to act as the Saviour of Soccer. But he claimed to have brought in £12 million for the League, and a rather more adequate system of accounting of such sums than his predecessor Fred Howarth had provided. In his time the League headquarters were moved to Lytham St. Annes, a half hour's drive west of Preston, so, for whatever motive, staying faithful to the League's Lancastrian roots (Lytham is a few bracing miles' walk down the coast from Blackpool). He recognised that entry into European competitions would have advantages. In 1959 he masterminded the League's legal victory which secured big money for the Pools companies' use of the League fixture list. In the early 1960s he flushed out the rigging and betting scandals that had involved a large number of players, mostly in the lower divisions, but rumours of which were harming the game's image. In his time at the helm, under the Presidencies of Richards and then Len Shipman of Leicester and Lord Westwood of Newcastle, he gave the League a chance, 'coaxing, dragging and bullying' it 'from its dusty, tradition-bound state in the mid-1950s into a tough, commercially-minded giant which stood a chance (but only a chance) of surviving the even harsher, tougher days which loomed ahead' (Inglis, p. 291).

Hardaker was single-minded, ruthless and often abrasive. His opinionated response to professional problems was manna to the press. John Roberts recalls Hardaker's own reaction to the invasion of Derby by Manchester United fans in the 1970s, Hardaker's first direct experience of the 'arrival of a mob in a town': 'It was frightening,' said Hardaker, 'they came out of Derby station like rats out of a sewer, and when the psychiatrists and sociologists and do-gooders try to put it all down to the mothers of these kids not putting them on their potties when they were babies, I'm not having it' (John Roberts, 'Violent Knights of the League Table', *The Guardian*, 16 January 1980, p. 21). But if he condemned the masses, as he saw them, or the mob, he certainly did not court the élite. He had no time for the hauteur of the FA, and was even sent to Coventry for a period of six months by the diplomat supreme, Sir Stanley Rous. Rous's cosmopolitan aspirations, his public school moralities, his hob-nobbing with Jules Rimet, his Presidency of FIFA — all these urbane characteristics would cut no ice in Lytham. For in the end, for all his revisionist progressivism, Hardaker was defending long-established structures. He never sought, in Simon Inglis' words, 'to trim the numbers or create an élite' (p. 288).

Thirty years on from the thinking behind the 'Pattern for Football', the dispute continues to rage as to the relative claims and merits of the League, the individual clubs and the national interest. Much has changed. Many of the communities for which football was a vital form of cultural expression have very different profiles; new generations of soccer fans buy franchised strips of big-city clubs on the basis of their television viewing patterns and a glimpse at the top First Division positions on Ceefax or Oracle. The cost of their strip might have gone most of the way towards the price of a season ticket for their local club. The League could never have hoped simply to survive in its traditional form, with television and sponsor money directed at glamour clubs, and those clubs becoming increasingly hostile to any policy of mutual benefit. For such clubs, the metaphor of the benefit society or the extended family was giving way to that of the League as Robin Hood. Something had to give, and one spark was the Heysel Tragedy and the exclusion of English clubs from European competition. This led to immediate threats of breakaway and Super Leagues, with the Big Five — Everton, Liverpool, Tottenham Hotspur, Arsenal and Manchester United (London and Lancashire in league at last) — planning to invite another thirteen to fifteen clubs to form a new autonomous Super League with them, free to set up its own television and sponsorship deals. The marketing possibilities of such a small group were irresistible to these clubs.

Compromises were struck in the 1980s and the League staggered out of the decade shaken to its core yet bonded by the crises of hooliganism and the tragedies of the Bradford fire and the Hillsborough disaster. By the autumn of 1990 there was optimistic talk of unification of the two bodies. The League had appointed to a new post — Chief Executive — in the early 1990, and had a marketing/commercial director in post. And Alan Hardaker's protégé and eventual successor, Graham Kelly (League Secretary 1979–88), was now in the top job — newly defined as Chief Executive, but in 'essentially the same' post as earlier Secretaries, as an FA spokesperson put it — at the FA. But things reverted to form by the early summer of 1991, when FA plans to form its own Super League were revealed. The new Europe of post-1992 free trade was beckoning and the big clubs were not likely to object to a change of stewardship. Lytham was beginning to look undeniably antediluvian; with superb irony the sounds from the FA in Lancaster Gate were unambiguously contemporary, and the gatekeepers of the game's wider values were speaking the language of the modern.

Scenario one: Super Leaguers and League Saviours

David Dent, Football League Secretary since the defection of Graham Kelly to Lancaster Gate in 1988, knows his League. He was club secretary at Carlisle for eighteen years, and at Coventry for five. When the news of the FA proposal to recruit top clubs for its own Super League broke, the old FA/League tensions dominated the sporting press. Asked by the *Daily Mirror* whether a Super League would mean the end of League football, Dent replied: 'Yes, if it goes through the ramifications to the League will be far-reaching.' League President, Bill Fox, a Blackburn fruiterer, called up the spirit of Joe Richards, alleging that ordinary fans would be 'absolutely appalled': 'They are interested in their own team, whether it is Wolves, Crewe or Tottenham Hotspur, not the England team. We can ride along on the crest of a successful England team, but people want to put their own team first' (*Daily Mirror*, 9 April 1991, p. 28). Gordon Taylor, Chief Executive of the Professional Footballers' Association, defended the League:

I am proud of having 92 clubs and 2,000 full-time professionals and 1,200 on youth-training programmes. Our contracts and commitment is with the League. We hear a lot of criticism about the way our football is run, but the control of the players and clubs is better in this country than virtually any other country in the world. (*The Independent*, 8 April 1991, p. 28)

Graham Kelly's 'Blueprint for Football' received strong support from some sports writers. Jeff Powell praised the man who had once been 'perceived as the puppet of the ego-mongers at the League', and went on to endorse the plan:

The F.A. Super League is the future. The Football League is the monolith of the past and their bluff has been called. Their attempts to inveigle themselves into excessive power have little to do with their propaganda about representing the good of the game at large. The grass roots of the game are tended by the Football Association, through the junior, local and county levels of their administration, and not by one League, however overbearing ... 'What's got into Graham?', you could almost hear them asking between the squeals of protest. Perhaps it was their own self-importance when he was trying in vain to run a rational game. ('Kelly Coup Has League Running for Cover', *Daily Mail*, 9 April 1991. p. 39)

The League had developed its own proposals for reform the previous autumn in 'One Game, One Team, One Voice', but this was rejected outright by the FA Council and the FA's proposals immediately put in jeopardy deals worth £3.5 million which the League was working on. Trevor Phillips, the League's commercial director, accused the FA of plagiarism, its proposals being 'essentially a rehash of "One Game, One Team, One Voice". From a commercial point of view, every single item is the same — and I mean every single item. There are no new ideas — what is different is the structure in which to develop those ideas' (cited in Russell Thomas, 'League anger at F.A. "hijack" ', *The Guardian*, 9 April 1991, p. 14). The League also mounted its counter-offensive with a public attack on the FA's plans, launched in the form of an open letter from its own Chief Executive to his FA counterpart. In this letter the FA was accused of being 'unfair, un-ethical, un-British and unworthy' of representing the game, and of threatening to destroy '100 years of endeavour, not for a new dream but an illusion' (Russell Thomas, 'League condemn "unworthy" FA', *The Guardian*, 11 May 1991, p. 21).

The Independent gave one of its two editorial leaders over to the issue. Here it is in full:

In football's best interests

For anyone who does not follow English football — and perhaps for many who do — how the game is run in the country of its birth must seem baffling. Contrary to practice elsewhere, responsibility is divided between two competing organisations. The Football Association is responsible for the rules and laws of the game, for promoting it at grass-roots level, for running the England team and for the FA Cup. The Football League runs the four divisions into which England's 92 senior professional football clubs are divided according to their cumulative performance in League matches. It is from the players in the First Division of the League that the England team is mainly drawn.

The interests of the two organisations inevitably conflict. The FA is primarily interested in quality. The Football League, being composed of member clubs, is also concerned with quantity: clubs have to pay players and have heavy capital and running costs. Notionally, the more fixtures, the more revenue. The FA, by contrast, argues that too many games make for lower quality: the more First Division fixtures and additional competitions there are, the more lack-lustre the performance of the England XI is likely to be.

The conflict is encapsulated in the Football League's decision to put the number of teams in the First Division back up next season from 20 to 22; and in the contradictory proposal, endorsed yesterday by the FA's councillors, to create a Premier League of just 18 clubs. To that the Football League has given a venomous response — not surprisingly, since the proposed Super League would be run by the FA and would drastically undermine the prestige and revenue of the Football League. The Football League's counter-proposal, that it should have equal representation on the FA's executive board of directors, was thrown out yesterday by the FA. The Football League is in no mood to sign a suicide note and the FA is not about to share its responsibilities for its Super League brainchild with the Football League.

The FA argues that a successful side is the key ingredient in generating interest in the game and that fewer fixtures would tend to produce a better England XI. If top division standards were raised, they believe, more people would make the effort to attend. The Premier League's higher profile would, moreover, attract better sponsorship and television revenue. The most successful clubs favour the proposal, since it is likely to give them a larger slice of a larger cake.

The question at the heart of all this is: what form of structure of English football would produce the best results for the maximum number of people? Football is different from most sports in that it arouses fierce local loyalties. It would be sad if the existence of a Premier League had a demoralising effect on teams that remained in the Football League. But the game has to fight for its place in the competitive world of the leisure industry, in which public interest tends to focus on stars or star teams. In such a world, a continental-style Premier League makes sense.

The logical way to solve the conflict would be for the Football League and the FA to merge. Such a move has been mooted, but each party is, inevitably, afraid of being eclipsed in the merged body. Pending such an outbreak of unselfish good sense, the Super League concept deserves encouragement. (*The Independent*, 9 April, 1991, p. 16)

The targeted figure of the contemporary consumer dominates this thinking and analysis: the discriminating consumer, not the traditional fan; the leisure industry, not the local culture — these are the considerations that sway the argument towards support for the FA proposal.

The League's long-standing reluctance to reform, and so guarantee conti-nuity within change, had made it vulnerable. Indeed, in the non-specialist press the issue was bowdlerised to the simplest of proposals: 'Football's First Division is to be disbanded in favour of an 18 club Premier League, the Football Association has indicated . . . On 29 June in Torquay the 92 members of the FA Council will vote on the blueprint and if, as expected, there is an overwhelming majority for the plans, all the power in English soccer will be transferred to the FA' ('First Division "Hijacked" ', *Leisure Opportunities*, Issue Number 86, 15 April 1991). Charles Clegg had suggested that the professional game should go to the wall if it could not sort out its internal economic problems. That was back at the end of the first decade of the century; at the beginning of the last decade the game now looked to be truly up against the wall.

In its League form, the professional game had not so much been criticised as vilified at times in previous years, nowhere more bitingly than in the words of Robert Maxwell. The media magnate had nicknamed the Management Committee the Mismanagement Committee, after the 'Football League . . . called an extraordinary general meeting in January 1988 to stop the Maxwell family extending its influence' (Haines, 1988: 447). Maxwell had rescued Oxford financially in 1982, Derby in 1984, and had dabbled in shareholdings at Reading; reports in 1984 also linked him with bids to buy Birmingham City and Manchester United. In late 1987 the rock singer Elton John, Chair of Watford Football Club, offered Maxwell his majority share in the club for £2 million, and this precipitated the League's refusal to approve such transactions. Maxwell mobilised his media against the League: 'the Football League is now being run by small men with even smaller minds' (cited in Inglis, p. 357). And he continued to speak out personally: 'anything that the League's Mismanagement Committee takes the initiative about has a kiss of death about it. Nobody should pay any attention. These are the people that have allowed the game to be run into the ground. They're just nothing' (BBC 1, 'Sportsnight', 21 November 1990). Whitewashing or simply overlooking his own involvement in notoriously unproductive television negotiations on behalf of the League in the mid-1980s, Maxwell continued to postulate and pontificate on the shortcomings of the League, and even called for the Football League to apologise 'for questioning his motives in seeking a £13 million stake at White Hart Lane' (Joe Lovejoy, 'Maxwell's Threat to Withdraw His Millions', *The Independent*, 23 November 1990, p. 32). He had evidently lent Irving Scholar, the Tottenham Hotspur Chairman, £1.1 million for one of his companies, a sum then loaned on to Tottenham/Spurs to enable the club to pay Barcelona the final instalment of Gary Lineker's transfer fee. Asked whether fans of the club of which he had become Chairman in 1987, Derby, might consider the £1.1 million to have been better spent on their/his own club, Maxwell responded: 'If a supporter asked me about that I would tell him to get stuffed. What I do with my money is my business. Have I not done enough already for Derby? They were in the knackers yard when I was invited to help them' (Lovejoy, ibid.). That same season Derby fell into a steep decline culminating in relegation to the Second Division in 1991. In his discussion of Maxwell's entry into League affairs and club management, Simon Inglis quotes the warning words of the League's founder, William McGregor: 'Beware of the clever sharp men who are creeping into the game' (Inglis, p. 301). During the Spurs affair a League spokesman responded to Maxwell as follows: 'Regrettably, Robert Maxwell mirrors one of the unfortunate traits of the modern game — he can afford the entrance fee, but he doesn't seem to appreciate the value of decorum' (Lovejoy, ibid.). For all its obstinancy, intransigence and procrastinations, the League has represented a clear set of values. Its new

Chief Executive in 1990, Arthur Sandford, came from a background of football officiating, professional public administration and law, very much in the Sutcliffe/Hardaker mould. But more and more the magnanimous messiah to whom more clubs were turning would be revealed as a maverick or a monster.

Scenario two: Spurs, Shots and the Shay

The Football Association is the highest parliament in English football . . . Though an autonomous body with its own regulations, the Football League acts only under the licence of the F.A. The relationship of the FA and the Football League is a delicate one, indeed. Yet by patience and the understanding of each other's objects, friendly relations have been maintained across the years, for all the occasional differences of opinion. (Green, 1960: 47 and 55)

The delicate relationship is now stormy; the 'occasional difference of opinion' appears to be deep-rooted insoluble tensions. And it is the traditionalists of the League who are usually blamed. But as the FA looks to a lucrative future as an entrepreneurial promoter of money-spinning Super Leagues, it is worth looking at the fragility of a faith based almost exclusively upon the notion of financial salvation. Tottenham among the élite and Aldershot at the bottom of the League in 1991 are sobering case-studies. Halifax at the bottom of the League represents an alternative model. Between these extremes lie the values of regional pride, mutual support and local loyalty which have been at the centre of Football League philosophy.

Spurs

Tottenham Hotspur provided the biggest recurrent news story in football throughout the 1990-1 season, as its debts of £13 million or more were revealed, bursting the post-World Cup Italia '90 bubble. Spurs had been £5 million in debt in 1982 when Irving Scholar and Paul Bobroff, businessmen and long-time Spurs fans, bought up a controlling interest in the club by initially buying up the shares held by widows and daughters of deceased male fans. Bobroff and Scholar set up a rights issue to existing shareholders in 1983, and followed this up by making Spurs the first football club with a Stock Exchange listing. This wiped out the clubs debts of £3,287,952, with shares oversubscribed at 4.5 to 1. 'Football clubs are an Aladdin's cave but the riches inside are untapped,' Scholar told Neil Wilson (Wilson, 1988: 120). Scholar spoke the language of economic regeneration and enterprise. He was 'in the vanguard of the Thatcherite entrepreneurial revolution: commercialisation, diversification, aggressive marketing and merchandising were the solutions to the game's problems' (Manning, 1990: 10). Some solutions! By 1990-1, Scholar had risked criminal prosecution for his 'dealings with Robert Maxwell on behalf of Spurs' (Jason Nisse, 'Ex-Tottenham Chairman Ran Risk of Breaking Law', *The Independent* (Business & City), 13 November 1990, p. 26); the sports equipment subsidiary of Tottenham Hotspur plc (Hummel UK Ltd.) had proved an economic disaster, despite claims that it had been making profits after only one year; the club manager Terry Venables was trying to establish a consortium both to buy the company and bail it out of debt; and the club was having to consider selling its top players to cope with its level of debt.

The Spurs story in the early 1990s is one of the entrepreneurial dream turned sour. No FA Super League would have safeguarded Spurs from the consequences of the Scholar initiatives.

Shots

Aldershot Football Club — the Shots — was also in trouble in 1990, facing a winding-up order at the end of July. Saddled with debts the club ceased to trade after sixty-four wholly undistinguished years in the Football League. One week later they were back in business. A 19-year-old property tycoon called Spencer Trethewy had come forward claiming to be able to pour £200,000 into the ailing Shots. Within days the young saviour was on the board; within two weeks he was a guest on the national network 'Wogan' chat show on the BBC, introduced as the central figure in a 'fairy story'. His answers in the Wogan interview were naive and evasive in the extreme:

Wogan: What business are you in? Speculation . . .
Trethewy: Not really . . . I think that's a little too risky . . . Occasionally I do buy a few
          houses and then I sell them on.

('Wogan', 13 August 1990)

But such waffle didn't appear to matter. Trethewy claimed to have it made so he was acceptable: he flew around in helicopters, seemed to be chauffered in big cars, and the Shots seemed to be saved. It was in a Sunday tabloid paper, the *News of the World*, that it was revealed that the 'Soccer Saviour is a Fraud' (4 November, 1990). Trethewy had actually been working, up to the point of Aldershot's winding-up order, as a copy-machine salesman on £7,500 per annum. He was soon off the board, and Aldershot was actually saved by sources from elsewhere, including the club doctor and other associates ('Shots in the Dark', BBC 2, 'Southern Eye', 8 November, 1990).

The then Chairman of Aldershot, Colin Hancock — a television crew's dream subject at the time, in the working setting of his dental surgery — reminded enquiring journalists and broadcasters that 'those of us who involve ourselves at this level are crazy'. Local businessmen in football, he said, forget that they're businessmen, 'just to buy a pair of legs'. In a business sense they actually act illogically, irrationally: 'you do it because it's football, and that's part of the romance of football' (BBC 1, 'Sportsnight', 21 November 1990).

Crazy, irrational and illogical they might be, in terms of entrepreneurial criteria. But such eccentricities have a pedigree in the philosophy of the Football League, a cultural rootedness and genuine community base which guarantees a stability of sorts — unlike the wafer-thin guarantees of the economic messiah and the popular capitalist parvenu.

The Shay

Halifax Town play at the Shay. In the season 1990–1 they tussled with Aldershot themselves and the Welsh border club Wrexham for bottom spot in the League's bottom division. But the club is unique in the Football League. Whilst Birmingham Football Club, for instance, is looking to strike deals with McDonalds in developing new facilities in multi-leisure complexes, Halifax is owned by the local authority, Calderdale Council, which has the majority shareholding and also owns the ground. David Helliwell, Leader of the Council, speaks soberly and respectfully of the contribution of professional football to local cultural life:

Professional football is not about making profits, just as opera is not, just as ballet is not, just as orchestral concerts are not. The sooner we recognise that what's good enough for opera — that is subsidy, subsidised tickets — is good enough for football, the better. I have no doubt that as we approach the end of the century our model will spread, and in ten years from now people will not see it as odd. We've had a problem making people understand that it's normal . . . The commercial model of football — what I always term the butcher, baker, candlestickmaker model — has we believe failed miserably. Probably even now 80 of the 92 League clubs are insolvent and probably technically trading illegally. I'm glad to say that whilst we may be 92nd in the Football League we're one of the 12 that is solvent.

(BBC 1, 'Sportsnight', 21 November 1990).

Helliwell criticises traditional styles of management of League clubs, yet his vision and Halifax's experiment place football firmly within the local culture. Professional football has been too bounded by tradition at key moments in its history — a game with too inflexibly framed frontiers — but if modernisation is to mean marginalisation for the majority, under the supposedly caring embrace of an FA initiative, then the cultural values at the core of the professional game in Britain will have been abused.

All six League Secretaries who held the position from 1888–1991 were born in the North of England. The Football Association's first three and its fifth Secretaries were Southerners, the fourth one having been Derbyshire-born. When the League's fifth Secretary became the Football Association's first Chief Executive in February 1989, it looked like the relationship between the League and the Association would be closer than at any previous time. Graham Kelly had learned his trade well at the League, where he had leapfrogged into the primary post on merit. Men of the moment swim with the tide, and in the Thatcher years the League had many problems of image, credibility and continuity. It is interesting that the first League Secretary to take a top job at the parent body has turned so punitively on his mentor. It is to be hoped that the ambitious career move which sparked all this will not result in football historians looking back at the last decade of the century as Kelly's Folly.

Acknowledgements

I feel an enormous debt to Simon Inglis for a great deal of the material which I have used in this chapter. His history of the Football League is an exemplary blend of social history, cultural analysis and sporting gossip, moulded into a highly accessible popular history. The book is 'the official centenary history of the Football League', but it is also an objective piece of scholarship; official here does not mean whitewashed. It should be required reading in all professional football clubs, at the Football Association itself and in the office, perhaps, of Robert Maxwell.

I want also to thank Liz Crolley for providing me with background material on key people at the FA. I have also drawn on the writings of a number of sports journalists, and hope that I have represented fairly the positions that they were taking when I have in turn reported reporters' opinions.

Bibliography

Fishwick, Nicholas (1989), *English Football and Society 1910-1950*, Manchester: Manchester University Press.

Green, Geoffrey (1960), 'The Football Association', in A. H. Fabian and Geoffrey Green (eds), *Association Football, Volume One*, London: The Caxton Publishing Company Limited.

Haines, Joe (1988), *Maxwell*, London: Macdonald.

Inglis, Simon (1988), *League Football — and the Men Who Made It*, London: Willow Books/Collins.

Manning, Maria (1990), 'Tottering Hotspur', *New Statesman and Society*, **3**, 128, 23 November.

Mason, Tony (1980), *Association Football and English Society 1863-1915*, Sussex: The Harvester Press.

Tischler, Steven (1981), *Footballers and Businessmen: The Origins of Professional Soccer in England*, New York: Holmes & Meier Publishers, Inc.

Tomlinson, Alan (1986), 'Going Global: The FIFA Story', in Alan Tomlinson and Garry Whannel (eds), *Off the Ball: The Football World Cup*, London: Pluto Press.

Wagg, Stephen (1984), *The Football World: A Contemporary Social History*, Brighton: The Harvester Press.

Wilson, Neil (1988), *The Sports Business*, London: Mandarin.

3
Rich man, poor man: economic arrangements in the Football League

Tony Arnold

The pattern of development of professional football reflects changes over time in its social and cultural environment. In the early years of professional football the forms of communication, or media, were limited in scope and football clubs developed within their own distinctive national or even local–regional context. In recent years, as communication forms have expanded, football has increasingly come to operate within an international context in which local factors are of less importance. The development pattern in any particular country therefore represents an accommodation to the tension between those two elements; the distinctive national tradition and the new transnational imperatives.

This chapter will consider the importance of economic arrangements on the development of clubs in the (English) Football League, where an entrenched tradition dating back over a hundred years has interacted with a particular social culture to slow the rate of adaptation to emerging European norms. This involves considering the nature of the leisure market, the distinctive economics of the industry, and the way these have changed since the 1880s. Each era has its distinctive theme; in the 1980s, which are analysed in some detail, the policy changes lead towards greater 'industrial concentration', the possibility of (domestic) 'success concentration' and therefore a potential conflict between the interests of the national league and transnational, i.e. European, competitions.

The leisure market

The market position of professional soccer has, not surprisingly, changed considerably since its formative period, the last quarter of the nineteenth century. Industrialisation had changed the nature of the working week; previously the work rhythm had been 'self-imposed, and often leisurely, weekends had been elastic and holidays numerous',[1] but the strict controls of industrialism reduced leisure time, and also sharply demarcated work and leisure.

Spectator sports suited the new social and economic conditions: contests could be held on relatively small areas of land within urban areas, they could be concentrated into short periods of time, they offered excitement and release from work-a-day monotonies, they could take advantage of gradual increases in income, leisure time and the availability of transport and they were also generally acceptable to the improving classes as an alternative to 'pernicious pastimes' associated with drink and dance.[2]

In the period 1875–1914 several major British sports, including association football, became 'highly commercialised'.[3] During this period the boom in public interest was organised and institutionalised; many clubs became limited liability companies and their growing financial base provided the money, both from share issues and operating surpluses, to build the necessary ground facilities.

Between the wars the leisure industry experienced 'a pronounced post-war boom and slump, followed by rather modest expansion', interrupted by the sharp downturn of 1929–32.[4] During this period the leisure market was 'radically altered if not transformed' by new commercial amusements, including gramophone records, talking pictures, television, Butlins, and the football pools, each based upon new forms of publicity and mass production.[5]

Although football prospered during this period,[6] and markedly so during the golden age of 1945–51, the 1950s and 1960s were 'a watershed in the development of mass leisure. Trends which had first become apparent in the inter-war years were now consolidated'.[7] Increases in disposable incomes, in leisure time, and in personal mobility meant that the leisure market grew and diversified.

Leisure consumption increasingly displayed a positive association with household income and with decreases in the length of the working week; between 1974 and 1984 the leisure market grew 22 per cent in real terms, faster than the general growth in household expenditures, but recreation and entertainment took a smaller proportion (22.5 as against 31 per cent) of the enlarged leisure market. Moreover, within the recreation and entertainment sub-group the market became more fragmented with increases in both in-home entertainment and in active sports participation and the importance of mass spectator sports underwent a relative decline.[8]

Football was, therefore, not unique during the 1970s and 1980s in experiencing a decline in public interest, as indicated by on-site attendances, although it was at least able to avoid the serious financial difficulties and closures experienced by the cinema industry. On the other hand, the retention of the same number of Football League outlets throughout virtually the entire post-war period was far from typical of the leisure industry as a whole, where 'corporate growth and mergers have resulted in a high degree of concentration'.[9]

The economics of the football industry

The rules that govern behaviour in the Football League are quite unique; they represent a particular combination of approaches general to sporting leagues and those developed to accord with the League's own value judgements and traditions. Sporting leagues owe their existence to the benefits which they bring to member organisations; a centralised structure provides regulatory and promotional services, and the operation of policies that further the collective interests of member clubs.

The English Football League has exercised control over:

1. the size and composition of its membership and, until 1986, the location of franchises;[10]
2. input decisions, through the maximum wage and retain and transfer systems, and the specification of maximum payments to directors and other suppliers of risk-bearing capital; and
3. output decisions, by defining the fixtures that take place in the various competitions and stipulating, until 1982, minimum admission price levels.

The League has also administered revenue-sharing arrangements between member clubs since 1919 and handled negotiations with the pools promoters and with television companies. The overall decision-taking process has been highly conservative, for many years requiring a three-quarters majority for changes, in an attempt to ensure that group interests were protected.

These activities are entirely consistent with the distinguishing feature of a cartel, that it 'determines a structure of rules constraining the behaviour of the group's individual members to act in the interest of the group as a whole'.[11] In most industries the activities of an overt cartel would be opposed by the government, in the interests of competition policy, but the operations of the Football League (and other sporting leagues) have met with little government opposition. There are two likely reasons for this: the distinctive nature of the 'product' and the effect of this on organisational relationships in sporting leagues in general, and the nature of organisational objectives.

The 'product' and organisational relationships

Sporting leagues differ from most other industries because of the nature of the 'product' itself; member organisations must cooperate before there can be a product. It is for this reason that Sloane saw cartelisation in the sports industry as 'necessary for there to be a viable product at all'.[12]

Economic analysis of professional sport has drawn heavily upon the idea of uncertainty of outcome, hypothesising that public interest (and thus joint or industry revenues) will be greater if results are less certain. Neale described this as the Louis-Schmelling paradox, the need of a champion for a strong challenger to maximise his own income-earning potential, although in the context of sporting leagues there is an interesting contradiction or tension between attempts to maximise individual club incomes through continued success and joint income maximisation.[13] As Cairns *et al.*, observed, 'for any individual club, league uncertainty of outcome will be only a partial determinant of attendances. For a single club its own playing success will also be significant'.[14] Uncertainty of outcome can in turn be subdivided into a set of uncertainties of match outcome, seasonal outcome and long-run outcome, each of which may, in principle, have an income effect.[15]

If sporting leagues wish to increase the uncertainty of outcomes, they need to bring about a more equal distribution of the key resource, playing talent, than would be obtained by unregulated market forces. This can be achieved through direct measures, such as the 'college draft' system in the American NFL (where access to new professional talent is closely controlled, with a bias in favour of less successful sides), or indirect measures, such as controls on the wages payable to players (so that greater economic strength does not lead to a more attractive monetary offer to potential players) or requirements for member organisations to share income, so that the successful clubs cross-subsidise the less successful.

In the Football League, direct measures have hardly been used while the importance of particular indirect measures has varied over time. The controls on players' wages and mobility (the retain and transfer system) were important influences until the 1960s on the equalisation of playing standards between clubs, particularly 'city' and 'town' clubs with different audience potentials but thereafter, with the abolition of the maximum wage system, changes to the retain and transfer arrangement, the setting up of new competitions and the levying of higher charges to television and pools companies, it was the League's income-sharing arrangements that grew in importance.

Organisational objectives in the Football League

Football League clubs, which are all limited liability companies, have been described as utility rather than profit maximisers, within a minimum security constraint,[16] or as 'intent on achieving playing success while remaining solvent',[17] whereas clubs in some leagues, such as the American NFL, are generally thought to have more conventional, profit-maximising, business objectives.

It is unusual for limited liability businesses to aspire to utility rather than profit maximisation but this is not necessarily beneficial; Cairns *et al.* described sportsmen-owners who sought playing success as a dominant objective as 'more potentially damaging to the interests of the League than pure profit maximisers, as they may create greater inequality in playing performance among the member clubs and hence raise the degree of instability in the League as a whole'.[18]

Arnold and Benveniste carried out a questionnaire survey of clubs in the Football League which indicated that playing success (44.1 per cent) and financial success (37.4 per cent) were the most important business objectives and that their relative importance to clubs in the Second and Third Divisions was the same, while financial considerations were more important, or pressing, to clubs in the Fourth Division.[19] It was also apparent that 'financial success' meant, to most clubs, generating enough money to avoid compromising immediate plans for playing success, for example through having to sell an important player, rather than profit maximisation for the benefit of external suppliers of capital.

These unusual business objectives have shaped, or been shaped by, the financial restrictions which have existed since the early days of the League on maximum dividends, on directors' remuneration and on the allocation of any surplus on business liquidation. The Football Association required that these restrictions be included in the Articles of Association of all Football League clubs, presumably to prevent clubs from being operated for merely financial gain, but in so doing they imposed conditions that must have reduced the supply of risk-bearing capital and of managerial expertise.

Although the FA's limits on dividend payments and directors' remuneration have recently been eased,[20] very few football clubs provide a commercial return to shareholders.[21] As a result few football clubs, other than perhaps Tottenham Hotspur and Manchester United, have attracted sufficient long-term capital to fund their highly specific, long-term (stadium) assets. This has meant that the recent demands of government and consumers for safer, more civilised stadiums have, to the extent that grants, assets sales and retained profits have been insufficient, often been funded through short-term debt, which has left some clubs heavily dependent on the continued support of their creditors, particularly the banks. Such an arrangement has, however, persisted because, under conditions of capital rationing and low returns to shareholders, it has generally been relatively inexpensive for directors to obtain control of club policy.

The size, composition and location of membership

All football clubs must be registered with the Football Association. The Football League, as a member organisation, admits registered clubs in line with its overall policies, which have generally been as much strategic as purely economic. The extension of the League to two divisions in 1892 was a device to absorb the competing Football Alliance, while the establishment of Division Three (South) in 1920 meant the election *en bloc* of the First Division of the rival Southern League. After a parallel Division Three (North) was set up in 1921 there were eighty-eight clubs in the League, and the only subsequent increase, to ninety-two clubs, came in 1950, this time for economic reasons related to the post-war boom.

Until 1986 any changes in the composition of the agreed number of clubs took place between seasons when the clubs with the poorest playing record applied for readmission to the League, along with clubs outside the League who wished to join. This system gave member clubs the power to make their individual judgements by reference to geographical and traditional factors as well as the economic or playing attributes of the various applicants. Since then a more automatic arrangement has operated with the top non-League side replacing, subject to meeting certain ground and other conditions, the weakest League club.

Input controls

The Football League has operated four primary business input controls, on dividends, directors' pay, and players' wages and freedom of contract. The best-known controls relate to the contracts with players. When the Football League was established in 1888 its original objects included the 'regulation of players' terms of employment by agreement on a maximum wage' and a requirement that all players should be registered with one club, which would have a right of veto over any change of registration. These intentions were not, in fact, achieved until 1890 in the case of registration, and 1901 when the maximum wage was introduced, and even then it was despite the arguments of the wealthier clubs, who preferred an open market.

These constraints were objectionable in preventing players from achieving their market wage but they probably helped to equalise playing standards between clubs,[22] at least until the abolition of the maximum wage in 1961, and the modification of the retain and transfer system following the *Eastham* v. *Newcastle United* case in 1963. Freedom of contract was finally established in 1977.

The two pairs of controls have had very different effects; the low level of dividends and directors' pay has reduced the ability of football clubs to compete with other businesses for scarce resources, although this has probably been offset by the nature of the business and the prospect of a 'pleasing local prominence', which both encourage local businessmen to offer managerial expertise despite the lack of monetary compensation.[23] The restraints on players are less likely to have significantly reduced the availability of playing talent to the industry, but until the 1960s may well have dispersed that talent more widely over the industry than market forces would have done.

Since then, even after initial adjustments to the abolition of maximum wages, player salaries have risen far faster than inflation,[24] partly because utility-maximising firms have more difficulty than profit-maximising firms in identifying optimal salary levels. Although the absolute growth of salaries was more rapid in the First Division than in the other divisions, by 1985 wages were a much higher proportion of turnover for clubs in the Fourth Division (76 per cent) than in the Football League (60 per cent) as a whole.[25]

The transfer system also brought relatively little benefit to clubs in the lower divisions. The continued rise in transfer fees encouraged the larger clubs to invest in their own recruitment and coaching staffs, rather than rely upon smaller League clubs to carry out this function for them. In consequence only 6 per cent of the total transfer payments by First Division clubs were paid to Third and Fourth Division sides in 1988-9.

Output controls

The Football League controls the composition of each division, and thus the fixtures played by each club, using a promotion/relegation device in an attempt to equalise playing standards. The League computer is also pro-grammed to avoid competing fixtures at adjacent clubs, in order to prevent loss of revenue. From 1890 until 1982 minimum admission prices were stipulated,

Table 3.1 League match attendances and annual receipts, 1948–9[29]

	League attendances	Increase over 1937–8 (%)	Annual receipts	Increase over 1937–8 (%)
Div. 1	38,000	27	£64,000	100
Div. 2	24,000	20	£43,000	87
Div. 3S	15,000	36	£26,000	117
Div. 3N	10,000	43	£16,000	129

which left clubs free to charge more, particularly for seated accommodation, but also prevented price-cutting competition between League members.

Most clubs applied the League minimum to large areas of terrace standing accommodation. This minimum was set at a level which may not have been income-maximising but did ensure that football was available to the bulk of the population, particularly in the days before the proliferation of midweek fixtures under floodlights. Until the First World War the minimum admission price was 6d. (equivalent to about £1 nowadays) for men and 3d. for ladies and boys, and this was doubled in 1920. After the Second World War, as attendances boomed, the minimum was raised to 1s. 6d. until cuts in Entertainment Duty permitted a reduction in 1946 to 1s. 3d.

The League's pricing policy has, over time, been more successful than the industry's own publicity would indicate. Match attendances in 1888 averaged 4,500, rising in the First Division in 1908–9 to 16,000.[26] The continuation of low pricing policies meant that by 1937–8 First Division and FA Cup attendances were both twice the level of 1908–9[27] although the financial gap between large and small clubs also appeared to have widened.[28]

The general pattern in the post-war period is well known. At first attendances rose, in common with other entertainment outlets, to unprecedented levels, but then fell almost continuously from the peak of 1949. Due to pricing factors, however, trends in attendances do not, necessarily indicate the trend in club revenues, or even gate receipts. Between 1937–8 and 1948–9 the growth in takings substantially exceeded the (considerable) increase in attendances, a benefit which extended to clubs in all four divisions (see Table 3.1). During an era in which players' pay was quite closely controlled, low pricing represented a sensible policy of market maximisation, but at about the same time as players' wage restraints collapsed the League began to raise the price of football in real terms, and also to increase the number of fixtures, through the institution of new competitions aided by the widespread introduction of floodlights.

By 1981–2 the minimum entry price was sixteen times higher than in 1957–8, which more than compensated for the decline in League attendances, even after inflation is taken into account. High price policies inevitably reduced the (live attendance) market, thus reinforcing the effects of widening leisure opportunities on traditional spectator sports, but such policies were commercially rewarding.

Bird has argued that League football has been an 'inferior' good, with demand falling as incomes rose,[30] but the demand for football, over the range

Table 3.2 Annual variations in inflation-adjusted gate receipts in the ten years from 1972 (%)[34]

Aston Villa:	−7.7, −20.4, +31.3, +28.1, +35.6, −3.1, −19.2, −8.1, 0, +15.9
Wolverhampton:	−4.8, −7.8, −28.4, +15.9, −15.5, +36.5, −3.3, +52.5, −22.5, −33.3

of prices charged, also appears to have been income-elastic, so that the aggregate gate receipts of the football industry have increased rather than fallen during the post-war period. This conclusion is reinforced by Arnold's findings, using data over the period 1905–85 for four West Yorkshire clubs, that, even before the growth in ancillary incomes is taken into account, the clubs concerned were able to generate (at given levels of competition success) inflation-adjusted gate receipts that increased over time.[31]

Since the removal of the specified minimum, prices have continued to rise although there is now more price differentiation between clubs. In 1988–9 the average admission receipts per spectator were £4.75 in Division One (ranging from £6.15 to £3.90), £3.70 in Division Two (£6.43 to £2.75), £3.10 in Division Three (£3.96 to £2.53) and £2.70 in Division Four (£3.03 to £2.23). This has added to the unequal distribution of the decline in attendances; First Division gate receipts (in real terms) nearly doubled between 1958 and 1989 but Fourth Division gate receipts rose by only 10 per cent during the same period.[32]

The pattern of receipts in the Football League differs from most other industries in the extent to which receipts are responsive to success, and thus vary from one year to the next. Football attendances have always been sensitive to success and failure; in 1885 a committee member at Burnley said that 'the public will not go to see inferior players. During the first year we did not pay a single player and nobody came to see us'.[33] In recent years, as more competitions have been held, the benefit from success has increased, and so has the variability in receipts.

Two clubs, Aston Villa and Wolverhampton Wanderers, in the ten years from 1972, experienced annual variations in 'real' gate receipts (i.e. after adjustment for inflation), as shown in Table 3.2. For these two clubs, cup competitions, including FA Cup, League Cup and European club cups, provided, on average, 20 per cent of total attendances, but success or failure could change this percentage from 5 to 32 per cent in consecutive seasons (Aston Villa, 1980–2). These figures are not necessarily typical of the annual variation in League club incomes but they do indicate the unusual trading risks faced in recent years by clubs in the Football League.

The sharing of incomes between member organisations is also rarely encountered in business circles and is one of the most distinctive features of a sporting league. In the Football League income-sharing was introduced during the First World War to help clubs in financial difficulty. The measures were so successful that they were retained when official football resumed after the war, and persisted with only minor modifications until the 1980s.

Since 1949, for example, all clubs paid 4 per cent of gate receipts (net of certain costs) from all matches into a pool to meet the League's administrative expenses and other joint costs. Until 1983, in every Football League match the home club also paid the visiting club a fee per spectator even though the same fixture was to be played later in the season on the other club's ground. Other forms of gate money redistribution or pooling exist for cup competitions, over and above the basic principle that the two competing sides receive an equal share of the receipts from each tie. Television fees were also shared relatively equally until recent years, in spite of the marked preference of television companies to show matches featuring top clubs. Sums paid by the pools promoters for the use of fixtures have been shared equally, but cup and league sponsorship has generally been performance-related with the successful clubs receiving the higher return.

For many years the consequence of these arrangements has been a substantial transfer of receipts from the better supported to the less well-supported clubs, in line with the 'uncertainty of outcome' approach to sporting league competition. In 1986, however, the ten most powerful League clubs threatened to form a 'Super League' outside the Football League and used this prospect to persuade the smaller clubs to agree to substantial changes in the control of Football League policy and to its income-sharing arrangements. In specific terms, changes were made to the voting strengths of clubs from different divisions, to the sharing of television and sponsorship incomes and Football Association and League Cup pools, and to the level of contributions to the league and cup match pools.[35] Even more recently, there have been further changes in the allocation of television fees in favour of the leading clubs, whose matches are televised more frequently. Together, these changes have considerably reduced the importance of income-sharing arrangements, to the clear benefit of the leading clubs.

Industrial concentration in the 1980s and 1990s?

Economic arrangements in the Football League have changed considerably in the last thirty years, as attendances have steadily fallen. The most important changes took place in the 1960s and 1970s with the abolition of the maximum wage, the reform of the retain and transfer system and increases in the minimum price of admission. In the 1980s the growth of joint incomes from sponsorship and television fees, and reductions in income-sharing were probably the most important developments.

The effect of these changes on Football League clubs varied according to their income level, and has affected their ability to compete for scarce playing talent and thus to compete on the field of play. Moreover, this effect had both inter- and intra-divisional dimensions. The changes can be considered under four main headings: attendances, league gate receipts, pooling contributions and the distribution of total match receipts.'

Football League attendances from 1958–9 to 1988–9 fell by 45 per cent, with the decline in attendances being greater in Divisions Three and Four. By 1988–9, First Division club attendances were, on average, 1.92 (1958–9 — 1.71), 3.52 (2.97) and 6.34 (4.08) times those of the average attendances in Divisions Two, Three and Four respectively. The increase in the differential between clubs in different divisions is not particularly surprising, but far more interesting, and relevant to the nature of competition is the increase in the

Table 3.3 Increase (decrease) in match receipts, 1984–5 to 1988–9 (in 1988–9 £'000s)[39]

Div.	Season ticket	Football League	FL Cup	FA Cup	Other	Total matches	Match pools	Fixture copyright	TV fees	Total
1	704	(1,404)[a]	(79)	1,301	510	1,032	(35)	(169)	8,091	8,919
2	2,218	4,786[b]	220	783	468	8,475	(226)	(66)	(23)	8,160
3	96	1,998	28	91	302	2,515	(521)	(129)	(397)	1,468
4	164	1,226	88	148	240	1,866	(521)	(129)	(517)	699
	3,182	6,606	257	2,323	1,520	13,888	(1,303)	(493)	7,154	19,246

Had the number of matches in both divisions been the same in 1988–9 as in 1984–5, then [a] would = +1,811, [b] = 2,973.

differential between members of the same division. In Division One the attendances of clubs in the top half of the division were 1.55, 1.61, 1.65 and 1.92 times as high as those of clubs in the lower half in 1958–9, 1968–9, 1978–9 and 1988–9 respectively.[36] The sudden change in the differential in the last ten years is noteworthy.

The connection between pricing increases and the decline in attendances has already been discussed. League gate receipts in 1988–9 were 20 per cent higher than ten years before, after adjusting for general inflation, although the share going to the First Division as a whole has fallen (57 to 51 per cent), and to the Second Division has increased (25 to 30 per cent), partly due to the recent change in the number of clubs in the top two divisions.[37] In the First Division the richest five clubs now have gate receipts 3.25 times as high as those of the poorest five, as against 2.25 times in 1979.

The contributions made by clubs to the income-sharing pools have also changed sharply in recent years. This reduced the net contribution to the pool by First Division clubs, between 1984–5 and 1988–9, by £1,025,000 in total, and reduced the aggregate benefit to Second, Third and Fourth Division clubs by £260,000, £355,000 and £410,000 respectively. Once again, there has been a further intra-divisional effect; in Division One, for example, the net contribution levels of the richest fell from 11 to 4 per cent, and the net pool receipts of the poorest fell from 4 per cent in 1984–5 to 3 per cent in 1988–9.[38]

These indicators do not, however, take account of the considerable change in the sharing of joint incomes, particularly television fees. Football has steadily moved from being a 'live attendance' sport to one catering jointly for live and television audiences, but the level of television fees has only recently begun to reflect this; in 1988–9 First Division clubs received 20 per cent of their match receipts from television, as against 2 per cent in 1984–5.

The increase (in inflation-adjusted £s) in match receipts from all sources over the last five years, by division, is shown in Table 3.3. One structural change has taken place during this time, a decrease in the size of Division One and a corresponding increase in the size of Division Two by two clubs. Despite this, First Division clubs received 46 per cent of the increase in real match receipts of the last five years with 42 per cent going to Division Two, 8 per cent to Division Three and 4 per cent to Division Four. It is noteworthy, however, that 90 per cent of the extra money accruing to clubs in the top division has come from television, £7,100,000 in new money and £940,000 from changes in the distribution of existing television fees at the expense of clubs in the other three divisions.

By way of contrast, the substantial increase in the receipts of Second Division clubs has derived entirely from their live audiences, due to increases in the number of matches played, in average attendances per match and in admission prices. The more modest increases for Third and Fourth Division clubs also come from increases in the receipts from live audiences, which have exceeded the decrease in shared income revenues.

Within each division, however, the distribution of increases in (real) match receipts has been uneven. In Division One the increase for the top five clubs, allowing for inflation, was 2.5 times that of clubs in the less well-supported half of the division, which has helped to maintain the overall differential in favour of the richer clubs. The top five clubs in 1988-9 had receipts 1.5, 2.4 and 2.9 times as large as those of the second, third and fourth quartile clubs respectively in the First Division.

In the last thirty years the constraints on the market for players' services have been greatly reduced, but the increased importance of income-sharing arrangements during the 1960s and 1970s helped to prevent the larger clubs from exerting their full market power. In the 1980s, however, changes made to the sharing of joint incomes, notably television fees, increased the differences in average income levels between the divisions and, perhaps more importantly, between clubs in the same division.

The number of League 'outlets' is very large, due to historical factors, and it would be surprising if the income levels of clubs in the First and Fourth Divisions were not very different. Within divisions, however, one would expect 'outcome uncertainty' to be a more important policy objective and the increasing financial advantages enjoyed by the top sides over fellow-members of the First Division do nothing to increase the level of competition in that league.

Competition dominance

The ability of particular clubs to dominate league and cup competitions can be measured after choosing the relevant periods of time, and a definition of 'success'. A broad, overall view has been obtained by selecting four twenty-year periods, 1895-6 to 1914-15, 1919-20 to 1938-9, 1946-7 to 1965-6 and 1966-7 to 1985-6, and by defining 'success' as finishing in one of the top three positions in Division One, or reaching an FA Cup Final. (For consistency over time, other competitions have been ignored.)

The number of successful clubs, so defined, and the proportion of competition successes achieved in each of the four periods is shown in Table 3.4. This approach can indicate whether the size and composition of the élite group has been stable or changing over time. If 'élite' is defined as clubs finishing in the top three positions in Division One and/or reaching the FA

Table 3.4 Competition successes, 1895-6 to 1985-6

Number of most successful clubs	Cumulative proportion of successes			
	1895–1915	1919–39	1946–66	1966–86
1	0.13	0.13	0.14	0.20
2	0.24	0.25	0.26	0.31
3	0.34	0.32	0.36	0.40
4	0.43	0.39	0.43	0.49
5	0.50	0.45	0.49	0.57
6	0.56	0.50	0.54	0.63
7	0.61	0.55	0.59	0.69
8	0.66	0.59	0.64	0.73
9	0.70	0.63	—	0.77
10	0.74	0.67	—	—
11	—	0.71	—	—
Number with 4 or more successes (as above)				
	10	11	8	9
" 3 "	2	5	5	3
" 2 "	6	5	5	4
" 1 success	8	4	11	6
	26	25	29	22

Cup Final at least four times in any of the twenty-year periods, this produces a set of ten clubs in 1895–1915, eleven in 1919–39, eight in 1946–66 and nine in 1966–86. The total number of different clubs contained in these groups is twenty-five, out of a total League membership since 1888 of about 115. Given the élite of ten clubs established in 1895–1915, the leading group of eleven in 1919–39 contained six new clubs, the élite eight in 1946–66 included four new clubs, and the élite of 1966–86 contained five new clubs. No club has been dominant in all four periods, and only four (Everton, Liverpool, Manchester City and Arsenal) in any three periods. This seems to indicate that membership of the Football League élite has been variable, in response to demographic, economic and organisational factors, over long periods of time.

Table 3.4 also indicates, however, that the last twenty-year period appears to have been dominated by leading clubs to a greater extent than hitherto, which suggests that any overall increase in the degree of income-sharing (despite the decreases of the 1980s) has not compensated for the removal of the maximum wage system (and associated retain and transfer system modifications) in restraining a trend towards competition dominance by élite clubs.

Conclusions

The market position of, and economic arrangements in, the English Football League have changed considerably since its formation in 1888. The expansion of the leisure market and its diversification, to take advantage of new technologies and increasing disposable incomes, led to a decline in the importance of the traditional and once dominant spectator sports. The Football League responded to this with its own policy of diversification, involving the setting up of new competitions and the gradual acceptance of television as a legitimate audience sector.

Sporting leagues provide an unusual business setting because clubs need to cooperate with one another in order to produce their 'product' — matches. Within this setting it is likely that 'uncertainty of outcome' will increase public interest and hence the joint revenues of member clubs, although this is difficult to prove conclusively. In the National Football League (NFL) in the United States there is a definite intention to equalise the commercial strengths of clubs and their ability to attract star players, but in the English Football League, and throughout European football, 'uncertainty of outcome' policies have attracted only moderate support, largely because they conflict with the economic self-interest of the larger clubs. During the 1980s in England the leading clubs overturned the 'equalising policies' that did exist and now retain a larger proportion of their income than at any time in the past, which provides them with the ability to dominate the market for scarce playing talent, and their domestic leagues.

There are, however, good reasons for this; whereas in the United States the NFL is a competition without equal, for European soccer clubs there is an inherent tension between continued and successful membership of the domestic league and involvement in transnational competitions. At present, leading clubs are able to play in both their own domestic leagues and European knock-out competitions but the announcement in March 1991 of a new mini-league, basis for the latter stages of the European Cup, is a further step towards the emergence of a genuine European League. The same commercial logic that led the leading twelve clubs in 1888 to form a domestic league in England now points clearly towards new European arrangements.

During the last thirty years, the countries of Western Europe have been slowly adopting political mechanisms that transcend national boundaries and leading football clubs can hardly avoid moving in the same direction. Thus, although the market strength of élite national clubs may now be too great to benefit their domestic leagues substantially, this is likely merely to be part of a transitional process that will help them compete with their counterparts in other countries in the new competitions that emerge during the next decade.

Notes

1. Bailey (1978), pp. 11–12.
2. Wheeler (1978), p. 192.
3. Vamplew (1988), p. 77.
4. Jones (1985), p. 92.
5. ibid. p. 103. The decline in the working week from 54 hours in 1913 to 48 hours in 1920 was also helpful (see pp. 92–3).
6. Jones (1984), pp. 287–92.

7. Jones (1986), p. 336.
8. Williams (1985) p. 9.
9. Jones (1986), p. 344.
10. Through the re-election process; see also Vamplew (1988), p. 137, regarding a more direct control.
11. Cairns *et al.* (1986), p. 56.
12. Sloane (1980), p. 40; see also Sloane (1976), Schofield (1982) on the operations of a county cricket cartel in England, and Vamplew (1988), ch. 9.
13. Neale (1964). See also Sloane (1980), p. 25, and Jennett (1984), p. 197, who concluded that 'there is evidence to suggest that uncertainty of outcome is an important factor in making the decision whether to go to a football match'.
14. Cairns *et al.* (1986), p. 5.
15. Although the uncertainty of outcome effect is an important aspect of sporting league economics, its formal specification and testing is complex if not elusive; the results of hypothetical testing are accordingly somewhat inconclusive (see Cairns *et al.*).
16. Sloane (1971), p. 136; see also Cairns *et al.* (1986) and Vamplew (1988), pp. 78–80 and 326.
17. P. E. P. (1966).
18. Cairns *et al.* (1986), p. 71.
19. Arnold and Benveniste (1987b), p. 19.
20. The maximum dividend is now 15 per cent and one director may be paid.
21. This is not, of course, a new phenomenon. In the 1890s 'many clubs were finding it difficult to break even' (Mason (1980), p. 98); Edwardes thought in 1892 that 'as financial property football stock cannot be said to be very valuable', and the *Athletic News* suggested in 1909 that 'no-one who is out for a business return would look at football shares' (6 September 1909).
22. The maximum wage system was not entirely effective as wealthier sides had incentives to evade the regulations, even if this meant 'laundering' their accounts (Inglis (1985), p. 11; also Holt (1989), pp. 293–5).
23. There have, of course, been a number of other 'perks'; see Tischler (1981), pp. 70–1 and Mason (1980), p. 48.
24. Arnold and Benveniste (1987a), p. 197.
25. Based upon data in Football Trust (1985), Table 2.6, and (1989), Table 3.3. These levels were not new; Everton spent on average, between 1892 and 1901, 62 per cent of their gate receipts on wages before the introduction of the maximum wage reduced this proportion to 47 per cent in the following ten years (Vamplew (1980), p. 122). Vamplew also found that wage and transfer payments were 53 per cent of total expenditure for a set of eight clubs over the period 1906–14 (Vamplew (1988), pp. 84–5).
26. Jones (1984), p. 289.
27. ibid.
28. *Economist*, 8 April 1939, p. 75.
29. Based upon data in P. E. P. (1951), p. 168.
30. Bird (1982); see also Jones (1986). Cross-sectional analysis by Grattan and Lisewski (1981) and by Sloane (1980), however, casts some doubt on this conclusion.
31. Arnold (1991).
32. Based upon data in Football Trust (1989), Tables 2.2 and 2.4.
33. *Athletic News*, 10 February 1885, p. 3.
34. Based on data in Arnold and Webb (1986).
35. In 1988–9 the levies were 3 per cent of the net receipts of League matches (distributed equally over all ninety-two clubs), 10 per cent of FA and League Cup

matches (divided 50 per cent to Division One, 25 per cent to Division Two, 25 per cent to Divisions Three and Four). There were further 20 per cent levies in Sherpa Van and Simod Cup matches, and 50 per cent in League play-off matches, distributed among the clubs and divisions concerned. Pools fixture copyright payments are divided equally among all ninety-two clubs. About 60 per cent television fees are divided between clubs by division (75 per cent to Division One, 12.5 per cent to Division Two, and 12.5 per cent to Divisions Three and Four), with the remaining £4 million allocated on a match-by-match basis to the clubs whose matches are televised.

36. Based upon data in Football Trust (1989), Table 1.4
37. See Football Trust (1989), Table 2.2.
38. ibid., Table 2.5.
39. Based upon data in Football Trust (1985) and (1989) Table 2.6 in each edition.

Bibliography

Arnold, A. J. (1991), 'An Industry in Decline? The Trend in Football League Gate Receipts', *Service Industries Journal*, **11** (2), pp. 43–52.

Arnold, A. J. and I. Benveniste (1987a), 'Wealth and Poverty in the English Football League', *Accounting and Business Research*, Summer 1987, pp. 195–203.

Arnold, A. J. and I. Benveniste (1987b), 'Producer Cartels in English League Football', *Economic Affairs*, **8** (1), October/November 1987, pp. 18–23.

Arnold, A. J. and B. J. Webb (1986), 'Aston Villa and Wolverhampton Wanderers 1971/2 to 1981/2: A Study of Finance Policies in the Football Industry', *Managerial Finance*, **12** (1), pp. 11–19.

Bailey, P. (1978) *Leisure and Class in Victorian England*, London: Routledge & Kegan Paul.

Bird, P. J. W. N. (1982), 'The Demand for League Football', *Applied Economics*, **14** (6), pp. 637–49.

Cairns, J., N. Jennett and P. J. Sloane (1986), 'The Economics of Professional Team Sports: A Survey of Theory and Evidence', *Journal of Economic Studies*, **13** (1), pp. 3–80.

Edwardes, C. (1982), 'The New Football Mania', *Nineteenth Century*, **XXXII**, 1892.

Football Trust (1985), *Digest of Football Statistics*, London.

Football Trust (1989), *Digest of Football Statistics*, Leicester.

Gratton, C. and B. Lisewski (1981), 'The Economics of Sport in Britain: A Case of Market Failure?', *British Review of Economic Issues*, **3** (8), pp. 63–75.

Holt, R. (1989), *Sport and the British*, Oxford: Oxford University Press.

Inglis, S. (1985), *Soccer in the Dock*, London: Collins.

Jennett, N. (1984), 'Attendances, Uncertainty of Outcome and Policy in the Scottish Football League', *Scottish Journal of Political Economy*, **31**, (2), pp. 176–98.

Jones, S. G. (1984), 'The Economic Aspects of Association Football in England 1918–39', *British Journal of Sports History*, **1** (3), pp. 286–99.

Jones, S. G. (1985), 'The Leisure Industry in Britain 1918–39', *Service Industries Journal*, **5** (1), pp. 90–106.

Jones, S. G. (1986), 'Trends in the Leisure Industry since the Second World War', *Service Industries Journal*, **6** (3), pp. 330–49.

Mason, Tony (1980), *Association Football and English Society 1863–1915*, Brighton: Harvester Press.

Neale, W. C. (1964), 'The Peculiar Economics of Professional Sport: A Contribution to the Theory of the Firm in Sporting Competition and in Market Competition', *Quarterly Journal of Economics*, **78** (1), pp. 1–14.

P. E. P. (1951), *The Football Industry*, Planning Report Vol. XVII, No. 324, London.

P. E. P. (1966), *English Professional Football*, Planning Report Vol. XXXII, No. 496, London.

Schofield, J. A. (1982), 'The Development of First Class Cricket in England: An Economic Analysis', *Journal of Industrial Economics*, **XXX** (4), pp. 337–60.

Sloane, P. J. (1971), 'The Economics of Professional Football: The Football Club as a Utility Maximiser', *Scottish Journal of Political Economy*, **17** (2), 1971, pp. 121–46.

Sloane, P. J. (1976), 'Restriction of Competition in Professional Team Sports', *Bulletin of Economic Research*, **28** (1), May 1976, pp. 3–22.

Sloane, P. J. (1980), *Sport in the Market?*, Hobart Paper No. 85, London.

Tischler, S. (1981), *Footballers and Businessmen: The Origins of Professional Soccer in England*, New York: Holmes and Meier.

Vamplew, Wray (1980), 'Playing for Pay: The Earnings of Professional Sportsmen in England 1870–1914', in (eds) R. L. Cashman and M. McKernan, *Sport: Money, Morality and the Media*, Sydney University Press: University of Queensland, Australia.

Vamplew, Wray (1988), *'Pay Up and Play the Game': Professional Sport in Britain 1875–1914*, Cambridge: Cambridge University Press.

Williams, D. (1986) 'The Leisure Industries', *Midland Bank Review*, Summer, pp. 4–13.

Wheeler, R. F. (1978), 'Organised Sport and Organised Labour: The Workers' Sport Movement', *Journal of Contemporary History*, **XIII** (2), pp. 191–210.

Part 2
Playing

4
Putting on the style:
aspects of recent English football

Chas Critcher

Several themes dominated the public image of football in the 1990–1 season. One was the ubiquity of Paul Gascoigne, who could not be avoided in the pages of the national press. A second was the apparent decline of Liverpool, following Kenny Dalglish's decision that he was no longer prepared to tolerate the pressures of modern football management. A third was the uneven progress of British clubs and national sides in various European competitions. A fourth was violence on the field of play, symbolised when, for the first time in the history of the League, two clubs, Arsenal and Manchester United, had points deducted following a mass brawl during a televised match. Relatedly, there was controversy over referees' interpretation of a FIFA edict to send off those guilty of a 'professional foul'. Each theme in different ways spoke of the changes and continuities in the style of English football as it had been played out over the previous twenty years.

Just over a decade ago (Critcher, 1979) — at a time when writing academic articles about football was an aberration rather than the industry it has since become — I tried to offer an analysis of the way football had been changing since the Second World War. Though now superseded by other work, one strand of the argument has been less developed than others. Few writers have sought to address what I tentatively located as 'style'.

I want here to extend the argument that style is essential to football. Used in slightly different but related senses, style refers to styles of play (the tactics of the game), including stylised violence (as a tactical ploy but also a form of self-expression); and the style of footballing heroes (those characteristics they do, or are seen to, embody). I shall argue that these are cultural representations, in the sense that they represent to us particular versions of those themes which have always been central to the game, yet whose meanings alter significantly over time: those of masculinity, class and nationhood, along with the significant counterpointed sub-theme of race.

Football as a form of cultural expression has the uniqueness of all sports. The analogy sometimes made is with theatre, but actors work to or from a script, with a common interpretation which has been rehearsed in precisely the form in which it is ultimately presented. (The theatre audience often knows what will happen so is mainly interested in the manner in which it is executed, a perception shared only by Liverpool supporters in football.) By contrast, the essence of football — despite its frequent absence from the British game — is improvisation, the capacity to surprise the opposition and the crowd.

The selection of style as a theme can be partly validated through its frequent use by writers on football. Walvin (1986) consistently uses 'style' to analyse footballing stardom, black players, the self-images and patterns of spectatorship. This analysis will concentrate on playing and the player. Other aspects, such as changing styles of spectating, are discussed elsewhere in this volume. There is no claim here that football can be totally or adequately understood through the concept of style; only that some of its most salient aspects, frequently marginalised in other accounts, can be revealed by the consideration of style as a central motif of professional football. Much of what follows will be familiar to those who have read or written about tactical problems in the English game or about the contemporary footballing hero. It is readily available in some of the best sports journalism. My intention, and any claim to originality, lies in the attempt to read across apparently separate developments as interrelated aspects of style.

Tactics as style
Foreign fields

England's 0-1 defeat by Brazil in the 1970 World Cup was argued by some to be their finest performance under Alf Ramsey's managership but there was little international success following their subsequent quarter-final defeat by West Germany. The key indices are performances in the European Championship and the World Cup. In ten tournaments all told between 1972 and 1990, England failed to qualify four times and did not progress beyond the first phase of the main tournament three times. In the remaining three tournaments, all World Cups, England reached in succession the second phase, the quarter-final and the semi-final. There is a genuine improvement here yet the English national side's European record remained lamentable and the overall record unimpressive.

Nor was there much consolation in the fortunes of Scotland's national side. Perversely, Scotland failed to qualify for every European Nations Championship tournament between 1972 and 1990 but managed to qualify for every World Cup in the same period. They never progressed beyond the first phase because of a tendency to fail against rank outsiders.

Yet this same period of national failure was one of exceptional club success. 'English clubs, shaping talent from all over the British Isles into competitive and disciplined units, were undoubtedly the pace-setters in Europe until the Heysel disaster' (Butler, 1987; p. 311). In the sixteen seasons from 1970 to 1985, English clubs won the European Cup seven times, six times on the trot (1977–82), and had two losing finalists. Two English clubs won the Cup Winners' Cup and another reached the final. The UEFA Cup, properly in existence from 1972, was won by six English clubs in fourteen years, with two others in the final. Nottingham Forest (twice) and Aston Villa won the European Cup, Everton the Cup Winners' Cup, Ipswich and Spurs the UEFA Cup, but the club responsible for most of this success was Liverpool.

In my previous essay (Critcher, 1979) I suggested that the comprehensive defeat of Liverpool by Red Star Belgrade at Anfield in the European Cup of 1973 epitomised the tactical bankruptcy of British football. It has since been acknowledged that this provoked a rethink at Anfield. The precise solution adopted is less well understood than its effects. Until their explusion from Europe after the Heysel disaster of 1985, Liverpool were one of the most successful club sides in Europe.

Their success has been to harness the best of the English game, especially the constant pressurising of opponents, with the best of the continental, especially precision of passing and running off the ball. The frequent failure of Liverpool players to reproduce their club form when playing for their national sides indicates the reliance on blending players to produce a whole which is often greater than the sum of its parts. The Liverpool style is in some ways remarkably conservative. They look like a typical First Division side yet don't play like one. They have generally had a three-man forward line with a recognisable division of labour: a central striker (Johnson, Toshack, Rush), a winger (Heighway, Barnes), and a player who feeds off these two (Keegan, Beardsley). Their three-man mid-field changes names but not roles; fifteen years ago it was Hughes, Case and Callaghan; now it is McMahon, Whelan, Houghton or Nicol. The back four has generally been flat but with always one player of genuine pace or skill with the ball, the most obvious recent example being Alan Hansen. Occasionally a continental player has been used as a sweeper.

Yet the Liverpool story remains an exception; their secret remains just that. The only club to have come anywhere near emulating them has been Nottingham Forest under the managership of Brian Clough. At a provincial club with limited support and resources, he has nevertheless produced some outstanding players and teams, often reliant on subtle defensive strategies. Clough clearly has the ability requisite for an England team manager, to blend ordinary players into an exceptional side, but his abrasive personality has ensured that he would never be selected by the conservative gentlemen who run the Football Association. He has, in short, an inappropriate style.

The English disease

Many have tried to explain why English clubs have at least occasionally been able to compete with sides from Spain, Italy and West Germany in a way the national side cannot. Possible explanations include (1) the preference given to league competition in the organisation of the game, (2) the strategic import- ance in major clubs of players who are British but not English, and (3) an alleged excess of coaching.

The first explanation argues that the organisation of English football produces outstanding club sides rather than individual world-class players. The collective interests of the clubs as vested in the Football League predominate over national interests entrusted to the Football Association. The evidence is strong: the length of the English league season and an excessive number of games; the proliferation of sponsored tournaments; the reluctance to prioritise international matches (Fynn and Guest, 1989); the reversion to a twenty-two member First Division and so on. Hence the lobby to merge the two organisations and the FA's proposal, in the spring of 1991, to institute its own Super League. The roots of the problem, however, go deeper than the organisational structure.

The second line of argument is that English league football is dominated by players and managers who are British but not English. At the time of writing, players qualified for England were a minority in Liverpool's side and only just a majority in that of Manchester United. Both clubs had Scotsmen as managers, as did Arsenal. Add to that the Welsh and the Irish from both sides of the border and it becomes clear that the success of English club sides has depended on a blend of players from all over the United Kingdom and the Irish Republic. (This is likely to prove a handicap since FIFA plan to limit the number of players in European club competitions born in countries other than the one the club represents.) The overall force of this argument is diminished by evidence that other European leagues — in Spain, Italy and West Germany — have absorbed foreign players without adverse effects on their national sides.

The third line of argument is to decry the excess of coaching, natural talent being supposedly stifled by the imposition of systems which minimise individual initiative. Again, however, successful footballing nations have rather more complex coaching systems than England. For all its apparent sophisication in theory, in practice English coaching emphasises the untea-chability of 'natural' skill. Ability is seen as something the player is born with; coaching is about tactics, how to exploit existent skill, rather than the development of new skills. Coaching reflects rather than challenges the English definition of what constitutes skill in professional football: it is a question of style.

The evolution of tactical formations is revealing of this style. Only slowly did British football, in the wake of international humiliations in the 1950s, move away from the W/M formation which had dominated football from the inter-war period. 2–3–5 became 4–3–3, 4–4–2 and finally 4–5–1, without any discernible improvement in the capacity to improvise. Formations became a defensive straitjacket.

Perhaps if it was not possible to outplay good teams, then it might well be possible to outfight and outrun them; perhaps new techniques which put greater emphasis on defence, rather than looking towards attack, might be the answer . . . It was still not understood that systems can only be of merit if players who can work them are available. British football, with its emphasis on strength and aggression, struggled to adapt. (Rippon, 1983: p. 76)

In the introduction of the fixed formation, British football reached the end of its intellectual tether. A measure of its conservatism and inflexibility came in the early stages of the 1990 World Cup Finals. England manager Bobby Robson suddenly improvised. A fifth player was introduced into the back formation. This was not merely a defensive ploy though it did recognise that a 'flat' British-style back four was always vulnerable to opponents who could break suddenly. The 'new' idea was that the defence could be used as a platform for attacks. With five at the back, full-backs could venture upfield and overlap, confident that others would cover them. Additionally, at least some of the back five would carry the ball out of defence, interchanging with mid-field players and so introducing some patterned flexibility to attacks.

This recognition of a strategem which continental teams had used for years, of the 'libero' or free player at the back, was both belated and temporary. The expressed views of Robson's successor, Graham Taylor, do little to suggest that he recognises international football to be a different ball game, one English players are ill equipped to play. The basic sense of rhythm is different. I can still find no better explanation of the basic contrast between the British and continental styles of play then one given twenty-five years ago, of what was then an emergent slow/fast continental rhythm:

This style of play has two phases: the first includes the slow build-up of attacks by ball-holding, square passing and reverse passing, in mid-field; the second one is of fast movement and dash in and around the penalty area. Mid-field superiority is essential for the build-up of attacks in this style; thus any team attempting to play this type of game must have players in mid-field who are highly talented in ball control and short passing . . . the team aims to retain possession. The team makes slow progress towards the opponents goal: when in the region of the opponents' penalty area the forwards forget the number they are wearing on their shirt, and move in all directions at speed; meanwhile the ball is still being held and passed by the mid-field players, until a gap is found in the opposing defence: then the ball is passed quickly to the player in that gap or into the gap for a player to run onto. (Lozdiak, 1966: p. 52)

The effectiveness of this style has been learned the hard way by British teams in international competition. The question is why, in the nearly thirty years since Hungary first exhibited these basic skills in beating England 6–3 at Wembley, so little has been done to incorporate them into the English national game. The answer, though not the resolution, is simple: it's not our natural style.

There is a distinctively British style of playing football. Each continent — mainland Europe, South America, even Africa — generates its own distinctive style but the British is more different from all of these than they are from each other. Compared with overseas players, British players are technically deficient in the finer points of the game: ball control, passing, balance and positional sense. Too many players are unadaptable. Defenders frequently have trouble controlling or distributing the ball and centre backs are happier with the ball in the air than on the ground. Forwards are often one-paced and predictable in their movements. The old-fashioned centre forward is still around. Even Robson, when desperate, resorted to robust and unsophisticated players such as Mark Hateley and Mick Harford. Taylor has likewise persisted with Steve Bull. At most, British teams can compensate for these deficiencies by exploiting their own virtues, constantly harassing opponents and subjecting them to an aerial bombardment, parodied in its essentials by the style of the contemporary national side of the Irish Republic under the management of Jack Charlton.

These technical deficiencies remain at all levels of the game, despite attempts to overcome them. Indeed, those with exceptional and untypically British skill, such as Glenn Hoddle or Chris Waddle, have been derided for their lack of 'workrate' and often found more appreciative audiences abroad. Players, managers and administrators are not alone in endorsing this traditional style. It is also what spectators expect and want. Supporters have a preference for direct rather than indirect football, for continuous changes of possession rather than keep-ball, for the quick high cross rather than patient manoeuvring for an opening, for effort rather than aesthetics. Home crowds will support a winning team, whatever its style, but they also want the excitement which a game based on speed, strength and aggression provides — as its popularity when televised abroad attests.

What we have here is a distinctively national style, intimately related to those virtues and skills the game is required to express. While the surface of the game appears to have changed, its essence has remained constant: impervious to change, obdurate in its commitment to the British style. One key component of this style is a definition of manliness, also evident in the role of aggression and violence in the game.

Rules Britannia

It is almost impossible to resolve the question of whether the amount of cheating in professional football has increased in recent years. Statistics of cautions and sendings-off reflect variations in refereeing practices, themselves determined by how the Football Association and the Football League perceive the problem.

The game itself has in theory become less violent. Shoulder-charging has been virtually eliminated and goalkeepers are protected from physical interference more than they used to be. However, this apparent elimination of what was previously routine physical contact has not necessarily decreased the amount of foul play. It has simply taken on new forms. Close observation of any professional match will reveal that there are precious few clean tackles. Pushing and shoving, holding an opponent or his shirt are routine, only penalised when excessive or obvious.

In a comprehensive review of different types of illegal behaviour, Desmond Morris (1981) argues that the referee can do no more than punish the most flagrant breaches of rules, such as obvious acts of dissent and foul play, though much deliberate violence is likely to happen off the ball unnoticed. Morris argues that the conflict between players and referees is a permanent feature of the game, since players are dedicated to the adoption of any means necessary to achieve the goal of victory.

Nevertheless, new and stylistically exaggerated forms of deviance do seem to have entered the game. Injuries or fouls are feigned, as players dive in the area or roll in apparent agony after a tackle. The 'professional foul', the use of any means to prevent an opponent scoring, betrays a new kind of cynicism.

Together with the open dissent from the referee's decisions, such developments point to changes in the style of cheating.

Wagg (1984: p. 154) has suggested that a cynicism towards the rules reflects the amorality of the business ethos dominant inside and outside the game, with the only countervailing pressure as the need to 'clean up' the game's image for the wider televiewing public. This may underemphasise the extent to which codes of behaviour have cultural roots, especially in versions of masculinity.

There is, for example, no precisely equivalent behaviour in either rugby code. Both have problems of foul play, though these are largely of a traditionally violent kind. The comparison is complex because of the different rule structures and rhythms, not to mention financial rewards, of the rugby codes but both seem able to avoid the overt displays of emotion and dramatic displays which have become part of professional football. The distinction may lie in different kinds of masculine style, that of rugby being in the more traditional mould of aversion to display, restraint of emotion and quiet satisfaction with the collective achievement of a score. Football, by contrast, has become dominated by displays of anger, elation and dissent. Walvin (1986: p. 40) attributes much of the modern emphasis on histrionic display to the expectations of the media. By contrast, Morris (1981: p. 140) argues that some at least of the emotional display of the modern footballer is a release from the unnatural self-restraint which had previously limited expressions of elation. Either way, there has been a significant shift in the licence given to emotional display within a changed style of masculinity.

Authority has come to be seen less as the implementation of a common and necessary morality than an alien imposition. Walvin has argued that this has a basis in the wider society, where other authoritative institutions such as school, family and work have lessened their hold of arbitrary power over youth, especially working-class males. The result has

left sport exposed as one of the few surviving institutions which continued to demand of its participants an unswerving loyalty to and an unquestioning acceptance of its codes, conventions, and punishments. Not surprisingly, young footballers (or tennis players for that matter) bridle at these demands when, in almost every other aspect of their social and economic lives, the nature of discipline — of authority and obedience — has changed so fundamentally. (Walvin, 1986: p. 110)

The change in behavioural style is clearly related to a shift in the wider society where there has been a decline in traditional working-class definitions of masculinity — its brutality and emotional insensitivity as well as its collective sense of control. The game reflects these changes and expresses a new style or masculine code.

Perhaps this is encapsulated in attitudes towards pain. The ability to take and receive physical punishment is an intrinsic part of all contact sports. Traditionally, in sport and in life, the working-class man knew a lot about pain. The code was not to show it; being a man meant that you could take it and come back for more. Now pain has become a ploy. Players writhe in apparent agony, mainly in the hope of gaining some advantage, a free kick at least and preferably the cautioning or sending-off of an opponent. After some token treatment, they run off apparently none the worse for wear. Once, such sly and unmanly conduct would have been seen as fit only for foreigners. Now it is an intrinsic part of a new kind of manliness in which psychological cunning has displaced physical confrontation.

That example may suggest the complexities of football as an articulation of manliness. The centrality of sport to masculinity is often underrated, especially in the proliferation of writings about masculine identity. What it means in our culture to be a man is often articulated around and through sport. The key masculine values are frequently identified as those of aggression, competition and achievement. Equally important, however, is physical style, for that is the demonstration of male status. Whether in stratagems within the game, attitudes towards authority or reactions to pain, sport acts out a particular validation of a masculine style. In his exaggerated deviance, the professional player becomes the bearer of some common confusions and contradictions in contemporary masculinity.

Players' styles
A passing interest in the game

From the mid-1960s onwards, the status of top-level professional footballers changed dramatically. Previously they had been retained within the economic and cultural confines of the everyday working-class world from which they were recruited and to which even the most outstanding of them would be likely to return. What they expected, and what was expected of them was that they would express the virtues and vices of the world of the working-class male. From that they drew their style: of playing, bearing and appearance.

Following the abolition of the maximum wage in 1961 and the absolute power exercised by clubs over players in the Eastham judgement of 1963, top-level professional footballers began to demand the kinds of salaries commensurate with the rarity of their skills. Combined with the rapid expansion of endorsement and media contracts in the 1970s, such developments soon divorced the top-level players from their previous status. How they dressed, where they lived, who they mixed with, and thus eventually what they represented, underwent change. As Walvin has noted, this was a transformation of style:

The *style* affected by large numbers of footballers was dictated by the image of the footballer portrayed by TV and the newspapers, and by those commercial interests which rapidly latched onto the game and its most prominent (i.e. commercial) stars. The end result was the emergence of the modern player, acutely conscious of his earning capacity, on and off the field, highly susceptible to lucrative and tempting offers and increasingly committed to a style of life and behaviour which was in many crucial respects new. It was a style which cut him off from his footballing forebears and perhaps, most importantly of all, from many of those working-class fans who formed the traditional bedrock of the game's supporters. (Walvin, 1986: p. 33–4, original emphasis)

In my earlier discussion of this transformation (Critcher, 1979), I offered a fivefold typology of the footballer as hero:

1. traditional/located in the working class;
2. transitional/mobile on his way out of the working class;
3. incorporated/'embourgeoised' into the 'new' middle class;
4. superstar/dislocated from any cultural milieu;
5. superstar/relocated in the world of show business.

In the 1960s and early 1970s the move from one to another of these statuses was experienced by many professional footballers. They now coexist at different levels in the world of professional football. Players in the Fourth, Third and even Second Divisions remain 'traditional' in style; some in the Second and the lower reaches of the First aspire to become 'mobile/transitional'. A good number in the First Division may become 'incorporated/embourgeoised', identifying with the ethos and lifestyle of the self-made businessman. Their fame remains largely contained within the footballing subculture. It is in the appropriation of a player's fame outside the world of football that 'superstardom' operates. When recognised by those with little intrinsic interest in football, the footballing hero has become a celebrity labelled a 'superstar' and adopting what Walvin (1986: p. 32) has called 'the style of the élite'. Others without the substance may try to emulate the style. As Tommy Docherty has recently and cruelly put it: 'In the fifties we had players trying to be stars; now we have stars trying to be players.'

Tendencies in the media and especially television contribute to the process, though their precise role is a matter of debate. Goldlust (1987) blames them for a tendency to report on the match or the state of the game itself in terms of 'controversial' individuals, but Chandler (1988) suggests that the media merely debunk our illusions about heroism. Few, however, could disagree with the analysis that 'in many cases the selling of certain footballers' images took over from and transcended the very phenomenon which made it all possible — the game of football' (Walvin, 1986; p. 34). In Wagg's words 'football culture has been largely annexed to media culture' (1984: p. 113).

Shooting stars

Stardom is as much to do with style off the pitch as on it. The player must meet the excessive and often unreasonable demands of the media — that he be a character yet behave himself, that he appear in public and have no private life to call his own, that he be as articulate off the field as he is on it. Fortunately, the most extreme of these demands are made only on a few. Most top-level footballers have developed their own ways of dealing with and even exploiting these pressures, aided by a panoply of agents, lawyers and accountants. They are comfortable as 'standard bearers for the new consumer capitalism' (Wagg, 1984: p. 141).

None of these tendencies and tensions is confined to soccer or even sport. They are also evident in popular music where fame may be more transient but even more difficult to handle when those involved — star and public — are so young. It is not unknown for pop stars to disintegrate when fame comes suddenly and without limit. But unlike other celebrities, the sportsperson has to keep performing to standard to maintain his status. Films can be recut and records remixed to disguise those occasions when the star performer has an off day, but in sport the goods must be produced continuously, live and unedited, before a critical audience. The tragic decline of George Best and the trials of Ian Botham are well known but the price of stardom can be heavy even in amateur sport. Barry John, a folk hero of Welsh Rugby, retired from the game in 1972 at the height of his fame when only 27. His autobiography (John, 1975) graphically recounts the pressures of stardom — 'the intensifying public movement towards my own deification' (p. 29) — which he felt unable and unwilling to absorb. Will Carling, captain of England's rugby team in the late 1980s and early 1990s, experienced problems of a similar magnitude though slightly different in kind, many stemming from the Rugby Football Union's attempt to resist the logic of professionalism. Others, inside and outside football, found fame easier to handle. Symptomatic of these was Kevin Keegan.

Born into a mining family in Doncaster in 1951, Keegan signed for Scunthorpe in 1968 and was bought by Liverpool for £35,000 in the spring of 1971. With him in the side until 1977, Liverpool won the league championship three times, the FA Cup, the UEFA Cup and the European Cup. Keegan was then transferred to Hamburg, who won the Bundesliga in 1979 and lost to Nottingham Forest in the European Cup Final of 1980. He played sixty-three times for England between 1972 and 1982, was selected as the Football Writers' Association Player of the Year in 1976 and, uniquely for an English footballer, was European Footballer of the Year twice. In the summer of 1980, he unexpectedly signed for Southampton, leaving them two years later to join Newcastle United, whom he helped gain promotion from the Second Division. At the end of the season, on his 33rd birthday, he announced his retirement from the game.

Keegan was an exceptional goalscorer. At Liverpool and for England, he averaged almost a goal every three games; at Southampton and then Newcastle, a goal every two games. No one could argue with his record or those of his clubs yet our interest may be more in the control that Keegan exerted over his own destiny. His main professional contracts each had a clause stipulating the amount of his transfer fee on the expiry of his contract, effectively giving him choice over which club he joined. At the height of his European fame with Hamburg, he had a salary of £125,000 and endorsement deals grossing a quarter of a million pounds a year. Yet when he agreed to the deal which took him to Newcastle, underwritten by a promotional deal with Scottish and Newcastle Breweries to pay him a total of £3,000 a week, he stipulated that he would not advertise beer drinking directly.

Keegan was no paragon, disgracing himself when sent off in a Charity Shield final, rowing more than once with England managers and putting his name to a provocative column in the *Sun* newspaper. Such conduct in other players might have been signs of instability but in Keegan they were consistent with a tough sense of his own interests and identity (Gibson, 1984).

Keegan may have been one of the first to show that the status of superstar could be exploited by the player himself as much as by others. But it required determination, a sense of personal stability and the acumen to know when to move on. These were comparatively rare qualities in professional footballers. Fortunately, only a few have to cope with the strains of being a superstar, for only some are so elected.

Myth appropriation

Extraordinary and measurable talent is a necessary but not sufficient qualification to become a star outside the game as well as within it. To be recognised as an outstanding player and thus a footballing hero is by no means the same as becoming a household name. One significant index of success within the game is to be nominated as Footballer of the Year by the Football Writers' Association.

The list reflects the transitions in style noted earlier: from the star players of the 1940s and 1950s (Matthews, Finney, Lofthouse, Blanchflower) through those of the 1960s and 1970s (the Charlton brothers, Banks, Keegan, Dalglish), to the more modern era of the 1980s and beyond (Rush, Lineker, Barnes). Finney, Matthews, Blanchflower, Dalglish and Barnes all managed to win it twice. Yet in all four decades, there are many — Syd Owen, Tony Book, Terry McDermott, Neville Southall — known only to those who follow the game.

Even judgements within the game do not concur. Since 1972, the Professional Footballers' Association have voted for their own Footballer of the Year but only occasionally has their judgement coincided with that of the FWA. There is, however, a consensus about what kind of player is recognised. Both the FWA and the PFA choose their stars from attackers or mid-fielders rather than defenders. Of forty-three FWA winners, seventeen have been forwards, fifteen mid-fielders and just eleven defenders. The PFA has chosen nine forwards, three mid-fielders and four defenders. Journalists and players share with the general public the expectation that the star player will be a forward.

The star footballer is likely to be one who regularly scores or makes goals: he must generate excitement, not merely technical recognition. Even this, however, does not explain why some players have appeal outside the game. In the last decade, the players who have had most effect on English national performance, whose absence could not immediately be compensated for, have been Peter Shilton, Bryan Robson and Gary Lineker. They are highly paid, have played for leading clubs as well as England and have been noticed outside the game. Yet it has been an arguably inferior player, at least one who has yet to prove himself at the highest level, who has become a 'superstar': Paul Gascoigne.

Asking what it is that Best and Gascoigne have which other players do not is rather like asking what Marilyn Monroe and Madonna have which other female entertainers do not. It is, in the literal sense, a mystery. We cannot define it so we call it charisma ('charisma': a favour specially vouchsafed by God; a grace or talent'; *Shorter Oxford English Dictionary*, 1972). It is at once something more than, yet the ultimate realisation of, style: it is a kind of presence.

Gascoigne's rise to fame was startling. By the end of 1990, even those who had never been to a game could recognise the name and the face or recall the clip which showed him on the verge of tears during the 1990s World Cup quarter-final. His footballing ability is in English terms exceptional with an extraordinary capacity for the unexpected which may in itself turn the course of a match. Yet, as his uncertain status in the English national side shows, he also has long ineffectual periods, especially if his team is forced on to the defensive. Other less fashionable players, such as Gordon Strachan of Leeds United, had a more sustained capacity to control a game in the 1990–1 season.

What Gascoigne offers is an appeal to those whose interest in the game is tangential. His attractiveness to the general public is evident, yet Gascoigne, fair and squat, looks like neither athlete nor pin-up. His personality is what matters: cheeky, disrespectful, street-wise, he looks and sounds like the Geordie lad next door. On and off the field he is a natural showman yet with a disarming sense of his own ordinariness.

What makes Gascoigne and not Strachan a star is what endangers him. The danger arises because often it is the flawed volatility which propels someone to the status of superstar. It is the lack of discipline in their play which makes them exciting and the lack of discipline in their personalities which makes them vulnerable. Those who are disciplined on and off the field may not become superstars because recognition of their qualities is confined to the game. They may be known outside the game but they have no wider appeal, a status nicely caught by Gary Linekar's admission on 'Desert Island Discs' that he is 'a rather boring sort of person'. Stars are not made of such stuff. By contrast, in the few months each side of Christmas 1990, Gascoigne was pictured with Prime Minister Thatcher and had a record in the Top Ten, yet was dropped by England for an important match against the Irish Republic and sent off in a televised match for swearing at the referee, ironically complaining about an alleged foul on the immaculately behaved Lineker. His career, especially an impending transfer to Italy, was then jeopardised by an injury in the 1991 FA Cup Final caused when he fouled an opposing player.

What matters in the transmutation to superstar is persona or style. As long as the player and his fame are contained within the footballing subculture, the problems he faces will be those traditionally faced by professional footballers: drink, gambling and sex (Crick and Smith, 1989). The style is prescribed by the subculture of professional football and the expectations of other players, management and supporters. Once he moves outside those confines, however, a whole new set of expectations come into play — those of agents, promoters, advertisers, the public and media, more interested in the status of stardom than its source. Boorstin's analysis of stardom suggests that a male hero is authentic, defined by who he appears to be. The two are not necessarily compatible. 'When a man appears as hero and/or celebrity, his role as celebrity obscures and is apt to destroy his role as hero' (Boorstin, 1963: p. 82).

As we have seen, this problem is faced only by a tiny minority of professional footballers. Most have a readily available style to inherit. But one group of footballers have no such inheritance and may experience considerable uncertainty about their status inside and outside the game. These are the new generation of black British footballers.

Race for the title

From the late 1970s black men and women emerged as top-level performers in British sport, initially in athletics and boxing, then in soccer. Viv Anderson became the first black footballer to play for England in 1979 and Garth Crooks the first to score in a Cup Final two years later. But the first black footballing superstar was John Barnes. Signed by Watford in 1981, his early development owed much to the foresight of general manager Bertie Mee and team manager Graham Taylor. His playing ability outgrew the confines of a small town club and he was signed by Liverpool for £900,000 in the summer of 1987.

With Beardsley, signed from Newcastle, he was to join Aldridge as the spearhead of a team which needed to compensate for the loss of Rush to Juventus. Barnes was the first black player to be signed for either Liverpool club (at the time of writing, Everton still have no black player in their first team).

In his significantly unauthorised biography, Dave Hill argues that 'there could not be a less typical black footballer than John Barnes' (1989: p. 57). Born and brought up in the Jamaican middle class, sent to an English grammar school, Barnes appears to show little consciousness of his race, preferring the term 'coloured' to black as a self-description. This background and the attitudes it nurtures contribute much to Barnes's style, on and off the field, especially the air of detachment which serves him so well, except when the English national side seems unable to harness his talents.

Three fundamental issues have arisen from the emergence of the black footballer or athlete. The first is how and why Afro-Caribbeans should be so disproportionately prominent. Cashmore (1982) has argued that sport and music offer career opportunities to young blacks largely excluded from success in the educational system, a tendency reinforced by the ready availability of role models, from Mohammed Ali to Pele. Thus sport becomes associated with internationally recognised black achievements, often in a style which explicitly validates black identity. These factors are specific to the Afro-Caribbean community and experienced less by Asians, who consequently are less involved in top-level sport.

Within sport, however, the progress of the black performer is often subject to discriminatory practices, the second issue. Hill, amongst others, gives examples of the crude racist stereotyping which informs managers' and coaches' assessments of black players as temperamentally suspect, lacking in 'bottle' and likely to take offence at 'harmless' racial jokes. While Woolnough's account (1983) largely reproduces such stereotypes, Hill emphasises the dilemmas of the black footballer:

Consider the politics of the field of play. Rule One: don't retaliate when the opponents bait you. The ref. will send you off, not the other guy. Rule Two: don't lose your rag with the crowd when they shower you with spit as you back away to take a corner kick, when they goad you with monkey chants and throw bananas on the pitch just to let you know they think you are no better than an ape. Rule Three: don't get upset when your own team-mates behave in exactly the same way. Break any of these rules and they say you've got a temperament problem. (Hill, 1989: p. 93)

Complementing Mason's (1988) preliminary analysis, Maguire (1988) tested whether English football would reproduce the tendency of American sport, known as 'stacking' to relegate black players to marginal playing positions. Maguire noted that Afro-Caribbeans represent 1.4 per cent of the general population but 7.7 per cent of professional footballers. Both analyses showed proportionately more black attackers than defenders but the real dearth of black players was in mid-field and in goal. Defining the spine of the team as comprised of goalkeepers, centre backs, central mid-field players and central strikers, Maguire claimed that black players were twice as likely to occupy marginal rather than central playing positions. Mason also emphasised that at the end of the 1980s no First Division club was regularly captained by a black player. No blacks were to be found in management or coaching. It may also be observed that in 1990 there were at least two league referees of Asian origin but no Afro-Caribbeans.

The third issue is the overt racism of football crowds, who habitually use the term 'nigger', throw bananas on to the pitch and greet black opposing players with monkey noises. While some such as Morris see such insults as no different from others common within the game, Hill argues that this is unadulterated racism, to be found, along with sexism and xenophobia, as much in the directors' box as on the terraces.

There seems to be an inherent limit on the status accorded to black footballers, even compared with other sports. Linford Christie in athletics and Frank Bruno in boxing have achieved recognition as national heroes, their colour secondary to their sporting achievements. Perhaps because these are individual sports, where black success is an accepted tradition, they have been adopted as honorary Britons. No such common recognition has yet been given to a black footballer. Racial ideas pre-empt the black player from fully representing English working-class masculinity.

The styles of recruitment, management and crowd response provoked by the black player tell us much about what lies beneath the surface of white sporting culture. Yet there may be hope, if only because ultimately football has to be a meritocracy. Black players are now common in national and club sides, notably Arsenal's mid-field. It is not necessary to subscribe to racist stereotypes about innate ability to recognise the distinctive contribution of black players to the English game. While some black players may have an orthodox style when playing as central strikers and defenders, there is also evidence in mid-field players of balance, ball control and a capacity for improvisation which does not come easily to their white counterparts. The pace of Parker and Walker in England's current back four, the erratic brilliance of Barnes, the proficiency of Arsenal's mid-field, all suggest that more than black faces have appeared on England's professional football pitches: they have brought with them their own distinctive style, nurtured and retained despite the racial hostility of those who manage, play and watch the game.

Conclusion: style clash

How, then, can we make sense of these different kinds of style: of tactical styles, of real and stylised violence, of the style of the footballer as hero, of the style of the emergent Afro-Caribbean footballer?

We may not have any language adequate to analyse the processes I have been trying to identify. Style has been developed as a concept in cultural analysis but has been largely confined to such areas as fashion or youth culture. Attempts to identify style as a distinctive attribute of 'post-modernist' consumer culture (Tomlinson (ed.), 1990), or as a form of bodily discourse (Frank in Featherstone *et al.* (eds), 1991), seem unable to encompass styles in sport. We have not progressed far beyond the classic articles by Goffman and Geertz, reproduced in a recent collection (Alexander and Seidman (eds), 1990) which takes a wider view of culture as a symbolic form.

John B. Thompson (1990) has recently argued that cultural forms need to be resituated in their social context. Culture should not be seen as separate from society but as integral to it. Football, according to such an argument, does not merely reflect society, but is part of how the society symbolises its central themes. There is not football style here and some separate entity called masculinity there. Rather, football articulates or represents masculinity.

According to Thompson, symbolic forms have five essential characteristics. The first three — that they are motivated communications, draw on conventional codes and have an internal structure — have been well established by figurational sociology (Elias and Dunning, 1986). Even more relevant for our purposes are the other two characteristics specified by Thompson. The first is the referential aspect, that 'symbolic forms are constructions which typically represent something, refer to something, say something about something' (Thompson, 1990: p. 143). Secondly, both the symbolic form and its referents are situated within a socio-historical context.

There is no immediate reason to deny football the status of a symbolic form. Hence we can ask what it is that football refers to. The language of semiotics can be tentatively mobilised for this purpose. Barthes (1973) has suggested that our understanding of what is signified or referred to often depends upon our understanding of generalised 'myths' embedded in the culture. In the case of football, there are three basic sets of interrelated myths which football signifies or refers to, though they may be easier to nominate than to analyse.

It is not difficult to see what football refers to: versions of local identity, from local club to national side; masculine pride and achievement; working-classness in both its 'rough' and 'respectable' forms. Football thus appears to represent in complex ways variations on these theses: the enigma of the working-class Englishman. Yet what is important here is to recognise that the values or ideals expressed by football are not immutable. The process is more complex, traceable through analysis of style.

We can see at least four aspects of this process of signification. There is, to begin with, a clear continuity in what football signifies and clear limits to what it can ever to be made to signify. But within those real limits, there are, secondly, changes in style and what it signifies, traceable to sources inside and outside the game. Thirdly, there is a variable interplay between what the game intrinsically signifies and the signification systems dominant in the wider society, producing a permanent tension between the unofficial discourse of football and dominant definitions of what it represents. We can consider each of these in turn.

Firstly, some of the continuities are self-evident. It is difficult to specify anything, other than war and royalty, which articulates national identity quite so powerfully as the England team competing in the latter stages of a World Cup competition. Despite an apparently growing band of female supporters and players, football remains a celebration of masculine identity, its style and achievements. Class may be a less visible presence but it can be heard: the language of the football terrace and pitch is unequivocally that of the mainstream male working class.

These themes as articulated by football are subject to pressures of change as well as continuity. Some pressures are external. The traditional English style of playing inherited in the post-war period was rendered anachronistic by the evident superiority of 'foreign' styles of play. Some pressures are internal, as the shifting economies of the game and the wider society open out to the very best players rewards and lifestyles which challenge any simple definition of them as irredeemably working-class. Other pressures are simultaneously external and internal, as Afro-Caribbeans bring to the indigenous game physical styles and graces derived from a distinctive cultural heritage.

Football, it may be objected, is only a game: a physical and competitive activity designed to realise an arbitrary goal. Yet the goals realised may be more than the immediate features of the game; they are also the goals of the wider culture. What is embodied in football, even or especially as I have tried to show in the style in which the game is played, is more than mere technical expertise. For what constitutes excellence in the English game — the direct approach, the constant effort, the unremitting pace — is not merely a sporting but a cultural definition. In endorsing the English or British style of playing, as opposed to that of continental Europe, South America and now Africa, it also appeals to a wider sense of Englishness: belief in effort, an aversion to theory or fancy ways.

So, too, the player is defined in part by the culture outside football. His capacity to perform is expected and anticipated in ways particular to football but his presence off the field, the trappings and media excursions, are those of the celebrity. He is both football hero and media superstar. The Afro-Caribbean footballer is also perceived and treated in the racist terms of the wider culture. He can never be just a player; he is always a black player.

Nevertheless, the identities of Englishness, masculinity and class expressed by the game are not in any simple sense the dominant official versions. There is always a tension with more respectable articulations. The official version may predominate at moments of national ritual like the Cup Final, though even here the crowd does not always observe the official niceties. Members of élites may try to appropriate the game but must do so selectivity in order to disown its more profane and disorderly elements. This is not the England of rustic charm or social harmony: urban conflict is at its core. This is not the manliness of the stiff upper lip: it is more likely to snarl or curse. This is not the class which knows its place but the one which celebrates its commonness.

These processes — of continuity with tradition, reflection of change, infusion by the surrounding culture and tension between profane and sacred elements — are evident in quite different national and local contexts. Football has an extraordinary cultural plasticity. The game and its cultural role can be transposed all over the globe. In each case, the precise meaning of masculinity, national or regional identity and class will take on local variations. We can find the role of football in signifying and articulating cultural identity in Brasilia or Birmingham, Milan or Manchester, Lusaka or Leeds. The particularity of each socio-historical and cultural context is realised through a recognisable style of playing and watching football. The game may be constant but the kind of style and what precisely it refers to will vary; it is both universal and particular.

In the contemporary English context, football style seems to be in a state of some confusion. The English football media are never happy unless there is a sense of crisis, often spuriously pursued on the sports pages (See Stephen Wagg's chapter in this volume). The current crisis identified here — of and in style — is nevertheless real and pervasive. It is manifest in the continuing inadequacies in international competition, in controversies over codes of behaviour, in the often ruinous effect of the status of superstar, in the perpetuation of racist stereotypes which obstruct recognition of the potential contribution of the black footballer.

Some of these crises are potentially resolvable within the game. Coaching may become more adventurous; the professional foul may be eliminated. However, the forces of conservatism are ubiquitous: from the arcane structure of the Football League to the demand from the terraces to 'get it up the field'. Nor is it easy to see how footballers protect themselves from the stresses of media stardom or that, magically, football crowds and management would become blind to the colour of the players.

The essential problem is that football has merely adapted its traditional style to wholly changed circumstances inside and outside the game. In particular, it stands for a kind of national culture, an ideal of manliness and a class identification which can no longer inform the game with the confidence they once had. There are simply too many contemporary challenges to those comfortable definitions. Raymond Williams (1987; p. 178) has neatly pointed to the paradox of strident versions of nationalism and racism in a world whose economy recognises no boundaries of states or races. John Hargreaves's incisive analysis of the ideological role of modern sport identifies sport as an attempt to preserve conservative ideals of masculinity and class which are being dislodged as tendencies towards home-centredness and consumerism displace older kinds of working-class community: 'involvement in sports becomes one of the few remaining ways working-class men's identity can be reaffirmed and their identity shored up' (Hargreaves, 1986; p. 106).

We find in football an attempt to retrieve some ancient certainties of nationhood, masculinity and class within a socio-historical context no longer so favourable to their continuation. In this sense, football and its style may be seen as an index of cultural uncertainty.

If that seems too fanciful, I write these words in the immediate aftermath of a quite appalling performance by the English national side in a European Championship match against Turkey, notable for its good fortune, technical deficiencies and physical crudity. This could be interpreted narrowly, as merely another indication of the flawed techniques and management of English football. The argument here has been that the underlying problem remains that of the English style, which has causes and consequences outside the game itself. It is the style of a culture in a state of tension. Football is one of its most powerful if least understood manifestations.

Bibliography

Alexander, J. C. and S. Seidman (eds.) (1990), *Culture and Society*, Cambridge: Cambridge University Press.

Boorstin, D. J. (1963), *The Image*, Harmondsworth: Penguin Books.

Barthes, R. (1973) *Mythologies*, St. Albans: Paladin.

Bulter, B. (1987), *The Football League 1888–1988*, London: Queen Anne Press.

Cashmore, E. (1982), *Black Sportsmen*, London: Routledge and Kegan Paul.

Chandler, J. M. (1988), *Television and National Sport*, Urbana, IL: University of Illinois Press.

Crick, M. and D. Smith (1989), *Manchester United: The Betrayal of a Legend*, London: Pelham Books.

Critcher, C. (1979), 'Football Since the War', in J. Clarke, C. Critcher and R. Johnson (eds), *Working-Class Culture*, London: Hutchinson.

Elias, N. and Dunning, E., (1986), *The Quest For Excitement*, Oxford: Basil Blackwell.

Fynn, A. and L. Guest (1989), *The Secret Life of Football*, London: Queen Anne Press.

Frank, A. W. (1991), 'For a Sociology of the Body' in M. Featherstone, M. Hepworth and B. S. Turner (eds), *The Body*, London: Sage.

Gibson, J. (1984), *Kevin Keegan: Portrait of a Superstar*, London: W. H. Allen.

Goldlust, J. (1987), *Playing for Keeps: Sport, the Media and Society*, Melbourne: Longman.

Hargreaves, J. (1986), *Sport, Power and Culture*, Oxford: Polity Press.

Hill, D. (1989), *Out of His Skin: The John Barnes Phenonemon*, London: Faber and Faber.

John, B. (1975), *The Barry John Story*, London: Fontana.

Lozdiak, C. (1966), *Understanding Soccer Tactics*, London: Faber and Faber.

Maguire, J. (1988), 'Race and Position in English Soccer', *Sociology of Sport Journal*, **5**: 257–69.

Mason, T. (1988), *Sport in Britain*, London: Faber and Faber.

Morris, D. (1981), *The Soccer Tribe*, London: Jonathan Cape.

Rippon, A. (1983), *Soccer: The Road to Crises*, London: Moorland Publishing.

Rollin, J. (1979 onwards), *Rothman's Football Yearbook*, London: Queen Anne Press.

Tomlinson, A. (ed.) (1990), *Consumption, Identity and Style*, London: Routledge.

Thompson, J. B. (1990), *Ideology and Modern Culture*, Oxford: Polity Press.

Wagg, S. (1984), *The Football World*, Brighton: Harvester.

Walvin, J. (1986), *Football and the Decline of Britain*, Basingstoke: Macmillan.

Williams, R. (1983), *Towards 2000*, London: Chatto and Windus.

Woolnough, B. (1983), *Black Magic: England's Black Footballers*, London: Pelham Books.

5
Can play, will play? Women and football in Britain

John Williams and Jackie Woodhouse

If football were dangerous, some ill-effects would have been seen by now. I know that all our girls are healthier and, speaking personally, I feel worlds better than I did a year ago. Housework isn't half the trouble it used to be, because there is always Saturday's game and the week night training to freshen me up.

(Mrs Barraclough, captain, Huddersfield Atalanta FC, 1921)

Booze, betting and birds

During the England team's surprisingly successful campaign in the 1990 World Cup Finals in Italy, two 'personalities' emerged to satisfy the apparently unquenchable appetite of the news journalists of the British tabloid press who were out in Italy (Davies, 1990). One of these was, of course, the England midfield star Paul Gascoigne — 'Gazza' whose 'continental' skills and patriotic — and, therefore, not wholly unmanly — tears provided for a rather untraditional but wonderfully marketable commodity in the post-Finals national glow. (See Critcher, this volume, for more on the 'Gazza' phenomenon). The other major World Cup 'personality' focus for the British national news media came in a much more traditional guise, though her fame — and marketability — were also rather more fleeting. The figure of Isabella Ciaravolo, a worker in the Is Molas Gold Hotel in Sardinia, covered British tabloid front pages on 14 June 1990, following allegations of what one newspaper euphemistically described as 'high jinks with (English) players' (*Daily Mirror*, 14 June, 1990). Pursued with near-religious tenacity by British journalists making cash offers for information on those players allegedly involved, Ms Ciaravolo, denying any such impropriety, was eventually transferred to a less exposed position and location. Her public trauma over, her life thus reassumed its tranquil course.

During this, to English eyes at least, by now routine interlude of press coverage of a major football excursion, the editor of one British national tabloid newspaper had his passport confiscated by Italian police, reportedly as an insurance against further harassment of the hapless hotel worker. (*Independent*

on Sunday 17 June 1990) The 'Isabella affair' — a story with no apparent
foundation in fact — signalled the arrival of the England team and, more
effectively, of the British press, in Italy. More to the point, however, the story,
once again, confirms key aspects of contemporary ideological relations
between women and football in Britain. In footballing parlance, women are,
traditionally, the 'birds' in that unholy triumvirate which also includes
betting and booze and which threatens to drag down into the mire the game's
most audacious and unpredictable talents. In tabloid discourse, while 'the lads'
battle it out on the terraces, women typically display their own 'patriotism' or
allegiance to the football cause via those Page 3 adornments of bobble hats,
scarves and strategically positioned footballs, which invariably emerge as props
around the time of major football tournaments. (At other times, of course, 'the
girls' get to 'model' jockey caps, flaunt tennis rackets, etc., etc.) In tabloid-
speak and in the sorts of 'male talk' which more widely characterise discussion
around football in England (Taylor 1990) women do not much watch, play or
otherwise support the game. Instead, they most frequently constitute the 'sex
angle' or are implicated via the more bizarre of the footballing widows/sexual
apartheid news stories ('Man Assaults Wife in Coronation Street v. World Cup
Television Tragedy'), which news journalists now seem to make an integral
part of the coverage of almost all major championships. Little wonder, then,
that it is in England that the tabloid *Sunday Sport* combines sport coverage with
surreal fictions *and* pages of topless 'models'.

It is, perhaps, not surprising, either, that those who work inside the football
industry, but who fail to measure up to the masculine traits demanded of this
notoriously closed occupational culture — perhaps because of their 'over-
theorising' or their demonstrable lack of 'bottle' — are frequently dismissed,
in language heavy with sexual censure, as 'fanny merchants' (Dunphy, 1976),
or are otherwise damagingly feminised. (Consider, for example, the case of the
export to France of the delicate and much underused skills of 'Glenda' née
Glen, Hoddle).

Despite their encouragingly low-key hooligan performance during the 1990
World Cup Finals, the profile of England's 'barmy army' of travelling fans
seemed pretty much to confirm the sorts of masculine exclusivity described
above. There was no shortage of 'Lock up your daughters' T-shirts in Cagliari,
or of the casual, sexist abuse which seems to have become part and parcel of
the travelling English football condition over the past fifteen years or so. Nine
out of ten English fans in Italy were young, white males, though numbers of
female England followers are rising slightly (Williams and Goldberg, 1991).
Women and children were much more prominent in Italy among the ranks of
the Irish, Scots and Italian fans and were even so among those of the feared
German and Dutch contingents. (Indeed, only fan groups from the United
Arab Emirates seemed quite so dominated by young men as were the English.)

Understandably, few English families would have been willing to undergo
the reported police 'Siege of Sardinia', even to watch World Cup football.
Indeed, a more accurate impression of the spread of interest in the England
performance in the Finals might be taken from viewing figures of television
coverage back in Britain. A record TV audience of more than 24 million
watched England's semi-final tie against West Germany. Reportedly, over one-

half of these viewers were female, a fact which demonstrates the widespread interest across the gender divide as the tournament unfolded. It did so via the sort of TV coverage — particularly on BBC — which seemed designed to promote the aesthetic and dramatic qualities of the event above the overly narrow and sometimes mean-spirited partisanship which, arguably, too frequently characterises football support and the presentation of football on British TV.

It has been widely suggested since the Finals that TV coverage of the World Cup has also encouraged more women to watch live matches in England (Crean, 1990). If this is the case, it would be interesting, indeed, to discover how women's experience of English football culture and spectator facilities compares with those promised on television, for example, by the 'carnival' of the World Cup and by grounds like Gregotti's new Luigi Farraris Stadium in Genova which hosted one of Scotland's matches. (Of course, the Taylor report promises improved facilities at British football grounds, of which more later.) More generally, these developments in female spectatorship, coupled with the recent growth of interest in Britain in women's football — with TV audiences of up to 2.8 million, the women's game is now apparently more popular with viewers than Channel 4's flagship NFL grid iron coverage — promise something of a mini-revolution in relations between women and the game in England.

Channel 4's fictionalised series, 'The Manageress' which, implausibly, has as its central premise a woman as the manager of a Second Division League club, even hints, perhaps a little ironically, that the 'glass ceiling' which limits the advancement of women into managerial positions in almost all professions, might even be penetrable — given the right contacts — in this most impenetrable of male preserves. A more 'realist' perspective is provided, however, by the compelling BBC 2 documentary series 'United!' which was made soon after the first series of 'The Manageress'. The former charts the fortunes of Sheffield United FC during the 1989–90 League season. It convincingly demonstrates the cultural chasm which exists between the fictional football world of 'The Manageress's' Gabriella Benson and the unforgivingly harsh and masculine textures of a real and successful Football League club in the 1990s.

But if we are standing on the brink of a new beginning in relations between the game and female players and spectators, how, precisely, did we get here? Have female spectators had a role to play, a history, in 'the people's game'? Where do they figure now? More especially, why in a country which was absolutely central to the spread and growth of football around the world at the turn of the century has football for women been so contentious an issue as to make its development amongst the slowest in comparable countries around the world? The British undoubtedly love their football, but they haven't much liked — and mainly still do not like — the prospect of the 'fair sex' donning boots, shirts and shorts and taking the plunge from the terraces and the stands on to the field of play. What this chapter tries to do is to excavate some of the history of the links between women and football, links which go back at least to the late Victorian period but which, as yet, remain little explored by academic writers.

The first women footballers

At the time of the establishment of the first professional Football League, in England in 1888, organised sport for women in Britain and elsewhere was little advanced and women's football — or the involvement of women in any physical contact sport or sports deemed 'unladylike' — was hardly advanced at all. 'Ladies' of suitable social status first played at Wimbledon in 1884, but it was to take almost a quarter of a century more, for example, for women to overcome the objections of the male founders of the modern Olympics, such as Baron Pierre de Coubertin, that it was 'against the laws of nature' for women to compete in any Olympic sports and it was into the third decade of the new century before women athletes — 'The most unaesthetic sight human eyes could contemplate' — first competed in limited track and field events (quoted in Hargreaves, 1984). The 'new scientism' of the Victorian era, reflected particularly in opposition from eugenics and social Darwinist theorists, served to buttress the view that sport was 'unnatural' for women and that strenuous games, especially during puberty and menstrual periods, drained energy from vital organs, damaged women's bodies and, thus, threatened the survival of the race (McCrone, 1987: p. 116). Willis has pointed to the way in which in discussions about sport 'the natural' is one of the grounds of ideology because of its apparent autonomy from biased interpretation (Willis, 1982: p. 117), a point taken up by Klein in her description of the ideological force in patriarchal societies of sports as essentially masculine, thus requiring physical and psychological attitudes and behaviour which is 'unnatural' to women and therefore, beyond their proper sphere (quoted in McCrone, 1987: p. 116).

Coupled with these powerful social and cultural constraints backed by 'science', was the ideology of Victorian familism, an intrinsic part of a system of patriarchy bound up with ideas about family arrangements, gender identities and sexual mores (Hargreaves, 1987). Involved, too, were the progressively masculine associations drawn in the public schools in alliance with British imperial expansion, between the games-playing ethos and a form of 'muscular Christianity' which asserted that 'a woman's only role in sport was to watch and applaud' (McCrone, 1987: p. 102). Finally, and almost inevitably, fears were expressed by men — and, indeed, by some women — over a physically public role for women in sport and games and the likely consequences of such roles for female (and male) sexual identities. Links were drawn between tendencies towards prostitution and the 'bodily display' demanded in some sports, providing a confusion between sport's expressiveness and sexual depravity (Mrozek, 1987: p. 286). As a consequence, at the turn of the century, in all forms of exercise for women, a properly prudish demeanour, decency and modesty were required; the avoidance of over-exertion, bodily display and sensual pleasure was absolutely essential, requiring that sporting attire was distinctly shapeless and 'sexless' (Hargreaves, 1987: p. 136).

A partial exception in late Victorian England to the general associations drawn between sport for women and damaging physical and moral consequences was provided by the public schools of St. Leonards (in St. Andrews) and Rodean (in Brighton), where it was asserted that even so-called 'rough-games' — hockey, lacrosse, cricket — could be played without participants becoming at all unwomanly and in ways which could generate moral qualities as well as mental lucidity and good health (McCrone, 1987). Sport for females, at this time, was very much the preoccupation of privately educated middle-class girls; a case of 'games for the classes and gym for the masses'. Under the separatist — if not feminist — philosophy of physical education for women promulgated by Mme Bergman-Osterberg's Dartford College of Physical Education, the training of bourgeois girls was aimed at improving the racial quality of the élite (Holt, 1989: p. 119). Inside the public schools, where the headmistress had a considerable degree of autonomy, girls could enjoy their sport in relative peace. However, even in these pioneering enclaves, institutio-nalised sporting activities for women required some accommodation to expectations about 'appropriate' behaviour for females. Some sports, including football, were strictly off limits because of their masculine, and almost certainly their class, connotations, though, briefly, in 1894, Brighton High School for Girls apparently boasted a football club. More usual, however, were the views like those held by Miss Lawrence, the sports-supporting headmistress of Rodean, that football was totally unsuitable for girls on account of its roughness (McCrone, 1987).

In contrast to the playing opportunities provided by the robust and privileged education of sections of the female élite, sport remained a near-closed world for working-class women and girls of Victorian England. Richard Holt and others have shown how the ordinary social lives of workers in the cities of late nineteenth-century Britain were dominated by sociable drinking and sporting institutions and associations for men in a society where segregation of the sexes remained very much the rule rather than the exception. In such communities, organised football clubs provided a bridge between the world of the child and the adult male world, a world in which

boys learned how to drink and tell jokes as well as the language of physical aggression. Sport was part of this process . . . Football clubs were only a part of the wider process of male socialisation which took place in the workplace, the pub and the world of hobbies . . . Pubs were places where men both played games and talked about them. (Holt, 1988: p. 73)

This description seems equally apposite today. However, penetrating these masculine networks and associations either as football players or spectators must have been an especially forbidding proposition for the female enthusiasts of 100 years ago, perhaps particularly for working-class women. There were other practical problems, too, for married female fans of the growing professional sport, not least the requirement of providing their spouses promptly with a hot post-match meal (Mason, 1980: p. 158)! Nevertheless, Mason reports that until the mid-1880s, when money lost at the turnstiles became too great, women were admitted free of charge to matches, and that at Leicester in 1899 'the fair sex' were present 'in every part of the ground' (Mason, 1980: p. 152). Apparently, too, Newcastle United had a 'Ladies Outing Club' organised by the club's female fans in the early years of the new century (Mason, 1980: p. 152).

On the playing side of sport, 'considering Victorian and Edwardian social prejudices it was no surprise that women were virtually excluded from participation in professional sport' (Vamplew, 1988; p. 209). However, in 1895, in the wake of the establishment of the All England Women's Hockey Association, and of exhibition cricket matches for women, a challenge match between women footballers was staged at Crouch End, organised by Nettie Honeyball, first secretary of the English Ladies (see Crampsey, 1978: p. 19). Mirroring the new schisms in the male game, the match was contested between the North and South of England, the former running out comfortable 7–1 winners. The *Manchester Guardian*'s account of this pioneering fixture predictably focused less on the game than on the players' attire, commenting extensively on the 'rational dress' of the women concerned. 'When the novelty has worn off.' the reporter concluded, starchily, 'I do not think that ladies football will attract crowds', though, contrary to popular prejudice against women players, he also agreed that football provided 'a new and healthy form of recreation' for women. In Newcastle, later in the year, a women's match attracted a reported crowd of more than 8,000 spectators (Williamson, 1991: p. 4).

In Scotland, charity exhibition games for women, held around the same time, were organised by Lady Florence Dixey. Lady Dixey was a poet, novelist and explorer as well as a keen advocate of women's rights. She championed the cross-saddle for female riders and was war correspondent for the *Morning Post* during the Boer War. Despite such determined female opposition, by 1902, the Council of the Football Association, viewing women players with what was to become a familiar, jaundiced eye, thought it necessary to issue a warning to its member clubs not to play matches against 'lady teams'. As Ward points out, this decision set a precedent for what was to become a long-standing policy of separateness in football — men against men and women against women — though this pattern of division by sex is, admittedly, hardly uncommon in other sports (Ward, 1989: p. 3).

Attracting little obvious support from the professional male game, for which crowds in the expanding cities of England were growing season by season, football for women players in the early part of the new century remained little more than an amusing eccentricity. Briefly, at least, the onset of the First World War changed all that. With most professional male players on contract up until the end of April 1915, and amidst plenty of official murmuring about 'lack of patriotism' amongst football players and spectators, the professional male Association game continued to be played, in front of much diminished crowds, for the first year of the conflict. The eventual suspension of the League and Cup programme, and the drawing of more and more women — the nation's 'hidden army' — into work in the war industries, coupled with the wider, ongoing political struggles for female emancipation, seemed to provide something of a catalyst for a previously unimaginable growth in the popularity of women's football. When attempts were first made to provide sport for 'munitions girls' it was found that 'they had never been accustomed to take part in team games, or, indeed, any form of exercise for pleasure' (Holt, 1989: p. 118). However, female experiences in the Great War eroded some of the old ideals of female gentility and passivity, especially amongst those middle-class women who had experienced the harsh realities of munitions work and the pleasures of female comradeship at the work-place. Opportunities, provided by the war effort, for women from different social backgrounds to mix and work together seems to have been crucial in stimulating the organisational impetus necessary for the establishment of the new factory and charity women's football teams, which boasted women both from working-class and middle-class backgrounds. Official sanction was provided for the new venture on the bases of the essentially 'patriotic' nature of the teams' fund-raising activities and the fact that women were no longer competing with the established men's game for the national football audience. Many of the matches played during this period were also mixed-sex and were performed in novelty costumes, thus insulating those women involved from possible accusations that they might be taking their sport involvement 'too seriously'.

Serious, indeed, however, were the women who made up Dick Kerr's Ladies, a team formed in 1917 by a group of female munition workers at Kerr's engineering works in Preston. Kerr's ladies, like many similar female 'charity' teams of the time, had humble beginnings, playing their early matches on waste ground outside the factory gates. As news of their exploits spread, by the early 1920s Dick Kerr's were playing in front of large crowds at Football League grounds. The use of the League's facilities were surprisingly sanctioned by the FA in 1920 as audiences for women's games grew unmanageably large.

The female works teams gained support for their activities by bringing good publicity for their employers and by helping to keep home morale high in the face of the carnage across the channel. The McConnel sisters — Agnes and Elizabeth — played for Wallsend Slipway Marine, a wartime engineering team which played in the North East Woman's League. According to Agnes: 'There were always good crowds. We travelled by train and sold batches of tickets to fans ourselves, which made sure we had a few supporters of our own [at the match]' (*Northern Echo*, 5 January 1989). The Wallsend team wound down its activities at the end of the war, but the impetus provided for the women's game by the new social and occupational relations of the war period continued to fire the growth of women's football into the new decade. Teams sprouted particularly in the North, the Midlands and the South West. During the early part of the war an English 'representative' side had played 'international' matches in Scotland and Ireland using players drawn from the thriving North East League. One of these matches — in Ireland — attracted 38,000 fans. In 1920 alone Dick Kerr's Ladies played a total of thirty matches, winning twenty-five of them. By 1920, however, Dick Kerr's had, in effect, become the unofficial England women's national team, astutely adopting a small Union Jack on its playing strip and twice, early in 1920, thrashing a women's team representing Scotland by an aggregate score of 22–0. Moreover, in April of that year, and eschewing some of the post-war isolationism of the men's game, the Dick Kerr's entertained a French female national side over four matches in England, including one experimental 'floodlit' match at Deepdale. An aggregate of 61,000 spectators watched the Preston side remain unbeaten during the series, a performance it repeated when touring in France in October that same year. On returning triumphantly from the continent to Lancashire, the welcome for the Ladies was 'rapturous and very much in the style of FA Cup Winners returning to their home town' (Williamson, 1991: p. 28).

The national enthusiasm for the Dick Kerr's in the early 1920s seemed in some ways to parallel that revealed by the rapid expansion of the professional male game during the same period. In 1921, Division One and Two of the Football League were each expanded to twenty-two clubs (from twenty) and a new Division Three was formed, mostly from southern clubs, soon to be followed by a Division Three, North. It was a boom time for both male *and* female football, with some professional players even taking time out to coach their female counterparts (Williamson, 1991, ch. 3). At Goodison Park on Boxing Day 1920 an astonishing 53,000 spectators saw the much awaited meeting between the impressive St. Helen's Ladies and the near-invincible Dick Kerr's. A reported, 10,000–14,000 fans were locked out of the packed ground, and the match realised over £3,000 in gate receipts for local charities. The showdown proved to be the zenith of the female game in England, although Williamson is still able to report that:

By early 1921 it was as if the country had been gripped by ladies' football fever. Teams now covered the country with every major town having its own side and the major cities having several, especially in the north. Whether at the weekend or in the middle of the week there was a ladies' match being played somewhere. (Williamson, 1991: p. 15)

It is unlikely, even at 'boom' times like these, that football for females ever became a mass participation sport in Britain. Nevertheless, by now the national interest in women's football was substantial if still localised. It was a state of affairs which could not, of course, be allowed to last. A number of things conspired in the game's sudden downfall. For one thing, the charitable causes and the social context of wartime Britain upon which the female game was built, and which remained its *raison d'être*, were by 1921 beginning to fade from the collective memory. For another, and more importantly, the relative success of the female game and the very seriousness with which some female players and their supporters were now approaching the sport, grated with those powerful opponents who continued to preach about the 'de-feminising' dangers of female athleticism. Finally, and most importantly of all, the women's game offended the middle-class propriety of the FA's ruling Council and, more particularly, it threatened to continue to grab some of the local limelight from the lower ranks of the male game, which was by now fully reconstituted after the break in 1915, for the playing of the 'sterner game for England' (Mason, 1980).

The warning signs were clear late in 1921 in the *Football Special* which carried a column written by 'The Football Girl'. Produced by a woman and devoted almost entirely to the female game, the column began to reflect what appeared to be substantially male anxieties about the alleged 'obsessiveness' of some female footballers which was making them, simply, 'short-sighted and selfish' and neglectful of other 'reasonable amusements'. 'Unless some girl (*sic*) footballers are very careful,' the article continued darkly, 'they will find their over-enthusiasm leading them into danger' (quoted in Williamson, 1991: pp. 43–4).

The FA Council seemed unreflectingly, to agree with this diagnosis of the female game's ills. The pretext for the critical withdrawal of FA support for the

staging of women's matches at League grounds was the alleged maladminis-
tration of charity funds. But, clearly, other priorities were now in play. On 10
October 1921, the FA Council instructed clubs staging women's games to take
full responsibility for receipts and payments from these matches. On 5
December, the Association's Consultative Committee referred to unspecified
'complaints' about the conditions under which women's matches were staged
and to the 'appropriation of receipts to other than charitable objects'. Money
may well have gone astray during these events, but this was down to loose
accounting procedures rather than corruption. The real, chauvinistic nature of
the FA objections to the women's game were made more clear in the Council's
expressed 'strong opinion' in the same statement 'that the game of football is
quite unsuitable for females and should not be encouraged'. The FA,
accordingly, instructed its member clubs to cease the staging of matches
involving female players.

The loss of official sanction, and of the use of grounds capable of holding the
sorts of crowds which were frequently attracted to women's charity matches,
was a crippling blow to the female game. But, it was also a development which
might have provided the impetus for the better organisation and the restructuring of women's football, which still tended to be *ad hoc* and rather
directionless in terms of the manner in which matches were arranged and
staged.

Estimates suggested that towards the end of 1921 there were around 150
women's clubs in England, with the strength of the women's game remaining,
substantially, in the North and Midlands. Many of these clubs probably knew
little of each other's existence because of the localised nature of charity
competition. However, Williamson reports that on 10 December 1921 representatives of twenty-five women's clubs met in Blackburn to form the first
English Ladies Football Association (ELFA). The second meeting of the
Association, at Grimsby, attracted a reported sixty clubs (Williamson, 1991: p.
83).

Statements issued by the new Association on its determination that there be
'no exploiting of the teams in the interest of the man or firm who manages
them' (Williamson, 1991: p. 83) reflect both the growing confidence of the
clubs and views on the apparent 'inevitably' of male control in a world — and a
sport — in which male sanction for the activities of women remained, for
most, simply a routine fact of life. However, the ELFA lacked the necessary
support and the organisational base, and the women's game lacked the venues
and the strength in depth — it was still difficult to raise competitive teams
from the South — to manage successfully the transition from the staging of
frequent, but irregular, charity matches to an autonomous regional league
structure. As the previously dominant Dick Kerr's Ladies began to falter
against rising female opposition in England — though, typically, the club
responded in 1922 by embarking on a pioneer tour of North America to take on
men's teams — so the women's game itself slipped into steep decline. By the
end of 1922, and with women's participation in other, more 'appropriate'
sports on the increase, the post-war boom for the Association game for women
was virtually over.

The fate of football for women in Britain over the following forty years or more remains, as far as we can tell, almost wholly unreasearched. Information about this long period is, accordingly, very sparse indeed. Undoubtedly, the women's game continued in a more or less 'underground' fashion, staging matches at local festivals and for fund-raising and charity events. Dick Kerr's Ladies made periodic 'come-backs' to national prominence, particularly during a short spell in the 1930s, but the activities of most teams remained localised and largely out of the public eye. That some continuity prevailed is clear from the fact that Dick Kerr's Ladies finally disbanded only in 1965 — more than forty years after the club's international successes — having played more than 800 games and raising over £70,000 for charity (*Lancashire Evening Post*, 14 May 1984).

Briefly, the Second World War promised to revive much of the previous wartime interest in women's football, with a women's international match between England and Belgium being staged in August 1939. However, when, in 1946, the FA confirmed its 1921 position in relation to the women's game, prospects for a more sustained growth once again disappeared. At local level, the struggle continued. In 1950, the Essex FA warned all its member clubs against staging a match between Chelmsford and Maldon Ladies. The ban — and its attendant publicity — drew a crowd of over 4,000 spectators to the match, eventually played at a Chelmsford park. The North West and Lancashire continued for much of this period to be a stronghold in a considerably weakened national football scene for women. The Manchester Corinthians club, in particular, was reputed to be the major force in the sport in the 1950s and early 1960s, playing matches in South America, Jamaica, Italy and elsewhere, often attracting five-figure crowds (Ward, 1989: pp. 8–9). But the women's game was to wait until England's World Cup triumph in 1966 for the necessary stimulus for a major national surge to rival those of earlier periods.

Between the wars — and in contrast to the later experiences of women players — the involvement of females as football spectators seemed to grow. We can suggest a number of reasons why. Facilities and spectator provision at grounds improved after the Great War, and the game gradually became more 'respectable', losing some of its reputation as a focal point for drinking, 'rough house' behaviour and gambling. Women were also buoyed by their political successes and the confidence drawn from their penetration of other key masculine enclaves during the period of special conditions provided by the war. Why not, then, in these 'new times', watch football? In November 1920, the *Daily Express* reported that some female fans had even begun to 'take a hand' themselves in spectator disturbances at football (Dunning *et al.*, 1988: p. 99). In the main, however, the attendances at matches of more female fans was generally associated with slowly improving behavioural standards among football crowds. Newspaper reports of the build-up to the 1927 FA Cup Final noted as a 'remarkable feature' the number of female fans travelling to the game, many with babes in arms (ibid., p. 100). Two year later, press reports suggest that 'at least 50%' of the train loads of spectators who were travelling to Wembley to watch Bolton Wanderers and Portsmouth were women. Such was the number of female fans who travelled to Leicester to watch their team, Brentford, in a cup tie in 1936 that the local press dubbed the London Club 'the ladies team' (ibid., p. 101). If, as some claim today, the game has a 'family tradition' involving substantial numbers of female fans, the 1920s and early 1930s surely seem as good a reference point as any in its history.

This partial 'feminisation' of the football audience between the wars was not of course, uncontested by the sorts of men who saw the game as a welcome retreat from unnecessary female 'interference' and domestic responsibilities. Women fans were very often accused by men — as, indeed, they are now — of lacking commitment to, and knowledge of, the game. Fishwick points to the example of male Sheffield Wednesday fans accusing their female counterparts in the city in the 1920s of being affluent, 'fair weather' supporters who 'butt into men's affairs'. They received a spirited reply for their trouble in the local press from the city's female 'shilling' supporters (Fishwick, 1989: p. 58). In fact, photographic evidence from the period suggests that women may have made up to 20 per cent of 'popular side' support at some grounds, some of them attending 'in small female groups, suggesting, perhaps, that young, unattached women were more likely to enjoy the freedom to go to a match' (ibid.). This was a 'freedom', however, which was still strictly limited and which, inevitably, had its price. Press and 'popular' attitudes towards female football spectators in the 1930s seems to have been that, like suffragettes, they were alien, unnatural Amazons (ibid.).

Our knowledge of the composition of the 'live' football audience in the immediate post-Second World War period remains slight. Fishwick points out that the trend, since 1950, towards more family-based leisure pursuits coincided with a substantial decline in football attendances, and there seems little doubt that the rise in 'privatised' consumer and leisure options drew substantial numbers of female followers off the terraces and out of the stands (Fishwick, 1989; Dunning et al., 1988). It was a development which would not have disturbed 'unreconstructed' players like the Welsh international, Trevor Ford, who probably spoke for the majority of men when, in 1957, he opined that, 'Football is not a woman's game, it's not a pastime for milksops or sissies, it's a man's game' (Ford, 1957, quoted in Fishwick, 1989: p. 147). The growing incidence of, and panic about, football hooliganism, which started to grow from the late 1950s almost certainly worked in the same direction, but it seemed not to discourage the doughty females who made up the Ladies Committees on local supporters clubs. These women, relieved by male supporter club members of the onerous task of making policy decisions for fans, spent much of their time, instead, raising funds for their clubs and, in a number of early cases, raised money to buy houses for players and their families (Sport Weekly, 21 August 1948, p. 15). Despite some objections from women, the conservative National Federation of Football Supporters Clubs continued to organise a national competition to unearth the season's 'Football Queen'. The award was designed to reward committed female support, but as a number of female opponents pointed out, it mysteriously tended only to be the younger and conventionally 'attractive' women fans who stood any chance of winning the prize (National Federation of Football Supporters Clubs, 1954: p. 27).

The new age of women's football

The staging of the World Cup Finals in England in 1966 provided an opportunity for the game to stem the drift of 'live' support away from matches and to reconstruct the game's image in the face of widespread concern about growing crowd violence at football. Women were one focus of this new campaign, with television coverage offering, specifically, female fans — presumably *all* men knew the laws — the opportunity of instruction on the complexities of the offside rule and on more of the game's imponderable nuances. But it was on the playing side that opportunities for women grew most markedly after the footballing summer of 1966. Bale points also to the influence of the rise of the women's movement in encouraging women in the 1960s to play 'masculine' sports, and he further notes the importance of proselytising individuals in establishing women's football in particular areas (Bale, 1980). This seems certainly to have been the case at Southampton, a club which dominated the women's game throughout the 1970s. Sue Lopez, then on the brink of a representative playing career for Hampshire in hockey, was, instead, captivated by England's footballing success: 'It was England's World Cup win that did it. After that, no other game could suit me' (*Book of Football*, 1972: p. 592). Lopez helped to launch the WFA, with friends formed a successful club in her home town and also became the dominant female player of her generation. She played as an amateur in the professional women's league in Italy in the early 1970s, refusing many offers from abroad to turn professional because to do so would have disqualified her from selection for the (amateur) England national team.

As the number of women's clubs grew, out of diverse origins (Bale, 1980) but under the enthusiastic driving of women like Lopez, the need for a national administrative body became more pressing. Accordingly, the Women's Football Association (WFA) was eventually established in November 1969 under the secretaryship of a man, Arthur Hobbs. The new body had no formal sanction from the FA which, as recently as 1962, had confirmed, once more, its opposition to female play, but it attracted forty-four original member clubs. By the beginning of 1972 this figure had reached 182 and was rising.

Reflecting some of the structural tensions which have been apparent almost throughout the entire history of the English men's game, the volunteers who ran the WFA favoured a grassroots, gradualist approach to the development of women's football, though opposition to football for girls in schools remained considerable, even into the 1990s. Opponents of this accommodative, 'softly, softly' policy advocated a more high-profile, aggressive and 'professional', international launch to the modern women's game. Conflict was inevitable. In 1970, an 'unofficial' World Cup for women was staged in Italy, where the women's game already had a professional footing. The six nations involved were represented by female club sides, England by Chiltern Valley, the champions of the East Midlands Ladies Alliance. Crowds were large, but the play was sometimes overly physical, drawing complaints from the outmanoeuvred WFA that the tournament had thrown the whole of the women's game into disrepute. The WFA later outlawed the East Midlands Ladies Alliance, but to no obvious effect and, in 1971 Chiltern Valley travelled to

Mexico to contest the second women's World Cup in as many years.

In Mexico, some of the worst fears of the WFA were realised. The tournament, backed by South American business interests, was run on crassly sexist, show biz/commercial lines. The women involved played into pink goal frames, beauty parlours were installed in dressing rooms, and some teams were encouraged to wear hot pants and blouses in place of the normal football strips. As a prelude to matches there were rodeos, baseball games and displays by semi-clad majorettes. Predictably, perhaps, the tournament was a huge commercial success. A capacity 108,000 crowd, mostly men, watched the opening match in the Aztec Stadium between Mexico and Argentina. Black-market ticket trade was, reportedly, brisk.

Women's football in England in the early 1970s suffered no shortage of exploitative male 'interest'. A charity women's match organised in London in February 1971, for example, was advertised as a clash between 'the world's most beautiful players'. Fleet Street turned out in force. 'I can watch a man's match,' commented Patricia Gregory the WFA's assistant secretary, in 1972, 'But, if a man comes to watch us, all he sees is girls' (*Book of Football*, 1972: p. 590) But here the similarity between women's football in England and the Mexican jamboree ended. There was no razzmatazz and precious few spectators for the women's game back home. Instead, top women players changed for matches in cars, washed themselves off after games with buckets of cold water and struggled to book park pitches when opposed even by the lowest local male clubs (SNCCFR, 1989).

Though these first 'championships' were challenged by the WFA, the international links advertised in Italy and Mexico, as well as the earning potential of the women's game, sufficiently alerted UEFA at its annual conference in June 1971 to pass a motion requesting that national associations take control of the women's arm of the sport in their own countries. Denis Follows, the FA Secretary, showed patrician sympathy but had difficulties persuading the ossified ranks of the FA Council to take the women's game seriously. However, fearing censure, or worse, from UEFA, when the Council met on 29 November 1971 it made a minimal commitment to recognise the WFA, lift the 1921 restrictions on its member clubs, and set up a joint consultative committee with the WFA. Despite its own huge reserves, no financial commitment was made by the FA towards the development of the women's game. It took a further twelve years for the WFA to gain formal affiliation to English football's controlling body.

With growing, but still slight, assistance and support from the top levels of the English game — a situation hardly improved, in 1973, by the appointment as FA Secretary of the ex-Charlton Athletic defender (he played eight League games) and businessman, Ted Croker, a man determined in the view that it was 'unnatural' for women to play, or even to watch the national sport — the WFA looked to the development of football for girls in schools as an effective means of popularizing the sport and defusing widespread prejudice. It proved no easy task. Ironically, in many ways lack of progress at club and national level curtailed prospects at schools, too. Doncaster Belles and England international goalkeeper, Tracey Davidson, was one of many who did not push to play football at school because she knew nothing of the existence of the women's

game until she discovered the sport, aged 19. Joanne Broadhurst, another
current international, echoes in her school experiences those of many women
who later became top players:

I used to play hockey as well [as football], so they [teachers] used to try to make me
play hockey instead. They said that I should choose to play hockey because with
football I wouldn't get anywhere . . . They just said women had nowhere to go in
football and I should play hockey. (SNCCFR, 1989)

There is a substantial academic literature, of course, on the manner in which
the 'sport is male' convention is established at an early age and is reinforced in
school via a combination of the effects of established ideologies, the channell-
ing of males and females into sex-appropriate sports and the force of peer group
and parental pressures. Scraton has noted, for example, how female P.E.
ᵡteachers oppose girls playing football because of its 'masculine' connotations
(Scraton, 1986). One recent England international, who later played professio-
nally abroad, remembers how her parents threw out her football boots, accused
her of being 'unfeminine' and told her to 'grow up' when her playing interest
in football hardened (SNCCFR, 1989). Willis has also pointed out how success
for males in sport serves to strengthen male identity because of the 'natural'
assumption that achievement in sport means success at being masculine. For
women, however, to achieve in sport — particularly in 'masculine' sport — is
to fail as a woman because in certain profound symbolic ways she 'becomes' a
man (Willis, 1982). In this sense, for many men — and women — according to
another England player, Marieanne Spacey, women footballers are 'just a
bunch of dykes running about a football field; women trying to be men'
(SNCCFR, 1989).

    In those few schools where football for girls as well as boys was promoted —
or at least allowed — girls were actually prevented *by law* from playing in the
same team as boys. The 1975 Sex Discrimination Act exempts from the Act's
provisions 'Any sport, game or other activity of a competitive nature where the
physical strength, stamina, or physique of the average woman puts her at a
disadvantage to the average man'. In 1978, 11-year-old Theresa Bennett, an
outstanding female player in a boys' junior club, was told by a Deputy County
Court judge that she could compete with boys of her own age. The verdict,
however, was overturned by Lord Denning in the Court of Appeal, who ignored
medical evidence on the prepubertal similarities between boys and girls and,
instead, stuck perversely to the average man/average women distinction drawn
in the Act. A *Daily Telegraph* leader following the appeal concluded with the
words, 'The heresy of sexual equality in all things is nowhere more invidious
than in the realm of sport' (quoted in Grayson, 1985: p. 41). Rose Reilly, star
of women's football in Scotland in the early 1970s, probably had her own
thoughts on this issue. When she was fourteen and playing in an informal
'boys' match, a Scottish League club scout mistook her for a promising male
player and tried to sign her for his club on schoolboy forms (*Book of Football*,
1972: p. 591).

    Senior staff at the FA, under Croker, almost certainly agreed with the
Denning ruling, which prevented any girls from playing in competitions

involving boys and run under the auspices of the FA. In fact, the adoption of the Appeal ruling effectively prevented almost any junior female football because of the difficulties in raising all-girls teams. Complaints about the ban continued to arise, however, particularly when the Equal Opportunities Commission judged that, until puberty, no such inequalities as were referred to by the Act existed. In May 1987, two 8-year-old female players from the Putney Corinthians club picketed the FA AGM, following their ban from the final of a London under-11 cup competition. Their cause was taken up by the prospective Labour Party candidate for Putney, Peter Hain, who characteristically described the ban as an example of 'sexual apartheid' (*The Guardian*, 6 April 1987). Hain's two sons also played for the depleted Corinthians. The FA agreed to reconsider its position.

In August 1988, the ESFA reported on a national survey it had conducted of schools which revealed that at 82 per cent there was a demand for football for girls; at 38 per cent a demand for girls' teams; and that at 60 per cent of schools, football activity involving girls was already going on (ESFA, 1988). The ESFA pledged to change its charitable status, which put it in care of 'schoolboy' football, at its next Council meeting. Croker commented, with resigned disappointment, 'We just don't like males and females playing together. I like feminine girls. Anyway, it's not natural' (*The Times*, 26 August 1988). In fact, it took a further two years for the changes in the ESFA's charitable constitution to be completed.

In March 1991, thirteen years after the Theresa Bennett case and four years after the Hain intervention, the FA was finally in a position to rescind its Rule 37 which forbade female players from playing in football competitions with boys up to the age of 11 years, though it was still opposed in its intentions by County Associations. In some counties, secondary schools were simply ignoring the Denning ruling anyway. 'Girls have been playing along with boys in our school teams for several years,' a head of physical education at an Oxfordshire Comprehensive told *The Observer* in 1991, 'It is about time the FA woke up to the reality of secondary comprehensive education' (*The Observer*, 24 March 1991). Commenting on the success of mixed football in a school in Ponders End, London, a female teacher told Kate Berry for *The Guardian* on 23 April that,

By introducing mixed football we have found that the boys readily accept that girls aren't just interested in traditional schoolgirl pursuits. Football, therefore, plays a fundamental and valuable role in shaping school attitudes.

In November 1980, the WFA appointed its first paid, full-time Secretary, Linda Whitehead, who had had some commercial experience at Blackburn Rovers FC. By the early 1980s, however, the women's game in England had enjoyed little success in its attempts to establish a strong country-wide base for the sport. A small number of top players enjoyed some international success but found little competition in the struggling regional leagues. In 1983, Norwich and England Striker, Linda Curl, scored a record twenty-two times in her club's 40–0 WFA Cup destruction of Milton Keynes. Soon after, the emerging Doncaster Belles beat Leek Leaders 34–0 in the same competition. Probably wisely, the Belles' next opponents withdrew from the tie. The women's game's lack of any strength in depth and effective grassroots development was proving to be damaging and embarassing. Who could take the sport seriously? Once again, help, when it eventually came, came from international pressure. In 1983, FIFA instructed football's national governing bodies to take greater responsibility for the development of the female game, a situation which already existed in some of the more successful European female footballing nations. Accordingly, in May 1984, the WFA was invited to affiliate to the FA. In the same year, the FA agreed to the staging of a women's five-a-side match at Wembley prior to the Charity Shield meeting of Everton and Liverpool. It was the first time women footballers had trodden the hallowed turf of the national stadium, though female hockey matches had been a Wembley fixture for some time. Also in 1984, the England's women's team reached the first UEFA Cup Final, beating the powerful Danes to do so. The 'WFA News' described the achievement as 'a significant turning point of the tide for women's football in the United Kingdom' ('WFA News', 9 July 1984) England lost the two-legged final (against Sweden) on penalties. The first leg, in Stockholm, was televised live in Sweden. For the second leg, at Luton Town the Swedish team arrived with a TV crew and thirty-six press personnel. The game was barely mentioned in the British press, a point which was not lost on experienced England players like goalkeeper, Terry Wiseman, who was astonished by the reception the English players received in Sweden. By way of contrast, preparation for a major women's European match in England might involve a weekend's training in Batley and the entire England squad sleeping in a single room in a gym or hostel in sleeping bags (SNCCFR, 1989).

But change was coming for the women's game. The establishment of the Community Programme-funded PFA/Football League 'Football and the Community' initiative at Football League clubs in 1985 brought with it a commitment to work with all sections of the community, including girls and women. As a consequence, coaching and playing opportunities for females increased substantially, and League clubs were encouraged to support the establishment and affiliation of women's teams. At the last count, more than thirty League clubs lend their names to, or provide support for, women's clubs. In the late 1980s, Arsenal became the first League club to hire women on their YTS scheme — a replacement for the club apprenticeship scheme — in order to promote coaching for girls in the Islington area. Other 'independent' community schemes based at League clubs — notably at Millwall — also began to promote play for girls and women more strongly. (Millwall's women's team, the Lionesses, won the WFA Cup in 1991.) Most of the successful schemes involving women attracted local authority support and finance, and almost all of these involved Labour-controlled local authorities, where a commitment to equal opportunities came hand-in-hand with the promise of cash or the use of facilities.

In January 1987, a BBC 2 documentary 'Home and Away', provided national exposure in Britain for the women's game almost for the first time. Ironically, its subject was the latest drain of English female footballing talent to the professional league in Italy. In the same month, a letter in 'WFA News' recalled similar, unsuccessful, attempts by the Italians to recruit English talent in 1976. It warned of the consequences of the loss of six top female players to

Italy, including the highly rated England striker, Kerry Davis. Top players like Davis and the England captain, Debbie Bampton, earned £150 per week in Italy, plus kit, food and accommodation. Later in the same year, Michele Cockburn from Guiseley, Leeds, became the first woman to qualify for the Advanced Coaching Licence, a qualification already held by over 1,000 men. (Sue Lopez remains the only other female 'full badge' holder.) Soon after, she became the first Sports Council-funded female Football Development Officer, promoting football for girls and women in the North West. (The FA has recently appointed three female Assistant Regional Development Officers for the women's game.)

More was to follow. In April 1988 the first women's international match at Wembley — though restricted to just thirty minutes each way — was staged during the Football League's miserably unsuccessful centenary 'celebrations'. Later, during a summer in which the England men's team was suffering humiliation during the European Championships in West Germany, the England women brought off a major coup by winning the *Mundialito* (the little World Cup), beating the hosts, Italy, 2–1 in the final. This extraordinary performance against the highly trained professionals on the continent unexpectedly won the women's national side *The Sunday Times* Sports Team of the Year Award, providing more vital exposure for a sport which, even at the highest levels, was still largely played in England on windswept park and school pitches with facilities and crowds to match.

It is still premature to talk about a decisive 'breakthrough' for the women's game in Britain even given the evidence of recent progress, particularly in 'grass-roots' coaching and playing opportunities. However, two developments in the late 1980s have, perhaps, proved to be of particular significance. Channel 4's decision to screen a series of one-hour programmes on the women's game in 1989 was prompted by the enthusiasm of a female player and employee of Mark McCormack's Trans World International production company, which made the programmes for TV. The series' determination to 'personalise' its coverage and its rather leaden production techniques apparently did not detract from its popularity with Channel 4 viewers. Indeed, the slower pace and the more open football of the women's game contrasted strikingly for many viewers with the negative, helter-skelter patterns of much modern male play. An 'emotional' 1989 WFA Cup Final which, a week after the Hillsborough tragedy, had another Merseyside team, Leasowe Ladies, beating Friends of Fulham on a weekend when all male football had been postponed produced a television audience of almost three million and substantial press organised around the Hillsborough theme. The WFA reported that the Channel 4 series provoked hundreds of letters and requests from new female converts including sixty enquiries on how to start a women's club. It provoked, too, some predictable hostility from sections of the football media establishment. TV football commentator, Archie Macpherson, commented:

I'm not saying a women's place is purely in the home — though some skivvying does not do them any harm. If Channel 4 wants to show us how entertaining football can be outside the senior game, then let them put the cameras at other places. Like any school playground. (*The Times*, 28 April 1990)

Notwithstanding the continuing prejudice and resistance of this kind, it was no coincidence that the increased national exposure for the women's game and the slow development of a more 'constructive' relationship between the WFA, the FA and the Football League occurred at around the same time as Richard Faulkner, First Deputy Chairman of the influential Football Trust, was elected to his position as the new Chair of the WFA. Faulkner, a professional lobbyist, ex-Labour parliamentary candidate and a key administrator in the men's game — the Trust allocates grants to Leagues and non-League clubs for stadium improvements and 'community' activities — provided the sort of 'insider' contacts and power brokerage which was probably necessary to subdue at least some of the anti-female football sentiment which continues to pervade League and FA circles. Coping with, and opposing, the strongly residual sexism and casual condescension which seem to be structural characteristics of these organisations is likely to prove a much longer and much more difficult process. At a recent major women's match, a senior League official who was presenting the trophies spoke fulsomely in his after-match speech of the 'fine looking lasses' who had played in the match. On another similar occasion an FA official admitted that 'like it or not' the women's game was probably here to stay. The English players visibly cringed. One indicator of Faulkner's likely influence at the WFA came with the announcement in 1990, that the Trust had allocated £150,000 to the development of the women's game, some of which would go towards the establishment of a National Women's League for the start of the 1991–2 season. By 1991, 334 women's clubs were registered with the WFA, accounting for around 9,000 players. An estimated 700,000 women players are registered in West Germany. Italy, France, the Netherlands, the United States and, especially, the Scandinavian countries, all have a stronger women's game than Britain in terms of numbers of teams and registered players. Was it possible that the proposed new national League might propel women's football in Britain, once again, towards the kind of national popularity enjoyed by Dick Kerr's Ladies and celebrated by the men and women of 1920s Lancashire?

Can play, will watch?

It is only really in the latter part of the 'modern' (post-1966) era of the history of the English game that the role and visibility of women within male professional football have substantially increased; but developments in this arena have also proved to be painfully and predictably slow. While female administrators and officials have clawed for a foothold in club offices and, latterly, even on the field of play itself, the profile and function of female fans — when in the public eye at all — have generally been viewed through the prism of debates about violence and disorder by young male spectators.

In fact, most of the early 'official' reports about the game and its problems, which were published in the 1960s and early 1970s, give little clue that women attended football matches at all (Harrington, 1968; Lang 1969). The more imaginative Scottish office McElhone report of 1977 breaks ranks in this respect by recording that it took oral evidence for its inquiry from four 'punters' — 'three men and one girl' (p. 3) but this is the lone female input out of forty-six oral contributions. By the time of the Popplewell report of 1986, football's spectator agenda was slowly in shift. The use of the rhetoric of 'the family' was already widely in play as part of the neo-liberal Thatcherite assault on state 'dependency' and collectivist ideologies. It was also surfacing regularly in football talk, usually as a signifier for dissatisfaction in club marketing departments with traditional supporters, and the preferred pursuit of a high-spending, respectable and discerning football customer. Popplewell, himself, in near-parody of this general trend, defended the provision of executive box facilities inside League grounds by arguing that 'Families, too', are using these facilities, and their support is essential to a well run club and needs to be encouraged' (Popplewell, 1986; p. 40). Perhaps Popplewell is thinking here of his own family's resources and preferences? Female support, ah, yes, but a voice for women? Popplewell commissioned research for his inquiry from the University of Surrey. It involved interviews with 1,000 football attenders. None of those interviewed was females (see Canter et al., 1989).

In the wake of Heysel, and a number of other less calamitous, disturbances involving English fans at home and abroad, the British Government stepped up its campaign to regulate further and segregate the troublesome football audience. Its support for 'family areas' and its insistence that clubs introduce membership schemes primarily as a more effective means of isolating and identifying hooligans proved unpopular with many fans. Many female fans, for example, resisted the invitation to watch matches from these 'safe' spaces arguing, instead, that the traditional home terraces already provided the sort of secure 'family' atmosphere promised by the new membership area (Williams et al; 1987). At the same time, however, the popularity, particularly of family terraces and stands, also revealed much about the intolerance and unpleasantness displayed in sections of major grounds, especially, but not solely, by younger men. (It said much, too, of course, about the general provision of facilities for women inside grounds.) Perimeter fencing also came down along the family terraces, which were soon used as a means of encouraging limited desegregation inside grounds. Crèches are also on offer at a, still small, number of clubs. This was a challenge to football's 'aggressive male ethos' which, argued Robert Armstrong in The Guardian on 25 July 1985, was resented by women and their disapproval had made even watching football on television a 'closet activity' for many beleaguered men.

As Armstrong suggests, the 'male ethos' associated with the game also found regular expression, not only at 'live' matches and in the treatment of the game in the popular press, but also in the increasingly tabloid-like television representations of the sport. Perhaps the bar-room banter of 'Saint and Greavsie' and the hysterical defensiveness of populist TV commentators such as Emlyn Hughes are the most obvious offenders here. But, the kind of assumptions which underpin this sort of 'male talk' were also never far from the minds and mouths of the game's administrators. In 1986, for example, the FA, under Croker, briefly launched a 'Friends of Football' campaign, designed to recruit more 'live' fans to the game. Its 'family' focus highlighted young boys who play football, fathers who take their sons to matches, and mothers who, dutifully, wash the dirty football kit. The campaign was scrapped almost instantaneously. In fact, contrary to the FA's ideas about the 'proper' role of women as football's 'backroom staff', women spectators on average probably made up between 10 and 15 per cent of football crowds in the 1980s. At some clubs — again, Brentford seem to be prominent here – up to one-fifth of the 'live' audience is female (Williams *et al.*, 1987).

The rise, in 1985, of the 'radical' national supporters movement, the Football Supporters Association, seemed to offer the promise of new forms of access for female fans. However, the FSA also seemed to have some difficulty in recruiting female members and, initially, in providing access for women to senior positions in the organisation's executive structure. Similarly, the burgeoning fanzine movement, and fanzine culture, seems almost uniformly *male* in its orientation, both in terms of the people who put fanzines together and those who buy and read the magazines (Bucke, 1989). A small number of fanzines have, however, run occasional items on the women's game and on women spectators (see *When Saturday Comes*, No. 51, May 1991). Many fewer seem able to recruit female contributors. The only football fanzine written by women primarily for women, *Born Kicking*, has made only irregular appearances despite considerable national interest in the concept and in its originator, Jane Purdon. Interestingly, in Italy — a country hardly noted for its drive for sexual equality — football culture seems rather more accommodative to women. At one Series B club, Regina, for example, the acknowledged leader of the local Ultras (fanatical young supporters) is female.

The national response to the Hillsborough disaster of 1989 — a tragedy which claimed the lives of nine female fans — provided a rather different focus for the role of 'family values' in the national sport. The networks of belonging which were invoked by the losses at Hillsborough were about community, class and region in particular, but they were focused especially through a sense of injury to the collective 'civic family' (Brunt 1989: p. 23). Hillsborough, too, especially via the liberal Taylor Report (1990) and its discussion of the aggressiveness of English football culture as well as the appalling facilities on offer to English fans, provided a concentration on women fans as a possible fulcrum for change in the Association game. Speaking of the major recommendation to come from the report — that all British stadiums become all-seated by the turn of the century — Taylor comments, 'When a spectator is seated . . . small or infirm or elderly men and women as well as young children are not buffeted smothered or unsighted by larger and more robust people on the terraces' (Taylor, 1990: p. 12). Around the same time, suggestions about the role of women spectators as a 'civilising' influence on potentially volatile male football crowds (Murphy *et al.*, 1990) were criticised for their lack of concern for the effects of such a policy on women (Talbot, 1989) and for their supposed shifting of the responsibility for collective male violence away from men (Scraton, 1990).

Research on female fans suggests a considerable and predictable role conflict between their identities as women and as football fans (Woodhouse, 1991). Female fans *do* identify damaging forms of sexism within the sport, but at the same time they resist attempts to recruit more women to matches on account of their sex rather than their commitment to football. At a time when some of the most valued traditions of the game seem, to many, to be threatened by processes of modernisation — traditions, for example, associated with location, identity, supporter styles and conditions of spectating — female fans seem cautious about, or even hostile towards, changes which threaten to 'feminise' football culture and which thus may raise accusations from male counterparts about their status as 'real' fans. Many of them also clearly like the 'masculine' edge to the football milieu (Woodhouse, 1991). Many, too, however, recognise that changing football culture in ways which might make it more responsive to the values and ideals of female — and many male — fans will require more than flip-up seats and salad on the half-time hamburgers. As one female Cardiff City fan told Woodhouse,

Attracting women to football is not just a question of safe grounds and seating stadiums. It's a whole process of breaking down stereotypes. I was bored with football at first and felt alienated in a completely male and sexist situation. My enjoyment of the sport itself had to be strong enough to confront this sexism and challenge it. (Woodhouse, 1991: p. 28)

Female fans are largely agreed in their wishes to see more women adminis-trators and officials within the game (Woodhouse, 1991: ch. 5). In February 1989, Kim George, a 28-year-old maths teacher, became the first women to referee an FA Cup tie, a preliminary round match between two non-League clubs. (The first female class-one referee, and the first woman line official for an FA Cup tie, Elizabeth Forsdick, had taken the line some eight years earlier, in 1981; *The Guardian*, 9 October 1981.) In the 1990–1 season a woman was, for the first time, a reserve official for a Football League match. Hounded for a story by the press, George reassuringly confirmed that she was 'not a strident feminist carrying the banner for women in sport' (*The Times*, 2 September 1988) and that her footballing activities did not clash with other, more 'feminine' concerns because 'luckily, my boyfriend thinks it's good that I have my own interests' (*Woman*, February 1989). Despite this advance, at FA headquarters, referees, reports — from males and females — are apparently marked. 'This report contains offensive language', in order to 'protect' the female staff who open the mail (*Off the Ball*, 16, 1988). Female FA administrators, however, notably the impressive Pat Smith, were in the front line of FA/fan operations during the often difficult times in Italy during the 1990 World Cup Finals. Some 'stiff' language was almost certainly in use here.

The rapid growth of family enclosures, and the increase in marketing and commercial activities of clubs during the 1980s provided increased and 'appropriate' opportunities for work for women inside clubs, on a voluntary, part-time or, less usually, even on a full-time basis. More than a dozen League club secretaries are now women, though most of these are employed in the lower divisions where their role is very much subordinated to the whims of club chairmen and their boards. One woman, Annie Bassett, achieved the Chief Executive position at a major club, Birmingham City, but her stay proved to be short-lived following intense publicity and the introduction at St. Andrews of her ill-conceived membership scheme which aroused little local popular support (See 'Annie Adds to the City Supporters' Blues', *The Guardian*, 29 September 1990).

A handful of women are League club directors though a number of these seem to be 'sleeping partners' to their husband's board ambitions. Exceptions are provided by Vicki Oyston at Blackpool (where her husband Owen Oyston is the Chair) and Pam Burton at Halifax Town, a director appointed by the Labour-controlled local authority, which has a majority shareholding in the club. Ms Oyston, an articulate and outspoken director, was 'humiliated' after being barred from entry into the Tranmere Rovers boardroom at half time during a Littlewoods Cup tie in November 1988. Among the members of the home board upholding the bar was Susan Johnson, wife of the club chairman. Rovers claimed the boardroom was men only 'by tradition' not 'by definition', an 'explanation' which did little to impress the Oystons, who watched the second half of the match from the terraces (*The Guardian*, 23 November 1988). Pam Burton, surely uniquely for a club director, a school teacher, confirms that a number of League clubs continue to operate a policy of this kind with little attempt by the Football League or influential grant-giving bodies to disturb the 'men's club' mentality which underpins it. Burton is more than aware of the problems faced by women in aspiring to executive positions inside football clubs and other male-dominated institutions. But she is also convinced that women can contribute substantially to the well-being of their clubs.

It's the butch lady isn't it? Nobody can equate femininity with authority for some reason or other . . . If she's in power, then she's a lesbian, a dyke or whatever. And yet, a perfectly ordinary female is quite capable of having high authority and high power and not losing anything of her characteristics . . . I think they'd bring a totally new perspective [more women directors]. I think the supporters would actually benefit more. I think they [women] see more, see wider issues. I actually think the players, possibly, would benefit more as well because you talk to them in a different way. You pick up on different aspects about them. You know more about their families quite often. (SNCCFR, 1991)

During the spring of 1991, women seemed to be knocking more loudly than ever before at the door of the male sporting Establishment. The MCC, that bastion of English male sporting privilege, was even forced to a vote on female members by the ex-England women's cricket captain Rachel Hayhoe-Flint. Though the breach against women was comfortably held this time, this particular assault is, surely, far from over. (Lancashire CC recently voted in *favour* of women members.) At the same time, the inaugural Women's World Rugby Union Cup was held in South Wales and it attracted considerable media interest if not substantial 'live' support. A woman jockey, Alex Greaves, also became the top race rider on all-weather race tracks in Britain (*The Observer*, 3 March 1991). In British football, too, the possibilities for change and for a new role and status for female fans, players and spectators is enormous as the game struggles with the requirements of modernising stadia, rationalising the game's antiquated structure and preparing for the new challenges of Europe. A Home Affairs Committee Report on *Policing Football Hooliganism*, published in February 1991, calls for a greater democratisation of decision-making processes within the game as well as for a more interventionist role for central government in the financing of stadium redevelopment programmes. It concludes with the following words:

Soccer is the most popular sport in England and Scotland. Hundreds of thousands play the game or watch it regularly. Even more identify with a team or their national side. The national football authorities owe it to these people to ensure that they can regard themselves as partners in the game not as fodder for exploitation by those who cream off soccer's rich pickings . . . The 'them and us' attitude of the past must be buried. (p. xxviii)

Women football players, spectators and officials would agree — wholeheartedly. In March 1991, Ros Coward visited Honeywell School in Battersea, and the Allen Edwards school in Stockwell, south London. Her brief was to find out how, if at all, the ambitions and aspirations of young girls had shifted from the conventional ones to be nurses, hairdressers and ballet dancers. 'The most pressing ambition of many of these girls', she reported, 'which surprised me, was to play football' (*The Guardian*, 19 March 1991). Signs of the times?

Acknowledgements

We owe a special debt for this chapter to David Williamson, who let us look at a pre-publication copy of the manuscript of his book, *Belles at the Ball*. We are reliant on Williamson for much of our information on women's football between 1900 and 1922. Andy Ward provided us with much useful advice and information on women and football. He is also one of the pioneers in this area. Kate Berry and Patrick Murphy conducted some of the 1989 interviews with members of women's national football squad, and Linda Whitehead helped us with information on the WFA. Liz Crolley provided us with data on Lady Florence Dixey. Steve Wagg provided helpful comments on earlier drafts of this chapter. Thanks to all. This chapter has been written as part of a Sports Council/Football Trust funded research project on women and football in Britain.

Bibliography

Bale, J. (1980), 'Women's Football in England and Wales: A Social–geographic perspective', in *Physical Education Review*, **3**, (2), pp. 137–44.
Book of Football (1972), 'Femme Football', **2** (3), pp. 590–2, London: Marshall Cavendish.
Brunt, R. (1989), 'Raising One Voice', *Marxism Today*, September 1989, pp. 22–5.
Bucke, T. (1989), 'Football Fanzines and Fanzine Culture', unpublished paper, Sir Norman Chester Centre for Football Research, p. 15.
Canter, D., M. Comber and D. Uzzell (1989), *Football in its Place*, London: Routledge.
Crampsey, B. (1978). *The Scottish Footballer*, Edinburgh: William Blackwood.
Crean, T. (1990), 'Terrace Conversion', *20/20*, **2** (1), pp. 96–8.
Davies, P. (1990), *All Played Out*, London: Heinemann.
Dunning, E., P. Murphy and J. Williams (1988), *The Roots of Football Hooliganism*, London: Routledge.
Dunphy, E. (1976), *Only a Game*, London: Kestrel Books.
English Schools Football Association (1988), 'Survey of Football in Schools', ESFA.
Fishwick, N. (1989), *English Football and Society: 1910–1950*, Manchester: Manchester University Press.

Grayson, E. (1985), 'Split Decisions', *Sport and Leisure*, July/August, p. 41.

Hargreaves, J. (1984), 'Taking Men on at Their Games', *Marxism Today*, August, pp. 17–21.

Hargreaves, J. (1987), 'Victorian Familism and the Formative Years of Female Sport', in J. A. Mangan and R. J. Park (eds), *From Fair Sex to Feminism*, London: Frank Cass, pp. 130–44.

Harrington, J. (1968), *Soccer Hooliganism*, Bristol: John Wright and Sons.

Holt, R. (1988), 'Football and the Urban Way of Life in Nineteenth Century Britain', in J. A. Mangan (ed.), *Pleasure, Profit and Proselytism*, pp. 67–86, London: Frank Cass.

Holt, R. (1989), *Sport and the British*, Milton Keynes: Open University Press.

Home Affairs Committee (1991), *Policing Football Hooliganism*, London: HMSO.

Lang, J. (1969). *Crowd Behaviour at Football Matches*, London: HMSO.

McCrone, K. E. (1987), 'Play up! Play up! and Play the Game: Sport of the Late-Victorian Girls Public School', in Mangan and Park (eds), pp. 97–129.

McElhone, F. (1977), *Football Crowd Behaviour*, Edinburgh: HMSO.

Mason, T. (1980), *Association Football and English Society 1863–1915*, London: Harvester.

Mrozek, D. J. (1987), 'The "Amazon" and the American "lady": Sexual Fears of Women as Athletes', in Mangan and Park (eds), pp. 282–98.

Murphy, P., E. Dunning and J. Williams (1990), *Football on Trial*, London: Routledge.

National Federation of Football Supporters Clubs (1954), Minutes of Annual General Meeting.

Popplewell, O. (1986), *Crowd Safety and Control at Sports Grounds: Final Report*, London: HMSO.

Scraton, P. (1990), 'A Game to Make a Man of You . . . Unreconstructed, of Course', Letter to *The Guardian*, 29 January.

Scraton, S. (1986), 'Images of Femininity and the Teaching of Girls Physical Education', in J. Evans (ed.), *Physical Education Sport and Schooling: Studies in the Sociology of Physical Education*, London: Falmer Press.

Sir Norman Chester Centre for Football Research (1989), interviews with members of the England women's national football squad.

Sir Norman Chester Centre for Football Research (1991), interviews with female football administrators.

Talbot, M. (1989), 'Physical and Sport Education and Research', in *Women and Sport: Taking The Lead*, a Council of Europe Seminar, Bisham Abbey National Sports Centre, 11–14 September, Sports Council, pp. 23–35.

Taylor, I. (1990), 'British Soccer and Europe: Problems and Possibilities', Paper delivered at *Le Football et l'Europe*, Institut Universitaire Européen, Florence, 3–5 May.

Vamplew, W. (1988), *Pay up and Play the Game*, Cambridge: Cambridge University Press.

Ward, A. (1989), 'Some Notes on the History of Women's Soccer', unpublished paper, p. 10.

Williams, J. and A. Goldberg (1991), 'English Fans at Italia '90', paper for the Council of Europe, Strasbourg, p. 50.

Williams, J., E. Dunning and P. Murphy (1987), 'Young People's Images of Attending Football: a Preliminary Analysis of Essays by Liverpool Schoolchildren', Sir Norman Chester Centre for Football Research, p. 44.

Williamson, D. (1991), *Belles of the Ball*, Devon: R and D Associates.

Willis, P. (1982), 'Women in Sport in Ideology', in J. Hargreaves (ed.), *Sport, Culture and Ideology*, pp. 117–34, London: Routledge.

Woodhouse, J. (1991), 'A National Survey of Female Football Fans', Sir Norman Chester Centre for Football Research, Leicester, p. 62.

Part 3
Following

6
Walking alone together: football supporters and their relationship with the game

Rogan Taylor

I can't help liking football crowds. Few people seem to have a good word for them. Players . . . try to ignore them. Football Club management . . . tolerate them as a regrettable necessity. Certainly the bleak and unwelcoming aspect of some grounds suggests that the clubs concerned would be happier if the spectators tossed their money over the wall and went home . . . The only consolation the spectators have is the knowledge that they are essential.

(Cyril Hughes, 1957)[1]

It is easier to discover the conditions of the drains in Oldham in the late nineteenth century than to find out who went to football matches then. Football and history — serious, social history, that is — have only recently been introduced to one another.[2] As a legitimate topic for academic debate, the sport has been perceived traditionally as unworthy of attention, 'on the one hand too uncouth, on the other too "trendy" to achieve historical respectability'.[3] If this be true for the game as a whole, it is more so for its supporters. Today, as the eye surveys the packed shelves of a sports bookshop, encountering numerous, vague histories of almost everything, from clubs and players to shirts and shinpads, it will discover no account of the supporters themselves. Even the National Federation of Football Supporters Clubs (the 'Federation') — formed over sixty years ago — has yet to publish its history.

This essay cannot hope to fill the gap. It can only consider very briefly the context in which the professional game of football and its supporters emerged in the last quarter of the nineteenth century; the early 'relations' between clubs and their fans; the rise of supporters' clubs and the kind of people who organised them, and one or two celebrated examples of their collective action. It will trace the attempt by the Federation to provide a national platform for supporters' clubs. *En route* we will outline the role fans have played traditionally in supporting their football clubs and the game, and in seeking dialogue with those who owned the former and administered the latter. We will encounter the chronic difficulties facing any group of supporters seeking to represent themselves effectively and we will learn of the corresponding failure of football's administrators to develop any mutually fruitful relationship to the benefit of the game both parties help to sustain.

It is impossible to understand the way football supporters have been perceived — and the way they saw themselves — without some recognition of the somewhat unusual history of the emerging professional game itself, and of its social context. The first written codifications of the rules of football took place in the English public schools by the mid-nineteenth century, apparently as part of an attempt by the schoolmasters to gain control over a disciplinary system, autonomously operated by the pupils, known as 'fagging'.[4] The birth of association football — and the Football Association in 1863 — subsequently took place at the hands of ex-public schoolboys, attending university together and seeking to formalise a single set of rules so they could play one another.[5] Yet by the turn of the century, football had become a game watched and played, largely, by the ordinary folk of industrial Britain. Somewhere along the line, the game of aristocrats and the well-to-do was appropriated by the working class.

This is not the place to investigate the process, 'both problematic and significant', whereby an ancient 'folk' game was formalised and transmitted by the sons of gentlemen to the industrial workers of Britain.[6] We do know it happened, and that recognising this process is the key to understanding the strange relationship that has characterised football fans and the game ever since. For the developing attitude of those who owned football clubs, and those who administered the sport, towards the burgeoning crowds who came to watch, seems to betray some deep *embarrassment* that the public school game left in their charge had been clutched so passionately to the hearts of less advantaged people. As their amateur, Corinthian vision of football dissolved into a fiery reality of private limited companies competing against each other with professional players, the upper-class 'gents' who had midwifed the game swiftly abandoned the progeny on the nearest doorstep. Football was left 'in the custody of the lower middle class . . . a fractious alliance between clerks and self-made businessmen',[7] to struggle manfully for its lost 'respectability', like an orphan child in a Victorian melodrama. This dramatic sub-text helps explain with some clarity the style with which the game has been administered, and the atmosphere in boardrooms and committees of solid citizens who behave as if the local landed gentry stood at their shoulders, watching every move. As Stephen Wagg aptly puts it, football administrators found themselves 'left to run their affairs the way they imagined their betters would have wanted'.[8] The same came to be true of the vast majority of football supporters' clubs as they proliferated over the following fifty years.

The first football clubs were often simply clubs with 'members' who joined to get involved. These early enthusiasts might play one week, watch the next. They usually ran their clubs democratically, electing a committee for the purpose. As spectator support grew, so did the pressure to succeed and many clubs sought limited liability status to raise the cash required. The transformation of football clubs into private limited companies often worked to seal off the original supporters — once 'members' — from any significant involvement in their clubs' affairs. Ironically, it was the spectators' desire and insistence on seeing a winning team competing at League level that often provoked the transformation. Leicester Fosse joined the Second Division of the Football League in 1894, a commitment which involved increased expenditure to ensure fulfilment of fixtures and meeting of players' wages. Within months the club's Committee, democratically elected by its membership, began actively to seek new blood from amongst 'the influential gentlemen of the town'.[9] New rules appeared ensuring that anyone who wished to stand for the Committee 'would be required to provide a guarantee to the bank'.[10] Such conditions inevitably began to set the Committee apart from ordinary members and complaints that it acted dictatorially soon followed in the local press (some even suggested that a rival club be formed). As debts mounted, more well-off local 'gentlemen' were required to shore up the club and the distance between members and the Committee increased. At Leicester, limited liability status was sought in 1897 with a share issue of £3,000.

Some share issues priced shares clearly out of the reach of ordinary supporters, as at Sheffield United where £20 was the minimum required. When share prices were kept low to encourage wide ownership (5s. at Dartford and Southport; 10s. at Accrington Stanley), often too few local supporters took up the chance.[11] Even where shares were initially reasonably spread amongst working people, in time the bulk of shares seemed to concentrate in the hands of a few local well-to-do men.[12] Mason's survey of the shareholders of forty-seven football clubs (1886–1913) revealed most as distinctly middle-class, yet there was still a large 'sprinkling' of others of lower social standing.[13] The problem — in terms of their exerting any real influence — was that most of the latter took up only one or two shares as an expression of their support: a continuation of their 'membership' of a sporting club they may have joined years before.[14]

The emergence of supporters' clubs

For most football supporters, no doubt, their 'investment' — though lifelong in many cases — involved just their hearts, their habits and their regular sixpences. When they helped raise additional money, they tended simply to give it to their club. Even by the 1880s fans were involved in raising funds by running sports meetings, bazaars or promoting prize draws and lotteries.[15] By the turn of the century, supporters were already established in fund-raising roles. We know, for example, from the remarks of W. H. Squires, Director of Leicester Fosse, in 1904, that supporters 'In some towns I could mention . . . [have formed] . . . a finance committee . . .' to raise money for their clubs.[16] Leicester's 'Million Farthing Fund' was typical of the kind of scheme already in use to encourage fans and other members of a club's community to give cash. The history of supporters' financial contributions (over and above the money paid for admission) is almost certainly longer than the history of supporters' clubs themselves.

There were 'Brake Clubs', which organised travel parties, in existence from the 1880s onwards, but the earliest supporters' clubs appear to surface during the first decade of this century, though little record of their activities has survived. Watford SC is mentioned as 'one of the earliest', founded in 1911,[17] and Crystal Palace SC is also offered as a prototype.[18] Such sparse information, however, hardly precludes the previous existence of other supporters' organisations. Luton Town SC was formed in 1912, as the Minutes of the Football Club's Board show.[19] They reveal that a public meeting of supporters took place on 15 July 1912, when a subcommittee was elected, apparently with the approval of the Club. The 'Luton News' Football Handbooks of 1913–14 and 1914–15 include some detailed information about the supporters involved. There is a photograph of the officers of the supporters' club in 1914: twenty-one middle-aged gentlemen in suits and ties, looking remarkably like similar photographs of supporters' club organisers throughout the 1920s and 1930s. The leading lights of Luton's SC — again like so many of those who were to come after them — are all 'worthy gentlemen' of the local community, with local city councillors to the fore. The supporters' club President, in 1914, is Alderman Wilkinson. There are already four Vice-Presidents, including Mr Harmsworth, MP, Mr Oakley, Councillor and Justice of the Peace, and the Reverend Mahon. The headquarters of the supporters' club is at 'Edwards Restaurant' in Manchester Street. Little wonder the football club readily approved of the organisation. It was already looking rather like a mirror-image of the 'parent' body.

If supporters gathered under less 'respectable' leaders — often to criticise the Club for past failures — football clubs tried either to ignore them or to redirect the fans' energies into fund-raising. At Leicester in 1901, chronic discontent amongst supporters culminated in a boisterous public meeting attended by the Club Chairman who bemoaned the falling gates, while the fans bemoaned the footballing ignorance of the Board. A year later at another public meeting, Leicester's Secretary asked those gathered 'what sort of team they would like', urging them to raise 'a working man's subscription fund'.[20] Following relegation from the Second Division in 1904, angry fans were urged again — by W. H. Squires — to set up a finance committee, 'to provide the wherewithal for securing the services of (capable) players'.[21] For the next forty years, supporters at Leicester periodically raised money for the Club and pressed for some kind of institutionalised, proper dialogue with the Board of Directors. They did not gain it. The Board always repudiated such requests by reminding the fans that it was a *private* business.

This traditional argument, deployed by football clubs over many decades, would not make much sense to most supporters. The vast majority of football clubs, it seems, have rarely functioned as ordinary private businesses; otherwise most would be out of business.[22] Historically, many football clubs have survived thanks to a combination of public (usually supporter) and private benevolence. Cash to spend on players, for example, was rarely 'a function solely of gate-receipts but also of public appeals and philanthropic patrons'.[23] Private investors of course gained an institutionalised access, via the Board, to the Club's affairs, in accordance with a fundamental principle in the football world that anyone providing money to a club should keep 'a controlling hand during such time as his capital is invested'.[24] But in the vast majority of cases, the public/supporter 'investment' never bought any independent representation at the Club.

It probably appeared to many supporters that football clubs wanted to have their cake and eat it. When the clubs needed money (i.e. most of the time), they appealed, especially to supporters, as guardians of the community identity and ethos. When supporters appealed for relationship and openness (i.e. most of the time), the clubs quickly reverted to being private businesses.

In Leicester in 1911, the footballing equivalent of 'perestroika' was at the forefront of supporters' demands. Even one of the local journalists (who, then as now, appeared ever mindful not to jeopardise their often cosy relationship with the local club) had to admit:

If supporters knew more intimately all the trials and tribulations, they would be more forthcoming and patient. I think directors would be well advised to take the public more into their confidence. Reticence encourages neither generosity nor charity nor warm support.[25]

In 1913, fans were still complaining about their isolation:

I am sure the supporters of the Club in general would appreciate it very much if the directors would take them into their confidence and publish the 'gates' for every match and the amounts of transfers for players.[26]

Ten years later, letters continue to appear in the local press from fans seeking to justify their requests for greater involvement:

Surely we supporters are entitled to some say in the government of the game we support?

We are terribly interested in the game and its welfare in Leicester, though the City directors don't seem alive to the fact . . . they veil themselves in mystery . . . we grope in the darkness . . .[27]

Still the club refused to be drawn into any correspondence, provoking a further flood of angry letters from fans. The idea of forming a supporters' club — first attempted before the First World War — had resurfaced in Leicester in 1921. Some of its proposals were quite radical, including:

(1) That the supporters' club should consider its main role to involve representing supporters 'to the directors by means of a deputation';
(2) '. . . that a place should be found on the directorate for at least two members elected to represent the opinions of the very large band of supporters . . . *The Club is, properly speaking, an institution of the town and not a kind of private trading company, conducted at the whim of the few men who are at the moment immediately interested* . . . (my emphasis).[28]

This latter sentiment has a familiar ring to it and would hardly appear out of place in any modern fanzine editorial.

Supporters' clubs with aims to *represent* their members signally failed to flourish. Without at least some recognition from their clubs of the justice of their case, fans simply failed to organise themselves effectively.[29] Perhaps the majority of supporters were simply too apathetic, and the natural activists and organisers interested in articulating popular opinion were engaged elsewhere, in political and trade union activity, for example.

Stephen Jones has reviewed the activities of various sports-orientated, left-wing organisations during the 1920s and 1930s.[30] He describes the rise, in 1923, of the communist-inspired British Workers Sports Federation (BWSF), an 'internationalist' organisation with mottoes like 'Footballs instead of Cannonballs' and 'Peace Through Sport'. The BWSF saw the football world of private limited companies as an object of derision. It failed to read the subtleties of the British workers' locational bond of identification and devotion to professional football. The organisation was too dogmatic to recognise and evaluate the emotional investment of supporters in their clubs. Instead, it argued that professional football was 'boss' sport, already disintegrating (along with the rest of capitalism) into the dustbin of history, according to classic Marxist doctrine. Such an argument, difficult in any case to sustain in the face of football's growing popularity, inevitably depicted existing supporters as fools propping up a 'mug's game'.[31] The BWSF was more interested in organising football teams based around socialist organisations, like the North London Workers Union, than in organising the supporters of professional teams. Politics even entered the field of play, as BWSF teams practised 'socialist' tactics, described by one detractor (who styled the BWSF 'Bolshies with Sporting Feelings') as '. . . totally against individualism on the football field, preferring mass action, even mass shooting for goal . . .'.[32]

Of course, the BWSF was concerned with issues wider than football, encompassing all sport and recreation. It did get involved, however, in organising a match-boycott in 1930, when West Ham raised the minimum admission price to 2s. for a Cup Tie against Arsenal. The boycott failed to have any impact (and Arsenal won 3–0).[33] Three years later, the BWSF helped organise a successful campaign for Sunday League football against various defenders of the Sabbath Day, including the FA.[34]

In 1930, another politically motivated sports organisation appeared, the National Worker Sports Association (NWSA). It had grown out of the Sports Association (SA), founded by the London Labour Party in 1928, and had official TUC and Labour Party backing. In 1929, SA Chairman, Alec Macleod,

. . . initiated a 'Soccer for Sixpence' campaign protesting that, 'It is scandalous that football clubs should spend their large surpluses in securing 'fashionable' players under the transfer system instead of improving [supporters'] accommodation or reducing their prices.[35]

The idea of improving supporters' accommodation at the expense of transfer fees has, of course, recently been espoused by the current Conservative Government, following the Taylor Report on the Hillsborough disaster.

Throughout the 1920s and 1930s, supporters' clubs proliferated widely in both League and non-League football. Almost all appear to have been as eminently 'respectable' as Luton's in 1914. These supporters' clubs were rarely constituted to represent the views of fans to clubs; often the reverse, in fact.

They tended to see themselves almost entirely within the terms defined by their football clubs as 'proper'. Indeed, many supporters' clubs — possibly over half the total — were established at the direct instigation of football clubs.[36]

As we saw at Luton Town FC, supporters' clubs were 'recognised' principally as fund-raisers. The impression arises (from subsequent developments in the 1950s and 1960s) that many football clubs saw their supporters' clubs as the fund-raising arm of their private limited company — that, in a sense, the supporters' club (though of necessity a 'voluntary' body) really belonged to the 'parent' club. Consequently, when commercial managers appeared at football clubs in the 1950s and 1960s, some supporters' clubs were swallowed wholesale, along with any funds and assets they possessed.

In addition to raising money, supporters' clubs were often expected to organise travel to 'away' matches, produce and sell the match programme, act as unpaid stewards, counteract 'barracking' of players and criticism of the club. Taking Sheffield Wednesday and Sheffield United supporters' clubs as examples, Fishwick sees them as acting essentially in the interests of their respective football clubs, encouraging supporters 'to act as the club desired'.[37] When the role of supporters' clubs was aired in the press, the phrase 'a danger of the tail trying to wag the dog' frequently occurred, as writers warned of the perils of allowing football fans to act independently: 'Such organisations are good servants but bad masters — or even equals . . .'[38] This writer is prepared to allow a page in the programme (which the supporters produce!) for supporters to air their views, though 'Anything of a scurrilous nature would, of course, be severely censured'.[39]

Supporters' clubs the length and breadth of Britain did for decades precisely what was asked of them, sometimes with astonishing energy and commitment. It may be that the supporters' leaders — the various councillors and aldermen — gained some kudos from their role, but the majority of club members probably did what they did not for the love of anyone else's 'business', but for the affection and deep attachment they felt for their football clubs, and in the knowledge of how vital their contributions were for the survival of their clubs. In large part, the football clubs quite literally traded on the loyalties of their fans, offering little or nothing by way of reciprocation. If supporters pressed their case for more openness and involvement, it was usually seen as 'interference'.

There were some notable exceptions to the general rule. A few clubs did develop quite intimate relationships with their supporters' clubs, often triggered by an embarrassingly high level of supporter fund-raising. These tended to be (though not exclusively) smaller, amateur or non-league clubs. At Aldershot, for example, where £108,000 was raised by fans between 1949 and 1969, 'Liaison between us and the football board is that I, as Chairman of the supporters club, have been elected to the football board as one of the directors . . .'.[40] Rhyl FC, where in the early 1930s a staggering £10,000 was raised by supporters (a huge sum in modern terms), '. . . the football club who appreciate our efforts to such a degree that they actually allow us to have a representation of five on the directorate . . .'.[41]

At Southampton, too, following a financial crisis in 1934 when supporters' contributions helped to save the Club, the Chairman, Major Stanley Sloane, felt that '. . . we could not go on accepting these donations unless they had a representative on our Board and . . . we invited (the supporters' club) Chairman, Mr C. E. Hoskins to become a Director . . .'.[42] Similarly, at Wrexham and Plymouth Argyle in the 1930s, where supporters had raised large sums of money, room on the Board was found for supporters' club representatives.[43] More recently, at Coventry City FC in the early 1960s, and at Oxford United in the early 1980s, supporters were drafted on to the boards of their respective clubs, though with little impact. At Coventry, according to one source, the supporter on the board was 'useless . . . He never opened his mouth to the Club'.[44] At Oxford, following Robert Maxwell's takeover, the FC and SC were merged and three supporters' club officials elevated to the board. However, as Mr Maxwell now took all decisions personally, the board was an impotent anachronism.

Over the last decade, supporters who have gained representation on the boards of clubs have done so through the direct involvement of local authorities. At Halifax Town, where the Town Council now owns the football club, supporters advise the board.[45] At Leeds, too, the involvement of the City Council has opened the board to supporter input. Board representation for supporters may, or may not, work to advantage. The vast majority of clubs, however, have consistently refused (despite the history of financial assistance) to accommodate supporters in any meaningful way. They remain deeply suspicious of the fans' objectives, as outlined by C. L. Sutcliffe (described as a 'Famous Football Legislator') in 1934: 'Some supporters' clubs have strange ideas of their objects, and their chief concern seems to be . . . to discuss the players, their play, and the governing authorities . . .'[46] Heaven forbid!

The attitude both of football clubs and of the game's ruling bodies towards supporters who sought to organise themselves was very similar to that shown towards football *players*. When the Players' Union (PU) began to exert pressure and threatened a strike in 1909, William Pickford at the FA saw the issue simply as coming down to the 'question of who is to be the master'.[47] It was deemed permissible that players might have a union but, as William McGregor of the Football League put it: '. . . such an organisation should concern itself with reducing "rough play" on the pitch and endeavouring to make the calling of the professional footballer as high-toned as possible.'[48] Like supporters' organisations, the players, it seems, were welcome to get together, providing their objects were 'proper' ones — to serve the interests of the clubs and, if at all possible, to raise the 'tone' of their calling.

The first successful attempt to establish a national body amongst supporters was led by a small group of highly 'respectable' supporters' clubs from the south of England.[49] The impetus came from Northampton Town Supporters' Club secretary, Tommy Hodgeson and co-founder Mr Onley in 1926. In fact, according to an account by Mr Onley in 1958, it was Mrs Hodgeson who first suggested a 'National Federation' over a cup of coffee in her front room.[50] A preliminary meeting was held in London on 22 January 1927 at Lyons Restaurant, 2, Bridge Street, Westminster. The following clubs were represented: Northampton, Boscombe, Brentford, Charlton Athletic and Plymouth Argyle.[51] By the end of the year, over twenty supporters' clubs had joined up.

Information about the fledgeling organisation — full title: the National Federation of Football Supporters Clubs — is sparse until the publication of its first 'official organ', *The Supporter*, in 1934. This broadsheet-style monthly newspaper, expensively priced at 3d., was edited by Jack Williams of Wrexham SC, but it only ran for two years, until 1936.[52]

The flavour of the emerging Federation of supporters' clubs is captured in the photograph (on the front page of the first edition of *The Supporter*) of the delegates attending the Federation's AGM in 1934. The delegates are standing outside the conference venue, the New Civic Hall in Leeds, with the Lord Mayor and Lady Mayoress at their centre. To a man (which they all were, bar the Mayoress), trilbies have been removed for the photograph. Most are middle-aged or older; all dressed in Sunday-best suits, white shirts and ties. They appear the very embodiment of lower-middle-class English respectability of the 1930s.

The Federation's motto — 'To Help and Not to Hinder' (often shortened to 'Help not Hinder') — portrays the organisation's vision of its role. It is that of 'child' (supporter) to 'parent' (football club); there is an almost Victorian undertone too, that of the relationship between servant and master, re-emphasised by the Kiplingesque sentiments in Tommy Hodgeson's thoughts on it:

What a motto we have chosen for our National Federation.
What a message to live up to!
Put it into our daily lives,
See what a lot it means,
What a sermon it is.
Oh! If only it could be graven on all our buildings
Both national and local.
What a lot it would do if it were ever
In our thoughts and on our tongues . . .[53]

The officers of the Federation in 1934 — as at Luton in 1913 — were drawn largely from the ranks of local town and city councillors. The Chairman, J. Talbot Nanson, was the Mayor of Brighton, and the Northern Branch Chairman was the Lord Mayor of Leeds, who stands at the centre of the photograph of delegates. There were four Vice-Presidents, all of whom were councillors, and the Federation's President, F. C. Parker, Esq. was a JP from Northampton. (This tradition of leadership by local councillors continues today, with the current Chairman of the Federation, Tony Kershaw, a Conservative councillor in Loughborough.) The predominance of local council representatives no doubt provided the Federation with its organisational experience, the knowledge of how committees worked, and its abiding image of careful respectability and commitment. The Federation's membership fee was, of course, in guineas — and remained so until decimalisation in the early 1970s.

The aims and objects of the Federation outlined in *The Supporter* concern the bringing together of supporters clubs *for the mutual benefit of their football clubs*: 'It was hoped that supporters' clubs, by getting together and pooling

ideas and interests, would be of more material assistance to their football clubs
. . .'[54] Yet some voices in the Federation also hoped for a greater, more direct
involvement with the game's authorities: 'and at the same time, unity being
strength [supporters] would have more weight within the football world and
also be held in higher esteem by their own football club.' The trade union-like
phrase, 'unity being strength', perhaps indicates a feeling among some
Federation members that the organisation should act as a powerful representative of its members, giving them 'more weight' in football's corridors of power.

In addition, the Federation sought to foster 'good fellowship' and 'sports-
manship' between supporters, hoping 'to do all in its power . . . to stop
unfortunate happenings that mar Football'.[55] It offered advice to its member
clubs on income tax problems through the Federation's Honorary Solicitor, G.
S. Godfree, Esq., 'a member of the Income Tax Payers Association'.

As an organisation, the Federation saw the role of supporters' clubs in much
the same way as the football clubs did. At the heights of its membership, in
1948, when football's popularity peaked in England, the Federation included
nearly 200 member clubs, with an estimated total individual membership of
around one million supporters.[56] Yet even at this period, with the first Labour
Government in power, there was little sign of any rumbling 'militancy'
amongst the Federation's representatives; rather the opposite. In the *Football
Supporters Gazette* — the post-war version of the Federation's 'official organ'
— the Secretary, Leslie Davies, outlines the 'primary objective' of every
supporters' club: '. . . to create and foster enthusiasm in the Parent Club; to
encourage greater support at the matches; and by raising of funds to
financially assist the football clubs . . .'[57]

These are laudable aims, no doubt, but the absence of any request for — or
even expectation of, it seems — some reciprocatory gesture from the football
clubs is striking. The organisers and officials of so many supporters' clubs
appear to have swallowed whole their football clubs' definition of what a
supporters' club should be. At Watford, for example, the supporters' club
produced a monthly publication, in 1948, the purpose of which was, apparently, 'to provide helpful propaganda on behalf of the parent club'.[58] — the
complete antithesis, it seems, of a modern fanzine.

It is not that fans had little to complain of. At the Federation's AGM's
throughout the late 1940s and 1950s there are frequent complaints from the
floor about FA Cup ticket allocations, prices, amenities, catering licences,
coach transport and 'football clubs who insist on telling us how to run
supporters' clubs'.[59] Though the Federation, considering its size, sees itself as
'a power' in the football world, it is of course 'a friendly power', helping not
hindering, with no institutional relationship to the football authorities through
which it might exert real pressure or recommend policy.

The Football Association and the Football League were the appropriate
bodies to liaise with an organisation like the Federation. In the oldest
Federation document available — a Notice of the Third AGM, held at Slater's
Restaurant, High Holborn, on 5 July 1930 — it is apparent than an early
approach has been made to the FA, seeking recognition. Agenda items include:
'6. Delegates report on interview with Sir F. J. Wall. 7. Relationship and
Recognition by the Football Association.'

Sir Frederick J. Wall was Secretary of the FA until Stanley Rous took over the job in 1934; he was '. . . austere, top-hatted . . . an arch conservative who had longed for the days when football had been just a game and when he, as he often told people, had eaten a rump steak before playing the Royal Engineers in the F.A. Cup, so careless had he been of the result.'[60] It is not a meeting but an *interview* that the Federation reports on. Judging by later developments, one imagines it was entirely unofficial and 'off the record'.

The Federation's concern with gaining 'recognition' from the FA runs constantly through the minutes of its post-war AGMs. It was, of course, natural that a recently formed, national body of federated supporters' clubs should want to establish quickly a relationship with the game's national authority. In some ways, the Federation sought to be *like* the FA, or at least to mirror this august body. Within a few years of its birth, the Federation had almost as many Vice-Presidents and Life Vice-Presidents as the FA — and the age range of those involved was similar.[61] Soon, members are giving one another Bronze Medallions of Honour, and by 1964, special 'badges of office' have been commissioned for senior Federation personnel to wear around their necks, rather like lord mayors and councillors, which many of them were. Perhaps most of all, the Federation and the FA resembled one another in their shared, lower-middle-class propriety, in their concern to run their affairs 'the way they imagined their betters would have wanted'.

Like the FA, the Federation was as concerned with amateur football as with the professional game. Indeed, many (and at times most) of its affiliated members were supporters of amateur or non-League football. Of the twenty-one clubs listed as 'affiliated' in the Notice of the 1930 AGM, almost half are non-league and none comes from further north than Nottingham. For most of the period 1930–70, the Federation retained a distinctly 'southern' and 'amateur' constituency. Member clubs attending the post-1948 AGMs are preponderantly amateur and non-League. In 1948, for example, of 131 delegates present, over 120 appear to represent non-League clubs.[62] Of eighty-nine delegates attending the AGM in 1953 (with active membership already in decline), around fifty-five represent amateur clubs. Secretary Leslie Davies, with reference to the Federation's membership, says: 'I have not covered all the amateur and non-League clubs because they are so numerous and make up the balance . . .', but the Worcester delegate takes offence at this latter phrase and insists that this 'balance' makes up the overwhelming majority of supporters in the Federation.[63]

Throughout the 1950s and 1960s, delegates from amateur clubs consistently outnumber their 'professional' counterparts between 3 and 4 to 1. This preponderantly 'amateur' representation may account for something of the low public profile from which the Federation suffered, much to the annoyance of its more active members. Amateur club membership declined sharply after 1970 and the Federation became more specifically concerned with League football issues. By 1988, of forty clubs represented at the Federation's AGM, twenty-five were Football League clubs.

After its emergence in 1927, the Federation's real work soon developed around servicing its membership — the affiliated supporters' clubs. Despite the 'interview' with Sir Frederick Wall in 1930 (and many subsequent attempts to formalise a relationship with the FA), it would take almost fifty years before the doors of Lancaster Gate were officially opened to the representatives of supporters' clubs. Even then, one suspects that it was more the FA's desire to commercialise its activities in the late 1970s — and the pressure of dealing with a rising hooligan problem — that opened those doors. In 1978, Federation Secretary Tony Pullien writes: 'There is now a far more business like approach from the F.A. The need for cash is uppermost in their minds . . .'[64]

This half century spent largely ignoring the only national organisation that could at least purport to represent supporters' interests was a lost opportunity and a yardstick of the poor public relations management by those who administered football.[65] The Federation's vaunted 'respectability'; its occasionally almost cringing efforts to show it meant no harm (a 'friendly power') won the organisation no consideration by the game's authorities. Even at the height of the Federation's membership in the late 1940s, when it could claim to represent up to one million fans, the FA hardly deigned to notice its existence. The Football League was even less enthusiastic and failed to meet the Federation officially until 1981.

Occasionally, some supporters actively campaigned on issues of general concern. The FA's system of allocating tickets for Cup Finals — long felt to be anachronistic by many supporters — came under attack when Spurs fans organised a 'We Want Wembley' demonstration in 1962, demanding an 80,000-ticket allocation for finalists. A few hundred fans marched from Trafalgar Square to FA Headquarters at Lancaster Gate, where the system (which at that time allocated 38,840 tickets to the County Associations and less than 15,000 to each competing clubs' supporters) was 'explained' to them.[66] Interestingly, the Federation took umbrage at this protest action by the Spurs Fans. Cup ticket allocations had been a subject of complaint by the Federation's members from its earliest days.[67] Yet little had ever been done by the organisation to *publicise* its opposition. The action of Spurs fans in 1962 probably raised more publicity about the issue than the sum total of twenty years' discussion at Federation AGMs. The Federation was, throughout the 1950s, only concerned anyway with getting its *own* allocation of Cup tickets (just as the County Associations already had), rather than increasing the numbers allocated to supporters of the finalists.[68] Ironically, the objections expressed about the 'We Want Wembley' campaign included worries about the demonstration 'bringing the Federation into disrepute'.[69] One would have thought, as far as supporters were concerned, rather the opposite.

With supporters largely ignored by the football authorities or, if necessary (as fund-raisers) 'accommodated' by patronising football club boards, the only real pressure ordinary fans could exert was to stay away. This they did, increasingly, and for no doubt various reasons throughout the 1950s. The physical condition of the nation's football grounds deteriorated in parallel. On the terraces in 1954, '. . . the standard minimum price is 1s 6d; and there can surely be no other circumstances in which so little comfort and convenience is provided for the money . . .'[70]

For some of the youngsters who arrived on the fast-emptying terraces, there was another pressure they could exert on the game. In the late 1950s, and with apparent inexorability throughout the following decades, a modern form of hooliganism associated with football emerged. Though crowd disorder and violence had been connected with football matches since the late nineteenth century, the inter-war period had been less troublesome.[71] The outbreak of a renewed and virulent form of supporter misbehaviour, as it intensified throughout the 1960s, provoked a public debate about its causes and brought demands for a real partnership between the game and its supporters.

With the publication of the Chester Report in 1968 came suggestions for ways in which supporters could be included more effectively in the running of their clubs:

Within the limited company form it would also be possible to provide rights for two classes of supporters, upon which after all the success of the club depends — season ticket holders and the Supporters Club members. The constitution of the company could entitle season ticket holders of say, three years standing, to vote at annual meetings . . . The constitution of the club could be drafted so as to entitle the Supporters Club to appoint a representative on the Board. In these and other ways, clubs could link themselves more closely with the local community.[72]

The suggestion that football fans might have some 'rights' conferred on them in recognition of the vital role they played in the game was a novel one.

Further support for moves to 'democratise' the way football was organised and run followed, in 1971, with the publication of two articles by Professor Ian Taylor which set out a 'speculative sociology' of football hooliganism.[73] In short, Taylor argued that the recent outbreaks of violence amongst some supporters expressed their growing alienation from the changed values which the game was embracing. For Taylor, the heightened commercialisation and 'bourgeoisification' of football, beginning in the late 1950s and intensifying in the 1960s, left a resentful 'rump' of supporters who felt increasingly distanced from their teams' players and antagonistic towards the institutions which ran the game. He suggested that, especially during the inter-war period, there had existed (at least) the illusion of 'participatory control' amongst supporters. The loss of this illusion was now being expressed in a very direct form of participation — pitch invasions and violent territorial defence of a particular part of the ground — usually the 'end' behind one goal. Thus football hooliganism could be 'a sociologically explicable "democratic" response to the loss of control exercised by a football sub-culture . . .'.[74] It would continue until 'resolved by structural changes in the club's relationship to supporters . . .'.[75]

The proposition that football supporters had, in the past, experienced even an illusory feeling of 'participatory control' is debatable. It seems more likely that most supporters at most clubs would have had no illusion (either before 1914 or during the inter-war period) about the way their football clubs were run. But it may be true nonetheless that the football fans of the post-war period — and particularly the younger ones — felt *differently* from their forebears about football clubs and players. Whilst hardly 'explaining' football hooliganism (which takes a wide variety of forms), Taylor's provocative speculations may tell a lot about the meaning of some of its forms; they express alienation and impotence. The roots of such feelings run deep and beyond the boundaries of the football world, of course, but they are also eminently understandable within the confines of the game and its failed relationship with those who support it. Taylor might be right to see supporters' clubs, in their beginnings, as a possible 'means of affirming and institutionalising the control exercised by the soccer sub-culture'.[76] The problem is they never did. Instead, the football clubs and the game's authorities generally and repeatedly cashed in on the indefinable — hence 'religious' almost — enthusiasm that supporters showed for the game. But Taylor argues that it need not have been so. With a little more generosity and a little less concern for 'respectability', '. . . the needs and motivations of the supporters could have been taken seriously, and structural changes and reforms introduced accordingly'.[77]

Football's failure (when times were good and crowds were huge) either to affirm or to institutionalise a relationship with its supporters left the game highly vulnerable when attendances declined steeply throughout the 1950s and the 1960s. Yet at precisely this time, and with crowd behaviour a rising problem, instead of seeking closer, more effective ties with their supporters — or, at the very least, shoring up what relationships there were — many football clubs set about divorcing themselves from or dismembering their supporters' clubs.

By 1958, some football clubs were already setting up rival 'official' supporters' clubs to take commercial advantage of the Lotteries Act (1956). Ironically (and with considerable *naïveté*), the supporters' Federation had lobbied hard for this legislation which they believed would secure the ground of much fund-raising activity by supporters' clubs. Instead, and under growing commercial pressures, the football clubs saw it as an opportunity to take them over. By 1964, disputes between supporters' clubs and their 'parents' were so frequent that the Federation proposed (though it was never established) a national liaison committee to intercede on a regular basis.[78] Supporters' clubs fell like ninepins and, just a year later, the Federation's Secretary bemoaned the collapse of the network.[79] Few supporters' clubs had any legal or even written agreements with their football clubs. If supporters had raised the money for (and, as at Luton, had physically built) particular amenities, club rooms, tea bars, etc., inside the ground, who owned them?

At Coventry City in 1964–5, the supporters' club had financed the construction of extensive premises for its members, located in the Sky Blue Stand, at a cost of £27,587. The supporters also took over responsibility for the Stand's overdraft (some £41,000). Realising that 'we never owned a brick of it', the supporters' club members began to worry about the 'gentleman's agreement' which gave them access to the amenities they themselves had built: 'We asked for some security of tenure . . . Jimmy Hill refused to give us it . . . we'd built every brick . . . it was *our* ground . . . we were the workhorses and the club had taken all our money.'[80]

Ipswich Town's supporters' club representative, in 1967, told a sorry tale:

Two years ago we gave the football club £42,000 in twelve months . . . We have paid for every thing on the football ground: the stands, the offices and the dressing rooms . . . Without warning a notice in the press appeared saying they no longer recognised our

supporters' club and that a new one had been formed . . . This came as a complete
surprise. We went to the Boardroom and were given our notice — the Secretary and
myself after 31 years and 35 years service. We were not thanked . . . we did not ask for
thanks and we certainly did not get any . . .[81]

It was not only the larger, professional clubs which dealt so unsympathetically
with supporters who had voluntarily raised money over long periods. At
Bedford Town, where more than £175,000 had been donated by supporters
between 1959 and 1965, 'we were kicked off the ground'.[82] At Corby Town in
1973, the football club went bankrupt and was only rescued when the
supporters' club raised £12,500 to pull it round. The British Steel Corporation
(BSC) were majority shareholders of Corby Town FC and also owned the
ground on which they played. Following the supporters' rescue of the club,
BSC peremptorily demanded a rent for their club premises (which the fans had
built themselves inside the ground) of £10,000 per annum, plus 75 per cent of
the net profits on the bar. The supporters refused, began legal proceedings and
eventually won their case.[83]

Not all football clubs behaved with such cavalier disregard for their
supporters, some of whom, as at Ipswich, had volunteered half a lifetime,
helping in effect, but often without representation, to keep their football clubs
afloat. Some clubs did take the trouble to work out reasonably amicable deals
which allowed their new commercial managers to take over the lotteries whilst
ensuring a good working relationship with supporters' clubs.[84] If the football
club could run fund-raising schemes more efficiently than supporters could —
not necessarily the case — and make more money for the club thereby,
supporters could readily see the sense of it. But too few clubs bothered to deal
sympathetically with what was bound to be a difficult transitional period. It
would have been an ideal time to formalise some proper relationship, some
effective representation, for a club's supporters; to recognise and pay tribute
to their emotional and financial support over the years by institutionalising the
bond between clubs and fans, in place of the latter's traditional and indicative
fund-raising role. But too many clubs saw it as an opportunity to downgrade
what relationships they had with their supporters. Now able to develop their
own commercial activities and competitions, many saw little in their own (self-
) interest that required an effective dialogue — and this at precisely the time
when, in the face of growing crowd disorder, their own interests might have
been better served by rapidly *deepening* relationships with their fans and the
communities from which they were drawn.

Football had failed consistently to discover, or even to seek, what the
appropriate relationship might be with its supporters. It was not a simple task.
As the game grew to such enormous popularity, it penetrated the national
consciousness — the nation's idea of itself.

Football was a phenomenon; prodigious, surprising, for some, disturbing.
The most fascinating element of it for many who attended the game — and for
most of those who did not — was the behaviour of football's supporters: their
rituals, costume, dedication, sacrifice, joy and despair. Their feelings for the
game were clearly complex, often rooted in close social and geographic ties,
sometimes to the extent that they were more akin to devotees of a 'localised

religion'.[85] This is what picked football out of the mêlée of other spectator sports to make its particular mark. Football may not owe its existence to its supporters, but as Fishwick recognises, '. . . it was the *relationship between the supporters and the game* that made such an impact on English society'.[86]

That relationship was never significantly reflected or reciprocated, except to the extent that fans were 'allowed' a fund-raising role, which many performed prodigiously. Yet the desire to participate (and celebrate), and not merely witness passively, was evident for all to see. It may have looked to the 'Old Boys' the very antithesis of their Corinthian ideal, but there was something idealistic in the enthusiasm football's fans showed, utterly disconnected as it was from any possible material gain.[87] Was it their class origins — and identifying passion for the game — that not only fascinated but at the same time disturbed the guardians of the game's respectability? Despite the passage of time and the eminent worthiness of the middle-aged men who ran supporters' clubs, still the lingering image of football's fans remained of 'their workaday dirt and their workaday adjectives very loose on their tongues'.[88] There were, after all, no official meetings between anyone who could claim to represent football supporters; and the Football Association and Football League in nearly one hundred years of the professional game.

Such a serious failure on the part of the football authorities to engage in any real relationship with the representatives of football supporters' clubs can only be comprehended in the context of the game's origins and social history: its nineteenth-century codification in the public schools; its subsequent professionalisation and fierce popularity with the working class; its management by 'an alliance between clerks and self-made businessmen'. In football's passage through aristocratic halls to the tradesmen's entrance at the rear, the game's supporters became a simple, though disquietingly essential, embarrassment to those in charge. They were in Fishwick's phrase 'the Labour Party at prayer'.[89] Yet, despite the huge sums of money they raised and donated, the constant (and once enormous) flow through the turnstiles, and the sheer, undeniable passion for the game that fans communicated, they could not elect one single representative to voice their concerns in the parliament of football.

Notes

1. *F.A. News* (1987), **VI** (7), February.
2. See, for example, T. Mason (1981), *Association Football and English Society, 1863–1915*, Gt. Britain, 1980; Brighton: Harvester Press; W. Vamplew (1988), *Pay Up and Play the Game*, Cambridge: Cambridge University Press; C. Korr (1988), 'West Ham Utd F.C. and the Beginnings of Professional Football in East London, 1895–1914', *Journal of Contemporary History*, **13**, pp. 211–32; E. Dunning (1971), 'The Development of Modern Football', in E. Dunning (ed.), *The Sociology of Sport*, London: Frank Cass; J. Walvin (1975), *The People's Game*, London: Allen Lane.
3. Walvin, ibid., pp. 2–3.
4. Dunning, op. cit., p. 136.
5. See Geoffrey Green (1953), *Official History of the Football Association*, London: The Naldrett Press; see also Steven Tischler (1981), *Footballers and Businessmen*, New York: Holmes and Meier.

6. See Tischler, ibid., p. 34.
7. Stephen Wagg (1984), *The Football World*, Brighton: Harvester, p. 6.
8. Wagg, ibid., p. 7.
9. Patrick Murphy, 'Notes on the Relationship between Directors and Supporters of Leicester Fosse and Leicester City F.C., 1894–1960', unpublished paper, p. 5.
10. Murphy, ibid.
11. See Mason, op. cit., p. 39. The most recent share issue, at Newcastle in October 1990, required a minimum purchase of £100. It failed to attract sufficient interest and the share issue was abandoned.
12. ibid., p. 41.
13. ibid., p. 38.
14. ibid., p. 38.
15. ibid., p. 37.
16. Quoted in Murphy's unpublished paper, p. 15.
17. *The Supporter*, (official organ of the NFFSC) (1935), **2** (2).
18. Personal interview with Tony Pullein, Secretary of the NFFSC in the 1970s, April 1990.
19. Dated 25 July 1912.
20. Murphy, op. cit., p. 11.
21. ibid., p. 15.
22. A BBC TV 'Sportsnight' report in November 1990 estimated eighty of the ninety-two League Clubs in England to be technically insolvent.
23. Vamplew, op. cit., p. 17.
24. *Athletic News*, 16 March 1903, p. 1.
25. *Leicester Mercury*, 23 September 1911. I am particularly grateful to Patrick Murphy of the Centre for Football Research for access to his primary research and collection of press cuttings from the *Mercury*.
26. Letter to the *Leicester Mercury*, 1 May 1913.
27. Extracts from letters in the *Leicester Mercury*, 16 January 1924.
28. Extracts from letters in the *Leicester Mercury*, 10 May 1923.
29. As Murphy argues in his unpublished paper, many fans only got 'active' during particular crises at the Club. Once the problems died down, so did supporters' activities.
30. S. Jones (1988), *Sport, Politics and the Working Class*, Manchester, Manchester University Press, pp. 74ff.
31. ibid., p. 90.
32. ibid., p. 94.
33. ibid., p. 83.
34. ibid., p. 152.
35. ibid., p. 107 (quoted from *Daily Herald*, 9 and 13 August 1929).
36. National Federation AGM Minutes, 1965, p. 61.
37. N. Fishwick (1989), *English Football and Society, 1910–1950*, Manchester, Manchester University Press, p. 57.
38. 'Is Prejudice Against Supporters Clubs Justified?', correspondent in *Topical Times*, 10 September 1927, p. 231.
39. ibid.
40. National Federation AGM Minutes (1969), p. 69.
41. *The Supporter*, **1**, (1), September 1934, p. 3.
42. *F.A. News* (1957) **VII** (2), September.
43. See *The Supporter*, op. cit., pp. 3–8.
44. Personal interview with Jim Hamill, President, Coventry City SC, February 1990.

45. The Advisory Committee for the Club retains one place for the Chair of the Supporters' club, 1990.
46. C. E. Sutcliffe, 'Supporters Clubs with Strange Ideas', *Topical Times*, 10 March 1934, p. 339.
47. Tischler, op. cit., p. 112.
48. Quoted in ibid., p. 117.
49. There does seem to have been at least one previous attempt at federating supporters' clubs before 1914, in the north of England (see *The Supporter* (1934), 1 (1), September).
50. National Federation AGM Minutes (1958), p. 18.
51. *The Supporter* (1934), 1, (1), p. 2.
52. See National Federation 'Conference Notes' (1964), p. 29. This writer has photocopies of but four issues of *The Supporter* — the first edition, of October 1934, and three editions (September, November and December) of 1935. It seems unlikely that any other issues have survived.
53. *The Supporter* (1934), 1 (1), p. 5.
54. ibid., p. 2.
55. ibid., p.2.
56. The figures, inevitably, are estimates as the National Federation had little information about its member clubs. In the National Federation AGM Minutes of 1948, there are recorded 131 supporters' clubs represented with thirty-one apologies for absence. In other National Federation literature in 1948, 'some 200 Supporters Clubs' is mentioned as the membership.
57. *Sport Weekly Magazine*, 21 August 1948, p. 14. (The Federation used two pages in this magazine as its *Gazette*.)
58. *Sport Weekly Magazine*, 28 August 1948, p. 14.
59. National Federation AGM Minutes, 1948.
60. Wagg, op. cit., p. 32.
61. In the Mayor of Scarborough's address to the 1965 AGM, he urges the delegates to bring their children to the seaside then adds: 'looking around I ought to say your grandchildren'. Minutes, p. 5.
62. National Federation AGM Minutes (1948), p. 1.
63. National Federation AGM Minutes (1953), p. 6.
64. See the Federation's *Newsletter*, March 1978, under the headline, 'F.A. Support at Last'.
65. In the *Official History of the Football Association* there is no reference to any relationship with the game's supporters.
66. See *F.A. News* (1962) **XII** (5), December.
67. It is mentioned in the first edition of *The Supporter*, 1934.
68. This topic was discussed at many AGMs including 1948, 1953, 1954, 1956, 1958. In 1961, the Everton SC representative rejects the idea of the Federation getting its own allocation.
69. National Federation AGM (1963), pp. 28–9.
70. Morris Marples (1954), *A History of Football*, London: Secker & Warburg, p. 214.
71. See Dunning, Murphy and Williams (1988), *The Roots of Football Hooliganism*, London: Routledge.
72. *The Chester Report* (1968), pp. 61–2.
73. Ian Taylor (1971), 'Football Mad: A Speculative Sociology of Football Hooliganism', in E.G. Dunning (ed.), *Sociology of Sport*, London: See also Taylor (1971), 'Soccer Consciousness and Soccer Hooliganism', in S. Cohen (ed.), *Images of Deviance*, Harmondsworth: Penguin.
74. 'Football Mad . . .', op. cit., p. 372.

75. 'Soccer Consciousness . . .', op. cit., p. 160.
76. ibid., p. 145.
77. ibid., p. 158.
78. National Federation AGM Minutes (1964), p. 15.
79. National Federation AGM Minutes (1965), p. 12.
80. Personal interview, Jim Hamill, Current President, Coventry SC, recorded in February 1990.
81. National Federation AGM Minutes (1969), p. 81.
82. National Federation AGM Minutes (1969), p. 83.
83. National Federation AGM Minutes (1978), p. 13. See also AGM Minutes (1979), pp. 25-6.
84. For example, at Fulham FC. See National Federation AGM Minutes (1967), p. 71.
85. See R. W. Coles, 'Football as a Surrogate Religion', in *Sociological Yearbook of Religion in Britain, 1975*, Vol. 6, pp. 61-77.
86. Fishwick, op. cit., pp. 58-9 (my emphasis).
87. Fishwick makes this point. See ibid., p. 66.
88. C. Edwardes, 'The New Football Mania', *The Nineteenth Century*, October 1982, p. 627.
89. Fishwick, op. cit., p. 150.

7
Playing at home: British football and a sense of place

John Bale

British football is currently witnessing a series of developments that promise (or threaten) to sever the sport–place bond which has traditionally linked the football club with the locality in which its ground is sited. These developments may be interpreted as modernising tendencies and may include the continuing nationalisation and internationalisation of the game. Manifestations of such modernisation include (a) the spatial expansion of the geographical margins within which players are recruited, (b) the large number of scenarios which have been drawn up for more rationally located stadiums which, following the Taylor Report, are presented as being suburban and multi-purpose, and (c) the changing architectural styles of stadiums whereby the incrementally developed traditional ground is threatened with replacement by 'container architecture' or the concrete bowl. It is against the background of these tendencies that this chapter is set. It is already evident, however, that such events will not simply 'happen'. The various actors on the urban stage on which British football is set are not passive pawns at the mercy of the rationalistic tendencies currently at work, and this chapter's aim is to illustrate how the future map of British football is likely to emerge as a contested outcome of action by a variety of football-related activist groups in the urban environment.

The chapter falls into three sections. The first reviews the ways in which the football (soccer) ground can, despite tendencies which create what Meyrowitz[1] calls 'no sense of place', nevertheless be viewed as a source of what Yi Fu Tuan refers to as 'topophilia',[2] or a sense of place. Secondly, it stresses that, for many, the stadium presents a contrary image and that for many the stadium contributes to 'landscapes of fear'.[3] In each case the behavioural implications of such attitudes are explored by looking at cases of resistance and local political activism in the football context. A third section explores the implications of such attitudes and such activism for the currently debated possibility of the suburbanisation of the British football industry. Many recent studies have focussed on the feelings of a smaller minority of fans ('hooligans'), and the meaning of the game to other fans, and more particularly non-fans, has been underresearched; this chapter makes a tentative move towards filling this gap.

The football stadium and topophilia

The word 'topophilia', as defined by Tuan, refers to all the human being's 'affective ties with the material environment' and, in the present context, the situations in which football 'couples sentiment with place'.[4] While it may not be the strongest of human emotions, place-attachment or a sense of place is regarded by many as certainly contributing to the quality of life.[5] Edward Relph has stated that landscapes and places matter. They are not just incidental visual backgrounds to other social concerns but are part of our being that enter directly into the quality of our lives by providing countless small pleasures.[6] I will concentrate here on five kinds of sources to support the view that the British football ground is a potent source of topophilia, concentrating on both its physical (i.e. buildings and physical spaces) and the more mystical (or quasi-religious) landscapes. These categories are not mutually exclusive and are intended solely for convenience and organisation.

(a) The stadium as a sacred place

Football has often been viewed as a surrogate religion and it has been argued that if it fulfils the same human and social functions as real religions it should be analysed as if it were one.[7] Many observers have alluded to the stadium as a much loved place or a sacred place, analogous to a cathedral. One American observer, for example, calls the baseball park a 'sacred space', players seen as priests who represent us in a liturgy (the game) that is 'part of a sacred tradition'.[8] Coakley adopts a more cautious view, seeing team sports as having some religious characteristics but lacking others.[9] yet from a topophilic perspective, few would deny that Tuan's recognition of a sacred place as one being identified with overpowering significance[10] must undoubtedly apply to the football stadium. And such sentiments do not only relate to the great football stadiums; modest grounds, threatened with closure as part of the commercial imperatives presently characterising the sport, elicit responses such as that quoted in a match programme of humble Fourth Division club Chester, whose traditional ground (Sealand Road) was vacated in 1990. A dedicated supporter commented:

Sealand Road has been part of my life for 30 years; it's more than a football ground; it's a way of life not just to me but to thousands of people alive and dead whose lives have revolved around a match at the stadium. It is more than bricks and mortar, it's almost something spiritual.

A recent book on English football between the wars concluded that the football ground was the Labour Party at prayer.[11] While such a view may overstate the percentage of the working class who actually visit a football ground, the religious analogy remains valid in the early 1990s. Perhaps the nearest that football came to what Ian Taylor called a mass popular religious rite[12] was in the post-Hillsborough scenes at both the Sheffield Wednesday ground itself and at Anfield where one goalmouth, bedecked with flowers, wreaths and other football memorabilia, was turned into a memorial to those killed in the Sheffield disaster. Mourners filed slowly past as they would at a cemetery. The stadium, not a church, was selected for this rite, making it a sure site for topophilic sentiments.

Anfield has also been the scene of other quasi-religious events, signifying its much-loved character. The ashes of deceased fans have been scattered over the pitch or buried beneath the terraces; even a stadium cat lies buried beneath one goal line. Such identification of the stadium as a sacred place is not restricted to Liverpool.

(b) The stadium as scenic space

Although it is undoubtedly true that, in the football context as elsewhere, a sense of place has less to do with the aesthetic appreciation of landscape than with mixing with people whom one likes,[13] it can nevertheless be argued that there is a current tendency to turn distinctive places into anonymous concrete spaces. There is little doubt that the majority of grounds possess a sense of place (or *genius loci*), the nature of which has been brilliantly caught by Simon Inglis.[14] Over time, places develop a character that transcends the behaviour of particular people at one point in time,[15] possessing a symbolism that the architect had never intended.[16] But the love of the stadium is not rooted in a conscious awareness of any merits of design. It possesses, instead, what Relph calls an authentic sense of place which is, above all, that of being inside and belonging to your place both as an individual and as a member of a community, and to know this without reflecting on it.[17] Such authenticity may become increasingly lost in the architecture of the developments which threaten to change the landscape and location of British football.

American geographer Karl Raitz[18] has argued that enjoyment and gratification from the sport experience is, in part, derived from the landscape ensemble in which the game is played. The overall ensemble is made up of several elements — the layout of the terraces, the stands, odd bits and pieces of architecture and, in many grounds, views of the town in which it is found. Replace the traditional English stadium with a concrete bowl and the number of elements — the sources of gratification — are reduced. So too is the visual connection between the stadium and the town. In aspiring to a rational, universal space, 'sports saucers' succeed only in defining 'a non-place, rather an antiplace, hostile to the bounds imposed by locale and history'.[19]

Such reduced gratification from the football experience would be seen by Relph as typifying the paradox of modern landscapes — paradoxical because while intending and appearing to be beneficial (cleaner, safer, more comfortable, more convenient), the analytical and scientific planning and design has resulted in 'over-humanised landscapes possessing reduced potential for spontaneity and diminishing the quality of life, sadly, quietly, unobtrusively'.[20]

Such comments have been viewed as being academic and élitist,[21] seemingly distanced from the views of the footballers and fans who actually frequent the stadiums. The views of 'insiders', however, confirm the reduced gratification obtained from the brave new world of British football. The new (1989) suburban stadium of Fourth Division Scunthorpe United is seen by fanzine columnist Steve Beauchampe as 'a production line stadium, like a Ford; good quality, compact, functional and characterless'.[22] Similar comments, laced with traditional masculinity, had appeared in *Foul* (Britain's first 'alternative' football magazine) almost twenty years earlier where it was noted that 'football is not about covered stadiums, padded seats, ice cream and women and kids. It's about hitching, getting pissed, shouting, standing . . .'.[23] A decade later, *Off the Ball* observed that 'in promoting itself as just another arm of the wider entertainments industry . . . the game is reduced to ritzy-glitzy hype, heavily commercialised with forced and ordered excitement.'[24]

Players also dislike the multi-purpose, anonymous grounds with running tracks separating the game from the crowd, a layout which also exceeds the optimal viewing situation for spectators[25] for whom it might be interpreted as a sport space, rather than a football place. What is more, the landscape of the stadium has increasingly assumed that of a fortress, a place to be defended and, at the same time, a place of containment, surveillance, and what Michel Foucault called 'disciplinary partitioning'.[26] Indeed, *Discipline and Punish*, Foucault's book on the development of the modern penal system, sometimes seems to be describing recent changes in the football stadium as much as the birth of the prison.

(c) The stadium as home

Tuan noted that familiarity breeds affection when it does not breed contempt[27] and many football fans possess bonds with 'their' stadium which can be likened to ties with home. One example illustrates this form of topophilia. In 1985 London's Charlton Athletic commenced a ground-sharing scheme with Crystal Palace whose ground, Selhurst Park, was located 11 km away from their own, The Valley. The affection for the 'home turf' was reflected in comments in the Charlton fanzine, *Voice of the Valley*, following the move to Selhurst Park:

> It was just a football club leaving its ground, but to many, many people it was so much more. For the older fans it was the destruction of something that had run like a thread through their lives and for those of us who knew The Valley's past only at second hand it was the crushing of a dream. Charlton's moonlight flit was a cruel human tragedy that found no expression in the accountant's figures.[28]

Feelings against the move were extremely strong, the details of the campaign against it being described fully from the insiders' perspective in the fanzine. The successful campaign to return the club to The Valley was fought at an explicitly political level with a 'Valley Party' fighting local elections and obtaining a surprising percentage of the vote (exceeding 20 per cent in some places). *The Voice* was able to announce, 'we're going home!' Following plans to return to The Valley, the fanzine editorialised thus:

> We know that there are people who argue that they support the team and not the

ground, but they miss the point. The two cannot be separated without compromising the club's identity. Do that and you lose the deep emotional hold that even today football clubs exert over their supporters. Now, in the nick of time, the soul of Charlton Athletic will be recovered.[29]

It is often the ground, not the area within which it is found, that is home. A recent example which typified such a love of place was the battle for Craven Cottage, home of Fulham FC, in west London. But fans' sensitivity to 'place' and geographic distance were illustrated by the way in which, having lost the battle for 'the Cottage' to property developers, fans fought to keep the club in its own borough, rather than move to more distant pastures. Similar struggles are typified by the desire of Bristol Rovers fans to have the club move back to its 'home' from its (temporary) location in Bath and the successful lobbying by fans of Scottish clubs Heart of Midlothian and Hibernian against a possible merger. In 1984, Luton FC considered moving 25 km north to the new city of Milton Keynes; the proposal caused a furore in Luton. It was a decision which was said to be tearing the club from its most loyal supporters.[30] Such intense identification between people and places suggests that football grounds are, for many, examples of Relph's authentic places (about which fans have an unselfconscious sense of place), given the sentiment and attachment generated by them.

A 1970s study revealed that the London club Chelsea would simply not be 'Chelsea' if it relocated over a few kilometres in within the borough.[31] Examples of fan resistance to the relocation plans of clubs like Oxford, Reading, Fulham, Brighton, Luton, Bristol and Chester (to name a few) confirm a strength of attachment to place in which (part of) the community seems to be competing, with a degree of success, with the forces of capital, something apparently almost impossible in the United States where franchise moves are commonplace.[32] Such commitment to a football club is the conversion of a relatively passive form of topophilia to one of resistance and political activism and can be viewed as a reaction to the consumer-commodified orientation of football, symbolised by the shared or relocated suburban stadium.

(d) The stadium as a tourist place

Although Relph tends to deride tourist places because they are directed towards outsiders,[33] it has been suggested that tourism is, almost by definition, a pleasure trip.[34] In several cases the football stadium has become a tourist attraction, irrespective of any game being played there. For DM1 the tourist can enter the 1972 Olympic Stadium in Munich; the Berlin Olympic Stadium is on the itinerary of many tourists, and guided tours are provided at Wembley Stadium, Anfield and Old Trafford, the latter also having its own museum. In the tourist office in central Liverpool, the visitor is invited to enjoy a 'soccer city' weekend and it is argued by the Merseyside Tourist Authority that Anfield is a 'category 1 tourist attraction', that is, one that is 'unique to Merseyside or capable of attracting national or international visitors'.[35]

The number of football grounds presented as tourist sites, based on what are (at least presented as) much-loved places, would increase if the suggestions of Canter and his associates were implemented. They see the football heritage as a potent source for education about the game and suggest that 'this can be achieved by means of exhibitions, trails, audio-visual shows, theatre, interpretive panels, events, leaflets and bookings at heritage (football) sites'.[36] Pressures for preservation and museumisation may lead to post-modern architectural forms for new or renovated stadiums. At what stage it will become difficult to destroy stadiums because of their heritage potential remains to be seen; no precedent exists in Britain.

(e) Place pride and local patriotism

The role of football in producing pride in place (and its perversion into football hooliganism) has been thoroughly documented and needs little labouring here. Allusions to football, place-pride and social bonding have tended to be non-research-based, however, and studies which explore the actual feelings and attitudes of people towards their local team's success (or even survival) are few in number. A study by Derrick and McRory into Sunderland's (surprise) FA Cup Final win over Leeds United in 1973 remains an isolated example of research which explored residents' enhanced self-image through sports success. The Cup victory of an unfashionable club put the town on the map; one company executive commented on the effect of the club's success in this way:

Speaking for our company, [it has had] a tremendous effect. There's a different atmosphere in the whole place, they're all working a damn sight harder. They're much more enthusiastic. They've got something to talk about, rather than just moan. I envisage it will go on for a while yet.[37]

How long such sport-induced place-pride lasts, or who benefits from it most, remains to be fully explored.

Such place-pride traditionally resided in the local club — a focus for community bonding and the source of 'reconstruction' of some former *Gemeinschaft*. One result of modernist tendencies within the sport has been the undoubted reduction in the extent of spatial circumscription of many clubs' support. The concentration of television coverage on four or five major clubs permits the distant, as well as the local, viewer to become an instant fan. Manchester United has fan clubs nation-wide and over half of Liverpool's supporters are said to travel over thirty miles to watch a home game. Such distancing of support has been aided not only by television serving to reduce — even eliminate — the 'tyranny of distance', but also by the abolition of the maximum wage for professional footballers in the early 1960s (whereby clubs in large population centres could maximise their market potential and increasingly 'buy success'). In addition, the increase in car ownership in the post-war period and the growth of the motorway network have allowed the more discriminating spectator to by-pass the smaller clubs.

Even so, it is difficult to find anything other than the national sport which so readily provides a sense of place-pride. No other regularised ritual exists to project a place-name to a national audience each week. It is hardly surprising, therefore, that places without League clubs actively seek their presence while the civic leaders of places likely to lose a club through demotion or extinction rally in support of its survival.

Football and landscapes of fear

While football and other sports have frequently been promoted as 'representing' the communities within which they are found, doubts exist about the extent to which they are actually 'authorised' by members of the locality.[38] With changing social structures in the vicinity of grounds, the shift of the urban population towards the suburbs and the well-documented 'embourgeoisement' of the game itself,[39] the relationship between the club and its immediate public has changed. There is increasing evidence that some fans and many members of the local community perceive the football club and its activities as landscapes of fear or sources (not of topophilia, but) of topophobia.

Canter's recent work indicates that about one-third of football fans have been worried at some time while attending a football match.[40] Misbehaviour by fans and crushing by crowds or by mounted police in enclosed spaces were the most frequently cited sources of fear and violence. Research at the Leicester University Centre for Football Research has shown that of a sample of members of supporters' clubs, over half had, at some time, felt threatened at games. The most frequently cited (21.3 per cent) venue at which they perceived such fear was Anfield. Nearly 12 per cent stated that they would not visit Stamford Bridge (home of Chelsea) because of fear of hooliganism.[41] For many people, therefore, the stadium has become a modern landscape of fear.

A very large proportion of the general public also seems to view the vicinity of the stadium in such a light. In 1989, one hundred randomly selected members of the public were asked if they would expect to experience 'nuisances' and 'serious nuisances' if they lived within 2 km of a League ground. As many as 96 per cent felt that they would experience (at least) nuisances while 52 per cent thought serious nuisances would be experienced. As distance of hypothetical residence increased from the ground, the proportion of respondents claiming that nuisances would be felt declined.

It is very likely, however, that such perceptions are based on a moral panic because only 2 per cent of the population actually visit a football match with any regularity. The reactions cited above need, therefore, to be compared with those of people who actually live near League grounds. To do this, interviews were held in early 1989 and 4,597 residents (53 per cent male, 47 per cent female), each of whom lived within 2 km of one of thirty-seven of the ninety-one English league grounds. Compared with the 96 per cent of the general public who felt that football-induced nuisances might be experienced living near football grounds, the figure for those who actually did was only 41 per cent, with only 8 per cent feeling that football created a serious nuisance. The difference between the anticipated and actual ('public' and 'resident') view of football nuisances might be termed the 'moral panic effect'.[42] Although far from absent, the negative impact of football matches is greatly exaggerated by the general public.

The nature of football nuisances

Several studies have shown that hooliganism is cited as a nuisance by a smaller number of residents than spillovers such as car parking and traffic,[43] providing further evidence of a moral panic effect, i.e. media amplification of infrequent outbursts of hooliganism and the avoidance of problems for residents created by other football nuisances. Near some clubs around 90 per cent of match-day vehicles are parked in residential streets. While less newsworthy than crowd disorders, such traffic effects are, nevertheless, likely to impose significant stress on local people.

A recent study indicated that whereas 10 per cent of those interviewed claimed that football hooliganism was a nuisance, the respective figures for car parking and traffic were 18 and 22 per cent. Such figures obviously obscure a good deal of variation between localities but in only two cases out of thirty-seven was hooliganism mentioned as a nuisance by a larger proportion of residents than parked cars or traffic. Around some grounds the presence of pedestrians and even noise were also cited by more people than hooliganism.[44]

It is not only residents who consume football's negative effects and it is well known that some retail outlets close down on match days. Of 766 retailers interviewed in the vicinity of thirty-seven grounds, however, 65 per cent claimed that no apparent change in revenue occurred on average match days. Just over a quarter (27 per cent) experienced an increase and only 8 per cent stated that they experienced a decrease. Fifteen per cent of shopkeepers said that they found an increase in shoplifting on match days. Again it would seem that the negative impact on the retail, as well as the residential, environment may have been exaggerated in previous accounts.

Considerable variations exist in the extent to which people identify a particular event as a nuisance. Evidence from residents living around three London grounds shows that non-fans (75 per cent of those interviewed) are more likely to view matches as nuisances than fans. If all local residents were fans (which increasingly they are not), the number perceiving football nuisances would be halved. Little evidence exists, however, to suggest that significantly more women than men perceive football matches as nuisances.

The most obvious geographic factor influencing the likelihood of consuming football-induced nuisances is the distance of residence from a stadium (see above). The spatial limit of such nuisances is usually defined by a 'nuisance field' with the intensity of nuisance gradually declining towards its limits. Such impacts vary considerably in extent and in intensity. A First Division club set in a residential area may possess a nuisance field extending over 2 km away from its ground. The intensity of such negative impacts may range from those creating a mild nuisance to those producing severe annoyance and resulting in various forms of local resistance and activism. Although generally declining in intensity with distance from stadiums, in some cases the limitation placed on parking in the immediate vicinity of the ground, the nature of local land use, and more stringent policing which may have displaced hooligans to less obvious parts of the urban area, have resulted in 'outliers' of football nuisance being found at greater distances from the stadium.

Another source of variation is between, rather than within, urban areas and results from the changing geography of the Football League. Broadly speaking, the geographic centre of gravity of footballing success has been shifting south in recent decades.[45] Clubs in the north of England, with obvious exceptions such as Liverpool and Manchester United, have been experiencing declining fortunes. These geographical changes have had two effects. First, numbers attending games in the traditional centres of the north have declined and those visiting several grounds in the south have relatively increased. The shift in emphasis to the south has brought unprecedented crowds to some grounds where large attendances were traditionally unknown, e.g. Wimbledon, Bourne-mouth and Oxford. These are League clubs on sites more appropriate to non-League clubs. Not only is there a positive relationship between the percentage of local residents who perceive football nuisances and divisional status of clubs, the average percentage scores for the four divisions being 45 (Division One), 39, 29 and 22 (Division Four); in addition, the average nuisance score for areas around clubs in the south (45 per cent) exceeds the respective score for clubs elsewhere (27 per cent). For each division of the League, the average nuisance scores for southern clubs exceeds those for clubs in the remainder of the country.

At a time when ground-sharing is being regularly suggested, it is also salutary to note that of the thirty-seven grounds surveyed, the one around which (i.e. within 2 km) the largest percentage (73 per cent) of local residents claimed to perceive football nuisances was Selhurst Park — 'home' of both Crystal Palace and Charlton and the only ground in the League used by two League clubs. Local residents therefore experience football every (rather than every other) weekend during the season.

Resistance and activism

Only 0.16 per cent of respondents who claimed that they found football a nuisance obtained any direct form of compensation (i.e. tax reductions). This does not mean, however, that residents are powerless to resist the more noxious activities of football clubs. Indeed, given changes that are currently taking place in British football, resistance through local activism seems to have been remarkably successful. Such activism seems to have occurred in two kinds of situation. The first is where clubs have been involved in certain *in situ* attempts to diversify their economic activities; the second is where clubs have considered relocation.

Clubs at almost every level of the League are currently involved in seeking ways of diversifying their economic base in order to improve their precarious financial states.[46] Diversification may involve the development, near the ground, of such facilities as sports halls, hotels, convention facilities, offices, retailing, social clubs, etc., or the use of the stadium itself for purposes other than football, e.g. other sports, religious gatherings or rock concerts. A study in the mid-1980s showed that fifteen of forty-two clubs (36 per cent) surveyed used their grounds for non-footballing activities.[47] More recently a survey conducted by the Royal Town Planning Institute found that about one-quarter of all League clubs were considering commercial developments on, or adjacent to their grounds.[48] It seems likely that in such cases the negative effects of site usage would be less noxious than those generated by football, though as yet evidence is very limited.[49] Some potential uses for football stadiums, however, may involve converting the relatively passive acceptance of nuisance and may give way to forms of micro-political activism.

A good example is afforded by a coalition of twenty-one community groups living in proximity to the imposing Villa Park, home of Birmingham's Aston Villa FC. In 1988, Aston Villa, as part of their plans to broaden their economic base, hosted a Bruce Springsteen rock concert at their stadium. While residents, many of whom had not the slightest interest in football, had accepted with relative passivity the bi-weekly nuisances induced by football (recognising that the football club was there first), the club's newer, non-footballing activities tipped them over the threshold from passivity to activism. When the football club applied to the local authority for permission to hold two more such concerts in 1989, the coalition of residents' groups undertook a carefully orchestrated campaign to oppose the application. For them, they claimed, the 1988 event had led to a 'state of siege' in the local area. The environmental impact of the event was graphically described by the solicitor acting for them in these terms:

For the duration of the performances and extending in various ways through the preceding and following 24 hours, floodlights, noise, traffic and the mass of people coming into the area brought ordinary activity to an end. Some businesses had to close through lack of parking space. Residents over a substantial area had great difficulty reaching home. Once there they could not sleep or hear ordinary speech. The presence of a mass of people, far exceeding football crowds at the ground, sometimes behaving badly under the influence of alcohol, was intimidating. There was widespread urinating in doorways and a deluge of litter. Elderly people were frightened.[50]

The effect of the campaign was that Birmingham City Council rejected Aston Villa's application, a case of one part of the community triumphing over the financial interests of another group claiming to represent the locality.

Activism against football as a potential (rather than actual) nuisance may come from residents who view with alarm and concern the prospect of a football ground in their 'back yard'. For such people a football stadium is perceived as a noxious facility and in such circumstances local defence of an unspoilt area is readily activated. The example of Oxford United's attempts to suburbanise is a good case study.

Between 1965 and 1986 nineteen different sites were explored by the Oxford club as possible alternatives to their existing Manor ground, a site more appropriate to Oxford's former non-League status than for a club aspiring to the First Division. Despite the club's ambitions to move, opposition to suburban relocation has come from both the planning departments (of Oxford and neighbouring authorities) and from articulate middle-class suburbanites possessing antagonistic attitudes towards football grounds. A typical comment from such opposition appeared in the *Oxford Mail* in 1985:

We are told that Oxford needs a new football stadium. Who is 'Oxford' in this context? What is the average number of spectators at a match? Ten thousand would be an over estimate, and not all of these would be city dwellers. What about the views of the other hundred thousand city residents? I suggest that the vast majority of these would be against the proposal . . . There must be many who are silent but would be happy with no so-called 'first-class' football in Oxford at all.

Similar opposition came from residents of Milton Keynes at the time of Luton Town's proposal to locate there. Despite assurances from Luton supporters of the move that no visiting fans would be allowed, 'fear of violence and vandalism by football hooligans' by local councillors in Milton Keynes resulted in a unanimous rejection of the proposal.[51] Similar objections were also raised by rural residents to a proposal by Luton for a sports complex at a village north of the town, and by those living in a Bristol suburb to the proposal by Bristol Rovers to build a modern stadium there. Suburban objectors to football stadium development possess a well-developed negative (and inaccurate and exaggerated) image of the sport. A letter to the *Bristol Evening Post* in early 1989 summarised many residents' objections to the proposal (which was subsequently rejected) to site a new stadium for Bristol Rovers in the suburb of Mangotsfield which is, in fact, in the borough of Kingswood, not Bristol itself.

Violence, vandalism and abuse are common in all localities which have soccer stadia. We do not want that in Kingswood — especially when people from outside the district try to foist it upon us. The infrastructure of the area . . . will not support the influx of many thousands of people. There is no nearby railway station to cater for visiting supporters, and therefore all traffic will be confined to the roads. Parking will be random and affect a much wider area than the environs of the stadium . . . We do not want our roads and streets clogged with hundreds of extra cars . . . The noise level will be intolerable. (*Bristol Evening Post*, 1989)

Despite the observation of the Taylor Report that suburban sites possessed several advantages, opposition such as that noted above is broadly supported by the British planning system. For example, following the Taylor Report a mini-debate on football ground location took place in the pages of *The Planner*. The president of the Royal Town Planning Institute noted that there remained a case for inner city locations and that the importance of tradition and 'roots' should not be underemphasised, football grounds being seen as powerful urban symbols which are readily accessible to young and car-less fans. It was also stressed that the post-Taylor explosion of proposals for peripherally sited football grounds were often thinly disguised attempts to push retail schemes through an otherwise inpenetrable planning system.[52]

Senses of place and scenarios for stadium relocation

The feelings of local residents will need to be taken into account in the kind of scenarios for the suburbanisation of British football which were widely discussed following the Hillsborough disaster. *The Economist* argued that the need for larger, all-seated stadiums and adequate parking for today's car-owning spectators would force many clubs to acknowledge that, with their present locations, they were simply in the wrong places. Ancient club loyalties were described as 'sentimental' and shared grounds in low-density suburban sites were advocated.[53] The US model of big stadium complexes was seen as the brave new world of the 'peoples game', a world inhabited by rational, discriminating consumers who would be prepared to travel over considerable distances for a game. They would tend to possess what Relph termed 'inauthentic attitudes to place . . . essentially no sense of place, for it involves no awareness of the deep and symbolic significance of places and no appreciation of their identities'.[54]

Despite the scenarios for British football, outlined above, few clubs have actually taken the step of locating in new stadiums at the urban edge or beyond. In recent years the only ones to have done so are Scunthorpe and St. Johnstone, Walsall's move being hardly 'suburban'. Of significance to the present chapter, however, is the fact that when plans for such developments are drawn up resistance is likely to come from restrictive planning practices on the one hand and articulate suburban action groups on the other. Further-more, objections to relocation will be made by hard-core fans who prefer their club to remain in its traditional site. The essential point is that relocation of football grounds will be contested between those with topophilic attitudes towards the game and those for whom it presents a source of topophobia.

Should the future of football be in suburban stadiums, they will have to be located within compatible land uses. Siting decisions will have to be particu-larly sensitive to the distance of the stadium from existing residences. The new suburban stadium on the edge of Perth and home of St. Johnstone FC has generated more negative spillovers than local residents would have wished, the result of not simply more traffic than was expected, but the limited distance of the stadium from the edge of the urban area.[55] Sites in modern industrial zones might be the most logical solution, assuming that factories would not be operating at the times matches were being played. Such locations could provide double use of existing parking space. Such sites, however, would almost certainly be loathed by fans. New stadium proposals are therefore likely to attract active political involvement from several sources. Post-Hillsborough speculation about new stadium complexes has used the language of economic rationality. When decisions to site new grounds are debated, there will be a need to take account of the varied forms of activism and possible conflict which such proposals may provoke.

Of course, the forms of neighbourhood activism, either by fans in order to retain a club (e.g. Charlton) in its existing location, or by NIMBY-motivated residents to resist a stadium in their 'back yard' (e.g. Bristol Rovers), are invariably viewed as the outcome of contested space.

Conclusion

This chapter has shown how football can provide for some members of the public a source of topophilia, its stadiums being landscapes of pleasure, and for others a source for topophobia with football's landscapes of fear. I have focused on the meaning which football generates for different groups in society. The role of the fan should certainly not be marginalised and, as Osgerby has noted, the game's ideological realignment towards commercial consumerism has never circumvented the possibility of fan influence.[56] At the same time, I have shown how the pressures for modernisation and consumerism with the promises of suburban stadiums have served only to alienate the very people whom the 'modern' game would wish to attract, namely the suburban middle classes.

The apparently successful number of community initiatives to resist change in the geography of British football contrasts dramatically with the situation in North America where professional team sports are typified by an almost permanent state of locational flux. Comparative studies of the football–community nexus, the nature (and strength) of feeling towards both positive and negative spillovers from the football stadium, and the varying pressures for locational change, might provide valuable insights into the changing nature of football in Europe.

Notes

1. Joshua Meyrowitz (1985), *No Sense of Place*, New York: Oxford University Press.
2. Yi-Fu Tuan (1974), *Topophilia*, Englewood Cliffs: Prentice Hall, 1974. The word 'topophilia' was apparently used earlier in G. Bachelard (1969), *The Poetics of Space*, Boston: Beacon Press.
3. Yi-Fu Tuan (1979), *Landscapes of Fear*, Oxford: Blackwell.
4. Tuan, *Topophilia*, op. cit.
5. John Eyles (1985), *Senses of Place*, Warrington: Silverbrook Press. Edward Relph (1989), 'Responsive Methods, Geographical Imagination and the Study of Landscapes', in Audrey Kobayashi and Suzanne Mackenzie (eds), *Remaking Human Geography*, Boston: Unwin Hyman, pp. 149–63.
7. Robert Coles (1975), 'Football as a "Surrogate" Religion', in Michael Hill (ed.), *A Sociological Yearbook of Religion in Britain*, vol. 8, London: SCM Press, pp. 61–77; note also Siegfried von Korzfleisch (1970), 'Religious Olympism', *Social Research*, **37**, pp. 231–6.
8. Richard Lipsky (1981), *How We Play the Game*, Boston: Beacon Press.
9. Jay Coakley (1985), *Sociology of Sport*, St. Louis: Mosby.
10. Tuan, *Topophilia*, op. cit.
11. Nicholas Fishwick (1989), *English Football and Society*, Manchester: Manchester University Press.
12. Ian Taylor (1989), 'Hillsborough: 15 April 1989. Some Personal Contemplations', *New Left Review*, **177**, pp. 87–110.
13. Eyles, *Senses of Place*, op. cit., p. 26.
14. Simon Inglis (1987), *The Football Grounds of Great Britain*, London: Collins.
15. D. J. Walmsley (1988), *Urban Living*, London: Longman.
16. Mark Harrison, (1988), 'Symbolism, "Ritualism" and the Location of Crowds in Early Nineteenth Century English Towns', in Denis Cosgrove and Stephen Daniels (eds), *The Iconography of Landscape*, Cambridge: Cambridge University Press, pp. 194–213.
17. Edward Relph (1976), *Place and Placelessness*, London: Pion, p. 65.
18. Karl Raitz (1987), 'Perception of Sports Landscapes and Gratification in the Sport experience', *Sport Place*, **1**, (1), pp. 4–19.

19. Brian Neilson (1986) 'Dialogue with the City: The Evolution of the Baseball Park', *Landscape*, **29**, pp. 39–47.

20. Edward Relph (1981), *Rational Landscapes and Humanistic Geography*, London: Croom Helm.

21. Eyles, *Senses of Place*, op. cit., p. 73.

22. Steve Beauchampe (1989), 'Scunthorpe Living on the Edge', *Off the Ball*, **16**, pp. 5–6.

23. Quoted in Steve Redhead (1987), *Sing When You're Winning*, London: Pluto, pp. 47–9.

24. Steve Beauchampe (1986), 'Family Fodder', *Off the Ball*, November, p. 6.

25. Inglis, *Football Grounds*, op. cit.

26. Michel Foucault (1977), *Discipline and Punish*, Harmondsworth: Penguin.

27. Tuan, *Topophilia*, op. cit.

28. Rick Everitt (1989), 'Battle for the Valley', *Voice of the Valley*, **11**, pp. 22–8.

29. Editorial (1989), *Voice of the Valley*, **11**, p. 2. This and the previous example are only two of many more examples of topophilic sentiment found in insiders' comments in fanzines when ground changes are mooted. See also Inglis, *Football Grounds*.

30. Sir Norman Chester Centre for Football Research (1987), *The Luton Town Home Only Members Plan: Final Report*, Leicester: Leicester University, p. 8.

31. Jeff Bishop and R. Booth (1974), 'People's Images of Chelsea Football Club', *Working Paper* 10, Architectural Psychology Research Unit, Kingston Polytechnic.

32. Illustrated in John Bale (1989), *Sports Geography*, London: Spon, pp. 87–95.

33. Relph, *Place and Placelessness*, op. cit.

34. John Jakle (1987), *The Visual Elements of Landscape*, Amherst: University of Massachusetts Press, pp. 9–10.

35. Quoted in Richard Hill (1990), 'The Power of Place in Professional Soccer', unpublished undergraduate dissertation, Loughborough University, p. 52.

36. David Canter (1989), Miriam Comber and David Uzzell, *Football in its Place*, London: Routledge, pp. 160–3.

37. Derrick and Judy McRory (eds) (1973), 'Cup in Hand; Sunderland's Self-Image After the Cup', *Working Paper* 8, Centre for Urban Regional Studies, University of Birmingham.

38. Alan Ingham and Stephen Hardy (1984), 'Sport, Structuration, Subjugation and Hegemony', *Theory, Culture and Society*, **2**, pp. 85–103.

39. Chas Critcher (1979), 'Football Since the War', in John Clarke, Chas Critcher and Richard Johnson (eds), *Working Class Culture*, London: Hutchinson, pp. 161–84.

40. Canter, *Football in its Place*, op. cit.

41. Sir Norman Chester Centre, *Luton Town*, op. cit.

42. Stanley Cohen (1973), *Folk Devils and Moral Panics*, London: Paladin.

43. John Bale (1980), 'Football Clubs as Neighbours', *Town and Country Planning*, **49**, pp. 93–4; David Humphrys, Colin Mason and Steven Pinch (1983), 'The Externality Fields of Football Grounds: A Case Study of the Dell, Southampton', *Geoforum*, **14**, pp. 401–11.

44. John Bale (1990), 'In the Shadow of the Stadium: Football Grounds as Urban Nuisances', *Geography*, **75**, (4), pp. 325–334.

45. Bale, *Sports Geography*, pp. 96–7; John Connell (1985), 'Football and Regional Decline: Some Reflections', *Geography*, **70**, pp. 240–2. See also Peter Waylen and Andrew Snook (1990), 'Patterns of Regional Success in the Football League, 1921–1987', *Area*, **22**, (4), pp. 353–67.

46. Peter Sloane (1980), *Sport in the Market*, London: Institute of Economic Affairs.

47. Guy Oliver (1986), 'The Location and Relocation of Football League Clubs in

England and Wales', unpublished undergraduate dissertation, Geography Department, Southampton University.

48. Chris Shepley (1990), 'Planning and Football League Grounds', *The Planner*, **76**, (38), pp. 15–17.

49. Colin Mason and Richard Robins (1989), 'The Spatial Externality Fields of Football Stadiums: The Effects of Football and Non-footballing Uses at Kenilworth Road, Luton' (forthcoming).

50. Quoted in solicitor's statement at meeting of City of Birmingham General Purposes sub-committee, 13 April.

51. Sir Norman Chester Centre, *Luton Town*, op. cit.

52. 'The Game That Died', *The Economist*, 22 April 1989, p. 13.

53. Anthony Fyson (1990), 'Should Football Suburbanise?', *The Planner*, **76**, (5), 1990, p. 3; Chris Shipley, 'The Post-Taylor Bonanza', *The Planner*, **76** (16), p. 9.

54. Relph, *Place and Placelessness*, op. cit.

55. Andrew Moncrieff (1991), 'The Effect of Relocation on the Externality Effects of Football Grounds: The Case of St. Johnstone FC', unpublished undergraduate dissertation, Geography Department, Southampton University.

56. Bill Osgerby (1988), ' "We'll Support You Ever More": Conflict and Meaning in the History of a Professional Football Club', *British Society of Sports History Bulletin*, **8**, pp. 68–73.

8
An era of the end, or the end of an era? Football and youth culture in Britain[1]

Steve Redhead

This essay looks at aspects of the relationship between football, popular music and youth culture in Britain since the 1950s. It is predicated on the view that such 'history' is produced by competing discourses, texts and practices, as well as 'events'. This particular piece of work emanates from a larger, more comprehensive study of the nature of these social relations and their contemporary significance for football research in the New Europe. In the autumn of 1990, Glyn Ford, a Labour Euro-MP, caused a considerable stir in the mass media, and the European Parliament, by making allegations that the racist activity of skinhead gangs at football matches was an increasing problem and that a coordinated European response was necessary. In countries such as Holland and Germany it is certainly the case that this particular style of what the international media have dubbed 'football hooliganism' has manifested itself in recent years. In parts of Continental Europe much of the activity surrounding travel to, and attendance at, football matches in the mid–late 1980s and early 1990s constituted an almost satirically accurate impression, or caricature, of British football hooligan styles of the 1970s. However, despite the continued existence of racist chants and abuse at football matches in England in the 1990s (and clear evidence of increased racist street violence), there is little sign of much specifically skinhead soccer gang activity. In a sense that is partly, as this essay shows, because skinhead styles have fragmented historically in Britain and the subcultural theorists' claim for a homology — or fit — between a skin haircut, Doc Marten boots and fascist leanings has long ago been refuted. Moreover, and more importantly, there is reason to be cautiously optimistic about some of the changes in English soccer's 'style wars'[2] over the last few seasons. Carnival rather than fighting has become fashionable in Britain at sporting events — especially football — since the mid-1980s. At Italia '90 most English fans, as well as Scots and Irish, behaved in a way which was closer to the styles of spectating commonly found in Italy every

Sunday, testifying to the sea change since the days of the Heysel tragedy in May 1985. It was not, as some critics have suggested, that Italia '90 was the cause of this shift; it simply demonstrated the magnitude of the difference that such facets of football spectatorship (for instance, the explosion of football fanzines in Britain between 1985 and the present) had made. There are still many special differences between football spectating in Britain and Continental Europe, but there is a greater cross-fertilisation and homogenisation than ever before. What is significant, too, is that as a result of these changes a more peaceful return to European competition for English clubs including Liverpool over the next few years — after a ban of (excluding Liverpool) five years — can be anticipated than many ill-informed press critics and government spokespersons have suggested. Apart from odd incidents, such as the misbehaviour of Wales fans in Belgium and English fans' attack on an Irish pub in London, the 1990–1 season has been relatively trouble-free, thereby justifying UEFA's decision to lift the ban on English clubs and suggesting that they could allow more clubs back into Europe than is presently the case.

Part of the reason for this confusion is the continual association of skinhead style with football hooligan style, a mistaken connection made by academics and media commentators alike but not by fans who have regularly attended British football matches during the last twenty years. British skinhead youth styles only relatively briefly coincided with football hooliganism on any mass scale: from the seasons following the World Cup tournament in England in 1966 to the early 1970s. By this time the shaven heads, Doc Marten boots, Ben Sherman check shirts, half-mast, turned-up blue jeans and tight braces had all but disappeared from the football terraces and town centres because the style itself had metamorphosed into 'crombie' and other neo-skinhead, hard mod styles best exemplified in the Richard Allen 'cult' trash novels of the 1970s published by New English Library. This popular paperback series spawned titles which reflected the range of styles into which 'skinhead' had split — 'smoothies', 'sorts' (girls could play, too), 'boot boys' and inevitably, eventually, 'punk rock' — and were recalled in an ironic, parodic fashion by Stewart Home in his late 1980s reworking of the Allen tradition to historicise the rise and fall of the 'casuals' in a paperback pulp novel called *Pure Mania* published by Polygon. Skinhead styles were by then more frequently signifying 'anarcho-vegetarian hardcore punk' life style than anything remotely to do with the National Front. Furthermore, once he had disbanded The Smiths, the band's lead singer Morrissey, ever an obsessive pop archivist of the 1960s and 1970s, knowingly entitled a solo single 'Suedehead' to complete the picture.

By the onset of the early 1970s, too, 'glam rock'[3] had married together previously opposed subcultural styles. There was skinhead (Slade, for instance) and 'hippie' represented in the figures of David Bowie, Marc Bolan and Tyrannosaurus Rex — shorn of rock's counter-cultural mystique and pomp, Marc Bolan became, appropriately, just T. Rex. Garry Glitter, Glam's most tacky, and everlasting, star became a cheer leader for the British terraces up and down the country from 1973 onwards, as the chorus 'Come On, Come On' from the 'I'm The Leader of the Gang (I Am)' chart hit rang out inadvertently via 'Match of the Day' microphones and, deliberately, as the preferred soundtrack for countless TV documentaries on football and its hooligan problem long after even punk had come and gone. The Bay City Rollers pheomenon in 1974, also, quickly, manifested itself in terrace culture. The name of the game, even at this stage of the historical cycle, was diversity. Match days have long been a time for spotting a multitude of styles in a crowd, many of whom regarded — until relatively recently — the supposedly star professional players' hairstyles and clothing tastes as particularly 'naff'. The phrase 'footballers' perm' has been made into a four-letter word by football fanzine writers.

When punk exploded, or rather imploded, pop culture in 1976, and briefly into 1977, the game was in many ways up. Heavy policing in, around, and on the way to and from British soccer matches was well and truly institutionalised; segregation of away fans from the rest gave football grounds of this period the look of a training ground for a military exercise. Punks and teds (themselves survivors from an earlier clash between soccer and youth culture in the 1950s) may have fought running battles with each other in London's high streets but the English football terraces were, for once, becoming sharply politicised as right-wing neo-fascist groupings sought to extend their always fragile hold on young, mainly white working-class male fans. The Anti-Nazi League response was never as significant at football matches as it was on the streets, or at well-attended Rock Against Racism gigs[4] where *Temporary Hoarding* was the precursor of many football and music fanzines of the 1980s, but it undoubtedly helped to raise consciousness about the slide to the New Right which was already taking place in Britain — and elsewhere — and was consolidated with Margaret Thatcher's ascent to parliamentary power in 1979. Skinhead gang activity, and the 'return' of its style-leadership for many white, working-class males, was evident again in this mid–late 1970s period. Punk bands such as Jimmy Pursey's 'Sham 69, which took its name from abbreviated graffiti recalling skinhead territorial gang battles in the late 1960s, were constantly plagued by the crossover of skin style and neo-fascist organisations, though punk and skinhead figurations were often interchangeable by the late 1970s.[5] As the politics of youth styles became ever more confused, the efforts of 'two-tone' bands like The Specials, The Selecter, The Beat and Madness (another band plagued by neo-fascist hangers-on) managed to continue to break down the barriers between black and white, especially in terms of musical styles. The continued association of British skinhead style with racism and fascism manifested itself through the 1980s, though rarely at, or around, football stadiums. The connection was displayed first in some instances through 'Oi' music in the early 1980s and then, later, through specialist shops and low-key gigs, in a particularly lyrically nasty variant of 'hardcore' punk music which resonated in similar ventures amongst neo-nazi skinheads in European countries like Germany.

This much of the structure of the narratives which make up the histories of popular music culture and football in Britain is reasonably well known. What has, so far, been hidden from history is the relationship between casual youth culture and soccer and its eventual connection to a late 1980s 'mass' youth cultural phenomenon which, in 'global' culture terms, became represented in the imagery of 'Manchester' or more accurately 'Madchester'. This relationship, at one level, has also been important for attempts to justify the addition of the epithet 'postmodern' to youth culture since the 1970s. Much of the legitimation for this has come from a sense of playfulness with which British youth styles plundered the past of youth culture history and the debris of the urban streets, a claim for youth subcultures consistently made by writers like Dick Hebdige in the 1970s and 1980s. Yet its most obvious 'subversive' aspect has rarely been tackled; that is the complex challenge youth culture has made to established (and changing) notions of masculinity and sexuality in specific contexts such as pop and football. To excavate this we need to go back slightly in time to pick up the threads of youth cultural styles and football culture.

It is around the time of punk that we can rejoin the narrative; but it is not punk which gives us the signpost. By this period two significant factors were in operation. One was the continued phenomenon of 'Bowie boys' — and girls — who came under the influence of David Bowie's much-changing stage pop persona. This was, significantly, a 'gender-bending' persona which, along with Divine, predated by some years Marilyn and Boy George, as well as Marc Almond and others in the 1980s; as did Bowie's ambivalent pronouncement of his own 'bisexuality'. Bowie boys and girls acted out a multitude of exotic street performances. The 'fan as star' mode of youth culture had visibly come of age in the mid-1970s. By the time of Bowie's 'Low' album — with a cover showing the star in a duffle coat — both new musical territory (the LP experimented with European electronic styles which were to be influential in the 1980s) and fashion style poses were to be breached. Bowie's crossover mass-market entrance into film stardom came in the making of Walter Tevis's 'The Man Who Fell To Earth'. The film by Nicolas Roeg which was the origin of the duffle coat, helped to solidify a 'casual' style which was already picking up on remnants of mod from the mid-1960s as well as the fall-out from glam and the general apocalyptic mood of rip-up and wear from punk. The other important factor for the emergence of what is now referred to as casual style was the influence of Continental Europe.

The continued success of British football clubs in European competition was a crucial jumping-off point for the development of the casuals. Since — especially — Celtic's European Cup triumph in 1967, but arguably going back before that to West Ham United's Cup Winners' Cup success and Manchester United and Liverpool's stirring mid-1960s performances in Europe, British clubs had provided the opportunity for supporters to enjoy relatively cheap trips to the Continent. By 1977, Liverpool (most prominent amongst the leading clubs) were going for a historic treble of League, FA and European trophies. Manchester United's unexpected 2–1 victory at Wembley robbed Liverpool of the chance, but the unrestricted opportunities for fans to travel to and from the Continent of Europe were of more enduring significance. Increasingly, from the 1977–8 football season, which marks the 'official' birth of the casuals as a youth culture in pop history, European shops were divested of their wares — sometimes legally, more often illegally — as brand names such as Lois, Pringle, Lacoste, Adidas and so on started to take off on the terraces on a Saturday afternoon, as well as in the music clubs at night. Designer labels were ripped out, or razored off, in an ever increasing desire to get ahead. Cities such as Manchester, Liverpool, London, Glasgow and towns like Aberdeen became known for rapidly changing casual styles, the ebb and flow of such changes partially dependent on the relative success of the football clubs in the region, and how much of an entry into 'Europe' this had given them in any particular season. Casual itself as a label hid sharp and obsessive regional differences: London's 'chaps', Merseyside's 'scallies' and Manchester (Manc)'s 'perries', formerly Fred Perry Boys after Fred Perry shirts, soon just 'boys' or 'lads', reputedly terrorisers of a young Morrissey in late 1970s Manchester. By the late 1980s such original differences had been eroded in a mass-media application of the stereotype 'scally', originally meaning street-wise youth, possibly but not always delinquent, a derivative of 'scallywag', to almost anyone under 21 wearing baggy T-shirts, flared jeans and sporting a floppy fringe. Late 1980s differences, between and within, regions also became conflated by a hyper-hysterical labelling of the 'labellers'. According to the mass media, 'Scallies' were apparently everywhere: nicking goods, starting pop groups, selling pop concert tickets at inflated prices. One Manchester-based fanzine, *Bop Cassettes*, even coined — as a joke — the term 'scallydelia' and suddenly the musical phenomenon of a crossover between football/dance music/drugs such as marijuana, LSD and Ecstasy (E) had a place in a new discourse about law and order, football hooliganism and juvenile crime. 'Moral panic' is the concept which is most frequently used when deviance and youth culture have been explored but there are many problems with its application to explain the discursive connections between the histories of football and youth.

A more satisfactory approach is to conduct an archaeology of the 'texts' which make up these histories, often involving material such as fanzines, local archive material, oral testimony and so on. This technique has been success-fully employed in oral history projects on the more distant past (say thirty or forty years ago) but less frequently in looking at more recent times. To some extent the narrative of casual youth style in the closed media world of football, youth and pop culture can be documented textually. *The Face* magazine, *Sounds* and *NME* weekly pop papers, and other artefacts from the early to mid-1980s, do provide something of an archive, but most of it is woefully behind the phenomenon which it was documenting, or else is highly misleading. *The End* magazine from Merseyside, however, though riddled with wind-ups and false names of mythical casual football terrace (service) crews, remains the best first-hand account. From the early 1980s Peter Hooton (as co-editor with, originally, Phil Jones) and others produced a fanzine whose content was largely football-fan-related, though it was initially billed as 'The North's Finest Music Paper'. By the time of its own 'end' — when football had tended to be almost completely superseded in its pages by music and fashion — in the late 1980s, it had witnessed, and helped to contribute to, the massive explosion of football fanzines in Britain and Ireland, not to mention a few rare examples throughout Continental Europe. Hooton, whose group, The Farm, became the fanzine's 'house' band in the mid-1980s and deservedly cashed in on the British mass media's obsession with 'scally' culture in the late 1980s and early 1990s, achieving an international pop chart success with their singles 'Groovy Train' and 'All Together Now' and LP 'Spartacus', wrote a scathing history of the 'trainer wars' in *The Face* (November 1990). Under the heading 'The Good, The Bad and the Ugly', Hooton claimed that:

the obsession with training shoes for the youth of this country began in the late
Seventies and not in the late Eighties, as some would have us believe. It came from the
football terraces and the council estates of the big cities, and who gives a George Best
who started it — it happened and that's a fact. In the post-punk revolution of '78/79,
Adidas Samba ruled the terraces of Anfield and Goodison, quickly followed by Stan
Smith's, before Puma struck back . . . This was real fashion, and the competition was
intense. A revolution was going on that had absolutely nothing to do with the streets of
Brooklyn or the Bronx. In all the years that *The End* magazine was printed in Liverpool,
we never received a single letter about 'trainers' in America, but we did get hundreds
about the training shoes the different football crews were wearing.

The Farm's rise to fame was, in the end, sudden but a long history predated it.
The Face documented the band's back catalogue, as they eventually achieved
overdue commercial success, in a comprehensive article by John McCready in
April 1990. The popular music media generally started to catch on to what had
been happening on Merseyside and in Greater Manchester some five years
earlier, produced dozens of *End* retrospectives. One of the best was Pete
Naylor's well-researched 'In Search of the Scally' in *Sounds* in March 1991 and
its sequel 'The World of The End' (never printed because of *Sounds'* demise).
Liverpool University's student magazine, *Guild and City Gazette*, in November
1990 took a 'Trip on the Groovy Train' and interviewed Keith Mullin, guitarist
with The Farm. The article was prefaced with a frequently cited editorial quote
from *The End* in 1981 which proclaimed, 'for too long now London and the
establishment have taken lightly the threat of Scallyhood. Now the nation has
been warned. The End is proof that there is new light at the end of the tunnel.
Follow us and we will take over your world'. When asked about The Farm
being dubbed 'The Original Scallies', Mullin argued, 'It was over five years ago
. . . it was just a word that was bandied around . . . someone who went to
football matches, robbers and that . . . me grandma used to call me old fella a
scally.'
    Back copies of *The End* itself reflect a continuing debate about the origins of
'scally' youth culture and a deep suspicion of attempts by academics and the
media to incorporate it. In Vol. 6, for instance, an issue which carried the
readers' quiz 'Are You A Scal?' answered in thirty questions, a correspondent
from Crumpsall, Manchester, responded to a recent (24 April 1982) NME
article on 'scallies':

At long last national recognition for scallies. Although forced to live in Manchester, my
origins rest in Runcorn (a true woolie) and I've been an observer of the development of
this marvellous youth cult for many years. I remember the first stirrings around the
time of Liverpool/Man United Charity Shield Match in 1977, the black cords, adidas T-
shirts and blue snorkels. I've been trying to explain for years to people the subtleties
and intricacies of Merseyside dress sense — all I got was a bemused puzzlement.

There followed a description of styles of 'scally' walk, and tortured musings
about the possible detrimental effects of the late 1970s mod revival on 'scally'
culture. The letter went on:

However, my fear proved groundless as these old parkas were quickly discarded in favour of the Artic (*sic*) 'Biften' Jacket (with detachable hood) — the bulkiness of this jacket emphasising the match stick like legs. The old Stanley jacket saw a revival at this stage also. As you will probably be aware the natives of Manchester have over the last two years been trying to copy the style and while reproducing it convincingly (so much so in fact I mistook several Mancs for scousers on match day in Manchester . . .) it is obvious that the style is now a fashion and not a WAY OF LIFE. In my opinion the true Scal looks as if he was born that way, and will never look any different — the clothes trapping may change but the actual style never does.

This letter, as with so many others during *The End*'s existence, received the barbed response from Hooton and Jones, 'I bet you go to University and study psychology and have got 'A' levels in "Scallies lifestyles syllabus C" '! 'Woolies' (Wollybacks — particularly directed at Leeds United fans, but strictly 'out of town') and students received almost as much stick as Southern 'dickheads' in the pages, letters and poetry corner of *The End*. London's self-styled 'chaps' ('down here scallies are called chaps') occasionally wrote in but were often dismissed as 'Cockney hooligans' who couldn't read.

The letters pages of *The End* were also a testament to the violence of the so-called soccer 'style wars' that dominated early–mid-1980s football culture. Until the mid-1980s, at least, football violence by various 'terrace' or 'service' crews was highly fashionable. Correspondents to *The End* from various parts of the country delighted in marking out both the latest fashion and the scores in the recent 'matches' between the crews. In Vol. 8 in 1982 (complete with the quiz 'Are You A Real Wool? in twenty-nine questions and fictitious interviews with amalgams of former scouse footballers 'Terry Mac Darracott' and 'Tommy Smythe') we were told, 'Blackpool are starting this season (1982–3) in bright green t-shirts, Lee Cooper stonewashed jeans and Adidas Summit (plus Black Slazies if it's cold). Preston were starting in Motorbike helmets and greasy leather jackets . . .' and (in another letter) 'tell your scals that their glory days on the terrace and field are over', and (from a Chelsea North Stand fan) 'it seems you lot up in Liverpool are trying to get to the top of the stabbing tables. Still Mancs don't count, 200 stitches or not . . . all me mates have read the End and its taken over from the "Face" as our favourite magazine'. Years later, by Vol. 19, much of the correspondence was devoted to spotting the 'real' terrace crews and laughing at the send-ups. 'The Swindon Town Kamikaze Suicide Assault Squad' wrote — in spoof — to proclaim that

altogether there are 14 of us in the firm and our ages range from 8½ to 37. Dresswise we're into expensive diamond pattern Pringle sweaters, skintight Lee cords, white Fila tennis socks and pricey Nike 'Vandal Supreme' sports boots, also we're well ahead in hairstyles and currently we're all into the brand new wedge style. So as you probably realise we're well ahead of the rest of the country's soccer yobs with their DA's, donkey jackets and kangaroo skin Gucci mountaineering boots'.

The letter appeared next to a more authentic commentary from the 'Lincoln Transit Elite' who claimed to be 'sporting Reebok trainers, Marc O Polo jumpers and flat tops'.

The End editorial team itself produced an article in Vol. 14 under the banner headline 'In Search of the Casuals' which defined the development of the various, forever changing football styles as regional reactions to skinhead styles. In the FA Charity Shield contest between Liverpool and West Ham, *The End* argued that 'to a man those East End "Casuals" were a mass of boneheads, flying jackets, them beloved Lonsdale and Dr Martens . . . 99% of the West Ham casuals had Sham 69 badges'. After disposing of the claims to football fashion leadership of Chelsea, Leeds, Arsenal, Tottenham and, to a lesser extent, Manchester clubs, the editors gave an account of the 'present stage of the History of Football Fashion Part 1, the sports gear':

Firstly the reasons why 1978/79 was mentioned was because we at The End believe this was the start of the present trendy look. Those heady days of Ritzy, Fiorucci, Lois (all at sometime abused, becoming the obligatory cut-downs). When these names became played out it was decided by all to broaden one's horizons, and the cry went up Europe! Pre-season tours, unexplored territory, in other words, easy pickings to be had. Hence the bringing home from the continent, of smart looking garments with strange sounding names. The situation now has got really out of hand, it's just a throw back to the three-star jumper days (the cockneys will admit they wore them around 1953!) when no group of supporters was distinguishable from another. When the likes of Oxford, even Chester have a so called trendy crew you have to say enough is enough.

Inevitably, such a summary inspired many more correspondents to deny this particular Merseyside football youth culture history lesson. For a fan from the Old Kent Road (writing in Vol. 15), 'Fiorucci's were first being worn in London in '73 or was it '72 . . . and in 1973 up till 1976, all teenagers were wearing Burberrys, Daks Cashmere jumpers, Fila, Italian callards and croc shoes and plenty of tom', and in Vol. 16 alongside 'In Search of the Casual, part 200', the story of 'Johnny Casual' (the Final Word) was told by a 'novel' (story) contribution from South of Watford which acknowledged that 'Robbin Scallie joyously points to the fifteen consecutive seasons ragging Europe. Which is all quite true, but it must be said that Lillywhites have been selling exclusive sportswear to the discerning Londoner since the days of Bertie Wooster (now there is a casual dream)'.

Most media accounts of *The End* have been second-hand, at one remove from the discourse created by the fanzine itself. This is partly because the magazine, like many of its contemporaries, was not available from high street stores and was sold outside football grounds or in music shops, or could be bought by mail direct from the editors' homes. Pop 'histories' of fanzines are now written as if this was a hooligan magazine, or as if it sensationalised and emphasised the deviance of the football supporter in the era from the late 1970s up to the time of the Heysel disaster in the manner of a tabloid newspaper. 'Moral panic' theory in the sociology of deviance fails to take account of the precise nature of the discourse of such fanzines and assumes it constitutes the object of social reaction itself. As Peter Hooton has strenuously pointed out, *The End* was never a football hooligan magazine. Though it does not fit easily into the lineage of more commercial football fanzines (such as *When Saturday Comes* or *The Absolute Game*) it constituted an important intervention in football and fashion 'street' politics in a decade when 'style' came to signify a burgeoning affluence amongst the young upwardly mobile ('yuppie'). A different kind of sexual politics was being proffered here, offering new identities for young males interested in the 'holy' trinity of soccer, pop and clothes. As Hooton saw it, the politics were always to the fore, and The Farm's stance against conformist conceptions of style politics in the 1980s, once they achieved pop-star billing, confirms a changing, but consistently radical, view of the pop and football crossover which they promoted.

Much of the argument about who wore what where, and who ran from whom, at least by the beginning of 1985, was governed by the widespread media coverage (especially in tabloid papers like the *Sun*) of the 'casual' youth culture and its connection to football hooliganism as if it was a new phenomenon. Then came the highly publicised disorders of that year at Luton Town versus Millwall, Chelsea versus Sunderland, Birmingham City versus Leeds United and the horrific Heysel disaster at the European Cup Final of 1985 between Juventus and Liverpool. A new direction in football spectator-ship then started to take hold culminating in the formation of an 'alternative' football fan organisation, the Football Supporters' Association (FSA). *The End* itself had always carried pieces on ins/outs, bad policing, clubs' (usually bad) reaction to their fans, professional footballers' frequently laughable haircuts and clothes, as well as popular music, politics, youth culture and fashion. These are all topics which have become the staple diet of the 'new' football fanzine movement since 1985 when the magazines *Off The Ball* and *When Saturday Comes* helped to spawn the 400 (and rising) sports — mainly football — fanzines to have emerged in Britain and Ireland by 1991. Prior to 1985, apart from *The End*, football fanzines consisted mainly of 'one club' supporters' magazines like *Terrace Talk* (York City), *Wanderers Worldwide* (Bolton Wanderers) and *City Gent* (Bradford City) and could virtually be counted on the fingers of one hand. By the late 1980s *The End*'s place at the forefront of the music, youth and soccer crossover had been superseded not by football fanzines in general but by the new 'club' culture, the origins of which it had done so much to document and stimulate earlier in the decade. As one magazine writer put it in late 1990:

The End, the granddaddy of the fanzines, which had documented the rise and fall of Puma, Adidas, Gallini and Lacoste, had always covered music and its followers as much as fickle football fashions. Inspired by this, two south Londoners started Boy's Own, which has been pivotal to the terrace/fashion/rave crossover. Its two instigators, Terry Farley and Andrew Weatherall, are now respected young dance DJ-producers, and recently returned their debt to The End's creator Peter Hooton by producing the first hits for his band The Farm.[6]

Boy's Own was to *The End* what the 1970s *Private Eye* lookalike *Foul*! was to the 1980s and 1990s *When Saturday Comes*[7] and the best of the other modern soccer fanzines. There is a direct lineage even where the participants in the later model had not so much as read the earlier version (though writers like Kevin Sampson contributed to both magazines as well as *The Face* and went on, with Suggs of Madness, to manage The Farm). For instance, a *Boy's Own* issue in 1990 had the magazine's guide to 'the good, sad and the ugly of the training shoe' in Top Ten form, acknowledging that

since the late 70s the training shoe has been the standard footwear of the chaps. The fashion standing of a town fell or shined on what was being worn by who and when.

Nowadays all manner of bods are on the trainee bandwagon — sloanes (wet-fish to you) ragas, hoolies, even plod.

However, as with the decade of difference between *Foul!* and, say, *When Saturday Comes*, the times had clearly shifted between the beginning of *The End* and the later *Boy's Own* issues. For instance, the widespread use of cannabis ('draw') at the football ground, as well as in many other public places, is frequently referenced throughout the pages of *The End*, from the early 1980s onwards, but in the intervening years 'old' psychedelic drugs such as LSD ('acid') and new concoctions such as MDMA (Ecstasy or E) became equally influential. By 1990 *Boy's Own* was involved in a general social reaction to 'excessive' indulgence in such substances, publishing an article entitled 'Five good reasons why it may be preferable to just go out and get drunk instead of spending a large part of the weekend in a chemically altered state'. The letters page of the magazine expressed similar 'Voices of Reason' and contained laments for the media's incorporation of a 'scene' which was better 'back in the old days' (that is 1987 and 1988, when the origins of *Boy's Own* itself and the Ibizan party-goers were more exclusive). In an issue in 1989, a Merseyside correspondent paid a 'Hillsborough tribute' to Liverpool fans, ninety-five of whom lost their lives in April 1989 as a result of the crushing at the Leppings Lane end of the ground at the start of the Liverpool versus Nottingham Forest FA Cup semi-final. Significantly, echoing the sentiments of hundreds of football fanzine articles, the letter went on to 'hope no-one is at this moment thinking up sick jokes and chants about Hillsborough. We've had enough of 'Munich '58' [referring to the Manchester United players killed in an air crash at Munich that year] and 'Shankly '81' [referring to the year in which Bill Shankly, former Liverpool manager, died].

Inevitably regional rivalries constantly surfaced, particularly involving London, Merseyside and Manchester. By the late 1980s, 'Madchester', as the Factory label recording group Happy Mondays christened it in 'Rave On', was seen to be part of a specialised, global image of youth and popular culture which even reached the front pages of *Newsweek*. Phil Thornton, in the same issue of *Boy's Own* as the Hillsborough tribute, gave a long personal account of 'Manchester: Centre of the Solar System' in terms of its fashion history over the last decade:

Some arguments will never be settled . . . who invented 'Scally/Perry' dress sense? The Scals naturally claim it was they; the Mancs are equally vociferous it was they. Both agree on one thing, however — cockneys were years catching up. As an impartial observer who shops, drinks and watches footy in both cities, I'll give you my memories of this period. It's 1981 and the Scousers had started growing their fringes into wedges and wore baggy jumpers, faded Lois and Dunlop 'Green Flash' pumps. They danced to OMD . . . Human League . . . Kraftwerk . . . and Funky disco, such as Rick James and Tom Browne. At the match, the newly-named 'Scallies' developed this Northern style of dress to encompass pastel jumbo cords, Keo and Kicker boots and every Scal's favourite garment . . . the sheepy. In the wink of an eye the Mancs adopted this style themselves and as the rivalry between the two tribes is so intense, they proudly claimed that they originated it. By 1982 the two were more or less mirror images of each other and the style spread throughout the smaller towns and cities of the Northwest. By now however the sporty foreign clobber craze had arrived from 'darn sarf' and Hurleys Golf Shop in

Manchester became the mecca for the boys and girls who gladly forked out ridiculous prices for Head, Cerutti, Kappa, Fila, Lacoste and Ellesse. The Face told everyone that the type of people who wore these clothes were called 'casuals' and everyone up here laughed . . . As this style remained popular amongst the working class kids around England, Manchester suddenly went into a scruffy backlash in 84. Flared jeans and cords were everywhere. This meant you didn't have to spunk £40 on a pair of trainers cos you couldn't see the fuckin things anyway. Beaten up cord shoes now became the big alternative to Adidas. 84 also saw the 'Snorkel craze'; everyone went frantic digging out their old school parkas . . . worn loose with a polo shirt underneath and with 20" flares below . . . Up until 86 you could easily tell who was and wasn't a student, but in the next year loads of scals/perrys adopted a more studentish style. Fringes got slicked back, polo necks were worn with extra baggy kecks and brogues. The scruffy but stylish Manc style of dress hasn't changed much over the years: the Happy Mondays are probably the best example of this mode . . . loose gear, baggy kecks, Rizla's, beards, short hair, tide marks, spunk stains and don't-give-a-fuck attitude!

The pages of *Boy's Own* in the late 1980s are, though, a testament to a new crossover between football, pop music and youth culture which marks out a fresh terrain for the 1990s, a formation I have elsewhere described as 'the end-of-the-century party'.[8] In this youth culture famous football names such as Boca Juniors (particularly associated with *Boy's Own* as the magazine spread out to become a dance record label), Eusebio and St. Etienne, for example, are ripped out of their previous context in football mythology and placed in the popular music realm as names of 'bands' and 'artists'. Continuing this *bricolage* the acid house/rave culture explosion of the late 1980s celebrated the rise of the DJ/producer/remixer — like Andy Weatherall, Paul Oakenfold and Terry Farley who were all associated with *Boy's Own* — as if they were football players or teams (literally in terms of the cheering behaviour of fans towards them at 'live' clubs). On the other hand, bands like Paris Angels, and many others, were really street/terrace fashion models getting up on stage. Peter Hooton of The Farm, when asked in *Melody Maker* (24 November 1990) if he agreed that the decrease in the amount of violence at soccer matches over the last couple of seasons was a direct result of 'Acid House' or 'Rave Culture', replied, 'Yeah, I'd say that's definitely true . . . A couple of years ago there'd have been a really bad atmosphere between groups of lads from Liverpool, Manchester, London, this city, that city, but that's unthinkable now.'

In the late 1980s and early 1990s the football terraces, then, experienced their own 'summer of love' which had been evident earlier at clubs like Manchester's Hacienda and London's Shoom. The carnivalesque — even surrealist — nature of this transformation in football culture was first symbolised by the inflatables craze started by Manchester City fans and their blown-up bananas, and speedily followed by virtually every other club (from Oldham Athletic's yard dogs to Grimsby Town's haddocks). The now defunct Manchester-based regional arts magazine *Avant* (Issue 6, September 1990) distinguished between this 'new wave' fan and the 'dinosaur' fan in a classic fanzine ins/outs style. *Avant* suggested that the 'new wave' fan had:

1. long centre parting or short two-dimensional (*not* skin or perm).
2. t-shirts Baggy (club shirts/slogans/James/Stone Roses/Happy Mondays etc.) *not* Lacoste, Perry, Union Jack, Gazza/England/tight fit.

3. parallel jeans or frayed flares/tracksuit bottoms. Baggy *not* tight fit stonewash/ drainpipes.
4. Puma trainers/kickers/lilac suede boots *not* brogues, Doc Martens, huge tongue trainers.
5. pin badges/bracelets/crystals *not* scarves/tattoos/Rangers hats.
6. fanzines/obscure flags *not* official programmes, bricks and cans.
7. cannabis not beer or lager.
8. other team — Cameroon *not* Rangers or Celtic.
9. Blue Moon/blissed up *not* Here We Go.

This fans' guide for 'Sensually Right On Supporters' obviously had its regional base as usual, and was underpinned by the contemporary global media concentration on Manchester and its youth culture,[9] but it accurately reflects the changing nature of football and youth culture in England in the early 1990s. Chants like 'Blissed up' ('Oh! we're all blissed up and we're gonna win the cup . . .') and 'Blue Moon' are what matter here, *not* Gazza and Lindisfarne's update of 'Fog On The Tyne' (Revisited), or even the considerably more palatable 'World in Motion' from New Order which featured England World Cup players singing and appearing in the video for the single. The singing of the words of the first few lines from Blue Moon, 'Blue Moon, you saw me standing alone, without a dream in my heart, without a love of my own', produced a Maine Road 'original', courtesy of Rodgers and Hart from 1934, but though often sung straight they are also adapted to read 'Blue Moon, We beat United 5–1!', a reference to the 1989 derby and, cheekily, sung in the original by Manchester United fans when watching the team play away in their 'blue' change strip. Terrace crooning is in vogue and the 'renaissance' fan is with us.

If the media and the Government of Margaret Thatcher *threatened* to undermine the football industry in England in the 1980s — especially after Heysel — this new football culture, fragmented and uneven as it is, is engaged in a remarkable celebration of 'fandom' and the rebirth of soccer spectating, undercutting widespread media and police predictions of violence by English fans in Italia '90. Reports[10] of the attraction of more women to football grounds in the wake of the World Cup spectacle (as well as overall increase in turnstile fans) overlook a tendency, which is clear in the pages of this archaeology of football and youth culture from the 1950s onwards, to problematise (and to 'play' with) traditional notions of masculinity, especially those which have been associated with football like defence of territory, a willingness to fight, and so on. Women are a largely unresearched part of the football crowd and their 'absence' is taken for granted in much literature, but the influence of dance club culture on the terraces (and vice versa) in the late 1980s and early 1990s undoubtedly had already produced a 'terrace conversion' of many female fans way before the television coverage of the World Cup 1990.

Certainly other texts, like the many soccer fanzines, constitute a similar series of representations of the way that football and youth culture fit together historically and geographically, in terms of time and space. But football songs used to be the lowest of low art. Not any more. Adrian Sherwood, long-time West Ham United fan, DJ and record producer and owner of the legendary On-

U Sound label, produced records in the mid-1980s which were to help reorient the whole assessment of football, popular music and youth culture. They were singles by Tackhead — 'The Game' — and the Barmy Army — 'Sharp as a Needle/England 2 Yugoslavia 0' — which were heavy dance-floor mixes of sampled terrace chants and community singing, plus fragments of TV and radio commentary. The musicians like bassist Doug Wimbish and guitarist Skip McDonald were used again later in a long-playing version called 'The English Disease', named with deliberate political irony so as to satirise the Conservative Government's legislative attack on football spectators in the Football Spectators Act, 1989. As a result new concoctions such as 'Leroy's Boots' (after Leroy Rosenior of West Ham United), and 'Brian Clout' (after Brian Clough, manager of Nottingham Forest, who had taken the law into his own hands and 'cuffed' pitch-invading spectators) began to echo around the nation's dance floors in a constant circulation, deconstruction, then reconstruction, of various contemporary elements of football, music and youth culture in its British context. 'Blue Moon', which appeared as a Manchester City football fanzine (Blue Print) flexi disc and on a vinyl record collection from On-U Sound, 'Pay It All Back Volume 3', saw Sherwood using the Manchester City fans' terrace croon, along with 'wicked' dance floor rhythms and TV commentator Clive Tyldesley's disembodied commentary of the 5–1 derby match in a celebration of the new 'musicalised' football-oriented pop culture.

BBC television cameras captured a fleeting glimpse of this new football fandom in April 1991 as it showed 'live' the joyful, celebratory response of West Ham United fans at Villa Park as their team (down to ten men after a sending-off) were thrashed 4–0 by Nottingham Forest in the FA Cup semi-final. Ironically, West Ham United were one of the clubs most focused on by academics and the media in the early and mid-1980s for their notorious football crew, the Inter-City Firm (ICF). After this display of extraordinary *bonhomie*, Ian Taylor argued that 'Style is important again. The crowd has a right to enjoy itself, to be a crucial, active part of the event. Hooliganism is suddenly decidedly unfashionable, *passé*, irrelevant.'[11] Whilst it mattered that there were no traditional enmities between the opponents that afternoon — indeed, both teams were united in football folklore because of their commitment to 'playing football' on the floor rather than in the air — the comments are significant. However unevenly, British football has played a part in a critical 'moment' in the social relationship between fans and cultural industries such as pop and soccer. The historical cycle of football's crossover with pop — a complex facet of 'postmodern' global culture — has turned again to produce a notable shift in British football fan culture. As a pamphlet by a Stockport County fan, Richard Turner, has recently put it:

The terraces have also provided a showground for many of the youth cults from the '50s onwards, a fashion parade for mainly young males. The closest ties between these trends and football has been in the 1980s, with the soccer 'casual' image that developed into the Acid House phenomena. Popular cultural images are an integral part of football culture, from the clothes to the chants derived from popular songs.[12]

The history of football and pop music culture in a specific political and geographical location such as Great Britain is not an easy formation to depict in written discourse. I hope that this essay has given some reason to be cautiously optimistic about English clubs' return to European competition, but the cultural stability of such a formation always hangs in the balance. It may not yet be the end of an era of football hooliganism which can be traced in its modern version to the 1960s (with historical antecedents into the last century), but the new identities and styles being forged are crucial to a potential breaking of the football/violence couplet.

Acknowledgements

I am extremely grateful to Alan Haughton, Research Assistant in the Unit For Law and Popular Culture at Manchester Polytechnic, for helping to assemble some of the materials drawn on in this essay and for the comments by Alan Haughton and the other Research Assistants, Toni Melechi and Richard Haynes, on an early draft version. I am also grateful to Pete Naylor for allowing me to see (after this essay was finished unfortunately) the articles he wrote for *Sounds* magazine on *The End* in 1991, and Peter Hooton and other members of The Farm for their cooperation in the production of the book *Football With Attitude*.

Notes

1. This is a short, and much revised, version of a Chapter which appears in my book (1991), *Football With Attitude*, Manchester: Wordsmith.
2. See for an ethnographic description prior to the 1985–6 League season in England, Steve Redhead and Eugene McLaughlin: 'Soccer's Style Wars', *New Society*, 16 August 1985.
3. See Ian Taylor and Dave Wall, 'Beyond the Skinheads: Comments on the Emergence and Significance of the Glamrock Cult', in Geoff Mungham and Geoff Pearson (eds) (1976), *Working Class Youth Culture*, London: Routledge and Kegan Paul. For good accounts of 1970s transmogrifications of youth styles into football, see David Robins and Phil Cohen (1978), *Knuckle Sandwich*, Harmondsworth: Penguin, 1978, and David Robins (1984), *We Hate Humans*, Harmondsworth: Penguin 1984. For a still useful oral history of skins and football, see Susie Daniel and Pete McGuire (eds) (1972) *The Paint House: Words From An East End Gang*, Harmondsworth: Penguin, especially chapter 9. For a view of a so-called 'golden age' of English soccer violence — which the author locates in the skinhead-dominated 1960s and early 1970s — see Robert Elms (1986), 'The Golden Age of Football Violence', *The Face*, May.
4. David Widgery: *Beating Time* (1986), London: Chatto and Windus, gives an insider's version which, as so often, differs depending on which political organisation of the left is being referred to.
5. See the writing of Dick Hebdige on skins and punks, especially (1979), *Subculture: The Meaning of Style*, London: Methuen. For Hebdige's writings about postmodernism and youth culture, see (1988), *Hiding In The Light*, London: Comedia/Routledge.
6. Tony Crean (1990), 'Terrace Conversion', *20/20*, **2** (1), Autumn, p. 98.

7. See Tom Baker (1987), 'Foul!' *The Face*, November, for a good account of the comparisons between a magazine which lasted from 1972 to 1976 and the post-1985 football fanzine movement. See also, for a review of the history written in 1985, Steve Redhead (1987), *Sing When You're Winning: The Last Football Book*, London: Pluto Press, and, a much changed account in 1991, Steve Redhead, *Football With Attitude*, op. cit.

8. Steve Redhead (1990), *The End-Of-The-Century Party: Youth and Pop Towards 2000*, Manchester and St. Martin's Press, New York: Manchester University Press.

9. See for one recent history, Sarah Champion (1990), *And God Created Manchester*, Manchester: Wordsmith.

10. For example, Crean, op. cit.

11. Ian Taylor, 'From Aggravation to Celebration', *The Independent on Sunday*, 21 April 1991.

12. Richard Turner (1990), *In Your Blood: Football Culture in the late 1980s and early 1990s*, London: Working Press, p. 8.

9
Having an away day: English football spectators and the hooligan debate

John Williams

You've got to fight, for the right to party

(Beastie Boys)

The party's in Europe

(Cas Pennant, West Ham Supporter)

Introduction

This paper is about English football spectators but, more specifically, it is about hooliganism. For a lot of non-football fans — and even for many who do support the game — hooliganism has become dangerously close to being the national sport's key defining characteristic for the past 25 years. Dalglish may resign, Gazza may even move to Italy, but those in search of 'a row' at football — 'the lads', 'the crews', 'the mobs', 'the top boys' — seem to be a constant fixture 'down at the match'. Their influence has been widespread. In 1989, for example, a number of 'quality' national newspapers in Britain, including the liberal *Guardian*, asked their foreign correspondents to report on how the continent regarded the English after ten years under the Thatcher administration. Were we still the stiff-upper lipped conservative stoics, the doyens of 'fair play' of years gone by? or had the new regime transformed us, in the eyes of our trading partners and competitors, into thrusting and business hungry free marketeers? Neither seemed to be the case. Instead, our near neighbours and fellow Europeans increasingly seemed to associate the English with young hordes of beer-drinking, threatening, thieving, sometimes violent and frequently abusive invaders. In short, a collection of *disruptive* travelling football fans — a serious 'crew', out on continental manoeuvres. Not just the dirty men, but the violent men of Europe, too. They (the continentals) also increasingly blamed the English, a little unfairly, for their own growing hooligan problems, though there seemed little doubt that many young 'city boys' on the continent were getting the message: 'Englishness means trouble'. From Gothenburg to Ghent there sprang up Union Jacks, English football

songs and English names for emergent 'hooligan' gangs. These young continental terrace fans also ransacked British TV and newspaper coverage of the
game for references to terrace (and stands) rivalries and the new English
hooligan styles. Some 'joined up' with the English during the latter's
continental expeditions (Ward reports on one brawny German convert setting
off to down twenty-five pints of lager to 'prove' his 'Englishness' to his heroes
who were then visiting the continent; Ward, 1989: p. 108). *The English* may
not have been exporting much in the fiscally barren 1970s and 1980s, but one
thing they did seem to be delivering abroad was a major lesson in the nuances
of abuse and combat inside and outside European football stadiums.

   I want to return, briefly, later to a discussion of the so-called international
hooligan network. Before I do that, I want to make a few comments about the
history of crowd disorderliness of football in Britain, more especially in
England. But most of what I have to say concerns hooliganism in the 'modern'
(post-1966) phase of the development of the English game. I also want to spend
some time looking at the associations drawn, from the late 1970s, between
racism and football-related hooliganism, and I will end with some comments on
more recent academic contributions to the hooligan debate. Throughout I will
also be considering the work done at Leicester University on the hooliganism
issue, much of which I was involved in researching and writing.

Before 1966 and all that

In starting with a brief look at the history of crowd troubles at football, it is
stating the obvious to say we tend to be nostalgic about the past. Perhaps
particularly in relation to emotive issues, such as those of crime and violence,
'the pale shadow of time is no match for the instant photo flash of the present'
(Pearson, 1983: p. 242). In some prominent sociological accounts of recent
British social history, the greater neighbourliness of the past, a sense of shared
structural and geographical circumstances and local identity, and the availability of a stable and coherent set of cultural and occupational traditions and
practices, are features which are *highlighted*. Against this is set a present which
is characterised, instead, by a series of cultural, geographical and occupational
dislocations which, it is argued, mitigate against the formation of 'organic'
local identities and, thus, effective community controls, perhaps particularly
those which have traditionally operated across the generations (see, for
instance, Cohen, 1972). Add to this the increasing social distance which has,
allegedly, grown between a technology-led police force and its local 'communities', and the extent to which the latter have themselves undergone
considerable ethnic as well as cultural reconstitution (Reiner, 1985), and one
has the recipe for the effective comparison of a relatively orderly and
'composed' past set against what is depicted as a considerably more
'decomposed' disorderly and volatile present.

   There is certainly something to this argument, I think. Who could doubt,
for example, that relations between the generations have been loosened and in
other ways re-ordered by the cultural and structural shifts in post-war patterns
of the family work and leisure, particularly perhaps for the sons and daughters

of working-class parents? It is difficult to question, too, that rising (official) crime rates, the inner city disturbances in Britain in the 1980s, the apparently endemic racist assaults in many of Britain's larger towns and cities and the near-continuous concern over the past twenty-five years about the collective disorderly behaviour of young men — especially, but not solely, at football matches — add considerable weight to suggestions that Britain in the 1990s is a long way from being the 'modern', egalitarian integrated, cosmopolitan and, to use a description which is popular with the present (1991) Prime Minister, John Major, *classless* society it is sometimes purported to be (see Murphy, Williams and Dunning, 1990: pp. 19–21).

But if this is the case, surely the vision of Britain's past which is invested in this comparison is also run through with assumptions which have begun to creak, just a little, under the weight of more detailed historical investigation. It is only relatively recently, for example, that modern historians, sociologists and other academics have begun to explore, in any detail, working-class delinquent subcultures and the violent and exclusionary forms of 'neighbour-hood nationalism' and 'popular sovereignties of place' (Cohen, 1988: p. 33) which seemed to be characteristic of many lower-working-class neigh-bourhoods before the Second World War. In doing so, a thriving collection of youth subcultural 'gang' styles and territorial rivalries have been uncovered, as has evidence of routine forms of violent contestation involving local young (and not so young) men and the police about 'who rules the streets' (see Pearson, 1983; White, 1986; Humphries, 1981; Cohen, 1978). In a similar way, the historical research at Leicester on football crowd disorders in Britain — though far from faultless in its methodology (see Clarke, 1991) — at least suggests an early set of disorderly terrace traditions which seem to be at odds with descriptions or assumptions of previous accounts about the professional game's early days (Dunning, Murphy and Williams, 1988).

Of course, demonstrating that professional football has something of a disorderly past for particular periods of its history is a long way from demonstrating that 'old' and 'newer' forms of football-related hooliganism are of a similar nature and scale or, indeed, that they even have the same 'causes' (see Mason and Crump, 1987). As Richard Holt has argued, 'hooliganism exemplifies to perfection the difficulty of disentangling what is new from what is old in social history' (Holt, 1989: p. 343). What *is* known from historical investigations of football crowd behaviour is that targets for spectator attack in the early part of the century, more usually than today, involved players and referees, as well as opposing spectators, and that outbreaks of hooliganism seemed to have been decidedly more spontaneous and individualised than those produced by the network of inter-gang rivalries which have come to characterise attendance at major matches in England in the modern era. The hostilities sometimes generated at local 'derby' matches, then and now, demonstrate the centrality of notions of 'territory' and 'community' to urban working-class sporting loyalties which were (and are) sometimes expressed in acts of violence at football and elsewhere. But if 'the continuity thesis is not without some merit if carefully defined', and 'football hooliganism . . . can never be explained in terms of simple continuities nor as an abrupt dis-continuity; the location and specific forms of juvenile riotousness were new, but the phenomenon itself was as old as the hills' (Holt, 1989: pp. 341–2), the profound discontinuities between 'older' and more modern forms of hooliganism also do require serious attention and explanation (Hobbs and Robins, 1990). Reviewing the data on earlier hooligan outbreaks — including a trawl by Tony Mason of the annual reports of the Chief Constable of Warwickshire between 1900 and 1940 which reveals no mention of football crowd disorders — Holt is probably correct when he asserts that

Nowhere in the vast press coverage and literature of match reports is there any reference to the growth of a violent, organised youth subculture within football. Casual, individual violence was almost certainly more common than today, but hooliganism in the collective and contemporary sense did not take place at football matches.

(Holt, 1989: p. 333)

The 'golden years'

If the early years of the game were notable for their gambling, drinking and the sometimes threatening and violent behaviour of local 'roughs', the inter-war years at football seem, by comparison, to have been considerably more orderly. I have no space here to examine in any detail the peaks and troughs in the history of crowd disorderliness at football matches (see Dunning, Murphy and Williams, 1988, for some discussion on this issue). It seems fairly clear, however, that out of the fairly routine but in the main, by modern standards, relatively small-scale disturbances of the pre-First World War period the game in England — and its audience — gradually, between the wars, became more 'respectable' and less tolerant and expectant of spectator violence. (The situation in Scotland seems much less clear cut. Here, sectarian rivalries, particularly those associated with the major Glasgow clubs, helped to provide greater impetus for the continuation of the violent traditions around the game; see Murray, 1984). In the immediate aftermath of the Second World War, arguably at a time of considerable national consensus of a kind seldom seen before or since (Davies, 1984) and prior to the onset of the increasing privatisation of leisure brought by rising wages and the arrival of television, vast crowds — the largest in the game's history — watched League football matches. They did so in crumbling football stadiums, many of which were already 50 or more years old, and in some cases little changed over decades. (By 1910, sixty-six League clubs had already moved to the location they continue to occupy today.) The stadium-modernising programmes, common on the continent where public ownership of stadium facilities was more usually the norm (Inglis, 1987), were little in evidence in Britain where stadium redevelopment was piecemeal and often dependent upon finance raised by organised supporters (see Rogan Taylor, this volume).

The potential dangers of staging matches in front of huge audiences in facilities designed, even then, for a different age, were brought home by the Bolton disaster of 1946 in which thirty-three people died following a 'break in' to the ground and overcrowding in a section of the Burnden Park stadium (though recommendations after Bolton that grounds be licensed were ignored by Parliament). What is, perhaps, most striking about the period, however, is, given the poor quality of facilities, the enormous and poorly banked and maintained terracing at many grounds, and the massive crowds which flocked to matches, how few incidents of disorder and how few accidents actually took place. Today, substantially the same shells of many of those grounds are licensed, in some cases, to accommodate less than one-half the spectators, they happily housed in the 1940s and early 1950s. Policing football in the 1950s was dramatically different too. At Bolton, 107 police officers took charge of a crowd estimated to be 85,000 strong (Popplewell, 1986: p. 11). In fact, even after the 1946 tragedy — which involved no reported hooliganism, incidentally — recommendations for policing ratios at matches stood at just one policeman per 1,000 spectators. Forty years later, one officer for every seventy-five spectators was widely regarded as an appropriate ratio, and in one, not wholly untypical, case in 1986, 500 officers were turned out to police a crowd of 7,000 spectators at a match at Millwall in south east London (Popplewell, 1986: p. 42).

Given the circumstances, why did spectator disturbances and, more especially, stadium accidents not happen more often at football in the 1940s and 1950s (the next major football disaster occurred at Ibrox Park, Glasgow, in 1971)? For one thing, football grounds in that period were not yet penned and caged as they were later, fatally, to be in the hooligan-haunted 1970s and 1980s. But this was largely, of course, because rival fans did not try to get on to the pitch at that time to fight each other. Why bother? Terraces and stands were unsegregated. Those who wanted to brawl with visiting fans had plenty of opportunities to do so where they stood or sat. Few seemed interested in trying. When incidents did occur they were often defused by other members of the crowd (see Robins, 1984: p. 148). The very size of crowds at the time make it unlikely that potentially troublesome customers were excluded. One can only conclude, instead, that patterns of spectating of the period were indicative of considerably more self-policing and internal discipline within football crowds compared with those of twenty years or more later and, indeed, those in the early years of the century. Relations between the police and working people were almost certainly also more harmonious then than they had earlier been or have since become (Reiner, 1985). It was likely, too, that these factors were connected to the relatively high levels of working-class confidence and stability of the early 1940s and 1950s (Holt, 1989: p. 337) and with the sorts of effective male generational controls which continued to operate within working-class communities and at football and elsewhere (J. Clarke, 1978; A. Clarke, 1991). As the post-war boom years for the sport began to give way to smaller crowds, and particularly as the game began to gain a reputation for attracting disorderly young fans, it was probably the older, more 'respectable', male working-class and lower-middle-class fans who were most easily attracted away. They were seduced by the sort of privatised leisure offered by the rise of Saturday afternoon televised sport and the widening range of leisure options made available by spreading car ownership and increasing relative affluence.

Finally, it also seems likely that the more committed sections of the football audience of the 1940s and 1950s may have experienced a more organic connection with, or even a symbolic cultural 'control' over, their local clubs and, perhaps, the game itself compared to the situation in the modern period in which major clubs seem to many to be distant 'businesses' and star players have inexorably become highly paid and, in class, geographical and cultural terms, literally dislocated footballing media 'celebrities' (Taylor, 1971; Wagg, 1984; Dunning, Murphy and Williams, 1988; pp. 147–8). One of the key issues here is the extent to which local clubs have ceased to become symbolic extensions of the local community, and patterns of community organisation which supported the forms of communal association involved in the localised financing of football clubs, later became disconnected by changing patterns of football ownership and finance and the game's cumulative fiscal crises (Clarke, 1991; Rogan Taylor, this volume).

Whatever the reasons, 'crowd control' at football for the decade after the war seems to have been largely a case of dealing with the occasional pub fight, or with individual offenders whose inclinations to fight may have had no football-related basis at all (see Holt, 1989: p.334), or, finally, of dealing with the sorts of problems which were occasionally produced simply by the sheer size of football crowds.

Bad boys, bad boys

The picture of large, and largely orderly, football crowds began slowly to change in England from around the mid-1950s onwards. As some older fans drifted away and amidst a more generalised panic about rising rates of juvenile delinquency and the increasing public and publicised misbehaviour of 'trouble-some youth' (Muncie, 1984), young football fans, initially those from the north west, began to attract publicity for their train-wrecking exploits. Football trains, it should be said, had also been attacked and damaged in the 1930s (see Dunning, Murphy and Williams, 1988: p. 109). However, that was a period in which localised teenage youth styles were regularly criticised for their attempts at imitating adult behaviour. In the 1950s, it was the spread of national youth styles, the greater cultural, stylistic and financial independence of working-class youths, and the national media coverage their sometimes disorderly activities drew which especially troubled older generations and the 'respect-able' classes. And, as Hobbs and Robins (1990, p. 17) point out, style travels through the media. The 'unmanageability of youth' became a constant, national media focus in the years which followed, shifting only as, within the changing political, economic and racial contours of British society, youth styles themselves evolved and changed.

Robins and Cohen (1978) argue that the 'youth ends' in north London emerged during the 1966–7 League season. It is perhaps significant, however, that it was on Merseyside in the early 1960s — then a focal point for the rising new British pop cultures — that the first publicised signs in the modern period of the activities of disorderly groups of young supporters were apparent (see Dunning, Williams and Murphy, 1988: pp. 142–5). It was probably in Liverpool, too, that segregation by age at the goal-end terraces received its strongest impetus, drawing as it did upon segregative new pricing policies for 'troublesome' young supporters, but more especially on the introduction by

fans of a repertoire of new pop-rooted football songs and chants. Penetrations
of the football world by aspects of what was, by 1964, a rapidly expanding
teenage leisure industry, had the effect of exacerbating territorial divisions, by
age, inside grounds. The new forms of terrace patois — songs, clothes, gestures
— were increasingly devised largely by, and for, young fanatics and they were
spread by television. Gerry and the Pacemakers' version of 'You'll never walk
alone' became the Liverpool FC anthem. Soon, few young goal-end regulars
were in danger of 'walking alone', but they did have to be sure of walking — or
running — with their 'own kind'. The battle lines were already being laid down
for the national struggles over 'who rules' at football; struggles which were to
become a near permanent fixture of the sport in England for the next twenty-
five years.

Sustained by the self-confidence and greater autonomy provided by the new
youth cultures and buoyed by the nationalistic excess inspired by the England
World Cup success of 1966, 'the lads' began to establish the Saturday
afternoon rituals which quickly attracted aspiring 'hard cases' from the
housing estates and city neighbourhoods. In the London area, the new recruits
were also drawn in from the working-class communities which had been
displaced to the suburbs, but the patterns of recruitment were different in
different areas, depending upon local traditions and local ecologies. By no
means all the young men who joined the ends did so to fight. As Willis points
out, the fundamental issue for most young working-class men in urban areas
and locations where violence is an everyday possibility is not some 'cultural
obligation' to fight (Hobbs and Robins, 1990: p. 20), but to fight as little as you
have to to maintain honour and reputation whilst escaping intimidation and
'being picked on' (Willis, 1990: p. 103). Football, however, provided the kind
of adventure and uncertainty and the possible dangers which are sought out by
many working-class young men and which transcend conventions and nor-
mally approved patterns of behaviour. Crucially, too, for the real 'hard cases'
and the 'nutters' who wanted it, terrace rivalries also promised a 'nihilistic
grounded aesthetic — the incomprehensible buzz of the momentary dis-
appearance of all meaning' provided by the real fight (Willis, 1990: p. 106).
For some the attraction was clearly compulsive, even addictive. As a West Ham
ICF 'member' put it: 'When you've run a firm and your adrenalin's gone,
know what I mean, and you — and you start (fighting). I mean, it's the best. I
mean, 60 quid's worth up yer nose won't, like, top that. Truth, no, it's the
truth! I mean sod the coke and the smack, you know. Because the *feeling*, the
feeling of doing something like that . . .' For those less compelled by the 'high'
provided by the violence and real pleasure in routing the opposition, there was
still the entertainment and pride in having local hard men who nobody messed
with easily. Everyone else could at least be there.

In the late 1960s, it was the skinhead who was identified most closely with
hooliganism in public perceptions. (Twenty years later, cartoons still depict
hooligans as skins.) The stylised hardness of the skins and their heightened
celebrations of some of the traditional concerns of working-class youth 'gangs'
— their aggressive and often violent masculinity; their community loyalties
and collective solidarity; their violent opposition to 'outsiders' and to ruptures
in traditional conventions of 'race' and gender — reinforced, and were

reinforced by, the emerging terrace orders. When Manchester United fans 'took' east London in May 1967, fighting and trashing in celebration as the north-west club beat West Ham to claim the League Championship, their actions set in motion regional rivalries around football which also later hardened around the politics of style and the masculinised imperatives of conspicuous consumption which took place against the backcloth of a divisive and debilitating economic recession (Redhead, 1987).

Firming it up

The central aim of the early travelling hooligans of the late 1960s and early 1970s was to 'take' the opposing end — literally to fight to occupy the terrace space which had been colonised by the local 'hard core.' At first, these activities, and involvement in them, seemed to demand at least some knowledge of the sport and, more especially, a football-related commitment to the local club. Such strategies initially promised the maximum exhilaration for the invaders and the requisite public humiliation for the vanquished. But they were also usually over pretty quickly, involved little opportunity for any real fighting, and increased the possibilities of arrest. As the police tightened up, the range of match-day activities involved in travelling with 'the lads' spread. Inevitably, the identity of the real fighters and those willing to 'stand' against opponents also became more distinct from that of the rest of the goal end. The 'top boys' set off earlier to matches — sometimes even days earlier — and challenged young men keen to make a name for themselves to survive, strut and, when required, to fight in the action-facilitating locales of unfamiliar, and therefore hostile, towns and cities. Names were adopted by the serious 'crews', or 'firms', frequently taken from their distinctive mode of transport to away games. 'Ordinary' service trains were initially favoured, marking out those men with the connections, 'the bottle' and the cash, from the 'mugs' who favoured the cheaper official football special trains and the inevitable and emasculating police escorts which awaited their arrival at the other end. Later, 'firms' moved on to cars and vans, then back to trains, etc., etc. — whatever seemed right to mess up the police.

The appalled fascination of the media with the named 'firms' only served to heighten the mythologies around them and increase their attractiveness to a growing number of young men whose primary interest seemed to be male comradeship and the possibilities for 'trouble' as much as the football. By the time the World Cup Finals were being staged in Italy, in 1990, 100 young Englishmen could, quite literally, become the centre of attention of the World's media, simply by parading drunkenly up the streets of Cagliari singing the national anthem. If you had been involved, the next day you could read about yourself on the front page of the English tabloids, which had been specially flown in to Sardinia for the occasion. This was fifteen minutes or more of instant fame. Its attractions proved compulsive. For 'the lads', of course, the press coverage was 'all bollocks' but, contradictorily, they studied and collected the reports avidly and danced around for the cameras. Later, as police claimed to be 'infiltrating' football gangs and sentences for hooliganism became alarmingly severe, journalists were fed false names and, particularly during English trips abroad, were physically attacked for 'writing shit' about the hooligan firms and their antics (see Williams and Goldberg, 1990). Forged in, and by, the glare of the national news media and thrown weekly into this compulsive drama of 'unsafe' adventure and risk-taking, it is not difficult to see how the fear and excitement generated by this kind of football-related camaraderie might be recalled later by those directly involved as 'a golden age, a paradise gone by' (Ward, 1989: p. 189). Also, at a time of increasing stress on traditional family ties, for young men like 'Animal' at West Ham, separated from his parents and rejected by his foster parents, mates like these in the ICF at the East London club, provided a sense of stability and 'family' support:

Well, West Ham [the ICF] became like a family, like, y'know. I mean, I could go out with 'em, train with 'em an' all that. Speak to them, you know, an' all that. Because I'd lost me parents, I didn't have no one else to turn to, so I could turn to West Ham who would help me out, like.

('Hooligan', Thames TV, August 1985)

The publicity given to the named 'firms' not only raised the national profiles of those involved — soon the firms were looking studiously only for the 'top boys' at rival clubs, and the names and faces of key 'hooligans' became common currency in such circles around the country — but they also undermined the local divisions in the home ends. Even in the late 1970s, most home 'ends' accommodated a number of discreet, small crews, which were identifiable by their local attachment via kinship networks, local estates or pubs. This is the situation recently described as existing in a Midlands town more than a decade ago (see Murphy et al., 1990, ch. 6). The increasingly testing national demands of the new football rivalries, however — top boys needed to be together to resist intrusions — and the compact established between the media and local 'hard cases' around the public promotion of the various football 'firms' meant that local divisions began to be superseded by the demands and the profiles of the major crews. As the latter took on a semi-permanent existence — their activities began to take in other events, away from football, for example — their city-wide credentials also provided 'membership' opportunities for hard cases and even sociopathic 'nutters' drawn from outside, as well as inside, the traditional estate networks. At the same time, the extending inventiveness and ambition of the major firms, which was occurring at the same time as the police were battening down at football, made indispensable to them not just the 'loyal mates' and 'good fighters' and the more ambiguously regarded involvement of the dangerous and unpre-dictable 'nutters', but also the skills of 'plotters' and organisers. The authorities and the media, always attracted to the lurid simplicity of conspiracy theory, soon had hooligan 'generals' contacting each other on walkie talkies and radioing in their 'battle plans'. In time, the police had their own high-profile intelligence system, the National Football Intelligence Unit, to combat this alleged growth in a technology-literate hooligan subculture (see also Armstrong, Hobbs and Maguire, 1991). On the ground, some pre-planning was becoming a requirement of the new scene and it drew respectful nods from opposing firms. But while it was important to meet up and discuss the tactics of the likely local police 'welcoming committee', when things 'went off', it was really back to basics. As West Ham's Big Cass says:

Well the fighting technique, a lot of it is born, I mean, people say it's organised, but really, actually, when it comes to fighting they (the ICF) just all know it and act spontaneously, because where they come from and their upbringing, right, when threatened, they all know exactly what to do. Which might appear that it's organised, but it ain't . . . But, this style of violence at football — there'd been violence before that, but a different style — that's one of the reasons how they keep it going. Every time someone comes up to beat it they've (the ICF) always found a way around it . . .
(Transcript for interview of Thames TV's 'Hooligan', 1985)

The 'new style' of football violence, and the 'organisation' which went with it, became more important when, as the attractiveness and news value of football visits to Newcastle, Manchester and the other English locations began to pale, the lure of continental Europe with its never-closing bars, reluctance to convict foreign offenders and ill-defended stadiums, began to beckon.

Serious hooligan incidents involving English fans in continental Europe began in earnest in 1974 when Spurs fans rioted at a UEFA Cup Final second-leg tie against Feyenoord in Rotterdam. Between that incident and the Heysel tragedy eleven years later, English fans were involved in football disturbances in almost all the major football playing continental countries (see Williams *et al.*, 1989). English-inspired hooliganism abroad is especially significant in the general development of the 'hooligan issue' for a number of reasons. Four seem to be especially important: firstly, as I have already said, such incidents helped to inspire and to shape hooliganism and also hooligan 'crews' on the continent, who routinely came to see the English as the yardstick against which their own performances could be measured. In such circles the English were 'a tough, sometimes outrageous group of people having an exciting time and cocking a snook at everybody' (Ward, 1989: p. 108; also, see Williams and Goldberg, 1990). Secondly, the grave international embarrassment and shame, as well as the physical damage, such incidents on occasions undoubtedly caused increased the determination of a right-wing British government to attempt to legislate hooliganism — and perhaps even the English game itself — away (see Ian Taylor, this volume). Thirdly, English hooliganism abroad served to underscore the links between the traditional territorial properties acted out at football, the sometimes violent excesses of young male fans, and racism. Finally, the English adventures on the continent also played a part in importing into English football culture some of the constituent stylistic features of the much discussed English soccer 'casual'. Let me now say a few things about racism at English football, and then about the rise of the 'casual'.

The race game

According to Holt (1989: p. 343):

Chauvinism, local and national, lies at the heart of hooliganism, and England fans seem to find in foreigners a convenient target for a vague resentment of Britain's diminished place in the world. Football has become a substitute for patriotism amongst the disaffected, half-educated white working class youth of a nation which, only a generation ago, was respected and feared throughout the world.

These forms of chauvinism also involved racism at football. As Cohen points out (1988: p. 63), racism is not something which is 'tacked on' to English history by virtue of its imperialist phase one of its aberrant moments: it is constitutive of what has become known as the 'British Way of Life'. Cohen's discussion of the 'rough racism' and the 'nationalism of the neighbourhood' which are typical of the rituals enacted through working-class street cultures by young men putting their aggression to work in defining and 'defending' their areas against real or imaginary attack is also useful in understanding the 'selective' operation of racism at football. As Cohen explains, racialised forms of ethnicity produced within working-class culture both supported spontaneous local upsurges of hostility against immigrants and prevented their political exploitation into any larger, more organised, movement (Cohen, 1988: p. 31).

Thus, the assertion of working-class localistic, proprietorial pride can in certain circumstances constitute a form of ethnicism which resists, or subordinates, racism (e.g. when black football players represent your town, your club, etc.). This is a key reason why racist organisations have had relatively little success in achieving support for their ambitions which cut across local club allegiances. However, in the 1980s the England national team — especially at matches abroad — became a particular focus for the activities of racists and racist organisations (see Williams et al., 1989). Elsewhere, I have discussed the rise of racism in the English game in some detail (see Williams, 1991). Here I am especially concerned with the situation as it developed in English football in the 1980s. Throughout this period, racist abuse and, at some venues, the activities of right-wing racist organisations remained a relatively routine feature of British football. The issue of racism in the game, however, was raised for public debate only spasmodically during this time, primarily when 'high-profile' black players were transferred to new and reputedly highly racist 'locations' for black athletes (John Barnes to Liverpool; Mark Walters to Rangers, etc.); when the activities of racist organisations were linked more directly to hooligan incidents (e.g. claims of NF involvement at Heysel; swastika-wearing Leeds United fans identified at the major disturbances at Birmingham City in May 1985); or when the televised coverage of major footballing events raised national questions about the attitudes and behaviour of English fans (e.g. the racist treatment of the substituted Dutch international, Ruud Gullit, at Wembley in March 1988).

Celebratory coverage of the violently racist activities of football terrace 'crews' continued apace, however, in the newspapers and leaflets of the National Front and other far-right organisations. It was inevitably shadowed by opposing exposure in the anti-fascist Searchlight magazine and is challenged today, once again, by a new generation of local anti-racist and anti-fascist organisations, a number of which focus their activities almost exclusively on racism at football. A number of professional clubs continue, however, to be prominent in the racist hierarchies drawn up by right-wing groups. In the National Front newspaper, *The Flag*, of May 1987, for example a 'review' of the domestic football season linked the continuing playing success of the two Merseyside clubs, Everton and the pre-John Barnes Liverpool, with the 'total absence of coloured players' in the two teams. Special mention was also reserved here for Leeds United because of the 'whiteness' of the Leeds side and the 'patriotic' (racist) nature of the club's supporters. Locally well-known NF and BNP members and organisers were by now a regular fixture distributing racist literature and memorabilia outside the club's Elland Road ground on match days (see Leeds TUC and Leeds AFA, 1987). In February 1986, two *Yorkshire Post* journalists 'infiltrated' the Leeds Service Crew hooligan gang, at that time among the most impressive and largest of all the named hooligan crews. One of their contacts told the reporters that 'The Service Crew are all NF supporters. We go to a lot of away matches and have battles with other fans . . . Sometimes, at weekends, we look for blacks and Paki's to do over' (*Yorkshire Post*, 18 February 1986). According to *Searchlight*, in January 1988, organised racist groups had, in the previous twelve months, been implicated in serious incidents of football-related violence at professional clubs including Newcastle United, Portsmouth, Hull City — where one of the club's players was reported to be unknowingly, having his playing kit sponsored by a 'front' for a white supremacist group — Liverpool, Everton, Chelsea, Bolton, Leeds United, the Manchester clubs and Glasgow Rangers (the last-named becoming something of a focus, especially for right-wing, loyalist alliances through football, linking fan groups from north and south of the border and from Northern Ireland).

A number of highly publicised and, ultimately, embarrassingly flawed police 'under-cover' operations at football in the late 1980s at Leeds, Chelsea, West Ham, Wolverhampton, Bolton and Manchester unearthed further evidence of the influence of racism and of racist organisations in the activities and ideologies of some of the best organised and most violent groups of English football hooligans (see *Searchlight*, July 1987, January 1988). Later still, in a new development, perhaps signalling another switch in the strategies of the far right at football, the Birmingham branch of the National Front was reported to be secretly attempting to purchase shares in Aston Villa Football Club. Front spokespersons claimed the aim of the purchase was to 'counteract' the influence of the Asian-origin Kumar brothers, entrepreneurs out of the Manchester-based textile trades, who had recently taken control at nearby Birmingham City and who were also about to appoint the Football League's first female chief executive. The NF group claimed that its Birmingham members included businessmen who already held shares at Villa and who were providing funds for further investment (*Sunday Mirror*, 28 January 1990).

Allied to the focus provided by domestic football competition for organised as well as for more 'spontaneous' racist displays, however, the 1980s, above all, signalled the increasing spread of football-related racist activity to venues abroad. As I have said, it is the English national side, especially at its matches abroad, which has been viewed by right-wing groups and sympathisers as the symbolically most appropriate site for the expressing of heightened nationalism and xenophobia, and a view of English national culture which is exclusively white.

Although the recent experiences of black players in Scottish football reveal clear signs of racism north of the Border, the Scottish national side has never attracted the violent, racist following now routinely associated with the England team abroad. Miles is probably right when he asserts that, since the 1960s and 1970s in Scotland, 'the "national question" has displaced (though not eliminated) the influence of racism in constructing the political agenda . . . suggesting that racism is not as central to nationalism as in England' (Miles, 1988: p. 40). It is also true to say that when the Scots travel abroad they seem to take with them little of the imperialist cultural baggage so apparent among sections of the young male army of fans which follow England. In addition to the well-publicised examples from the England tour to South America in 1986 when English fans returning on the same plane as the squad sang racist songs at the black English players, there is considerable evidence of racist, right activities at England matches abroad. In Luxemburg, Denmark and in Spain, during the World Cup Finals in 1982, English NF organisers were actively — and sometimes successfully — recruiting sympathisers before and after England matches (see Williams *et al.*, 1989). In the same year, following the selection of six black players for an England squad to play in West Germany, along with the usual cache of abusive letters from around the country about the importance of selecting only 'true born Englishmen' for the squad, the England manager Bobby Robson, also received a petition to similar effect, raised in the Birmingham area, and signed by more than 80 fans (Williams, 1991). During an England visit to Spain in 1984, a well-known NF activist was arrested and convicted following fights and missile-throwing before and after the match (*Searchlight*, April 1986), and Nazi salutes and slogans and displays of fascist symbols were common during England trips to West Germany (1987 and 1988), Sweden and Poland (1989) and, perhaps most bizarrely of all, even in Albania when, in March 1989 before a World Cup match against England in Tirana, a small number of a party of less than 140 accredited English fans gave Nazi salutes at the playing of the English national anthem before leaving the stadium as the match kicked off. In both Poland and West Germany, right-wing English extremists also visited the sites of concentration and extermination camps, leaving messages in support of Hitlerite doctrines as they went (see Goldberg, 1989).

Given the well-documented, cross-national contacts between right-wing organisations in other contexts (see e.g. Hill and Bell, 1988), it is perhaps not wholly surprising that similar racist contacts have also been made through links at international football. Information about the activities of football fascists in a number of European countries was published by the Socialist Group in the European Parliament at the beginning of 1986 (Bell, 1986). In 1987, however, research findings from Leuven University in Belgium posited a cross-national network of links between right-wing football hooligan groups in West Germany, Holland, Belgium, Sweden, Denmark, England and Scotland, though the Leuven 'evidence' for such liaisons — letters and occasional fan visits — fell far short of being sufficient to sustain the 'international Nazi terror' tabloid headlines which, inevitably, greeted their findings on publication in Britain (Van Limbergen *et al*, 1987). Certainly, at major international football tournaments these days the national differences and rivalries between hooligan crews and racists drawn from England and the continent seem quite sufficient to mitigate against the kind of cross-national conspiracy which is often predicted to be the likely result of contacts at football and elsewhere between members or sympathisers of racist groups drawn from different European countries (see Williams and Goldberg, 1990). There seems less doubt, however, that it is specifically English hooligan networks and far-right organisations in Britain which are currently identified on the continent as playing a central role in the spread of racist and violent subcultures across Europe. A recent report by the European Parliament's Committee of Inquiry into Racism and Xenophobia, published in 1990, for example, identified Britain as the major source of the 'export' of 'skinhead racism' to the continent and into Eastern Europe. Britain alone, the report concludes, accounts for more than 70,000 racist attacks a year (reported in the *Independent*, October 1990).

Signs of the soccer casual

Relating the issue of racism at football to the rise of the 'casual', Ian Taylor has argued that the shallow, jingoistic, chauvinistic and racist behaviour of some English football fans abroad is the product of the rise of a 'new' hooligan who is, in turn, the result of the emergence of a rampant competitive individualism among a post-war skilled labour aristocracy. These are the young working-class men who have done best out of the deregulation of labour markets brought by the free-market ideologies of Thatcherism. Lacking traditional working-class frameworks of support (neighbourhood, kinship, class institutions), the contemporary anxieties of the new bourgeois worker are revealed in the 'only possible development' available to them: a more intense, nihilistic form of racist, sexist and nationalist paranoia which is also fuelled by the xenophobic ranting of the British tabloid press. Hooliganism enacted by English fans abroad is, according to this view, simply beyond the reach of the pockets of the less skilled or unemployed working-class youth. The apparently high-spending and violent soccer 'casual' is, then, an entirely new departure in the hooligan phenomenon (Taylor, 1987).

I will return, briefly, later to these questions raised by Taylor about who is and who is not now involved in hooliganism at home and abroad. I am sympathetic to some of the points he makes. However, there is some evidence to suggest that in fact the work-less North West has a good claim in arguments concerning the origins of the soccer 'casual', confirming Frith's claim that 'Escape from hard times is a cultural necessity and the harder the times the more fantastic and precarious and desperate a business it becomes' (Frith, 1990: p. 179). By the late 1970s the 'casual' movement was already under way in Liverpool and parts of London. Other provincial towns and cities followed in their wake. Conversely, for the acutely style-conscious, some places have, simply, never caught on. Arguments about where and when the casual look began will almost certainly never be satisfactorily resolved. While Liverpool fans claim that they were 'looking smart' in 1978, Chelsea argue they began the fashion for expensive continental leisure wear in 1977. Liverpool fans had one of the first authentic local fanzines, *The End*, to advise on issues of dress and style (see Williams *et al.*, 1987; Redhead, 1987). Liverpool followers were regular European football travellers throughout the 1970s. London fans had better recourse to European holidays and to the continental range offered in sports outfitters like Lillywhites and were bigger active followers of pre-season tours and the national team abroad. What is clear is that the general trend began in these areas in the late 1970s when functional — but 'smart' and costly — imports from the athletics track — Adidas training shoes and hooded tops — were initially added to skintight jeans for the fashion-conscious and, according to the police, for those who wanted to be quickest 'on their toes' when the law came looking.

Locally available sports styles began to be shunned in Liverpool in late 1977, especially following the mass exodus from the city for the European Cup Final in Rome in the summer of 1977. Expensive sports 'designer' wear was an easy target abroad for light-fingered Liverpudlians, who are widely known in football circles in this country less for their fighting credentials than for their penchant for 'robbin'. It was the beginning of an illegal but lucrative cottage industry, drawn as a parody on Thatcherism's obsession with 'enterprise culture', and in resistance to national media stereotypes about the poverty-stricken, unemployment-riddled North West. Initially, the new continental styles fulfilled the same function of other European memorabilia — a sign of European adventure and club loyalty. Increasingly, however, soccer's style wars intensified, building upon traditional regional antagonisms (Cockneys are smarter/Cockneys are 'flash', etc.) but reflecting deepening economic and social divisions (London fans waving money at unemployed northerners or even revealing their designer underpants to their 'poor' northern rivals; see Ward, 1989: p. 97). In 1981, when Liverpool played Real Madrid in the European Cup Final in Paris, *Paris Soir* was astonished that the shoplifting targets of drunken young Liverpudlians included jewellers and sports shops, which were ransacked for Ellesse, Lacoste and Fila tracksuits and shirts. Meanwhile, at a time when other sorts of stores were struggling on Merseyside against the effects of a biting recession, the area became awash with security-guarded shops dealing in expensive sports leisure wear.

For the police and the press, of course, the 'casual' movement was predominantly a clever conspiracy designed to hide the 'real' hooligans among 'ordinary' respectable supporters. In cities like Liverpool, however, where work and its economic and cultural associations and certainties were simply not an available option to many young working-class men in the 1980s, this new football-centred 'life-style' spoke more of a defiant masculine celebration of economic depression and worklessness in the face of overwhelming pressure to consume. This new iconography — hardness = style *and* the power to buy — has been argued, by Frith, to pose problems for conventional sociological readings of youth subcultures as resisting bourgeois cultural hegemony (though earlier youth styles also celebrated hedonistic consumption *and* expressed it through their clothes and, in Liverpool at least, those central to the spread of the 'casual' style and 'scally' culture like the members of the popular local band, The Farm, were profoundly anti-bourgeois and highly politicised opponents of the Thatcher regime). Instead, the casuals are involved in a stylistic refusal to be excluded from the good life (Frith, 1990: p. 179). Importantly, too, if casuals were busy, in their narcissistic concern with self rather than class consciousness (Hobbs and Robins, 1990), in confusing the press as to their real origins — 'professional' people in 'good' jobs increasingly came up in media accounts about the 'new' hooligans — the backgrounds of many of the casuals in fact seemed strikingly traditional. The much-vaunted and massively hyped hooligan 'generals', who were described in the press as running businesses and managing banks, turned out to be self-employed window cleaners, couriers and irregularly employed clerks at best. Most others were in routine working-class jobs. As Hobbs and Robins argue, the casual style

relates to self-imagery and self promotion of working class youth through class specific hierarchies of violence and conspicuous consumption. The modern hooligan is very expensive and, in order to participate, he must identify himself, not only in terms of potential combat, but also by his ability to deal with scant monetary resources . . . The trajectory of this subculture takes with it a range of ever-changing icons of consumerism, but this should not detract from the unalterable class base from which the hooligan is propelled both to and from.

(Hobbs and Robins, 1990: p. 17)

This essential rootedness of the casual movement in football's traditional regional antagonisms and, indeed, in some of the traditional concerns of working-class youth for conspicuous consumption of the 'right gear' — it was certainly not cheap either to be an 'authentic' skin or a ted — makes it difficult to weigh claims that the new hooligan styles signalled significant post-modernist influences in the game and in working-class football culture (see Redhead, 1987). What was clear, however, was that the combination of muscle, 'gameness', articulate and sophisticated street smartness and style was becoming an eminently tradeable commodity in the new, media-saturated enterprise culture which was Britain in the 1980s. Members of West Ham's Inter City Firm, for example, were involved as consultants in BBC's 'The Firm' (1989) and delighted in representations of 'the lads' stockbroker belt life-styles and the trashing of the Golf convertibles and BMWs of rival hooligan gang leaders. The ICF were also looking, in 1988, at copywriting the 'firm's' initials in order to produce and market their own memorabilia. Members of the group, by now well-known faces to the police at football, were also involved in organising and running lucrative 'warehouse' parties in and around the London area. Big money was involved here, much of it untraceable. With typical panache, a number of members of the ICF turned up in style in Italy for the World Cup Finals in 1990, staying at the five-star Carlton Hotel in Bologna for the second-phase match against Belgium. On the street, however, they comfortably melted into the rest of the travelling English army.

Wise guys? Hooliganism, spectator behaviour and research

Recent academic debates about the hooligan phenomenon have become almost as lively, and as riddled with masculine posturing, as have been the dust-ups between the rival 'firms'. Some contributions seem to be in danger of becoming a mixture of the slapstick and slapdash. Others offer real insights and real advances. Many have offered well-reasoned critical comments about the approach to the hooligan issue adopted at the Centre for Football Research at Leicester University in the 1980s. I want, briefly, to look at some of these, and in doing so to outline my own views on the weaknesses — as well as the strengths — of the Leicester approach, while considering some of the alternative 'perspectives' which have now been put forward.

The rise of the apparently well-heeled 'casual' and speculation that the 'narcissims of minor difference' of the new youth cultures — an endless 'bricolage of style' (Cohen, 1988: pp. 38–9) — had explored the more traditional rules and rituals of 'community' and 'territoriality' which under-pinned the behaviour of young working-class men is one of the reasons why some of the Leicester work on hooliganism has come under attack. I have already said quite a bit about the class origins of the casuals and the continuities involved in their activities and cultural concerns. Indeed, among the various academic positions, I don't think there is too much disagreement on these issues. (More recent research in Scotland confirms that 'all the evidence points to the fact that "football casuals" come, predominantly, from the lower levels of the social scale and are, basically, working class youths'; see Harper, 1990). However, I think Taylor (1987) is probably correct to argue that recent changes in British political culture, in the structure of the labour market and in football's developing 'style wars' have contributed to making the firms attractive and accessible to *more* working class men from 'respectable' backgrounds who have money to spend. The more costly and sophisticated demands and attractions of riding with the 'top boys' — media, clothes, Europe, plotting up, messing up the police, etc., etc. — did make associations with hooliganism more fashionable, especially when the activities and utter-ances of those involved became ever more directed at opposing the pathologis-ing images of 'hooligans' carried and promoted by the media. (However, it should also be said that some working-class achievers have always been involved in hooliganism.) In this sense, Bill Buford's articulate Chelsea 'hooligans', including a Ph.D. student at London University (*Sunday Times*, 17 May 1987); Colin Ward's anti-racist, French-speaking, *Guardian*-reading hooligan guise (Ward, 1989); Hobbs and Robins' (1990) mythologised (and mythical?) schoolteacher member of Arsenal's 'Gooners'; and our own students at Leicester who were still 'involved' in hooliganism despite 'going to college', all have their place in the more recent manifestations of the phenomenon, which have been less straightforwardly 'knee-jerk' responses to violations of territorial rites than sometimes elaborate ploys designed best to engage (and outdress) identified rival firms. In more general terms, Ian Taylor's work is also useful for its determination properly to contextualise developments in football and the hooligan debate in terms of the particular historical and political moments of the game's recent struggles (Taylor, 1989).

The Leicester work on hooliganism, in any event, by no means excludes such cases of young men who have 'got on' but who are not beyond their cultural roots and male friendships networks. The Leicester research has often been mistakenly described as some variant of 'factor analysis' which argues for some simple and direct link, for example, between unemployment or deprivation and hooliganism. Instead, using Suttles' concept of 'ordered segmentation' (Suttles, 1968), the Leicester approach tries to describe the manner in which, under shifting circumstances for each new generation, the structure of lower-working-class communities seems, routinely, to generate specific cultural expectations about the use of violence in public spaces: the production and reproduction in effect of a cultural milieu which, in usually well-prescribed circumstances, demands or rewards physical violence between men (see Dunning, Murphy and Williams, 1988: ch. 9). The flexibilities in this account, particularly with respect to the range of locations, effects and penetrations of such milieux, have, perhaps, sometimes been underplayed in readings which have tried to link the origins of hooliganism in the Leicester work simply with some ideal-type, lower-working class community (see Dunning, Murphy and Williams, 1988; pp. 212–16). This is presumably one of the reasons why Hobbs and Robins ask, only partly, rhetorically whether a key member of West Ham's ICF, a man who once described himself as coming from an 'area where young men are "born to fight" and who has written about his football adventures, ably milking requests from television for interviews about football violence, can be usefully described as "lower class" ' (Hobbs and Robins, 1990: p. 8). It is tempting to say one might as well ask the question of another, rather better-known media star who has done reasonably well out of his own business and fighting acumen, Mike Tyson. What is it they say about being able to take the kid out of the street?

Less successfully, and less appropriately in my view, the Leicester work also attempts to explain the peaks and troughs in outbreaks of hooliganism using Norbert Elias's theory of 'civilising processes' (see Dunning, Murphy and Williams, 1988: ch. 10). I have already indicated in my brief review of the history of hooliganism at football some rethinking on my part of the issue of the scale and seriousness of earlier outbreaks of football crowd disorders. This reassessment sits uneasily with the 'latent evolutionism' of the theory of civilising processes (Horne and Jary, 1987: p. 100). In addition to this, the high level of generality at which the theory operates, its apparently universalistic applicability, and the sometimes rather fractious and defensive relations between 'Eliasians' and their critics (A. Clarke, 1991) also give the theory an aura of 'irrefutability' (Smith, 1984) and arguably leads, in the case of violence at football, to the underplaying of important national and cultural differences in patterns and forms of hooliganism. Finally, the theory underplays the more general importance of culturalist approaches, perhaps particularly those which examine the nature of, and shifts in, the cultural significance of the game in this country, and those structuralist perspectives which highlight key aspects of the constantly changing relationship between the state, football and the football audience (see, A. Clarke, 1991; Rogan Taylor and Ian Taylor, this volume).

Hobbs and Robins (1990: pp. 6–7) are also critical of the use of the civilising process to try to explain football hooliganism. They are on firm ground, too, when they lament the lack of hard data on the 'casuals', though these authors seem to believe that the only useful information on this issue is that which is gleaned from ethnographies. In criticising the methodologies adopted at Leicester, their own research on this issue leads them to simply, ignore the earlier ethnographic work done there (see Murphy *et al.*, 1990: ch. 6), and to understate substantially the nature and range of other data (e.g. from surveys) collected at Leicester about football supporters (Hobbs and Robins, 1990: pp. 7–11). Their contribution on the 'causes' of hooliganism seems disappointing, too. It seems to amount to little more than the assertion that violence is an apparently immutable 'fact of working class life' (Hobbs, 1988: p. 124), or, even more enigmatically, to the revelations like those provided to Robins by one of his subjects that 'its about mates, Dave, its about being with your mates, that's what its about' (Hobbs and Robins, 1990: p. 27). Having argued, contentiously, that 'there has been a steady stream of football-related deaths which we conservatively estimate at averaging six a year' (Hobbs and Robins, 1990: p. 3), Hobbs, in a later paper, incongruously, seems to resort to a crude variant of the moral panic/police conspiracy thesis in order to account for hooliganism's alleged unwarranted public prominence (Armstrong, Hobbs and Maguire, 1991)! Inevitably, given this sort of approach, social policy consider-ations are airily dismissed by Hobbs and Robins as just a 'yellow brick road' (p. 27) for self-seeking academics. New ethnographic work on a group of football 'casuals' from Sheffield (Armstrong and Harris, 1991) has recently been undertaken to add to the insights provided by accounts from football fans and followers of the firms themselves (Ward 1989; Allan 1989). Much of this work looks potentially very useful and interesting and it promises to update earlier studies and to add substantially to our knowledge about those currently described as 'hooligans'. However, judging from what has been made available so far, this material seems also to be rather short on sociological interpretation and theorisation. It seems, for example, to reject almost any structural analysis of the hooliganism question, in favour of one which rests, rather unconvinc-ingly, on anthropological assumptions about the alleged inevitability of clashes between committed rival fans (which fans? any fans?) at the sorts of 'dramas of rivalry' which constitute football matches. Armstrong and Harris also seem to be a little unsure about just how violent — and how regularly so — their subjects under scrutiny actually are (see Dunning, Murphy and Waddington, 1991). In a later paper (Armstrong, Hobbs and Maguire, 1991) Armstrong makes it clear he has little time for the new 'realist' criminologies stating that, for him, hooliganism is simply an overblown Trojan horse which has 'made it possible for the British police to introduce and normalise covert tactics and strategies of surveillance' (p. 41).

On the general issue of policy responses to hooliganism, the work at Leicester has also been criticised, more sympathetically, for being too social policy-oriented (Clarke, 1991; Horne, Jary and Bucke, 1991). On balance, I think this is fair comment, and reflects in part an over-corrective concern to produce a 'realist' response to hooliganism in the wake of the idealism of earlier approaches (see Marsh *et al.*, 1978). However, it is a criticism which also almost certainly overstates the Leicester influence in such matters, as well as underplaying the wide range of work about the game which goes on at the Centre for Football Research (see Williams and Woodhouse, this volume) but which is rather less 'newsworthy' than that on hooliganism. It is difficult to see, too, quite how the Leicester 'centre piece', *The Roots of Football Hooliganism*, a socio-historical study which deals with some of the structural underpinnings of the hooligan phenomenon, could be easily classified as a tome on social policy.

More specifically, Alan Clarke (1991) has argued that, despite the public opposition to them in the Leicester work, the Centre's research may have inadvertently contributed to the coercive penning and caging strategies which shaped football attendance in the 1970s and 1980s. I think there might be something to this argument to the extent that by stressing the structural roots of hooliganism to a right-wing authoritarian government which had been elected on a law and order platform, the Leicester work was unlikely, in doing so, to deflect such a regime from the fatally flawed and counter-productive policies of containment it so rigorously pursued. (The game itself could also escape responsibility for hooliganism, of course, by claiming, simplistically, that this research demonstrated that 'society', not football, was to blame.) But then one is tempted to ask just what sort of message might have had the desired effect — whatever that might have been — in such circumstances? In addition to this difficult problem, what is also missing, I think, from such criticism is any account of the supportive, enabling relationships established in the 1980s between Leicester and the articulate, progressive, democratising organisations within football — like the 'radical' national supporters organisation, the Football Supporters' Association, for example — which, rightly, figure prominently in Clarke's own thinking about a more ordered and hopeful future for the game. Let me, briefly, add some further comments on Clarke's position and on recent developments within football which promise the prospect of a brighter future ahead.

Clarke's central point is that much of the (published) Leicester work concentrates on a 'marginal minority' within the football figuration, the hooligans. In effect, he argues; the issue of hooliganism is one which concerns only a small number of fans, and a far more interesting sociological problem is raised by questions about which people become football supporters and why, and how, their patterns of support come into being. In this sense, 'In terms of achieving a detached view of the processes involved in the history of football, this focus on the "football figuration" rather than the "hooligan figuration" promises clearer insights into the patterns of support and webs of inter-dependence' (Clarke, 1991, p. 5). I have some sympathy with this view but, firstly, a number of qualifications. I would want to question the marginality of the hooligan issue which is stressed in Clarke's account. Hooliganism, and especially policy responses to the problem, has affected the football experiences of nearly all fans in this country in one way or another. Secondly, the Leicester work and its focus on issues external to football — the figuration examined is in fact much wider than 'hooligan' or 'football figurations' — took off as a response to approaches which adopted game-specific perspectives on the problem, i.e. ones which argued that match-day dynamics or changes in the game and in the relationship between the game and its audience alone were sufficient to explain the rise of hooliganism (see Taylor, 1971; Marsh et al., 1978). Clarke seems to me to be in danger of returning to his overly narrow position. Nevertheless, he is certainly correct to stress the need for more research on the football audience and on the cultural role of the sport and, by implication, for studies on the different traditions and responses to the game in different parts of the country. Such traditions might depend, for example, on different local occupational and political cultures; on different economic trajectories; on different local traditions of support; on differing local patterns of ethnic relations and player recruitment, etc. Clarke argues in relation to this point that what is crucially missing from the Leicester work is an exploration of the position of football in the community and the 'cultural power' which supporters can exert and have exerted, in shaping their relationship with the game and also the general cultural context within which the game is played and matches are staged (Clarke, 1991). Again, I think there is much to this argument though, once more, the Centre at Leicester is involved in research of this kind (see Rogan Taylor, this volume), and I want to conclude now by looking at recent developments in English football spectator culture which do perhaps promise a brighter future for the English game.

The people's game?

Since the Heysel disaster in 1985, but perhaps especially over the past two years and particularly since Hillsborough, the so-called 'alternative football network' has become more active in contesting the youth cultural terrain at football, much of which has previously tended to revolve particularly in press accounts more or less around the hooliganism/fashion axis. There are now, for example, more than 200 active supporter-produced football fanzines in Britain — most of them in England — which some estimates suggest have an annual readership of as many as one million fans (Horne, Jary and Bucke, 1991). Unlike some of their popular counterparts in Germany, for example, the vast majority of these independent supporter-produced and circulated magazines do not, typically, deal in exchanges between rival hooligan gangs (although a minority do seem to survive largely on the basis of stoking up local rivalries). Instead, they report on club and national football issues and, crucially, they also attempt to reflect the experiences and views of largely young, mainly terrace, non-hooligan football supporters. They are written mainly by, and for, male fans but many include articles by, and about, women and at least one fanzine, Born Kicking, is produced by a woman for a largely female audience. Almost without exception, such fanzines are also, explicitly or otherwise, non-racist. Editions of two 'World Cup' fanzines — one English, one Scottish — were also produced in Britain before the 1990 Finals. In the main, these publications celebrated the tournament and the place of the national teams in it. Predictably, however, the tabloid press in Britain concentrated its attentions before Italia '90 on a 'one-off', poorly produced, low-distribution 'fanzine' which urged hooliganism in Italy and which seemed to be regarded by most fans as a spoof (see 'This Evil Mag', Sun, 10 May 1990).

In some limited ways, the sense of collective and street-credible outlook which fanzines provide for young male fans who are caught between the ageing respectability of the supporters' club and the attractions of hooligan sub-cultures makes them very loosely analogous in their cultural role with aspects of the Ultras movements in Italy and Spain (although national fanzine readership seems largely confined to the better-educated segments of the football supporters' market; see Horne *et al.*, 1991). At the very least, many of them formally celebrate the wit and cultural invention of the terrace experience in a manner which, at least implicitly, challenges the more violent and racist aspects of the hooligan repertoire. The fanzine movement — or at least fanzine culture — has also been central to the, admittedly, recent spread and influence in English football of largely non-violent terrace styles (fancy dress, inflatables, etc.) and to the recent growth in England of a new, serious, literary interest in the game (see Taylor, 1990, also Hill, 1989, and Davies, 1990, as examples). It has also been important in stimulating a re-exploration of the relationship between popular musical genres and football. In this last case, the pacifying influence (on football fans) of the north west's so-called 'Scallydelia' movement (see Redhead, 1990) has probably been overstated. Nevertheless, it is perhaps significant that a popular and sophisticated north-west dance-oriented band, New Order, performed the official England World Cup song along with John Barnes and with inputs from one or two other England players. The song contained an explicit anti-hooligan message but at the same time, and perhaps more importantly, it was able to penetrate effectively credible football and 'street' cultures by being 'without doubt, the best pop record ever to be connected with football; perhaps the first such song that you can carry out of Our Price [record store] without self-combusting with embarrassment' (*New Musical Express*, 19 May 1990).

Although penetrating less directly into specifically youth cultural options, the continuing activities and public profile of the Football Supporters Association (FSA) in recent years, particularly in England, have also offered an alternative vision of experiences of the game and its future from that proffered either by hooligans (the struggle over the terraces) or by many major clubs (the high-spending 'family' audience). I have no space here to cover the origins and the growth of the FSA since Heysel (see, instead, Williams *et al.*, 1989). Suffice to say that the FSA was granted legal representation on behalf of spectators' interests at the Taylor Inquiry (the first time legal costs had been granted for such an organisation) and has continued to campaign in an articulate and informed manner in England for more formal recognition of the potential role of non-hooligan fans in limiting hooliganism and in helping to establish a new climate of greater mutual tolerance and respect amongst rival spectators. The organisation also played a key role at the World Cup Finals in Italy in providing information, guidance and support for English fans, particularly in Sardinia.

Added to these positive developments in the English game which have become more prominent since 1988, mention should also be made of the continuing spread of 'community'-related activities of English clubs over the past two years. A nationally funded community coaching and training initiative managed jointly by the Professional Footballers Association and the Football League is now in operation at more than fifty Football League clubs in

England and Wales. This scheme is about to be merged into a new Football Trust-funded national community programme which will be co-administered by the English Football Association and will cover all ninety-two (eventually ninety-four) League clubs.

Many of these schemes give specific encouragement to women players (more than thirty League clubs now have an affiliated women's team) and they are also involved in promoting match-day activities and facilities at clubs (family enclosures, membership schemes, supporter exchanges, etc.). Such initiatives seem to be slowly succeeding in building an infrastructure of 'community'-related contacts between Football League clubs and are arguably having an influence on changing the prevailing climate at some major grounds. Many, if not all, of the most successful of these locally based 'community' initiatives are substantially supported via the uses of local authority finance and facilities. Some of these relationships (e.g. at Leeds United, Preston, Halifax, and Millwall) bear similarities to the sorts of public-sector/private-sector partnerships which are more common in professional football in continental Europe than they tend to be in England. One of the most successful of the community initiatives, at Millwall, seems in fact to have a level of club commitment which goes some way beyond that typically experienced in some other northern European countries.

Such initiatives are unlikely to impact directly, of course, on the young men for whom fighting at football is much more interesting and important than simply (increasingly) sitting down to watch the game. But they do reflect a real cultural contestation within the 'football figuration' about some of the defining characteristics of what the game is actually about. Such issues are no longer just a struggle between 'the lads' and an 'intelligence'-obsessed police force. Hooliganism is not going to disappear from English football. But the manner in which it is contained, and the role of football fans in setting new agendas for the sport, will be crucial in its struggles to become, in the post-Taylor climate, a modern and reasonably pacified spectator sport for the 1990s and beyond.

Acknowledgements

I would like to thank Steve Wagg for helpful comments on an earlier draft of this essay.

Bibliography

Allan, J. (1989), *Bloody Casuals*, Glasgow: Famedram.
Armstrong, G. and R. Harris (1991), 'Football Hooliganism: Theory and Evidence', *Sociological Review*, forthcoming.
Armstrong, G., D. Hobbs and M. Maguire (1991), 'The Professional Foul: Covert Policing in Britain: The Case of Soccer', paper given at the Law and Society Annual Meeting, Amsterdam, June 1991.

Bell, A. (1986), *Against Racism and Fascism in Europe*, European Parliament: Socialist Group.

Clarke, A. (1991) 'Figuring a Brighter Future', in E. Dunning and C. Rojek, (eds), *Sport and Leisure in the Civilising Process*, London: Macmillan, forthcoming.

Clarke, J. (1978), 'Football and Working Class Fans: Tradition and Change', in R. Ingham (ed.), *Football Hooliganism: The Wider Context*, London: Inter-Action.

Cohen, P. (1972), 'Subcultural Conflict and Working Class community', *Working Papers in Cultural Studies*, **2**, pp. 5–52.

Cohen, P. (1978), 'Policing the Working Class City', in *Capitalism and the Rule of Law*, London: Hutchinson, pp. 118–36.

Cohen, P. (1988), 'The Perversions of Inheritance: Studies in the Making of Multi-racist Britain', in P. Cohen and H. Bains (eds), *Multi-racist Britain*, London: Macmillan.

Committee of Inquiry into Crowd Safety and Control at Soccer Grounds (1986) (Chairman: Mr Justice Popplewell), Final Report, HMSO, Cmnd. 2710. ('The Popplewell Report').

Davies, A. (1984), *Where Did The Forties Go?*, London: Pluto Press.

Davies, P. (1990), *All Played Out*, London: Heinemann.

Dunning, E., P. Murphy and I. Waddington (1991), 'Anthropological *Versus* Sociological Approaches to the Study of Football Hooliganism: Some Critical Notes', *Sociological Review*, forthcoming.

Dunning, E., P. Murphy and J. Williams, (1988), *The Roots of Football Hooliganism*, London: Routledge.

Frith, S. (1990), 'Frankie Said: But What Did They Mean?', in A. Tomlinson (ed.), *Consumption, Identity and Style*, London: Routledge, pp. 172–85.

Goldberg, A. (1989), 'English Fans in Poland', unpublished working paper, Leicester.

Harper, C. (Inspector) (1990), 'A Study of Football Crowd Behaviour', unpublished paper, Edinburgh.

Hill, D. (1989), *Out of his Skin: The John Barnes Phenomenon*, London: Faber and Faber.

Hill, R. and A. Bell, (1988), *The Other Face of Terror*, London: Grafton Books.

Hobbs, D. (1988), *Doing the Business*, Oxford: Oxford University Press.

Hobbs, D. and D. Robins (1990), 'The Boy Done Good: Football Violence, Changes and Continuities', paper presented to the British Sociological Association, July 1990.

Holt, R. (1989), *Sport and the British*, Oxford: Oxford University Press.

Horne, J. and D. Jary (1987), 'The Figurational Sociology of Sport and Leisure of Elias and Dunning: An Exposition and Critique', in J. Horne, D. Jary and A. Tomlinson (eds) *Sport, Leisure and Social Relations*, London: Routledge.

Horne, J., D. Jary and T. Bucke (1991), 'Football Fanzines and Popular Culture', *Sociological Review*, forthcoming.

Humphries, S. (1981), *Hooligans or Rebels?*, Oxford: Blackwells.

Inglis, S. (1987), *Football Grounds of England and Wales*, London: Collins Willow.

Leeds TUC and Leeds AFA (1987), 'Terror on the Terraces', mimeo.

Marsh, P., E. Rosser and R. Harre (1978), *The Rules of Disorder*, London: Routledge.

Mason, T. and J. Crump (1987), 'Hostile and Improper Demonstrations, Football 1880–1980' in J. A. Mangan (ed.), *Proc. xi Hispa. Int. Congress*, pp. 65–8.

Miles, R. (1988), 'Recent Marxist Theories of Nationalism and the Issue of Racism', *British Journal of Sociology*, **xxxviii** (1), pp. 24–43.

Muncie, J. (1984), *The Trouble With Kids Today*, London: Hutchinson.

Murphy, P., J. Williams and E. Dunning (1990), *Football on Trial*, London: Routledge.

Murray, B. (1984), *The Old Firm: Sectarianism, Sport and Society in Scotland*, Edinburgh: John Donald.

Pearson, G. (1983), *Hooligan: A History of Respectable Fears*, London: Macmillan.

Redhead, S. (1987), *Sing When You're Winning: The Last Football Book*, London: Pluto Press.

Redhead, S. (1990), *The End-of-the-Century Party: Youth and Pop Towards 2000*, Manchester: Manchester University Press.

Reiner, R. (1985), *The Politics of the Police*, Brighton: Wheatsheaf.

Robins, D. (1984), *We Hate Humans*, Harmondsworth: Penguin.

Robins, D. and Cohen, P. (1978), *Knuckle Sandwich*, Harmondsworth: Penguin.

Smith, D. (1984), 'Established or Outsider?', *Sociological Review*, **32**, pp. 367–89.

Suttles, G. (1968), *The Social Order of the Slum*, Chicago: University of Chicago Press.

Taylor, I. (1971) 'Soccer Consciousness and Soccer Hooliganism', in S. Cohen (ed.), *Images of Deviance*, Harmondsworth: Penguin.

Taylor, I. (1987), 'British Soccer After Bradford', *Sociology of Sport Journal*, no. 4, pp. 171–91.

Taylor, I., (1989), 'Hillsborough, 15th April, 1989: Some Personal Contemplations', *New Left Review*, December, pp. 89–110.

Taylor, I. (1990), 'British Soccer and Europe: Problems and Possibilities', Le Footbal et Europe Conference, Florence, 3–5 May 1990.

Van Limbergen, K., Colaers, C., and Walgrave, L. (1987), *Research on the Societal and Psycho-sociological Background of Football Hooliganism*, Leuven, Catholic University of Leuven.

Wagg, S. (1984), *The Football World*, Brighton: Harvester.

Ward, C. (1989), *Steaming In*, London: Simon and Schuster.

White, J. (1986), *The Worst Street in North London*, London: Routledge.

Williams, J. (1991), 'Lick My Boots . . . Racism in English Football', unpublished working paper, Leicester.

Williams, J. and T. Bucke (1989), 'Football and Football Spectators After Hillsborough: A National Survey of Members of the FSA', report for the Football Trust, Leicester.

Williams, J. and A. Goldberg (1990), *Spectator Behaviour, Media Coverage and Crowd Control at the 1988 European Football Championships*, Strasbourg: Council of Europe.

Williams, J., P. Murphy and E. Dunning (1987), 'Football and Football Hooliganism in Liverpool', report for the Football Trust, Leicester.

Williams, J., E. Dunning and P. Murphy (1989), *Hooligans Abroad* (2nd edn), London: Routledge.

Willis, P. (1990), *Counter Cultures*, Milton Keynes: Open University Press.

Part 4
Getting into Europe

10
The politics of football in the new Europe

Vic Duke

A new Europe is emerging in the 1990s with important economic, political and social changes occurring in both Western Europe and Eastern Europe. Football cannot escape the consequences of these changes, so that by the end of the century the European football map will look rather different. This chapter will examine the changes in both Western and Eastern Europe before addressing their likely impact on British football.

After a decade of off-field disasters in the 1980s, 1990 was a good year for English football. On the playing field, England reached the semi-finals of the World Cup in Italy, their best ever performance on foreign soil and second best only to winning the 1966 World Cup in England. More importantly, off the field there were no major incidents of football hooliganism involving England supporters in Italy.

This relative improvement in the behaviour of English football fans resulted in the ultimate triumph of 1990, namely the return of English clubs to European competition. English clubs had been banned from the three European cup competitions since the Heysel Stadium disaster of 1985. On 10 July 1990 this ban was lifted (except for Liverpool who had received an additional penalty) and the names of two English clubs (Aston Villa and Manchester United) were entered into the first-round draw for the European competitions.

At the time of writing the first two rounds of the European cups have been completed with no trouble of note involving English supporters. Over the same period, continental Europe has witnessed a fresh wave of football-related violence, much of it in Eastern Europe, where the combination of greater political freedom and a reduced police state is proving a volatile mixture. For instance, in a twelve-day period at the end of September there were major incidents in Vienna, Bergamo, Leverkusen, Belgrade, Split, Chemnitz, Leipzig, Rijeka and Prague. The culmination of this wave of violence was on Saturday 3 November in Leipzig where the (East) German police opened fire on rioting football fans and killed an 18-year-old supporter.

There is, however, more to the politics of football than the problem of football hooliganism. The next section considers the implications of 1992 for football in Western Europe. This is followed by a discussion of the impact of perestroika on Eastern European football. The final section examines the place of British football in the new Europe.

Western Europe and 1992

European integration will take a major step forward in 1992. Members of the European Economic Community (EEC) will become part of a single economic market. The status of frontiers between member states will be downgraded and individuals will be entitled to move and to work in any member state. There will no longer be restrictions on the movement of professional footballers from one member state to another. This development has enormous implications for the future of European football.

A political battle is under way between the European Commission (EC) and the Union of European Football Associations (UEFA) over freedom of movement for professional footballers. UEFA wishes to limit the number of foreign players (i.e. from another country) in each professional club team, a proposal which contravenes the free movement of EEC players within EEC countries. The EC insists that restrictions may apply to non-EEC players, but EEC players should be free to engage in their profession anywhere in the EEC.

UEFA has thirty-five member associations of which fifteen are located within the EEC. Because football developed first in Britain, there are four separate member associations for England, Scotland, Wales and Northern Ireland. Given the queue of countries wishing to join the EEC (e.g. Austria, Turkey, Hungary, Czechoslovakia and Poland), the balance of power is likely to shift in favour of the EC. An added complication, however, is that the UEFA headquarters are located in Switzerland and are, therefore, not subject to the rulings of the EC.

Currently, in most of the EEC member states, the number of 'foreign' players allowed to play in the domestic league championship is limited to two per club (in Italy it is three per club). UEFA controls the three European club competitions and has the political power to impose restrictions on them. Thus, from 1991 to 1992 clubs entering the three European Cup competitions will be restricted to naming a maximum of four non-nationals in a squad of sixteen players for each cup game. Clearly, there is a legal conflict between this ruling and freedom of movement for EEC footballers playing for EEC clubs.

After 1992 the definition of what constitutes a foreign player in EEC countries will change. According to the EC, a 'foreign' player will be a non-EEC national, whereas for UEFA the definition will remain that of a player who is not a national of that country. Players from other EEC countries will be foreign under UEFA rules, but not foreign under EC rules.

An example may be useful at this juncture. Assuming a restriction of three foreigners per club and applying the EC rules would permit the following scenario. Clubs are allowed to select a maximum of three non-EEC players, whilst the other eight (or ten including substitutes) must be EEC players. Thus a club could take the field (theoretically) with a multinational team composed entirely of foreigners in the UEFA sense, as long as no more than three of them are from outside the EEC.

Some commentators would suggest that this scenario has occurred already. During the 1985–6 season the Liverpool team which won the League and Cup double often contained not a single English player. Of course, the United Kingdom is a special case with four football associations in the one state, and the Liverpool team contained many Scottish, Welsh and Irish players. I shall return to this special case in the concluding section.

In practice, different member states already apply different interpretations of the current rules regarding players who are non-nationals. Belgium and Portugal have operated liberal interpretations of the term 'national'. Any player who arrives in Belgium before the age of 18 or who has played there for five years is deemed Belgian for club purposes. Portugal has treated all Brazilian players as Portuguese which has proved to be very convenient. Spain and Italy have tended to adopt more restrictive policies. Between 1965 and 1980 Italy permitted no foreign nationals. Some Spanish clubs have restricted themselves to fielding regional players only, such as Basque 'nationals' in the case of Real Sociedad.

Already, before 1992, there are established patterns in Europe of the flow of players from the poorer clubs/countries to the wealthier clubs/countries in football terms. Yugoslavia is the largest exporter of footballers with over 400 playing abroad. At the pinnacle of the importers' list and paying the highest salaries are the leading clubs of Italy and Spain, which have the financial power to buy players from anywhere in Europe (or indeed the world). Even leading West German players are tempted south to play in Italy and Spain. Argentina and Brazil are the two leading powers in South American football, but a majority of both their 1990 World Cup squads play in Europe.

The purchasing power of Italy and Spain as the leading importers of quality foreign players was confirmed again in the summer of 1990 following the World Cup. Transfers from abroad to Italy represented a vast array of international talent; namely four Brazilians, three Uruguayans, two Germans, two Soviets, two Romanians and one each from Argentina, Belgium, Czechoslovakia, Denmark, Hungary, Portugal, Spain and Sweden. Spain exhibited a slightly lower level of influx with two each from Bulgaria, Cameroon, England and Romania and one each from Argentina, Austria, Columbia, Uruguay, the United States and Yugoslavia.

UEFA fears that the flow of players described above will intensify if freedom of movement is conceded, and will have a detrimental effect on the development of domestic players in many countries. On the one hand, young nationals in net importer countries will find it difficult to break into the team and youth policies will be less important to these clubs. On the other hand, net exporter countries will lose all their leading players, which will result in a lowering of standards.

The impetus towards European integration has led to increased calls for the formation of a European League comprising the leading clubs in Europe (overwhelmingly in the EEC). No official statement has been issued on the subject by UEFA, who dismisses the proposition as pure media speculation.

Under UEFA rules an official proposal would have to be submitted by a national football association rather than by a group of interested clubs.

Significantly, both political and economic arguments for a European League are gaining momentum. The potential unifying force of a European League is not lost on the EC, notwithstanding the accompanying potential for disorder in terms of football hooliganism. Most European countries' national leagues display a conventional pyramid structure. At the top of the structure are the leading clubs in a national first division, followed (usually) by a national second division, regional third divisions and ever more regionalised sub-divisions. The logic of such a system is clearly extendable to the supranational level.

Economic arguments centre on the high cost of competing at the European level and the superiority for financial stability of a league structure rather than a knockout format. The existing European club competitions rely on a knockout format so that the leading clubs can be sure of revenue only for one round. By contrast a series of league fixtures against all others in the league provides a sounder financial base, and a consistently higher level of competition. Interestingly, very similar arguments were deployed in the period leading up to the formation of the world's first football league, in England in 1888.

The economic pressure against a knockout format has provoked a minor change on the part of UEFA and has opened up the possibility of a compromise solution. For season 1990–1 the first two rounds of the European cups were seeded in order to prevent major clubs from clashing too early in the competition. An extension to the seeding principle, which also moves in the direction of a league format, has been suggested by Real Madrid. The plan is to organise the first round of the European competitions on a mini-league basis with, say, four teams in each group, one of which would be a seeded club. The later stages would revert to a knockout format. The Netherlands FA may be prepared to propose a change of format on behalf of their leading clubs.

Other politico-economic changes in the new Europe are contributing to the pressure for a European League. Traditionally, television coverage of football was monopolised by state television companies. Western Europe is experiencing currently an era of deregulation and privatisation in the television industry. The resultant competition for football coverage has forced up the price football can command from television. Substantial rises have been negotiated in England, Scotland, Italy, France and West Germany (for a detailed discussion see Fynn *et al.*, 1989). Leading football clubs (and their owners) have come to realise that large profits can be made through the televising and marketing of professional football. In addition to selling television rights, there is money to be made through advertising, promotion and sponsorship deals.

It is no surprise that two of the leading clubs pressing for a European League are AC Milan and Olympique Marseille. Their owners, Silvio Berlusconi and Bernard Tapie respectively, are both heavily involved in independent television. For season 1990–1 a subsidiary of Berlusconi's empire (Fininvest) secured provisional television rights from over seventy clubs throughout Europe just in case they were drawn against Italian opponents in European competition. Meanwhile, Tapie has strengthened his sporting empire recently by buying Adidas, the leading German sports good manufacturer.

A further trend is the growing link between leading clubs and sponsorship by multinational companies. In 1986 PSV Eindhoven were totally integrated with Philips and became a profit-making subsidiary. Juventus of Turin are sponsored by Fiat and IFK Gothenberg by Volvo. Powerful interests lie behind many of the leading European football clubs and their pressure for a European League is considerable.

The setting up of a European League is, however, not without its problems. Not least of these is its relationship with UEFA. Without the support of UEFA, top players in the European League would risk not being able to play for their national team in the World Cup or European Championship. The leading clubs in the European League also risk expulsion from UEFA if they form a breakaway league without UEFA's approval.

Another problem concerns the relationship between the European League and the national leagues of the participants. Do the European élite clubs no longer contest their national leagues? Or do they compete in both? The latter option is liable to lead to conflicts of interest in a congested fixture list. In which league should the strongest team be fielded? In the past, both Boca Juniors and River Plate have fielded weakened/reserve sides in the Argentine league in order to save their best players for the South American (Libertadores) Cup, which begins with a set of mini-leagues.

Moreover, what are to be the criteria for inclusion in the European League? The proponents of the idea are tending to stress financial rather than playing criteria. The size and quality of the stadiums are likely to be an additional factor. There is a definite move towards demanding all-seater stadiums on the part of the Fédération Internationale de Football Association (FIFA). In principle, qualifying matches for the 1994 World Cup may only be played in all-seater stadiums. From 1993 UEFA may designate other high-risk matches as playable in all-seater only.

Already Italy has converted all its World Cup stadiums to seating. Clubs in the Netherlands have been ordered to cut the standing capacity of their grounds by 10 per cent each year, so as to achieve all seating by the end of the century. And in England the British Government has accepted the recommendation of the Taylor Report into the Hillsborough Stadium Disaster that all first and second division clubs must become all-seater by August 1994 (and all third and fourth division clubs by August 1999).

The speed of modern air travel renders the idea of a European League a viable proposition. However, the climatic variations of Europe make it difficult to agree on a playing season compatible with all the potential participants. The Soviet Union and Scandinavian countries play from spring to autumn with a long winter break. Most other mainland European countries now have a short winter break of between one and three months. Only the British insist on playing on throughout the winter. Could it be that the European League will be a summer league rather than a winter league?

Another problem arises where cities possess two leading clubs and the traditional rivalry between them is of crucial importance, especially for supporters. If Real Madrid enter the European League, what is to become of

Atletico Madrid? AC Milan are one of the driving forces behind a European
League, but what of their eternal rivals, Internazionale? In 1989–90 both
Milan clubs competed in the European Cup, a feat which no city had achieved
since 1968–9 when Manchester City and Manchester United appeared
together. Examples of other cities where choosing one club only for a
European League would cause local conflict are Turin, Genoa, Rome, London,
Liverpool, Glasgow, Lisbon, Athens and Vienna.

A more general point concerns the departures from the European cultural
tradition in the way proponents of the European League suggest it will be
organised. The proposed league fits more neatly into the North American
model of sport where television and advertising are as important as the game
itself, and the major cities obtain franchises in the league. Substantial
corporate investment is premised on the security of continued involvement at
the highest level.

The American professional leagues have no promotion or relegation, the
elements which form the cornerstone of the European tradition of sporting
competition. All of the European national leagues, with the exception of that
in Northern Ireland, cater for automatic relegation from the first division and
promotion from the second division. Much of the interest at the start of the
new season centres on how the newly promoted/relegated teams will perform.
A closed shop of élite clubs in the European league might soon appear stale to
the European palate.

Furthermore, admission prices are high in North America (except in the
case of baseball), which produces a more middle-class crowd in the stadium.
The working class must watch the game on TV. Again the European tradition
has been of a more mixed crowd, or at least of stadiums with differentially
priced sections to accomodate different strata of society.

Association Football (or soccer in the United States) is experiencing
attempts to Americanise the sport prior to the 1994 World Cup Finals which
are to be held in the United States. Recent suggestions such as widening the
goals to increase scoring, and dividing the match into four quarters to facilitate
advertising breaks on television, are totally alien to the history of the world
game and the European cultural tradition. This cultural tradition is common to
both Western and Eastern Europe, but the latter is facing problems of a
different nature, and it is to these issues I now turn.

Eastern Europe and 'perestroika'

Eastern Europe is currently experiencing a period of pronounced change —
economic, political and social. This whole process of change can be traced back
to the new leadership and new direction in the Soviet Union established by
Mikhail Gorbachev. 'Perestroika' has no clear-cut translation into English,
although it is usually summarised as restructuring or reconstruction. To
Gorbachev perestroika is a major programme of planned change in almost all
aspects of life (see Gorbachev, 1987).

With respect to economic policy, perestroika involves decentralisation and
expanding the role of market forces. However, as a renewal of the whole of

society, perestroika is not confined to economic change. Growth in the economy cannot be separated from democratisation and the principle of 'glasnost'. The latter refers to openness to new ideas and alternative viewpoints, a principle which is to apply to all aspects of social organisation. Football in the Soviet Union and Eastern Europe is therefore certain to change as a result of perestroika and glasnost.

Prior to perestroika, the official view in the socialist republics of Eastern Europe was that top-level football players were not professionals. They were registered as employees of the factory/enterprise/ministry that sponsored their club. In practice, they trained and performed as full-time 'professional' sportsmen. UEFA classified Eastern European players in a hybrid category as neither professionals (in the commercial sense) nor amateurs (in the part-time sense). Not until 1988 did UEFA alter the status of footballers in Czechoslovakia and Hungary to that of full-time professionals.

The changes in Czechoslovakia took place in two separate stages, the first before the so-called 'velvet revolution' of November 1989 and the second after it. The first stage was largely a response to pressures for change from within but was also partly influenced by the general context of perestroika (see Duke, 1990). The second stage completed the transition to an independent and professional football industry.

Starting from the 1988–9 season, Czechoslovakia first division footballers were recognised officially as professional sportsmen. They became contract players with their club and received a salary from the state according to the terms of their contract, which varied according to status and experience. The professionalisation of players represents a marked increase in status for the sportsmen involved. Differential pay scales strengthen the relationship between quality of work and salary obtained. The pay initiative enhances the role of incentives in improving performance.

Nonetheless, at this first stage, the salaries paid to the players were from the state and not from the club as a private concern. The pay scales were determined by the state bureaucracy rather than the market. At the time, football officials in Czechoslovakia predicted that they would emulate Hungary and the Soviet Union by allowing clubs to become commercially run, private organisations.

After the 'velvet revolution' the pace of change in all aspects of Czechoslovak society has intensified. The second stage in spring 1990 gave players freedom of contract and in May 1990 the Czechoslovak Football Association became independent of the state. A switch from total state finance to independent status and the accompanying need to be self-financing cannot be achieved overnight. Hence, the Czechoslovak FA are currently in a transition period with state finance progressively reduced until the summer of 1991. From that point on, the FA and the clubs will be totally independent private enterprises and the players will possess real professional contracts in the Western sense.

The Soviet case most frequently cited as an exemplar of future changes is Dnepr Dnepropetrovsk. In 1988 Dnepr became the first commercially run football club to win the Soviet first division championship. Three years previously the club severed its links with their trade union sponsors and became self-financing. Players were offered three-year contracts in the first instance. The success of the model is evident not only on the playing field but also in the bank. By the end of 1987 Dnepr had accumulated a profit of 300,000 roubles (roughly 0.6 of a rouble to the dollar).

Hungarian football has undergone more gradual changes over a longer time period, but the final stages of the process were completed under the influence of perestroika. The first steps towards professionalism were taken in 1979 and official approval was granted in 1983. Open professionalism was introduced in an attempt to overcome match-fixing and corruption scandals. The major scandal of the early 1980s involved 499 players, officials and organisers, some of whom were given prison sentences.

Despite the earlier start in Hungary, the move to an independent professional football structure was completed only recently, about one year ahead of the Czechoslovaks. In January 1989 freedom of contract was granted to the players and the Football Association became independent of the state in June 1989. As with the Czechoslovak FA there is a transition phase during which the state continues to provide some finance. In 1990, 7 per cent of Hungarian FA expenditure was covered by central government.

In addition to the professionalisation of players, there is a greater openness (glasnost?) to the transfer abroad of football players in return for much-needed Western currency. Initially, these transfers operated within strict limits. Footballers could move to the West only after reaching the age of 30 and if they had served the national team with distinction.

More recently, younger players have been transferred to the West. This trend to younger transfers started with Alexander Zavarov's transfer from Dynamo Kiev to Juventus at the age of 27 for £3.2 million in the summer of 1988. The flow of transfers to the West from Eastern Europe accelerated after the 1990 World Cup Finals in Italy. Fourteen of the Czechoslovak squad of twenty-two are now playing in the West and eleven of the Romanian squad have been transferred abroad since the finals.

Over 200 Hungarian footballers are currently playing abroad but around 85 per cent of them play in the Austrian second, third and fourth divisions. These are semi-professionals who continue to live in Hungary and receive match expenses in Austria, which are considerably better than the salaries of full-time professionals in the Hungarian first division. Similarly, for Czechoslovakia, there are 170 playing abroad of whom 80 per cent play for lower division teams near the border in (West) Germany and Austria.

Opportunities for leading players to seek a transfer abroad contribute to the development of greater openness and increased contact with the West. However, the glasnost policy of permitting official transfer to the West can be seen also as an attempt to stem the flow of unofficial defections. The most notorious case in Czechoslovakia recently was the joint defection of Ivo Knoflicek and Lubos Kubik from Slavia Prague whilst on tour in West Germany. After several months in hiding around Europe and a fruitless attempt to sign for Derby County, both returned eventually to Prague to negotiate compromise deals which took them to St. Pauli (West Germany) and Fiorentina (Italy) respectively.

During the initial period of change in both Czechoslovakia and Hungary, control of the transfer process remained bureaucratic despite the partial involvement of market forces in setting the transfer fee. Only when the Football Associations gained complete independence from the state were the transfer fees retained by the individual clubs themselves.

The most significant impact on the rate of transfers will occur if Eastern European countries attain associate membership of the European Economic Community and if EC rules on free movement of players prevail. The flow of players to Western Europe is then liable to become a flood.

In terms of sponsorship, the traditional East European model was for sports clubs to be sponsored by a factory, enterprise, ministry or trade union. The players were regarded as employees of the enterprise concerned. Now more commercial sponsorship involving Western firms is emerging and perestroika is seen as opening more possibilities in the near future.

At this point in time, many of the clubs continue to be sponsored by heavy industrial enterprises such as chemicals, steel and engineering. For instance, in Czechoslovakia Banik Ostrava are sponsored by the miners' trade union and Vitkovice by a steelworks. Eastern European leagues also contain a large number of clubs funded by the army such as Dukla Prague, Red Star Belgrade, Steaua Bucharest and CSKA Sofia. The Dynamo clubs were traditionally associated with the secret police but this connection has been discontinued (officially at least).

Several clubs have negotiated new forms of sponsorship with Western firms. In return for sponsorship, the company obtains advertising both on the club shirts and around the ground. Dynamo Kiev have signed a major sponsorship deal with Fisac, an Italian textile company. A further development concerns deals struck with Western equipment firms. Sports officials admit that the quality of Western equipment is better than their own products. Thus Western firms provide equipment in return for advertising rights. For example, Slovan Bratislava have arranged such deals with Adidas and Hitec.

In some countries, major sponsorship deals with Western firms have been restricted, thus far, to the leading clubs. For example, in Czechoslovakia in August 1990 Sparta Prague, who are the best-supported team in that country, were the first to secure a deal involving shirt advertising in return for sponsorship from Opel. Minolta of Austria followed suit by sponsoring the team from Nitra, now renamed Minolta Nitra. The name change unfortunately deprives us of one of the most evocative names in European football, that of Plastika Nitra.

Only the best-supported club in Hungary has negotiated foreign sponsorship thus far. Ferencvaros this year received 25 million forints from a French construction company (Bras) along with 5 million forints (there are approximately 100 forints to the £), from a Hungarian firm (Hargita). Hargita's name appears on their shirts. Not surprisingly these firms are involved in converting the club's ground into a 22,000-capacity, all-seater stadium by autumn 1991. At present Raba Gyor have the only all-seater stadium in Hungary.

Ferencvaros are making great strides towards the Western model of a football club as a commercial enterprise. To this end, the football section became separate from the original multi-sports club in January 1990. Turnover at the football club has increased phenomenally from 16 million forints in

1987-8, and 30 million in 1988-9, to nearly 50 million in 1989-90 and to an expected figure of over 100 million in 1990-1. The club intend to become a limited company within the next two years.

The new era of financial independence from the state is, however, taking its toll of the smaller clubs. Between 1988 and 1989 the number of multi-sports in Hungary decreased by 8 per cent and the membership of clubs declined by 19 per cent in the harsh economic climate of democratic capitalism.

All the various forms of commercial sponsorship are consistent with the principles of perestroika. New ideas from the West have been taken up. Commercialisation has intensified competition between clubs and stimulated the growth of market forces. The quality of equipment in use has been augmented. The scale of commercialisation is nevertheless far removed from that prevalent in major spectator sports in the West.

During the period of communist rule in Eastern Europe the names of the football clubs have reflected the political climate in each country. During the 1950s new ideologically sound names were imposed on the major clubs. In Czechoslovakia, Bohemians Prague were shackled with the name Spartak Stalingrad from 1951 to 1961, Slavia Prague became Dynamo Slavia from 1951 to 1965, and Sparta Prague were known as Spartak Sokolovo from 1953 to 1965. The fans, of course, continued to call the clubs by their traditional names.

The three Czech clubs cited above were able to revert to their pre-communist names in 1965 at the beginning of the 'Prague spring'. In Hungary, the liberalisation of 1956 prior to the October uprising enabled leading clubs to return to their original names. MTK Budapest were known as Voros Lobogo (Red Banner) from 1952 to 1956, and Ferencvaros had endured periods as Edosz and Kiniszi.

The more recent ending of communist rule has led to a further spate of name changes. In Czechoslovakia three trends are discernible: (i) a return to original names, e.g. SK Slovan Bratislava; (ii) dispensing with a name associated with the old regime, e.g. Union Cheb rather than Ruda Hvezda (Red Star); (iii) changing the name to match that of a new sponsor, e.g. Minolta Nitra rather than Plastika.

Name changes have been less evident in Hungary in the recent period. Dunaujvaros became Dunafeer to reflect their sponsorship. Honved, the army club, retained their name but replaced the soldier on their badge with a lion, the emblem of AC Kirpest which previously played at the Honved ground.

Elsewhere, East Germany has witnessed several name changes, e.g. Chemnitzer FC instead of Karl Marx Stadt and Sachsen Leipzig instead of Chemie Leipzig. Dynamo Berlin, formerly sponsored by the Stasi, rapidly became Berlin FC. Interestingly, in Romania, Dinamo Bucharest (linked to the notorious Securitatae) initially reverted to the name of a former club, Unirea Tricolor, only to reverse the decision and stick with Dinamo. More seriously, two teams associated with the Ceaucescu family (FC Olt and Victoria Bucharest) have been disbanded.

The most dramatic changes are taking place in the former East Germany. Political unification with West Germany occurred on 3 October 1990, to be followed by merger of the Football Associations on 21 November. As a result, for season 1991–2 the two leading East German clubs will enter the (West) German first division, another six will be placed in the second division, and the remainder will form a new regional division three north east. The merger will mean that an additional six disgruntled West German second division clubs will be relegated to the regionalised third divisions. Given that West Germany won the 1990 World Cup on its own, German unification is likely to increase further their dominance at the highest level of the game.

British football in the new Europe

The progress of European integration in both West and East will inevitably change the football map of Europe. At least the beginning of the 1990s sees English clubs back in Europe so that British football is not isolated from the arena of change. English clubs are on probation during their return to Europe, but there are positive suggestions that even Liverpool may return next season as a result of having their three-year additional ban commuted to one year.

The recommendations of the Taylor Report mean that the face of the British game will be rather different from that which was shown when the original ban was enforced in 1985. Stadium modernisation, relocation and ground-sharing are all more prominently on the British footballing agenda than they were six years ago. Here, models in continental Europe are an obvious and attractive source of reference.

Italy has led the way in terms of leading clubs sharing the same stadium, most notably AC and Inter in Milan, Sampdoria and Genoa, AS Roma and Lazio. Four Football League clubs are ground-sharing in a stadium owned by another club: Charlton Athletic at Crystal Palace; Bristol Rovers at Bath; Chester City at Macclesfield; Maidstone United at Dartford. All four intend to move to a stadium of their own nearer their home base eventually. (Indeed Charlton Athletic have just agreed plans to return to their original ground, The Valley.) Similarly, in Scotland, Clyde have moved in with Partick Thistle but are actively seeking a ground elsewhere.

England's record on the modernisation of stadiums is not good. In the years following the Second World War three clubs constructed new grounds on greenfield sites — Hull City in 1946, Port Vale in 1950, and Southend United in 1955. There followed a long gap of over thirty years before the next developments at Scunthorpe United in 1988 and Walsall in 1990. Both of these clubs sold their old grounds to supermarket chains.

Proponents of a European League argue that English clubs must improve both their stadium and the behaviour of their supporters before they can participate. Notwithstanding this caveat, there is no shortage of interest on the part of English clubs. The two names most frequently cited in the context of plans for a European League are Liverpool and Arsenal, a fact which does not please Everton, Tottenham Hotspur and Manchester United, the other advocates of a so-called 'Super League'. Another aspect of the debate concerning European League membership relates to the balance between selecting the wealthiest clubs (i.e. mostly Western Europe) and ensuring geographical representativeness. Are there to be any Eastern European clubs included such as Red Star Belgrade, Ferencvaros and Sparta Prague?

In Scotland, Glasgow Rangers are clear front runners for any place in a European League (see Moorhouse in this volume). This is based on a combination of their playing record, their financial strength and their ultra modern stadium. A total of £10 million was spent on redevelopment of Ibrox over a three-year period in the late 1970s. According to the leading expert on football stadiums, Ibrox is now 'one of Europe's finest and safest football grounds' (see Inglis, 1990).

The attitude of the football authorities would be a key factor in British participation in any European League. If a breakaway European League was outlawed by UEFA, leading players would be reluctant to jeopardise their international careers in the World Cup and European Championship. In the only historical precedent of note when the European Champions Cup (for club sides) began in 1955, the Football League refused to let Chelsea (the English champions) take part.

A British League is seen by some as an interim step towards participation in a European League. The history of crowd problems in matches between English and Scottish teams is a counter-argument to the obvious financial benefits to the leading clubs and their sponsors. The very concept of a British League leads us back to discussion of British football as a special case in European and world football.

The unique position of the United Kingdom, in having four Football Associations in the one state, has rankled for many years among African and South American countries, who feel that they are under-represented in the World Cup Finals. There have been threats to force a vote in FIFA, which would put an end to this (in their eyes) anachronistic anomaly. Perhaps one reason that the threat has never been carried through is the undoubted strength of a single United Kingdom national team in international competition.

Under new circumstances past advantages may quickly turn into future disadvantages. The special case of the four British FAs acquires fresh significance in the light of the UEFA ruling on the number of foreign players permissible in European club competitions. From 1991 to 1992 clubs can name only four non-nationals in a squad of sixteen players. Because the four parts of the United Kingdom are regarded as a separate nations in world football, these restrictions apply to players from other parts of the United Kingdom.

Earlier the example was given of the non-English Liverpool team which won the first division championship. There is a long tradition of English clubs fielding teams packed with Scottish, Welsh and Irish players. Clearly those clubs intent on participating in the European cups will have to select their players with greater caution in the future.

An alternative radical solution to the dilemma would be the creation of a United Kingdom Football Association, resulting in a United Kingdom national team in European/world football and possibly the creation of a British League. The opportunity to set up a new structure is evident. However, more likely is a cautious waiting game to see whether UEFA or the European Commission wins the political battle over the number of 'foreign' players allowed.

Ever since the beginnings of professional football in the last century, the main flow of leading players within the United Kingdom has been from Scotland to England. Glasgow Rangers have reversed the trend under the managership of Graeme Souness in the second half of the 1980s, when they purchased several leading English players. In the 1989–90 season no less than eight English players appeared for Rangers in the premier division.

Considering the greater fluidity in the international football labour market in the last decade, the number of foreign players in Britain has been surprisingly small (see Bale, 1990). Eastern European footballers have yet to make a major impact in British football, although the inflow is likely to increase if some of the Eastern countries attain associate membership of the EEC. One of the most interesting managerial appointments in 1990 was Aston Villa's appointment of Jozef Venglos, former coach of the Czechoslovak national team. Already one Czech player, Ivo Stas from Banik Ostrava, has followed Venglos to Villa.

Sponsorship is growing ever more important to British football, which reflects an earlier trend in mainland Europe. Barclays Bank is sponsoring the Football League at a cost of £11.55 million over a six-year period from 1987 to 1993. The Football League Cup has become the Rumbelows Cup in a four-year deal worth £5 million.

Income from television rights has increased rapidly in Britain with the advent of greater competition for football coverage. The Football League is receiving £11.9 million over four years from ITV in a deal which combines certain live first division matches and regional highlights of the lower divisions. A joint contract with BBC and BSB earns the Football Association £6 million a year for FA Cup and international matches.

On the other hand, television's influence on football is becoming more pervasive. Fixtures are rearranged to suit the demands of television rather than the desires of the clubs. For example, the Football Association broke a long-standing tradition in April 1990 by staging the two FA Cup semi-finals at different times on the same day to facilitate live television coverage of both.

Despite the current volume and variety of televised football in Britain (including a live Italian game on BSB every Sunday), attendance at Football League games has risen for each of the last four seasons. This statement brings me back to the beginnings of the essay and the relative healthy state of English football in 1990. British football as a whole has an excellent opportunity to construct a new future based on a long-overdue modernisation in the context of a new Europe.

Bibliography

Bale, J. (1990), 'Football Without Frontière: Some Questions for the 1990's', paper presented at Le Football et L'Europe conference, *European University Institute*, Florence, May 1990.

Duke, V. (1990), 'Perestroika in Progress?: The Case of Spectator Sports in Czechoslovakia', *British Journal of Sociology*, **41**, June, pp. 145–56.

Fynn, A. and L. Guest (1989) *The Secret Life of Football*, London, Queen Anne Press.

Gorbachev, M. (1987), *Perestroika: New Thinking for Our Country and the World*, London: Collins.

Inglis, S. (1990) *Football Grounds of Europe*, London, Collins Willow.
Rothmans Football Yearbook, London: Queen Anne Press, various.
Taylor Report (1990), *The Hillsborough Stadium Disaster*, London: HMSO, January.
World Soccer, IPC Magazines, various.

11

On the periphery: Scotland, Scottish football and the new Europe

H. F. Moorhouse

Scotland in Europe

Scotland is one of the 'submerged nations' of Europe. It is not a political state, not even 'a country' but a lot more than a region. Its inhabitants are proud of, endlessly discuss and strive to maintain their 'separateness'. To Scotland 'The new Europe' represents both a promise and a threat. The dream is that within a loose federation of equal (whatever their size) partners Scotland could take its own seat at the top table and have a direct say in its future. This is a scenario enticing even to the average non-politically nationalist Scot (virtually all are nationalists *culturally*) who perceives a move into some kind of federated Europe as a way of escaping the many irritations of being run by the present British Government which has never received much support in Scotland and which is materially and politically based on the South East of England, an area prone to presenting its own problems — an 'over-heating economy', 'run-away house prices' even 'football violence' — as those of 'the country as a whole'. The threat is contained in a Europe whose momentum is already pulling it away from its outlying provinces down towards the historic Mediterranean heart and now, suddenly, east into the less ancient but rather more explosive concerns of the last hundred years. The swathe cut by any Europe which really stretched from 'the Atlantic to the Urals' would stand a good chance of missing its northern outposts. Relatedly, a Europe preoccupied with size and growing ever bigger seems unlikely to acknowledge, let alone promote, the diversity contained in a 'nationalism' so culturally complicated that most people in Britain do not recognise its interlocking contradictory springs.

Scotland is characteristic of 'submerged nations' in that sport, and soccer in particular, has an overdetermined significance. There are the Catalans and Barcelona FC, the clubs of the Basque country and other problematic places — Naples, for example — where football and football teams stand for a good deal more than an exercise in moving a piece of plastic round grass. History ensures that the rhythms of the game in such regions are structured by much wider economic and political relations. I have discussed elsewhere (Moorhouse, 1984, 1986, 1987, 1989, 1990) four features which have served to structure Scottish football and its relations with popular culture. It has:

(i) had its professional competitions dominated by two clubs from one city — Rangers and Celtic of Glasgow;
(ii) clubs, including the two just mentioned, linked to ethnic groupings and antagonisms — 'Protestant', 'Catholic', 'Irish' — which exist in the wider society and which have other institutionalised forms;
(iii) been economically dependent upon transfers of players to the English League;
(iv) been a main force of expression of a dislike of 'England' and the 'English'.

There is one other structuring feature I want to add here. Scotland simply has a lot more clubs in its main League than most countries. This 'nation' of 5 million people has thirty-eight league clubs compared, for example, to England (plus Wales) whose population of over 50 million cradles ninety-two. Dumbarton (founded 1872), Clyde (1877), East Stirlingshire (1880), Albion Rovers (1881), Raith Rovers (1883) Forfar (1884) and a dozen others trace their histories back more or less as long as there has been modern football but they are scarcely names which trip off the most ardent non-Scots fan's lips. They represent the classic Scottish club: long pedigree, still part of the top breed, but so insignificant as to be almost a flea.

The point I want to make in this chapter is that the new Europe threatens to destabilise *all* the features which have structured, indeed created, the nature of the Scottish game and attitudes around the game for a century and more. My argument is *not* that the old frameworks of football north of the border are shifting simply or evenly — the forces of change and tradition interlock in complex ways — but it certainly is the case that Scottish football is being forced out of the mould in which it was formed into a new one in which an old balance of forces will be fundamentally recast. If in Scotland, as in many other places, football is truly 'much more than a game' then it follows that for this symbolically overloaded aspect of popular culture, the new *football* Europe presents itself as both promise and threat.

There is, for example, the constant fear that Europeans (i.e. the 'real' Europeans) might tar Scots with the same brush with which they coat English hooligans. If patience with the depredations of the English again wears thin then any subsequent ban might well be extended to Scotland by Continentals not conversant with the distinctiveness of Scottish 'nationality'. An associated fear is that through ignorance of the 'reality' of Scottish nationalism, jealousy, or just too great a zeal for tidiness Europe will insist that the United Kingdom, like any other state, plays only *one* team in the European Nations and World Cups instead of the four it enters at the moment. Such an eventuality, often discussed and often dismissed, would be a crushing blow not just to Scottish football but for Scottish nationalism since its basically symbolic (as opposed to political) nature requires the constant display of separateness, and soccer in particular supplies a good deal of ritual oxygen. At base, the cause for worry is a doubt about how long British eccentricity and exceptionalism, arising from its dominant position at the birth of the game, will be tolerated by a new bureaucratically organised, 'forward looking' Europe needing to balance many demands, and seeking fairness and legitimation through the calibration of precise rules and laws, not the softer measures of tradition.

However this may be, it seems quite clear that some arrangements in the new Europe will not allow various complexities of the Scottish situation to continue for long. For a century the English League and Scottish League have stood in a relation of buyer and seller. This constant movement of top players out of Scottish football has engendered both fatalism and pride north of the border and English cash has been and is a considerable part of the financing of Scottish clubs (Moorhouse, 1986). All in all, the century-long tide of players going south has spawned a whole complex of material and ideal interests in Scotland. Now new EUFA rules about the signing of 'non-indigenous' players seem set to shake this cultural structuring. To begin with, they threaten the new ambitions of Rangers. Where once clubs in Scotland used Scottish players almost entirely, Rangers, who had not signed one English international in their history up to 1986, now regularly play with six or seven top-class Englishmen in the side. If EUFA finally rule that 'England is a foreign country' (which, of course, in some respects Scots like to believe it is), Rangers (and their big ideas) would become very dependent on finding a lot of big fish from the rather small Scottish pool. However, if English sides are not allowed to play very many 'foreign' Scots, and it should be remembered that there is still a routine flow of players to England, the one source of income for most Scottish clubs will disappear. Conversely, strange alternative noises emanating from the European Commission about 'free movement of labour' and players having real 'freedom of contract', which, among many other things, would expose the defensive restrictions which the Scottish Football Association (SFA) puts on English clubs recruiting schoolboys north of the border (Moorhouse, 1987), also seem likely to threaten the income Scottish clubs obtain by trading in talent. Of course, one possible outcome of the new Europe is much greater migration of labour and it might well be that more Scots would move to Continental clubs but presumably only the best players, and in any case, culturally, movement to France, Italy, Germany and the like would not involve Scots in the same bitter–sweet relation as that much shorter trip across Hadrian's Wall. Anti-Englishness, the essence which defines 'Scottishness', would not be routinely renewed through the processes of the soccer market in quite the same way.

From scenes like these

In football terms the promise of Europe is, again, a place at, or rather in, the top table. The new willingness of Rangers to exercise an old financial muscle, break most of the unwritten rules of Scottish football and devote itself to truly grand ambitions, plus the EUFA ban on English clubs competing abroad, offered a real chance for Scotland to step straight into the main soccer spotlight outside the English shadow. Murray, the new owner of Rangers, fits

well into the new upwardly mobile, thrusting image of the entrepreneurs of the
new football Europe. It has become an article of faith in Scotland that within
five years there will be a European Super League, reflecting the Single Market,
and that, quite possibly in the headlines of a Scottish newspaper article,
'Rangers are the Only UK Hope for the European League'. Readers and
viewers have been made very aware of the doings of Berlusconi, the President
of AC Milan, the amount of Euro-media under his control and his apparent
reluctance to contemplate participation by the once powerful English in his
proposed Super League.

All this was quickly linked to Rangers' ending of their central 'tradition'
when they signed what was termed 'a high profile Catholic' or 'an arch-Tim' in
mid-1989 and one who had been on the point of rejoining Celtic just two
months previously. This was a huge symbolic shock (and choked hundreds of
clichés and jokes, though as many were soon created), for Maurice Johnston
was the first Catholic openly signed for the first team for at least eighty years.
There can be few countries where the purchase by one of its major clubs of the
star forward of the international side at a cost of over £1.25 million would lead
to immediate protests by some fans, the laying of a wreath at the stadium, and
to the secretary of the supporters' club association declaring:

It is a sad day for Rangers. Why sign him above all others? There will be a lot of people
handing in their season tickets. I don't want to see a Roman Catholic at Ibrox. They
have always stood for one thing and the biggest majority of support have been brought
up with the idea of a true-blue Rangers team. I thought they would sign a Catholic
eventually, perhaps in three or four years time, but someone from the Continent. It
really sticks in my throat.

(Glasgow Herald, 11 July 1989)

This immediate furore was all of a piece with that vision which sees the
'Protestant' Rangers and the 'Catholic' Celtic as involved in a violent 'war'
between two 'communities' in a 'divided city'. This interpretation is known on
the Continent, is very popular in Scotland, and possibly more so in England
where it exudes that enticing whiff of primitive savagery which it is one of the
cultural roles of the fringe 'nations' of the UK to provide (e.g. *The Economist*,
1989). In recent years several television programmes have been made in
England about the 'tribal' tension between the two big Scottish clubs and, at
the Johnston signing, the 'national' (i.e. English-based) TV news provided 'the
nation' with an intriguing, if quite preposterous, 'map' of the city of Glasgow
'divided' in two halves: blue and green (ITN, 1989). This whole notion, that
the two big Scottish clubs 'represent' two 'tribes' united only in 'unbridled
hatred', is insisted upon in numerous attempts at popular history and even in
academic analyses of Scottish football. At least three academics, all based
outside Scotland, regularly used to rush into the media to warn of the dangers
to the 'uneasy peace' between the 'serried ranks' if there was the slightest
upturn in 'the scale of hostilities' (*Scotland on Sunday*, 16 July 1989), or to
assert that the games of the Old Firm act as a 'safety valve' 'saving Scotland
from the greater evil of general civil strife' found in Ulster or the Lebanon
(*Glasgow Herald*, 20 August 1988, and see 5 August 1989). Now, any place

which really did contain 'communities', 'vendettas', 'potential bloodbaths', 'the beat of war drums' and so on would certainly be a lot more exciting than a city of wine bars, mortgages, bureaucracy, shopping malls, disabling poverty, contractual ties, office blocks, isolation, drugs and tourist provision, in short a city not unlike most others in Europe. The mythical and legendary 'Glasgow' is, in all truth, a good deal more interesting than the somewhat prosaic contemporary city where a majority of marriages are 'mixed', where there is no residential segregation, no widespread discrimination in employment, etc. Many analysts (and media portrayals which feed off them) actually wallow in a deep nostalgia for some 'good old, bad old' days, a characteristic kink of Scottishness. In Scotland, in popular and some academic literature, a simple moralising mixes with a parochial self-conceit and seeks to maintain some 'true Glasgow', and, by extension, some 'real Scotland', of the mind. And there is a quite underestimated double significance for Scots in the meeting of the Old Firm for it is not often realised outside how proud the Scottish football culture is of the clash of Rangers versus Celtic — 'the greatest club game in the world' as it is routinely referred to — as something the English have not got and cannot match.

In fact, when analysts start to use words like 'identity' (let alone 'tribe') in relation to football they need to be persuaded to provide much more robust concepts than they now deploy. Of course, 'identities' are situationally relevant, and people can move through levels speedily in certain eventualities, but talking of Glasgow as 'a divided city' with 'simmering hostilities' and so on has been pretty dubious for at least twenty years and now Rangers have suddenly exploded a lot of the old verities about this matter in relation to Scottish football. Indeed, some elements of the 'communities' did demur. Seventy to eighty people protested outside Rangers ground; representatives of the ninety-seven Rangers supporters' clubs in Ulster said that none of their members would attend matches while Johnston played and the wife of the secretary of the East Kilbride Rangers Supporters Club exclaimed: 'My blood is boiling. Is Mo Johnston going to run about with his crucifix? I have thought of nothing else all night.' Father Tom Connelly, the press officer of the Catholic Church in Glasgow, greeted the signing with a priestly moan: 'The deal is purely a financial one. Football today is not about loyalties, it is about money' (*Evening Times*, 10 July 1989), which hit the two rhetorics in play right on the head. For Johnston did explain his part in the affair through the language of 'contracts' or rather what exactly a 'contract' was, for while Celtic claimed he had already signed a 'contract' with them he insisted this was only a 'letter of agreement' with a list of conditions that had to be fulfilled before it was valid. Rangers, too, used the language of disengaged managerialism: 'investment in players', 'sound financial planning', 'maximising sponsorships' and so on. Generally Rangers now employ a cool, rational, sanitised, success-oriented business-speak, light years away from all those 'jihads' and 'bloodbaths'. The owners now point with renewed moral force to Scotland's segregated school system as the tap root of religious divide. This is not to say the club will rapidly lose its 'Protestant identity'. Stereotypes do not shift quickly or easily but, I will try to suggest later, that this 'tradition' of 'warring' 'communities', beloved not least by Scots determined to declare that their country has something truly 'unique' and crucially non-English, seems increasingly irrelevant to a new Glasgow.

The Scottish press hailed Johnston's signing as vital to Rangers ambition to enter Berlusconi's Euro-élite:

— his predominantly 'Catholic' clubs might not take kindly to an all-protestant team;
— the multinational big business sponsors necessary to survival at this height wouldn't want to be associated with a market-losing sectarian image;
— new EUFA rules on the number of 'foreign' players allowed after 1992 meant Rangers had to be opened up so as to attract the maximum number of talented young Scots.

A Glasgow paper put it plainly on its front page under a headline, 'Why It Had to Happen: Sectarianism Has No Place in the European Super League', about the few protesting Rangers supporters:

They are looking backwards, at a time when Rangers must look forwards. If the club was to follow their wishes its progress would be actively impeded, if not come to a dead halt. Rangers would remain a big fish in a small pond, instead of competing, on equal terms, with the great teams of European football.

(*Evening Times*, 11 July 1989)

In fact the fuss about the signing died away quite quickly. Johnston, who was going to be swept away by a 'volcanic' 'groundswell', has had some brushes with fans (though mainly, it would seem, those from Celtic) but the excitement of the time (and the doleful, hopeful 'predictions' of a petrol-bombed Ibrox and child kidnappings) now looks ridiculous. A second Catholic has now played in the Rangers team to no big fanfare. Meanwhile, Scotland has continued to be kept well informed about Berlusconi or 'the charismatic multi-millionnaire' or 'the richest man in Italy' as he is described, and his plans for soccer are still a regular topic for Scottish discussion. In February 1990 newspaper 'revealed' that a secret agreement had been reached on a sixteen team football European League. Attached was a pattern of fixtures, dates, television arrangements and comment from all manner of officialdom including the owner of Rangers: 'We have a fabulous stadium, possibly the best in the world, why should we be restricted to playing Hamilton Accies? The Superleague will mean lots of European games' (*Scotland on Sunday*, 18 February 1990). This promised place in the vanguard of a proposed new order is an unaccustomed but fabulous position for Scotland, more used to and, in truth, more comfortable with an underdog role. It would have been unthinkable just four years ago. However, just such a development, full of rich promise especially if English clubs failed to get in, would emphasise more of the dangers the new Europe might present to most of Scottish soccer.

Rangers in Scotland?

After a hundred years of being more or less ignored Scotland is suddenly receiving a great deal of prominence in various English publications including blueprints for the future of football. One recent text (serialised in *The Times*), co-written by the Deputy Chairman of Saatchi and Saatchi, sought to tell the story of English decline and loss of importance 'not only in the world, and in Europe, but in Britain itself, where Scotland now leads the way both in the quality' of play and administration of the game' (Fynn *et al.*, 1989: 8, and e.g. pp. 44 and 238). This would be news to most of those who actually live in Scotland but it is really just one club that is being referred to. From the depressed, seedy state of English football Rangers look like the nearest thing to a state-of-the-art operation run by the fast-track, street-smart, proactive, TV-wise tycoons who are *de rigueur* in the new soccer world. Not only is their ground — Ibrox — quite magnificent by British standards but it has been self-financed, perceived to be both a necessity and a sign of moral virtue in Mrs Thatcher's Britain of the 1980s. In plans which have football's future determined by financial logic, small-screen sponsorships and grid-iron parallels, Rangers seem to have the necessary big ideas and big stadium. In this company their possible plan to bid for a Scottish commercial television channel in 1992 looks extremely ideologically sound, showing the hidebound English the way forward into a world of media groups, product differentiation, pan-European consortiums, marketing tie-ins, commercial franchising and loads of ECUs. They are the British Berlusconis.

As Rangers seek a top European spot and constantly apply a profound financial pressure they seem likely to reduce all other Scottish clubs to second class status; hence a lot of resentment and not just from Celtic. Some papers wryly declared that the sensation when Johnson signed was not that the Rangers manager, Souness, had signed a Catholic but that he had signed a Scotsman. The SFA and Rangers have clashed on a number of issues in recent years, not the least of these being whether the SFA should adopt Ibrox as the new national stadium. The national manager has complained that the number of 'foreigners' playing in the premier division now means that chances for young Scots are being drastically curtailed and that, in the long term, this could sap the strength of the Scots side. On the other hand, Souness regularly declared that the response by other teams to his importation of talent and attempt to play 'a European style' had been a violent one, so that when the Russian Kuztnetsov, bought for over £1 million, lasted just one and a bit games before sustaining a serious knee injury Souness complained that 'too many hammer throwers' were being allowed to perform in Scotland (*Glasgow Herald*, 25 October 1990). The response to these accusations has been mixed, especially as both Rangers and Souness have long reputations to live down, but there is a broad agreement that the present Scottish game is too 'athletic' and discourages skill, so that neither its clubs nor the national side can hope to compete with the best abroad. Consequently, there has been talk that if Rangers do enter some Super League they will need to use 'two teams' tuned to the differing styles necessary for success.

Nonetheless, the new cultural rhythms are not simple here. Any resentment against Rangers is tempered by the fact that Scotland certainly does not regard itself as a football backwater and would hate to be left out of any major developments. Rangers activities have pulled others along in their wake and many a club now boasts some foreign international players, an Englishman, a few ground improvements, giving the whole of the Scottish game a much more cosmopolitan and confident veneer than it has ever had. Whereas not too long ago newspaper quizzes could ask, 'name the four players who have played in the Premier League this year who could not play for Scotland', now Rangers alone could often field a side of non-Scots. Scotland revels in all the 'world attention' it is told it is getting which, even if not true, is, quite as importantly, believed to be true. Already articles have appeared in the press asking if it really is possible that Rangers could be the 'national' champion of Scotland in a Continental League, a prospect made the more mouthwatering with the real chance that English participation could be zero. Moreover, as I have already suggested, Rangers ambitions are a sign of a rather more profound material and cultural change in Glasgow and Scotland more generally. The new interest of the English-based 'national' media often draws parallels between the rise of Rangers and what is known as 'the renaissance' of Glasgow (e.g. BBC Radio, 1989). Glasgow, and to a large extent most of Scotland, has lost its grip on heavy manufacturing industry. It now has (has to have!) 'post-industrial' ambitions within a united Europe and Rangers drive seems congruent with this. They call Scottish football to a new identity, towards managerialist, multinational, modernity.

However, some commentary, especially that flowing from England, noting that Rangers' cash turnover is more than all the other thirty-seven Scottish clubs combined, doubts whether 'the biggest club in Britain' can really rest content with staging the majority of its matches within the confines of a Scottish League (e.g. BBC2 TV, 1990). A number of Scottish grounds simply cannot accommodate the number of Rangers fans who want to see their club play away. Souness declared himself an advocate of a British League and a lot of those right at the top of the game in Scotland seem to believe that it is inevitable that the present structure of the Scottish League will be soon be disrupted, but it is not clear exactly what competition would remain nor what would happen to all those clubs which did not get into any European and/or British League.

This issue is becoming stark for Celtic for they are one club that has not stayed with Rangers' recent impetus. This is not simply a matter of relative success in major competitions but of a whole outlook and ethos. The Old Firm is beginning to look infirm as the keystone of Scottish soccer simply because Celtic have not even been able to make a convincing pretence of matching Rangers' ambitions. It is tempting to suggest that while Rangers stand for the 'new Glasgow' — glitzy, ambitious, pecuniary and brash — Celtic represent the 'older' Glasgow which still exists as part of what is, in reality, a 'dual city'. Beyond the gloss, press handouts and bright lights there remains another quite 'unregenerated', 'pre-modern' Glasgow, a place untouched by 'renaissance' and unconvinced by new slogans. Its inhabitants are still bound by relative or absolute poverty and traditional notions of what is appropriate action. It is the owners of Celtic who now trade, in increasingly desperate tones, in a language of 'communities', whose fans seek to have the new 'mercenaries' of Rangers matched by the 'passion for the club' of those 'who want to play for the jersey' (synonyms for Scottish and Irish Catholics), whose supporters recently hired a detective to compile a dossier on a cup final referee they believed to be an

Orangeman. They cling to a conventional view of what football 'is about' in Scotland, a posture which seems to block any initiative and to stultify any sensible response to the big changes which European developments seem likely to forge.

The club has been in some turmoil in the last few years due to their obvious financial inability to rebuild their ground to a manner befitting their presumed status and so to match Rangers in this and also in the purchase of top-class players. Pressure has taken the form of badgering the present board to let in new blood, for control of the club has been and is vested in the hands of three families whose male members tend to be accountants, lawyers and local politicians rather than frequent-flyer tycoons. So, there have been slightly odd calls to introduce 'businessmen of deep Catholic faith who would bring about some compromise between good business sense and traditions that are well worth preserving' (*Glasgow Herald*, 23 August 1988), but various major offers by Catholic businessmen have been rebuffed. Dempsey, a property developer, who was introduced to the board in mid-1990 (and who caused a stir as he maintained corporate entertainment facilities at both Celtic Park and Ibrox), was soon voted off in a quite unprecedented display of share power. There is a running debate in Scotland about whether Celtic should 'go public', selling shares not simply to find more of the money the club desperately needs, but also to give more of its 'community' a say, and to loosen the grip of the present, apparently unimaginative, owners. Pressed on this, after Dempsey's removal, one director spoke of 'the Celtic family', said that present shareholders were responsible to 'their consciences and traditions', that 'the Celtic way is, at heart, to conserve the club and preserve it for the future', a very different set of allusions to those employed by Murray and Souness (Radio Clyde, 1990). He insisted that Rangers were not a model that Celtic, 'with its different traditions and different values', could follow, that a share issue would not raise anywhere near the money the club required — only £10 million 'at best' (!) — and that, anyway, going public would 'put the club into play' so that it could, potentially, be bought by anyone. Celtic are deep in crisis, stuck with a dinosaur of a stadium, a far from star-spangled team, debts of £3 million and no clear plan of advance. They are in almost total disarray.

Now, if Rangers in Europe, indeed Rangers *and* Europe, threaten to ditch Celtic as relevant rivals the likelihood for most other Scottish clubs can be easily imagined. Despite the hype, Rangers' flow of finance, the strongest of any British club, compares unfavourably with most Continental clubs who are candidates for any Super League. This is why Rangers will need to play in as many big games as possible, and press to maximise and retain all available TV fees and on-screen sponsorships, thus setting in train new forms of football in Scotland and new ways of viewing it that will also probably serve to finish off many small clubs. It is poignant to compare the finances of East Stirlingshire with Rangers and to perceive how they already inhabit a very different world of 'football' (see Table 11.1). These figures should suggest how any new soccer set-ups which took away Rangers, or the chance of games with Rangers, which insisted on all-seated and covered grounds, which spread out a regular feast of glamour games on Euro-TV, which cut out the occasional windfall of a big transfer fee, or which threatened the sources of cash to the SFA and Scottish

Table 11.1 Extracts from recent balance sheets of Rangers FC and East Stirlingshire FC (£)

Rangers	1987	1988
Turnover of which:	4,193,175	6,600,812
football activities	3,072,862	4,356,987
commercial activities	1,120,313	2,243,825
Trading profit	555,075	1,489,387
Exceptional items (transfer fees)	−2,278,146	−3,147,573
Loss before tax	1,723,071	1,658,186
Extra income	—	586,350
Loss for year	1,723,071	1,071,836
Loss carried forward	3,150,483	4,222,319
Tangible fixed assets (mainly stadium)	11,776,263	23,354,874

East Stirlingshire	1987	1988
Total income	55,637	67,968.34
Net gate receipts	8,670	11,673.51
Pools copyright fee	25,340	30,005
Donations and sundry	12,871	14,885.98
Bank interest	6	3.85
Net transfer fees	8,750	11,400
Outgoings	55,252	66,180.96
Profit for year	285	1,787.38
Loss carried forward	36,168	34,380.62
Fixed assets (at cost) of which:		21,026
Land		8,412
Motor mower and tractor equipment		3,190
Floodlight system and covered enclosure		9,424

League which they then redistribute to small clubs as 'pools fees' or 'donations', would spell the death blow to a lot of Scottish clubs.

In all the talk so far about the Euro-League, even when it has become very expansive, those in control of Rangers have been at pains to insist that new competitions will coexist with indigenous ones: 'The day is not far distant when there will be a European Superleague Division 1, Division 2, perhaps for the likes of Hearts say, and even a Division 3 to be run in tandem with existing competitions in Scotland. There is a place for everyone in this game' (*Scotland on Sunday*, 18 February 1990). It is not clear that this really can be the case. If, as Murray also suggests, 'a Rangers–Moscow Dynamo match will be as commonplace as Rangers–Dunfermline', it is difficult to understand why the latter will attract much of a crowd, let alone why Forfar versus East Fife will attract anybody. Other extra 'glamour' competitions for the new times (and satellite dishes) have been suggested: a British Cup and a British League. They all 'make sense' financially but they cannot all be fitted in with what already exists. The SFA has always operated considerable restrictions against the showing of English (and Continental) football in Scotland, even in highlights form, recognising its danger for crowd attendance at the many mundane matches. Now new TV technologies which could skip over frontiers and unite the new Europe as a cultural as well as economic market threaten such protectionism regardless of any new Leagues. In 1990 the SFA struck a deal with a satellite company for the transmission of live Scottish games which also conceded the right to show live European and English matches in Scotland. Recent abysmal attendances at some crucial international matches seem to show that even the Tartan Army prefers to see the game piped into a pub as opposed to paying many pounds to enjoy all the discomforts of the national stadium.

Hearts and minds

One club that has tried to ride along with Rangers has been Heart of Midlothian. In June 1990 Mercer, the owner of Hearts, announced a takeover bid for the parent company of the other Edinburgh team Hibernian. This again was a thunderous assault on tradition. Besides the mismanagement the Hibernian board were accused of, the basic justification was that the teams had to unite in order to participate in forthcoming changes in the structure of soccer. One aspect of this concerned stadiums and the poor condition and lack of potential of both grounds. Another aspect was simply that the city was not large enough to support two major teams *and* book passage into the Euro-élite. The basis of that argument was the gap between actual attendances and what a club 'should' expect to get from its catchment population (Hearts, 1990: p. 8; see also Table 11.2). The vision was that an 'Edinburgh United' would have the assets and, in theory, the crowds to match the two Glasgow giants and to move amongst the best in Europe on equal terms:

It is our intention that Edinburgh and the Lothians will be represented at the superclub level by one major team, rather than continuing the dissipation of resources which applies at present. A European League is a very real prospect. Edinburgh and the Lothians must be in a position to be represented in such a League. We expect invitations to join a European League will be based on quality of stadia, size of supporting population catchment, financial strength and management.

(Hearts, 1990: p. 9)

The Hibernian defence document replied, among other things, with pictures of the team of 1921–2, 'The Famous Five' of the 1950s and a general rejection of 'vision' in favour of 'tradition' (Edinburgh Hibernian, 1990). Hearts' response accused Hibs of appealing to emotions and not reason:

At no point is there any sign of vision on the part of Hibs. Do Hibs really believe that

Table 11.2 Premier League home gates

	Population catchment basis* ('000)	Actual average attendance ('000)	'Actual' as % of 'population' catchment basis
Rangers	29.9	35.5	118.7
Celtic	29.9	28.8	96.3
Hearts	17.1	15.7	91.8
Hibs	17.1	10.9	63.7
Aberdeen	15.8	14.0	88.6
Dundee	8.4	8.7	103.6
Dundee Utd.	8.4	11.0	131.0

*cities with two clubs have their population equally divided.

Edinburgh and the Lothians will be able to accommodate two major football clubs in a European league? Do they really think that finance will be available for two modern football stadia in Edinburgh? . . . They are saying nothing because they know that an independent Hibs is doomed to a mediocre future.

(Hearts, 1990a: p. 4)

While this document did not go on to say so, the logical extension of that argument was that an independent and non-merged Hearts faced exactly the same future on a European scale and so by extension did all but probably only one Scottish club.

Mercer attempted to wage a battle of the suites. Day after day he appeared in the Scottish media moving through panneled rooms to Perrier-water-provided press conferences or seated by the limpid waters of Italian yacht marinas far from the Firth of Forth or speaking from his holiday home above Cannes. But there was a reaction of the streets. Among the Scottish public the bid was greeted with equivocation and incredulity, if not anger. Not only were these two of Scotland's 'big clubs' (though neither had managed to win a major competition for fifteen years), but they, too, linked into the ethnic divide though never in ways as pronounced as the Glasgow clubs. Indeed, in various interviews Mercer included the eradication of this as one element in his modernisation package: 'The benefits of a new stadium and the eradication of the tribalistic element in Edinburgh football will attract to the Scottish League new corporate customers who have declined to get involved in Edinburgh over the years' (*Glasgow Herald*, 5 June 1990). But by the next day he had been shocked by the feeling unleashed, with police and guard dogs sent to patrol his home, a window broken at his city centre offices, graffiti and other threats to him and his family: 'I say to myself, where are we at? Is this Scotland? Is this Edinburgh? I mentioned tribalism yesterday. I have experienced it in the past twenty four hours. Its so puerile and so short-sighted, and, in the end, its really quite sickening. I'm, staggered' (*Glasgow Herald*, 6 June 1990). This is not at all to say that Mercer was hit by a 'wave of violence' or 'sectarian hatred', but he did appear to be unprepared for the reaction provoked and, ruminating later, he certainly did believe this was an outburst from one of those 'tribes' that are supposed to pitch their tents across Scotland: 'The irony is that tribalism, the thing which we were trying to stamp out, to take the whole thing forward, was the thing that exploded.' (*Glasgow Herald*, 19 September 1990).

Mercer repeatedly claimed that he had won 'the business argument' but lost 'the social argument'. He would not talk about the 'religious aspect' but:

Privately though he does concede that the existence of 'Protestant/Unionist' Hearts and 'Roman Catholic/Republican' Hibernian was another factor he had failed to contend with. He says that in 15 or 20 years business and social life in Edinburgh, sectarianism was something which he had simply not encountered. This may be the case in Barnton, but not necessarily so in Gorgie or down Leith Walk.

(*Glasgow Herald*, 19 September 1990)

Which is an attempt to suggest that the middle-class sections of cities may not exhibit ethnic division in the same ways as working-class areas. Still, the middle class of this most middle class of cities certainly did get involved and seemed to reveal that their perceptions of the prospects for Scottish football were quite limited. A Queen's Counsel spoke of the importance of signalling to the world that football in Scotland remained the province of the people, not the plaything of middle-aged yuppies, while a solicitor, a Hearts shareholder, averred: 'Mr. Mercer talks about tribalism but whether he likes it not, football is a form of tribalism. The two clubs quite literally live off each other' (*Observer Scotland*, 10 June 1990).

Through the summer football supporters had to get used to concepts like: 'off the shelf companies', 'net book values', 'the third market', and to the polysyllabic names of financial advisers. It transpired that while the ideology was that Hibernian had gone public to allow fans to take a share in their club, the facts were that there were only 1700 shareholders, that eighteen professional investors owned around 80–85 per cent, and that two-thirds were held outside Scotland, leading to stories which ran: 'English speculators will finally kill off floundering Hibs . . . the money grabbing whizzkids from London's financial houses hold millions of Easter Road shares' (*Daily Record*, 6 June 1990). In the end some Catholic entrepreneurs stepped in to buy just enough shares to protect Hibs' independence while declaring they were not really concerned with football but thought Edinburgh should have two clubs, 'in the interests of the city's community' (*Glasgow Herald*, 13 June 1990). For whatever reason, and again to no big fanfare, Mercer recently appointed the first Catholic football manager Hearts have ever had. The remaining unresolved matter is the future and what it holds for clubs even as big on the Scottish scene as Hearts and Hibs if Rangers do pursue Euro-ambitions.

A tale of two cities and umpteen stadiums

One last set of pressures from Europe adds to the forces shaking Scottish soccer, for it faces all manner of commands to upgrade stadiums which emanate both directly from the Continent — one criterion for entry to the new

Super League(s) is said to be spectator facilities; there are EUFA directives on all-seater stadiums, etc. — and as mediated through the British Government's attempts to 'solve' the problem of (English) hooliganism and save the British (i.e. English) game. So in the 1990 report by Lord Justice Taylor on the Hillsborough disaster, Scotland figures as a 'good example' to the English. The Scottish authorities are commended for their success in the fight against hooliganism, including their tight ban on alcohol sales at grounds. The clubs are said to be in the van of showing the way to 'a better future for football'. In the chapter of that title Ibrox is held up as a model of ground redevelopment with good, wholesome, facilities (Home Office, 1990: para. 60). It is noted that the comprehensive remodelling had been done from the club's own resources and that the almost total seating is on offer at low prices so that the fans are not being driven away, one fear about all-seater stadiums in England (ibid.: para. 72).

Other Scottish clubs figure as exemplars, too:

The superior safety of seating has already persuaded a number of clubs in the UK to convert their terraces to seating either totally or predominantly. Following Hillsborough, Liverpool have announced their intention to adapt their famous Kop to seating. In Scotland, Aberdeen's ground at Pittodrie became all-seater in 1978; Clydebank followed suit; St. Johnstone's new ground at Perth is all-seated.

(Home Office, 1990: para. 73)

Here, the word 'seating' covers a multitude of sins. At Clydebank in the main and Aberdeen in some measure we are talking of 'seats' which are planks of wood. At Clydebank these seats are liable to be covered in green moss through exposure to the rain and/or bird droppings if under the cover of the stands. Soon after the publication of the Taylor Report the television viewer in Scotland could see the rain lashing down on the heads of those in the all-seated Pittodrie where quite large numbers of the seats are either uncovered or are not adequately covered against rain driven by the wind off the North Sea. Raised umbrellas often figure amongst the seated crowd. In Scotland, anyway, all-covered stadiums are rather more important than all-seaters if authority is really worried about what is best for most fans.

In effect, Lord Justice Taylor's judgement involves quite an idealisation of the situation in Scotland (the better to spur on the English) so that later in the report (para. 119) even the Scottish national stadium, Hampden Park, is described as: 'an imaginative example of ground redevelopment . . . in the course of being achieved', which is one way of indicating that a vast, mainly uncovered, bowl with timber and ash terraces has been converted to a rather less vast, mainly uncovered, bowl with concrete terraces. Rather, as a Scottish paper put it about the time the Taylor Report appeared: 'Hampden continues to creak in the wind' (*Glasgow Herald*, 10 March 1990). In the last two years the national stadium has been variously described in the Scottish media as 'a coup' 'marginally worse than a dump', 'a midden', 'a tip', 'a national disgrace', 'crumbling', 'decaying', shrouded in 'medieval gloom', 'dangerous', etc. which all capture the reality rather more accurately than Taylor. Hampden must be the only major European stadium which, in the last decade, has had to knock down a stand with 4,000-plus seats (before it fell down) and replace it with open terrace. There have been plans to redevelop Hampden since at least the late 1960s, and an official report in 1975 estimated the cost of producing a new covered 80,000-capacity stadium with 15 per cent seats at over £12 million and argued that the central state would need to pay at least £6 million towards this (Scottish Sports Council, 1975). As the 'floodtide of inflation' and 'need to curb public expenditure' which were noted in 1975 now dominate the central state's policies in the 1990s it seems most unlikely that 'the imaginative example' is actually realisable outside the Scottish football authorities discovering a spare £100 million or so lying about in their coffers. The SFA have been forced to think about other venues and in early 1991 were considering at least seven options, e.g. going to Ibrox, linking up with the Scottish Rugby Union to create one national stadium at Murrayfield in Edinburgh, creating new stadiums on any number of sites, mainly near Glasgow but including one at Bannockburn. Like Celtic, they are 'looking around' but searching hardest for the cash necessary to enable any new ground at all to materialize. In Scotland an outcry followed the SFA's decision to 'invite' the unpopular Prime Minister (Thatcher), on a political tour in March 1990, to visit Ibrox, marvel at its excellence and carry out the draw for the Scottish Cup semi-finals *before* the quarter-finals had been played. The reason for this curious event appears to have been a hope by the SFA that allowing Mrs Thatcher a good photo-opportunity might gain them more some state cash to redevelop Hampden or, more likely, get the central government to override local authority objections to a commercial exploitation of some of the Hampden site which would help finance more piecemeal renovation of the old stadium — hopes which have not transpired.

Lord Taylor's idealisation of the Scottish situation is no accident since the flaw in his plan for British soccer is the issue of finance. In his report various European stadiums are held out as examples but Taylor does not indicate how the gap implicit in the different pattern of the ownership of grounds between Britain and the Continent is to be bridged. In most of the rest of Europe the local authority or a sporting federation owns the ground and maintains it. This difference is noted in the Taylor Report but is smuggled out of the limelight since to ruminate upon it too long would bring to the fore the whole problem of football finance and how the facilities which the British Government and EUFA deem necessary are to be paid for. The Government recently enabled more money to go from the pools companies to refurbish antiquated grounds and this was immediately hailed as a great advance, but the cash made available is still not adequate to the task. The Taylor Report suggests that at least £130 million is required for all-seater and all-covered stadiums for the ninety-two English grounds (let alone any extra spectator, medical and police facilities). Let us add (what the English authorities and English-based media tend to forget) that there are about thirty-six rickety grounds in Scotland requiring upgrading from the same funds and we can see that 'an extra £100 million', which means about £150 million in all over the next five years, is not really going to get the job done. This ignores the special case (among others) of Hampden or various touted 'Skydome' successors where talk starts at around £200 million for one new, really big, stadium. In Scotland the state's new largesse has boiled down to £2 million or a lot less for each league club; hence a fair amount of extra money has to come from somewhere and for most clubs it is none too clear what that source could be. To the annoyance of local authorities the implementation of Taylor's safety recommendations have been watered down north of the border which will postpone the financial crunch, but EUFA and FIFA directives will not wait.

So the problem of how to finance any up-to-date national stadium is but one of many problems about grounds facing Scottish football where Rangers stand as almost the total exception rather than the rule. Hearts have been worrying about the costs of ground development for some time. In March 1990 they stated that complying with the recommendations of the Taylor Report would cost them £20 million if they moved to a new site and £6 million at their present ground, though it might not be possible to innovate enough there to make it worthwhile. In May it became known that Mercer had entered an arrangement for a new stadium with the owner of Rangers. Murray was planning a new £200 million housing, leisure and business development on a green belt site on the outskirts of Edinburgh, one element of which would be a new 25,000 all-seater stadium to be developed by Mercer with corporate facilities, greyhound track, potential as a pop concert venue and as a 'community' facility. The local authorities were most displeased. As the Labour leader of the council put it:

this is very little to do with football and much to do with making vast sums of money for Mr. Murray and Mr. Mercer which is hardly surprising given that they are property developers. The proposal is a massive invasion of a crucial part of the Edinburgh green belt, a major threat to the planning policies of the whole region.

(BBC1 TV, 1990)

Hearts bid for Hibs got inextricably mixed up with a tangle of possibilities of providing stadiums in Edinburgh fit to meet various European-based pressures. Part of Mercer's argument was that selling both existing grounds would yield up to £8 million towards the £12.5 million his projected stadium in the Murray plan was meant to cost. The convener of the district council's planning and development committee labelled Mercer and Murray 'millionaire casuals running amok through the green belt'. The proposed stadium accounted for only 8 per cent of the planned development and was a PR element designed to allow the rest. In any case, this scheme conflicted with the council's own development plans and their desire to create a 'world class sports complex' (on a site about a mile away from the Murray area) which itself was going to include a 25,000 all-seater and needed at least one major club involved to make it viable. At various times in the ensuing Edinburgh debate a minimum of six different sites for new stadiums have been mentioned and even actively promoted by local councils, while the plans favoured by free-market entrepreneurs move through the stages towards adjudication by the Scottish Office. Throughout Scotland the necessity to modernise stadiums has become inextricably bound up with local political rows, and with attempts to use stadiums as keys either to unlock the constrictions of the green belt (and since, depending on the level of planning permission, the value of land can rise from

£5,000 an acre to £250,000 it can be seen what the stakes are here) or to open the 'regeneration' of manufacturing areas which have fallen on rusty times. At least two of the plans for new natural stadiums lie on the now vacant sites of motor vehicle plants, and the Scottish Development Agency, various Development Corporations, Enterprise Trusts and committees of MPs have become involved in floating many of the plans. As with Celtic's dilemma about a new stadium, there is much talk of 'supremos' and 'consortia', plenty of feasibility studies and artists' pretty impressions but very little sign of brick-laying.

The need for new financial acumen in 'the football industry', which Rangers are held to embody, relates to another idealisation in the Taylor Report's plans for English (but in fact British) football. Since state cash is not going to be forthcoming to carry anything like the whole load of rebuilding stadiums then the picture of the club summoned by Taylor to provide good, modern, wholesome facilities has to be one with a stadium occupying a fair-sized, 'inner city' (itself, a usefully ambiguous term) site ripe for commercial development. To self-finance most improvements the club is supposed to redevelop that site or sell it and move to a new green field location with a strong hint that ground-sharing between clubs is another way that costs can be cut. Now, in some places in Scotland this could apply; in others, many others, it simply does not. The ground of Forfar Athletic was valued at £55,977 in its 1988 balance sheet. It sits on the edge of farmland in a small market town in the middle of nowhere. No one is likely to scramble to buy it for a leisure complex, science park or block of postmodern pads. Nor is any developer likely to go for the grounds of Albion Rovers, Alloa, East Fife or Stenhousemuir. There are very few yuppies in Cowdenbeath. Any number of the smaller clubs in Scotland face a bleak future in bleak places. Talk of the virtues of ground-sharing in Milan, Turin and Genoa is of little moment in Methil, Dumfries or Coatbridge or places where old ethnic antagonisms provide rough justifications against smooth rationalisation. Pressure from various political levels and/or from European football authorities willing standardised 'modernisation' packages but not the money to do it with is, in effect, likely to kill off many venerable clubs, and more in Scotland than elsewhere.

Meanwhile, it is Rangers who constantly up the financial stakes: a new £4-million 'office, dining and exhibition development' (with a 112-yard-long, pitch-viewing 'function suite') in February 1990, a £2-million property deal (within the Murray companies) so that the old training ground can be developed into a 'massive business park' in March, the issue of a 'Bond' to finance an £11-million-plus upgrading (with new top deck) of the old grand stand in summer, plus the purchase of a nearby small ground to take reserve games, and plans in autumn to add an extra deck on each end stand at £8 million to create a 58,000 all-seater stadium with all the modern trimmings. Murray has pointed out that when the current work is finished his club will have spent more on Ibrox than all the other thirty-seven put together. He wants the SFA to use Ibrox as the national stadium just as they went to Hampden when Queens Park were the biggest club. The SFA (and many others in football) are very reluctant and continue to search for 'their own home', quite foolishly according to a director of Rangers (see the letter 'A Stadium for Scotland' in the *Glasgow Herald*, 6 April 1991). Meanwhile almost no one in

Scotland comments on how bizarre it is even to contemplate the creation of *three* new, top-class football stadiums in the environs of one, rather small, city.

On the edge

Football has always meant a lot to Scots and has meant different things than it has for the English. But material forces, structural relations and, thus, cultural representations do change. They do not alter quickly but what soccer denotes in Scotland is changing. Simply put, it is moving under the push of unbridled economic power where the devil (of whatever persuasion) will take the hindmost. This shove seems likely to be reinforced by European politicians keen to stress both the efficiency of the free market and the image of a true 'community', where sport will provide one of the few cultural expressions available to build a Euro-consciousness. Those in charge of Scottish football stand awkwardly in the initial tremors of such forces; only Rangers really seem to believe that the future is theirs. Such is the 'health' of most Scottish teams that the national manager recently acknowledged that the League programme could not be postponed the Saturday before important internationals (as in most European countries) as the clubs simply could not stand the financial loss. In reality, there is unlikely to be a place for 'everyone' in the new TV-channelled, multinational-minded Euro-soccer. Often the explicit model here is the National Football League of the United States (Fynn *et al.*, 1989). The idea is that, somehow, the (English) Football League or each and every one of the clubs in Europe can unite like that but all cannot. The NFL is not beholden to national associations trying to protect national teams, national boundaries, old sensibilities and small clubs. In the new Europe there is bound to be a tension between the alert corporate lawyers of the free market and various 'governing bodies' seeking to assert 'rules' which have an unclear, if not dubious, legal standing. In any such tussle even a compromise will leave some blood on the floor of the hospitality suites. The clubs of Scotland seem to me to be among those most likely to perish.

In 1991, to the dismay of the major clubs in Scotland, there was a revolt of the 'have nots' against the 'haves' when most of the other members of the League voted to increase the number of teams, and hence games, in the Premier Division from 1992, further loading what is already agreed to be a crowded fixture list. This was a defensive manoeuvre designed to strengthen the position of the middle-ranking Scottish club. This could succeed, and the sudden departure of Rangers' manager, Souness, to Liverpool in April 1991 and his references to 'petty jealousies', 'politics', 'small-minded people' and 'no one wants a successful Rangers up there' (BBC TV, 1991) can also be interpreted as a victory for the forces of 'tradition' against those of 'enterprise', but the price to be paid might well be the guaranteed irrelevancy of Scottish football in Europe. In fact, the real battle has still to be fought and the result is very much in doubt, and for the small Scottish club (and this is a very large category) viewing from the periphery of a periphery, the emerging shape of European football reinforces an old, old worry: 'will we be able to survive?' Of course it is perfectly feasible to argue that this is no bad thing: that clubs must find their own level out of the main leagues if need be, that quality must overcome quantity in a new value-added Europe, that parochial concerns must be put aside in a brave new soccer world, etc. Still, quite a lot would go with such clubs, a lot of tradition, diversity, oddness, locality and, as I have tried to sketch here, a lot of what has served for a century to help make Scotland 'Scottish'.

Bibliography

Annual Reports (1987, 1988), East Stirlingshire FC, Forfar Athletic FC, Rangers FC, Edinburgh, Companies House.
BBC Radio, 'Sport on Four', 12 August 1989.
BBC1 TV, 'Reporting Scotland', 18 May 1990.
BBC1 TV, 'Friday Sportscene', 19 April 1991.
BBC2 TV, 'On the Line', 23 August 1990.
Daily Record (Glasgow), 6 June 1990.
The Economist, 'Fly Mo', 26 August, 1989, p. 22.
Evening Times (Glasgow), various dates.
Edinburgh Hibernian plc, (1990), *Response to the Cash Offer*, Edinburgh.
Fynn, A. *et al.* (1989), *The Secret Life of Football*, London: Queen Anne Press.
Glasgow Herald (various dates).
ITN, 'News at Ten', 10 July 1989.
Heart of Midlothian plc, (1990), *Cash Offer for Edinburgh Hibernian*, Edinburgh.
Heart of Midlothian plc, (1990a), *Reply to Edinburgh Hibernian*, Edinburgh.
Home Office (1990), *The Hillsborough Stadium Disaster: Inquiry by The Rt. Hon. Lord Justice Taylor, Final Report*, London: HMSO Cmd. 962.
Moorhouse, H. F. (1984), 'Professional Football and Working Class Culture: English Theories and Scottish Evidence', *Sociological Review*, **32**, pp. 285–315.
Moorhouse, H. F. (1986), 'It's Goals That Count? Football Finance and Football Subcultures', *Sociology of Sport Journal*, **3**, pp. 245–60.
Moorhouse, H. F. (1987), 'Scotland v. England: Football and Popular Culture', *International Journal of the History of Sport*, **4**, pp. 189–202.
Moorhouse, H. F. (1989), 'We're Off to Wembley: The History of a Scottish Event and the Sociology of Football Hooliganism', in D. McCrone *et al.* (eds), *The Making of Scotland*, Edinburgh: Edinburgh University Press.
Moorhouse, H. F. (1990), 'Scottish Shooting Stars: Footballers as Working Class Symbols in Twentieth Century Scotland', in R. Holt (ed.), *Sport and the Working Class in Modern Britain*, Manchester: Manchester University Press.
Observer Scotland, 10 June 1990.
Radio Clyde, 'Football Phone-in', 2 November 1990.
Scotland on Sunday (Glasgow), various dates.
Scottish Sports Council (1975), *Hampden: Report of the Working Party on the Future of Hampden Park*, Glasgow.

12
Playing the past: the media and the England football team

Stephen Wagg

Italy, Germany, Brazil — even Belgium, even Cameroon — *that* was football.
Whereas us — we were history!

(Pete Davies, All Played Out 1990)

This essay, as its subtitle makes clear, is essentially about the relationship
between the British media and the England football team. It concentrates on
the period 1982–90, so it covers the span of Bobby Robson's managership of
the England team. Robson became manager after the World Cup of 1982, in
Spain, took the team through two further World Cup competitions (Mexico in
1986 and Italy in 1990), and left as soon as the Italian tournament finished. He
is therefore a central figure here, but the article is not, ultimately, about him;
it's about football culture — in which team managers now have such a pre-
eminence; it's about the British popular press — especially the *Sun*; and it's
about the uses of Englishness. In trying to pursue and develop these themes I
draw on some of my previous work (Wagg, 1984, 1986) and the early part of
the essay is largely historical, showing how changes within the football world,
in the popular press, and elsewhere, may provide a context for understanding
the (often bizarre) happenings of the 1980s.

The football world: managers must manage

In contemporary British culture football managers enjoy a special status and
visibility. In the week in which this essay was written, for example, one
manager (Graeme Souness) was appointed by a major British club at a salary
reputed to be £350,000 a year, while another (the late Bill Shankly) has been
quoted by a leading cleric (Rt. Revd George Carey) during his enthronement as
Archbishop of Canterbury. (Carey cited Shankly's now famous dictum that
football was not a matter of life and death; it was more important than that.)
But this cultural prominence of the manager — indeed, the role of the football
manager itself — is a comparatively recent phenomenon which emerged, as I
see it, largely for two reasons.

Firstly, the internal politics of the English professional football world conspired to produce football managers in increasing numbers, until a point was reached, around the early 1960s, when a football manager, in the modern mode, was universally regarded as a necessity. Initially, in the 1930s, this had been because boards of directors had been anxious to devolve the more and more onerous responsibilities of finding, engaging and dealing with players on to a third party. This third party was invariably, up to the 1950s, entitled the secretary-manager. Moreover, board members were concerned to deflect some of the public anger, which, in many areas, greeted any lapse in the team's performance (Dunning, Murphy and Williams, 1988) on to someone else. Secretary-managers themselves undoubtedly welcomed the mystique woven around them by the press in the inter-war years, when they were increasingly represented as 'canny wheeler-dealers' going surreptitiously about their business in their trilby hats and belted raincoats (Wagg, 1984: ch. 5). This public prominence of football managers, and their exclusive control of team matters, was further reinforced by the popular press in the late 1950s and early 1960s. By this time, these newspapers were anxious to expand their football coverage beyond match reports and transfer news and managers were clearly the most likely source of extra copy. Increasingly from that time the performance of League football teams has been synonymous with the performance of their managers.

Secondly, there has been the factor of what I have elsewhere called the football 'technocracy' (Wagg, 1984: ch. 7). This refers to football as an area of expertise, dispensed by qualified coaches, and these technocratic ideas emanated from the Football Association, principally at the instigation of Stanley Rous who became FA Secretary in 1934. One of the aims of the coaching movement was to make English football better and more competitive in world competition — a clear departure from the policy of Rous's predecessor, Sir Frederick Wall, in whose time the FA had strongly espoused the 'amateur' ethos and had been prepared to resign from international bodies (such as FIFA) which they felt did not uphold it (Tomlinson, 1986). The theory and practice of coaching was gradually imported into League clubs in the 1950s and as qualified coaches became managers the notion of managerial responsibility was further strengthened, since most teams were now, apparently, being tactically prepared by their managers.

The FA's Director of Coaching has also, simultaneously, been the manager of the England football team, the first one being Walter Winterbottom, who was appointed in 1946. As I've shown (Wagg, 1986), the press took little notice of Winterbottom at the time, except occasionally to question the need for a 'boffin' to teach the crafty old pros of the England side how to play.

Thinking of England

In the 1950s British newspapers, as is generally accepted, began increasingly to appeal to the senses and gut feelings of their readers — hence the term 'sensationalism', which gained in currency on Fleet Street around that time. Many reporters, trawling the imagined subconscious of their readerships, found two highly promising anxieties: a wounded national pride associated with the dismantlement of the British Empire and a fear of communism, stoked by the Cold War. Such considerations became vital in an emergent circulation crisis, fuelled by the growth in television ownership, and they bore directly on football reporting since sport — especially football, along with horse-racing — was of major concern to readers.

Football was particularly assimilable to these themes, being, apparently, the perfect evocation of British imperialism. It's been an axiom in the British football world throughout its history that the British invented the game and taught other countries how to play it. Even the recent report by Mr Justice Taylor on the Hillsborough disaster, cogent and well received as official reports go (see Ian Taylor's article in this volume), finds space for the platitude 'Football is our national game. We gave it to the world' (HMSO, 1990, p. 5).

Since football was supposed, along with parliamentary democracy, to have been England's gift to the world, the English football team was widely assumed by Britons to be the best. In football terms this was, to say the least, a dubious judgement, but much was made by many people of the fact that England had never been beaten on their own ground — the Empire stadium at Wembley — and the fact that England had over the years disdainfully refused to play many teams, or to enter the World Cup before 1950, was widely overlooked.* This was the cultural seam which football reporters in the popular press began to mine in the 1950s. Desmond Hackett at the *Daily Express*, in particular, and Peter Wilson of the *Daily Mirror* began to inject a patriotic invective into their reportage of the England team. Comparatively little had been made of England's defeat by the United States — a country with no football tradition — in the World Cup of 1950, but when Hungary came to Wembley in 1953 the popular press predicted that England would make short work of them. Hungary, they asserted, had the regimented style of a communist country and this would be no match for the individualist spontaneity of the English. In football terms this was a judgement — albeit possibly contrived in order to 'sell papers' — of singular crassness. Hungary were known to people in the international game — including England manager Walter Winterbottom — to have an extremely good team, with several players of great skill: one of them, Ferenc Puskas, drew gasps from the crowd with tricks he performed with the ball even before the match had started. England lost 3–6 and Fleet Street was unforgiving. The England football team has, ever since then, been seen on the sports pages of the popular press as a metaphor for England itself. As Britain declined economically (Overbeek, 1990), shed its empire and faced up to a world dominated by two new superpowers, Fleet Street spoke as if a still great nation was being betrayed by the bunglers and shirkers who ran, or were, its football team.

This paradigm of supposed incompetence, backsliding and wounds to

* England were defeated on their own soil as early as 1877, when they lost 1–3 to Scotland at the Kennington Oval. They also lost 0–2 to the Republic of Ireland on Everton's ground, Goodison Park, in September 1949. Away from home, they had been beaten a number of times before the Second World War: by Spain in Madrid in 1929, by Hungary in Budapest in 1934 and by Czechoslovakia in Prague the same year, by Belgium in Brussels in 1936, Switzerland in Zurich in 1938 and Yugoslavia in Belgrade in 1939.

national pride remained substantially undisturbed in the popular press football discourse of the 1980s. While its expression became cruder, with shorter words and judgements more terse and abusive, its contrivance became more sophisticated, as market analysts probed the preferences of social classes C2 and below for editorial pointers. The packaging of atavistic Britishness was, of course, not confined either to football or to the popular press. It became an important element in political discourse in Britain in the 1980s and in the rhetoric of what was invariably termed 'Thatcherism': one thinks here particularly of Margaret Thatcher's post-Falklands speech at Cheltenham in 1982, and of the various political interventions of Norman Tebbit, which expressed his famed affinity with the mythic English saloon bar. But most of all one thinks of its main organ, the *Sun*.

The *Sun* and the politics of banality

The *Sun* grew out of the ashes of the *Daily Herald*, which closed in 1964. The demise of the *Herald* strengthened the already growing conviction on Fleet Street that affluence and attendant notions of 'youth' had made a leftish Labour popular newspaper unviable (Smith, 1975). Rupert Murdoch's News International bought the paper in 1969 and 'took it ruthlessly downmarket' (Jenkins, 1986: p. 48). The paper explicitly embraced the Conservatives in 1979 but had by then already established its distinctive editorial style — a sort of play-fascism: cheeky, monosyllabic, and anti-Establishment, apparently life-loving and massively reactionary. This style was wrought partly in consultation with Conservative politicians, especially during the years of Margaret Thatcher's leadership (1975–90), when leading Conservatives frequently 'popped in for a chat' (Chippindale and Horrie, 1990: p. 56) and senior *Sun* staff, in turn, advised senior Tories on campaign strategy (Grose, 1989: p. 37). But also, clearly, the style is the result of an imaginary dialogue with a generalised other: the *Sun* reader. This person is thought to be male (although women are nearly half of *readers*, as distinct from buyers) and working class. He has, all along, been assumed to be young: the paper itself, at the outset, promised to be 'young, new, virile' and '. . . on the side of youth. It will never think that what is prim must be proper . . .' (Lamb, 1989: p. 26). But the *Sun* does not forget its older reader, who is, according to Kelvin Mackenzie (editor since 1981), 'the bloke you see in the pub — a right old fascist, wants to send the wogs back, buy his poxy council house, he's afraid of the unions, afraid of the Russians, hates the queers and weirdoes and drug dealers' (Chippindale and Horrie, 1990: p. 148). There are three things about the *Sun*'s daily pursuit of this 'bloke' and his companion 'downmarket' categories that I want briefly to note.

Firstly, although it certainly contains conventional 'news', the *Sun* is not primarily a *news*paper, any more than its main competitors, the *Daily Star* and the *Daily Mirror*, are. It deals in publicity. That's to say it is concerned with fame — the known-ness of people — and the interplay between the public world of the 'known' and the private. It does not, on the whole, seek to report or explain events — Murdoch, when he bought the *Sun*, got rid of most of its

specialist correspondents (Chippindale and Horrie, 1990: p. 16). Such events
are for the broadcasting media. The *Sun* does not compete with television; on
the contrary, it is television-led. The things it says about public figures are
often not 'real', because publicity is not concerned with the 'real'. Indeed, if
something 'real' turns out not to be suitable — that is, not likely to be 'of
interest to our readers' — then, as writers on the popular press accept, it will
have to be swapped for something that is. For example, in a recent memoir, a
tabloid journalist describes having to write the reminiscences of the comedian
Dick Emery for which his newspaper had paid a large sum of money. To
Emery's protest, 'You've made all this up. I didn't say a word of it. I'm not
signing any of this garbage . . .', the journalist replies, 'Look, mate. You either
want thirty-five grand or you don't' (Clarkson, 1990: pp. 201–2).

Secondly, the *Sun* is centrally about social class: its essential character has
been forged in an unequal society dominated by a growing ethos of openness
and meritocracy; since the 1960s virtually all successful politicians, from
Wilson through Thatcher to Major, have paid lip-service to this. To the ranks
of the unsuccessful — that is, social classes C2 to E — the *Sun* offers symbolic
consolation: the apparent diminution of someone 'big'. Here the objective
merges with the subjective: whether of inherited wealth ('Royals', 'toffs') or
self-made, in the subtext of the *Sun* public figures equal hypocrites. When
even members of the Thatcher Government began to express doubts about this
kind of journalism and a bill to curtail it (the Privacy Bill) was before
parliament, a *Sun* editorial, written by Murdoch and others, retorted:

The Establishment does not like *The Sun*. Never has. We are so popular they fear our
success, since they do not understand the ordinary working man and woman . . . They
wish to conceal from the readers' eyes anything that they find annoying or embarrass-
ing to themselves' (6 February 1989, quoted in Grose, 1989: pp. 40–1).

In the trade this is known, rather less sanctimoniously, as 'slag off' journalism;
it is widely held that the Privacy Bill and public warnings by David Mellor, the
Minister at the time responsible for broadcasting, have had some muting effect,
but that the heyday of such writing was the 1980s. A recent account of life at
the *Sun* describes the paper's editor effing and blinding his way round the
office exhorting his staff to 'monster' their victims' and 'piss all over them'.
(Chippindale and Horrie, 1990: p. 309)

Thirdly, sport is vital to the *Sun*'s operation and to the stable four million
daily circulation it has enjoyed since the late 1970s:

Vast numbers of *Sun* readers start the paper at the back. To them the back page *is* the
front page — which is why it is laid out to look exactly like it with familiar red *Sun* logo,
big headline, sensational stories and all.
This is the paper's sports section and its flashy presentation shows how important it is.
In fact, when the sports writers talk about 'the front of the book' they mean the back.
(Grose, 1989: p. 80)

Football is the most important sport to the *Sun*, followed closely by horse-
racing. Both sports have a strong working-class following, of course, and their

popularity is bulwarked by television. This is thought to increase female interest which in turn promotes the pursuit of information about the love lives of footballers, along with jockeys, snooker players and so on. But the football reportage remains firmly within the paradigm of impatient, reactionary saloon-bar masculinity that was established in the 1950s.

The Murdoch *Sun*'s first sports editor, Frank Nicklin, declared at the outset that the paper's sports pages would have 'four rows of teeth' (Lamb, 1989: pp. 143-4). The quotation is from Harry Storer, a League football manager of the 1930s, 1940s and 1950s — days when managers were hard and unexpressive, talked constantly of 'guts' and scoured the dressing room for cowards and backsliders. They were sergeant-majors. When, in League football mythology, a player knocked timidly on his door and asked 'Boss, why am I in the second team?', such a manager always bellowed back 'Because we've got no bleedin' third team'. This managerial style became increasingly unviable after the players' wage emancipation in 1961 but symbolically, on the back pages of the *Sun*, it is kept alive. On behalf of the expectant C2s, Ds and Es the football writers of the *Sun* are watching the England team for a quality of football befitting the nation that invented the game. Anything less and they react as Harry Storer would have reacted: principal *Sun* football reporter John Sadler uses the suitably Freudian soubriquet of 'The Man Who Gives It To You Straight'. In 1989 *Sun* sports editor David Balmforth was quoted as saying proudly 'now we've got eight rows of teeth' (Grose, 1989: p. 88).

The England football manager, then, is a natural victim of the contemporary popular press: he is upwardly mobile, having left the social world which most *Sun* readers still occupy; he is famous; as a football manager he is responsible, by all the tenets of modern football thinking, for the performances of his team; he is a technocrat obliged in his job to deal with a press, many of whom have 'hype[d] the working class game into the realms of television-led fantasy' (Chippindale and Horrie, 1990: p. 276); and as steward of the national team he knows, from his experience of international football that press-enhanced public expectations of an England side are unreasonably high. He cannot expect to succeed. He lives, in a very real sense, in a world of madness, because both his team and his tormentors stand for an England that no longer exists — if, indeed, it ever did.

The 1980s: England in the *Sun*

Bobby Robson took over as manager of the England football team in July of 1982. He had all the credentials: an England player himself, a respected coach and tactician, the manager of a comparatively small club, Ipswich Town, to which, like one of his predecessors, Sir Alf Ramsey, he had brought trophies. The *Sun*, however, had already, six weeks earlier, persuaded an ex-League manager Malcolm Allison to testify that Robson would be 'the worst choice — he couldn't make a decision' (26 May 1982).

When Robson's appointment was announced, Frank Clough, one of several football writers on the *Sun*, judged that the existing squad of England players was 'sound, solid, competent, professional and functional' and he acknowledged that the record of Robson's predecessor, Ron Greenwood, had been creditable: played fifty-five, won thirty-three and lost only ten. But the way this had been accomplished had not been satisfactory: they'd averaged less than two goals a game, 'a depressing statistic'. What Robson 'MUST unearth during his tour of office', prescribed Clough, 'is a gem or two . . .' (7 July 1982).

The following day, the *Sun placed* Robson — in England and in English society. In the issue of 8 July, Robson is shown to be from mining stock in the North East and in his home village of Langley Park — here mummified in a conventional media representation of the northern working class — the 'cloth-capped pigeon men and leek growers . . . are all proud of their famous son'. But he has, of course, risen in the world and the same issue reminds readers, including any 'pigeon men', of his new salary: £50,000 a year and a five-year contract, which the pointedly misleading headline ('£250,000 PAY DAY FOR ROBSON') implies is a lump sum.

So what has the recipient of this salary to say for himself? The *Sun* induces Robson to offer a classic hostage to fortune: 'I know I'm the best man for the job. My track record is better than any of the other people interested in managing England.' Football managers, with their characteristically individual-ist ethos, often make such statements, and often the statements return to haunt them. The *Sun* meanwhile turned its attention to the World Cup Final of the coming Saturday, which Frank Clough's article reminded his readers would be contested by foreigners (West Germany and Italy): 'THESE GERMAN CHEATS MUST NOT WIN IT'. 'They're thugs and conmen,' observes Clough, but 'the Italians . . . are just as bad in their own way' (10 July 1982).

Bobby Robson was an earnest man. He was a patriotic man, conscious of the honour of playing, and selecting others to play, for his country. Like all international football managers he was a technocrat, priding himself on his knowledge of the game, and, as such, he preferred his press dealings to be with reporters from 'qualities' like the *Guardian*, whose football correspondent David Lacey he admired. But he soon found that, as England manager, he was the villain in a melodramatic fantasy being constructed by the tabloid newspapers.

Robson's first team selection omitted Kevin Keegan, England captain under the previous regime but now rumoured among managers to be fractious and prone to injury. Keegan 'sold his story' to a tabloid newspaper stressing that Robson had not contacted him with any explanation. On his next visit to his native North East, to watch Keegan's team Newcastle United, Robson was spat upon by an angry crowd (Robson and Harris, 1986: ch. 1).

The following year, at a press conference, Robson remarked that the West Ham player, Alan Devonshire, didn't do as well for England as he did for his club and 'went into some technical detail'. Tabloid reporters, impatient of such subtleties, rushed to the East End to speak to Devonshire in the hope of promoting a feud between the two. Then, in September 1983, at Wembley, England were beaten 0–1 by Wales. This triggered a campaign by the tabloids, complete with lapel badges, for Robson to be replaced by the Nottingham Forest manager (and sometime *Sun* football correspondent) Brian Clough.

Against the Soviet Union at Wembley in June 1984 England lost 0–2. At the height of 'Thatcherism', with its constituent notions of a restored British greatness and militant opposition to the Eastern Communist bloc, this result was unacceptable, especially to the tabloids. While copy was still being filed, however, there was more spittle for Mr Robson from indignant supporters, and chants of 'Robson out'. After the game Robson was interviewed by the BBC's Jimmy Hill. Hill 'put me through it,' recalled Robson later (Robson and Harris, 1986: p. 35), illustrating the capacity of the tabloids now to set the agenda for media discussion of the England team. Shouldn't England pull out of their forthcoming tour of South America, Hill suggested, and avoid humiliation?

The capacity of the popular press to surprise Robson remained un-diminished. The following May, while he was preparing to fly with the England team to Mexico, Robson was telephoned by a reporter on the *Daily Mirror* who said with some embarrassment, 'We are carrying a front page story tomorrow saying that you must go.' Robson replied ingenuously 'Go where?' (Robson and Harris, 1986: p. 59). Following the game against Mexico, Robson found, at his morning press conference, that some reporters had been consulting the record book and had produced statistical evidence to support their depiction of him as an incompetent. England, as it turned out, had not lost three international matches in a row since 1959. Did Bobby realise, asked one reporter, that 'if we lose to West Germany it will be the worst ever run by an England manager?' (Robson and Harris: 1986, p. 70).

With the World Cup of 1986 approaching, and England safely qualified for the finals, Robson nevertheless noticed that 'not everyone was satisfied, not by a long way. It was my misfortune to be caught in the middle of a newspaper circulation war and I was well used to some football writers who had not even attended our games attacking me and criticising our players' (Robson and Harris, 1986: p. 89). The battle had been joined, most importantly, by the popular papers owned by Robert Maxwell. His *Daily Mirror*, with the highly respected football journalist Ken Jones now departed to the *Independent*, fully embraced the paradigm of patriotic anxiety and abuse. Further they had conscripted Emlyn Hughes, a former Liverpool and England captain to comment on Robson. This was an important move because to have been a professional — especially at international level — is an important legitimation in the football world. Since most reporters had 'never played', much of what they wrote, though occasionally wounding, could be dismissed as 'paper talk'. The cooption of people like Hughes blurs this distinction. Hughes, who since his retirement from playing had briefly managed Rotherham United but worked mainly as a 'media personality', pronounced himself worried by Robson and accused him of mistaking one England player for another. In Maxwell's *Sunday People* the ex-Tottenham player Steve Perryman, who had played once for England, volunteered similar testimony. If England did well in Mexico all this sort of comment would be forgotten, but if they didn't, well, the papers could say, no wonder.

With the onset of the World Cup Finals of 1986 the *Sun*'s approach to the England team came into sharper focus. They had three leading football specialists — Alex Montgomery, Brian Woolnough and John Sadler — and they appeared, as they still appear, to operate like a team of police officers conducting an interrogation: at any given time one seems understanding and conciliatory, while another brandishes a stick. From mid-May to early June, *Sun* dispatches from the England camp are a mixture of the benign, the expectant and the ominous. England player Glenn Hoddle pays a personal tribute to Robson, in conversation with Montgomery ('MY DEBT TO ROBSON,' 16 May 1986) and Robson himself is quoted, improbably, as saying 'MY LADS SCARE THE WORLD' (27 May). The central concern for England is whether or not to play Bryan Robson, their inspirational, but lately much injured, captain. Sadler, on this question, is adamant: 'DON'T PLAY ROBSON'. He continues: 'Can we seriously anticipate the inclusion of a player who completed just seven League games in the last seven months of the season?' (31 May).

When Robson is declared fit, however, Montgomery is presented as cheerleader, his article headed 'CAPTAIN MARVEL' (2 June), and the following day there is a neutral 'I'LL PLAY'. This makes it possible, when England have lost 0–1 to Portugal, for Sadler to return to his earlier theme: manager Robson is dubbed 'FOOL ON THE HILL' (an apparent reference to England's training camp in the mountains) and informed that 'Risking Robbo was a mistake' (5 June). This mistake allows Sadler to reintroduce the matter of Threats-to-National-Pride, which now emanate, as he makes clear, not from the communist bloc, nor from Latin America, but from black Africa. England now play Morocco and Sadler's article of 6 June pleads 'DON'T LET 'EM LAUGH AT US'. 'Defeat by the Moroccans, of all teams, is unthinkable', he argues. 'But if it happened,' he suggests, reaching for a phrase much used on Fleet Street since the 1950s, 'I doubt if the England team would dare return home for weeks.'

The next day, with England having played a goalless draw against Morocco, it is the turn of Montgomery to get tough. 'England,' he announces, 'are the big name jokes of the World Cup — the Mugs of Monterrey.' Even if England do qualify for the next round of the tournament, 'that will not wipe out the humiliation of this result against a team with no pedigree and no tradition from the Third World'. Somewhat in contradiction of this, Montgomery refers in the same article to the punishing heat in which the match was played and describes the opposition as 'this hard-working, enthusiastic and skilful Moroccan side'. Nevertheless, 'too many England players have let the manager, themselves and the country down with performances far, far below what is acceptable from international footballers — certainly England international footballers.'

The following Monday, Sadler is now styled as 'the man who's been right every step of the way' — a title which appears above reproductions of earlier headlines. Today's headline, 'THE CRAZY GANG: They wouldn't beat the Sally Army', is in the time-honoured, saloon-bar idiom but the article is notably defensive of Bobby Robson:

If England fail to beat Poland on Wednesday, they will be flung out of the tournament and cost Bobby Robson his job as international manager. One of the nicest men ever to hold the post would surely be sacrificed — simply because of the sheer volume of public outcry.

This sudden concern for one of England's nicest managers could have been conjured with an eye to the next day's back page. Emlyn Hughes, in the rival *Mirror* and on ITV alongside another ex-England player Mike Channon, has been leading the field in criticising Robson. So the following day (10 June) with two days to fill before England's next match, the *Sun*'s story is about the manager and his critics: from Alex Montgomery in Monterrey comes 'BELT UP YOU BIG MOUTHS', a mischievous paraphrasing of Robson's impatience with his 'television tormentors', Hughes and Channon. 'Emlyn Hughes has tried to pick teams — and failed,' he is quoted as saying. 'Mike Channon has never had to pick one. I can't worry about them.'

Sun rumination on 11 June, day of the Poland match is both brittle and doomy. Sadler refers to 'BOBBY'S LAST STAND' and another headline asks 'CAN YOU CREDIT IT! *England are odds on to beat Poland tonight*'. England's 3-0 victory against Poland, however, brings out the ideologically inchoate nature of *Sun*sport. Its statements and positions over a day or two, or even on the same page, are unmarriageable. Every day, in true postmodernist fashion, the same reactionary cards — the 'SACK THESE DUNCES, the HOME, THE CONQUERING HEROES', the 'DON'T BOTHER COMING HOMEs' — are shuffled once again and dealt to the moment, irrespective of previous formulations. It speaks, therefore, like a manic depressive, with arbitrary extremes of temper. It expresses, not opinion but spasm. Thus, on 12 July, the 'CRAZY GANG' of three days earlier has transmuted into 'Robson lionhearts' who are 'on the march'. 'England were going to be buried in Monterrey,' reflected Alex Montgomery, 'but instead the lion roared defiantly again at the world' and the players 'produced the football we knew they could produce.' An apparent nationalistic euphoria now develops, enhanced by a further victory over Paraguay by a team now called 'BOBBY'S BEAUTIES' (19 June). This has brought them into the quarter-final where they face fresh South American opposition — 'BRING ON THE ARGIES' — and Montgomery has swung to a madcap optimism: 'we're on our way to the top of the world,' he trills.

England's subsequent defeat by Argentina on 22 June was mitigated in the eyes of the *Sun* by the fact that the first Argentine goal clearly entered the English net off the fist of their leading player, Diego Maradona. They had, therefore, according to Montgomery, 'been elbowed out of the World Cup by a little cheat': no disgrace, it was implied, should attach to wrongful defeat at the hands of a conniving Latin American. Of course, in the myth world of the *Sun*, cheats are always foreigners. Robson, a different sort of patriot, and a professional, acknowledged after the match that, had an England player done what Maradona had done, 'I do not suppose we would have argued with the referee' (Robson and Harris, 1986: p. 208).

From saloon bar to six-pack: from nice man to plonker

Two factors inform the *Sun*'s international football coverage in the later 1980s.

Firstly, there was now a consensus around xenophobia, attacks on the manager and blunt, arbitrary judgements to which their main competitors, the *Daily Mirror* and the *Daily Star*, fully subscribed. Since the circulation of any one of these could only increase substantially at the expense of the others, the

logic was for an escalation of this essential style. The *Sun*, therefore, moved
further and further away from the saloon bar and closer to the skinhead with
the six-pack, jettisoning more syllables and niceties as it went. There was, by
now, some disquiet in government circles about 'the new yobbish affluence
which the *Sun* represented', and this was expressed by the Home Secretary,
Douglas Hurd, in a speech at Tamworth in 1987. But it cut little ice with the
Sun, whose editor 'enthusiastically embraced the two fingers to society, "I
don't give a fuck" mentality' (Chippindale and Horrie, 1990: pp. 211, 78).

Secondly, the main football business of the period was the European
Championships of 1988, and Europe, to the *Sun*, was the home of 'Frogs',
'Krauts' and the hated European Commission. This latter counterposed a
bureaucratic, supranational reality to the Thatcherite fantasy of a renewed,
post-Falklands greatness for Britain.

In the prelude to the Championship there are familiar features. With
Robson unlikely to select his mid-fielder Glen Hoddle, there are a couple of
stories telling him that he should 'PLAY HODDLE OR YOU'RE DOOMED' (3
June) and 'DON'T WASTE ME, ROBSON' (attributed to Hoddle) (4 June).
And Montgomery and Brian Woolnough are apparently the 'gentle coppers'
assigned to Robson himself. He talks to them about his estimation of his
captain, Bryan Robson (better than Gullit of the Netherlands — 8 June) and
the stress of the job: 'I'VE BEEN THROUGH HELL FOR ENGLAND'. But,
with defeat by the Republic of Ireland in their first game, England find the
Sun's whole familiar vocabulary of national tragedy once again deployed:

DISGRACE TO THE NAME OF ENGLAND Alex Montgomery on the shame of
Stuttgart England were stuffed like Fourth Division nobodies here . . . This wasn't just
defeat, it was a disaster — and a national disaster at that.

The back page has 'BLAME ME' *says Bobby Robson* (seemingly to Woolnough)
while Sadler, now militantly unsentimental (no more 'one of the nicest men
. . .'), is jerking his thumb: 'ON YER BIKE ROBSON — *Get us out of this mess
or it's the end*' (13 June).

Two days later, Sadler not only repeats this ultimatum but broadens its
terms to include Robson's employers at the FA. Since the conceding of full
managerial control (to Alf Ramsey in 1963), less press notice has been taken of
the FA but now chairman Bert Millichip is given public notice to quit: 'BEAT
EM OR BEAT IT BOBBY — Barmy Bert and Co. can get on their bikes, too'.
His vote of confidence in Robson is interpreted as 'official permission to fail as
manager . . .' (15 June).

England's 1–3 defeat by Holland (a foreseeable one in football terms) is
acknowledged in the *Sun* with a one-syllable phallic metaphor — 'STUFFED'
(16 June) — and, the following day, a telephone poll for readers, with a choice
of candidates to succeed Robson. (On 18 June the poll's winner, Brian Clough,
threatens legal action beneath the headline 'I DIDN'T KNIFE ROBSON').

On Monday 20 June, with the England team eliminated and on its way home,
the *Sun* returns, once again to the 1950s, this time to the barrack room, for its
reproof: 'A GUTLESS, SPINELESS SHOWER!' Robson is pictured with a
dunce's cap drawn over his head. A series of optimistic remarks he has made

are listed beneath the caption 'Ramblings of the bungling boss who brought shame to England'. Brian Woolnough claims to have elicited from USSR captain Igor Belanov an 'astonishing blast' to the effect that 'ROBSON [is] TWENTY YEARS OUT OF DATE!' And there are pictures of FA officials Millichip, Dick Wragg and Peter Swales: at their next meeting, rages Sadler, Robson's job 'won't even be discussed'. So, he concludes:

The outrageous cover-up of England's slump to the level of European laughing stock has become a national scandal. As the players flew home, humiliated in a three match pointless exercise, the whitewash flowed as freely as the Rhine here in West Germany. There will be no changes, folks!

With Robson retained in post, as the football press surely knew he would be, this left a few short weeks' late summer break for the Wounded National Pride business before thoughts once again turned to the World Cup Finals, scheduled next for Italy in 1990.

With friendly matches and World Cup qualification games approaching in the autumn of 1989 an extraordinary exchange, strongly reminiscent of the casework of R. D. Laing (Laing and Esterson, 1972), appears in the *Sun*. Using a standard technique of asking a victim what it's like to be a victim, while victimising him on another page, the *Sun* sends Alex Montgomery to speak to Bobby Robson. He tells Montgomery of 'the hell he and his family have had to endure since England's disaster in the European Championships'. But, in the adjacent column, *Sunsport Opinion* responds:

Bobby Robson whinges that he and his family have been through hell since he led England to European Championship humiliation in Germany. He says we don't realise what it is like to be 'kicked in the teeth'.
We do.
He kicked us in the teeth when he named the wrong players, employed the wrong tactics, flogged his team with endless training sessions and warm-up matches against joke opposition, and, after boasting we could win the European Championship, left us the laughing stock of world football . . .
We know how Bobby can avoid further 'hell'. QUIT.

This is the language of what Laing called the schizogenic family. The *Sun* as antagonist turns on the butt of the family's hatred and deceit: it is not he but *they* who have suffered. You betrayed us to the outside world, they tell him, you let them beat us at football.

The logic of this stand is, of course, further and more severe punishment until Robson can, in a symbolic way, be certified as mad and taken away. So what ensues, through late 1988 and into the spring of 1989, is a growing clamour, increasingly psychotic in its tone, against the England football manager. When Robson says he will not 'be forced into submission by those who haven't the first idea of what they are talking about', the *Sun* interprets this as 'waving a "V" sign at his critics' (12 September). When he announces his next team selection the predominance in it of experienced players is described as 'SENSELESS! SPINELESS! HOPELESS!' and he is accused of 'insulting the nation's finest young footballing talent' (14 September). On 16

September a photograph of Robson holding the World Cup is printed with the caption: 'The *Sun* picture YOU'LL NEVER SEE AS LONG AS BOBBY ROBSON IS ENGLAND'S MANAGER'. On 17 September *Sun* readers, it is alleged, have been telephoning the newspaper to say Robson should 'GO!' (back page headline). On 20 October Robson is dubbed a 'PLONKER', again suitably phallic and vicariously culled from the popular television comedy 'ONLY FOOLS AND HORSES'. Other sections of the tabloid press sought to match this masculine vocabulary. In November, as if to keep the *Sun* on its toes, the *Daily Mirror* metaphorically 'squares up' to Robson: Robson's impatience with his critics is transmuted into the headline 'STUFF YOU LOT!', while on the facing page is printed 'STUFF YOU TOO! says *Emlyn Hughes*', who begins his article with the words 'Sorry Bobby, or should I say Booby' (14 November). Three days later, when England have drawn with Saudi Arabia in Riyadh, the *Sun* prints yet another mawkish lament: 'BOBBY'S A DESERT DISASTER *Even Saudis kick sand in our faces*' (17 November). On the same day the *Daily Mirror*, having a month earlier told Robson 'GO!' (when England failed to beat Sweden), now follow up with the inevitable 'IN THE NAME OF ALLAH GO!' The following week, the *Sun* is fighting on all fronts: 'BRITAIN'S CABBIES GIVE THE ENGLAND MANAGER A TIP . . . TAKE A RIDE ROBSON' is coupled with an attack on TV football commentators for accusing the *Sun* of waging a vendetta against Robson. Likewise FA Secretary Ted Croker, who has described the *Sun*'s campaign as 'deplorable' is given short shrift: 'Crackpot Croker's amazing message to the *Sun* . . . DON'T BE BEASTLY TO OUR BOBBY.'

Much argument has been adduced in cultural studies in recent years to the effect that neither audience understanding nor reaction can be straight-forwardly 'read off' from the content of media products. These products — the *Sun*, in this case — are 'texts', which are 'negotiated' by the people that use them (Pursehouse, 1987: p. 31). This important consideration can help explain why, despite the mounting printed onslaught upon him throughout the 1980s, in November 1988 53 per cent of *Sun* readers thought Bobby Robson should keep his job. Indeed, 41 per cent thought he was doing it well. It may have disconcerted *Sunsport* to learn that many readers didn't even see the manager as the problem, since 'almost half of those polled insist a change of manager would make no difference to England performances' (25 November 1988). Such apparently structural perspectives have no place in the *Sun*'s view of things.

The following March, England are in Albania for a match which, if they win it, will qualify them for the World Cup Finals in Italy. In the *Sun* Sadler writes:

The outrageous propaganda continues of course. There are no easy matches anymore, or so they'd have us believe. And as long as four months ago Robson returned from watching the Albanians to warn us: 'I haven't seen such a quick team for some years . . . so skilful, so capable of penetrating a world-class defence.'

Ex-England footballer, Mike Channon, obliged with a more familiar and agreeable judgement: 'Albania are a joke and if we don't beat them, we might as well stay out there!' (8 March 1989).

In much of this tormented discourse we can see the clash of two technocracies: the Football World and the Selling Papers Business. Common to both are ideas of Britishness and mission. But whereas the FA, under Rous and Winterbottom, encouraged the 'developing' world to play football, in the myths deployed by the *Sun*, 'Britain' *taught* the whole world to play and remains, like an autocratic schoolmaster, unalterably best. Back in the 1960s Winterbottom happily foresaw the day when an African side would win the World Cup (Davies, 1990: p. 157) and he promoted a world of football expertise and universalist judgement. The *Sun* is, of course, inflexibly particularist. England will always be teacher/parent; other football nations are children which, as in the families of Laing's schizophrenic patients, must never grow up. The Albanians *were* quick and skilful. England won 2-0.

When in Rome: Italy 1990 and the fight for football judgements

The British popular press has become locked into a style which is to a significant degree divorced from events. In their field of operations, there are events and there are 'stories', and the relationship between the two is tangential. For a World Cup Finals tournament these 'stories', in outline at any rate, are mostly known in advance. Any follower of British football through the tabloids could expect, aside from the twin peaks of National Humiliation and National Rejoicing, some cocktail of Players Seen Breaking Curfew/Player Had Sex With Hotel Maid/Yob Fans on the Rampage, supplemented where necessary with innocuous revelations from Today's Training Session. These have become the hardy perennials since the 1960s. Besides which, by 1990, so much hyperbole had been expended on Mr Robson that the *Sun*, with the *Daily Mirror* now matching it angry syllable for angry syllable, could have few rhetorical surprises left in its locker.

So it proved. Indeed, on the eve of the tournament, with its vocabulary of outrage exhausted, the *Sun* has barely the werewithal to acknowledge the granting of its long expressed wish. Robson, it emerges, is not to have his contract renewed by the FA and he will leave, immediately after the Finals, to manage the Dutch Club PSV Eindhoven. The *Sun* which in the preceding days has contented itself with instructing Robson to 'ditch' one player or not to 'axe' another, musters a graceless goodbye: 'PSV OFF BUNGLER BOBBY' (25 May 1990). A half-hearted attempt is made to link Robson's impending departure with the recent claim, by a woman called Janet Rush, to have been Robson's mistress. Rush's memoirs are currently being shared by the *Sun* and its brother paper in Murdoch's News International, *The News of the World*. Here the text, expectably, is faithlessness (Robson as 'soccer love cheat' — *The News of the World*, 27 May) but the subtext is manliness: Robson has shown dangerously feminine characteristics — he was 'a sensitive lover', Rush is quoted as saying. They often cried together.

Thereafter it is business as usual. A friendly against Tunisia (resulting in a draw, 1-1) draws from Alex Montgomery the verdict 'PATHETIC! ARROGANT! SMUG!' — and England weren't even playing 'a country of international standing'. All this, reflects Montgomery, 'in the North African port [Tunis] where the last big team to scuttle away was led by Rommel' (4 June). (Continuing this excavation of the 1940s, the *The News of the World*, who have been busy taking statements from other women claiming to be lovers of Bobby Robson, describe Robson as 'the most vilified Englishman since Lord Haw Haw' — 10 June).

A draw with the Republic of Ireland on 11 June brings the best opportunity of the Finals for the *Sun* to display its patriotic disgust. Once again the team become 'BOBBY'S BUNGLERS' (12 June) and, the following day, on its front page, the paper calls, a little bizarrely, for Mrs Thatcher to mark this 'most appalling performance by an England team in living memory' by summoning the players back to Britain. To Robson's suggestion that the Republic have the third best team in the world Sadler replies 'YOU'RE BONKERS BOBBY!'

All this heralds a lull in proceedings and mid-June brings a flurry of classic tabloid fill-in stories: two Scotland players are alleged to have been out drinking (*Sun*, 14 June); a Dutch player is claimed to have 'taunted' the England goalkeeper that he's too old (*Sun*, 16 June); and a [by tabloid and World Cup standards] half-hearted attempt is made to suggest that a tournament hostess, Isabella Ciaravolo, has had sex with three England players. The *News of the World* (17 June) decides to use the smear itself as their story and produces reassuring testimony from another hostess that Ms Ciaravolo is 'plain' and unlikely to attract one man, let alone three.

England's failure to be eliminated from these championships continued to confound the *Sun* reporters. A respectable performance against Holland brings Sadler to muse that: 'We are at last seeing a glimpse of the real Bobby Robson — sadly, perhaps, eight years too late' (*Sun*, 18 June). A succession of eulogies to England players, notably Paul Gasgoigne, then follows. England reach the quarter-finals, but John Sadler is still uncomfortable: 'England are now officially one of the best eight teams on Earth. But, damn it, they have still to produce a performance to make the world sit up and take notice' (*Sun*, 28 June). Victory against Cameroon brings England into the semi-finals against West Germany and enables the *Sun* helpfully to inform readers that 'we call Germans krauts because each eats 130lb of sauerkraut — pickled cabbage — every year' (3 July).

In the same issue, manager Robson and his West German counterpart are given comparative ratings on 'LOOKS', 'PERSONALITY', 'BRAINS', 'SEX APPEAL', 'LOVE RECORD' AND 'OWN GOALS'. Robson is described as 'ruggedly good looking'. He is 'good natured and forgiving, charming and easy going . . .', he is sexy in 'a little-boy-lost way' and this has facilitated a 'LOVE RECORD' worthy of the title 'Romeo Robson'. However, in the 'BRAINS' department, he is 'Bumbling Bobby' and his capacity for 'OWN GOALS' (a favoured term in publicity circles) is high, making him 'a real winner when it comes to putting his foot in it'. Beckenbauer is superior (by 47 points to 30, overall) because, in the world of publicity, the myth-making propensities of which are assumed to be part of the natural hazards of life, he is more efficient: he has 'good PR'. Getting 'a bad image' is seen as like getting pneumonia after going out in the snow without a coat: it's the product of ineptitude.

There is now a real problem here for the English football public. The *Sun* is the country's most popular paper, with a daily circulation of three and three-quarter million and an estimated readership of three times that. It employs a battery of football correspondents, but it does not talk football. Its primary interest here is not football, but football *people* — invariably football managers: using them, it seeks to provoke a reaction in its audience. It doesn't explain or discuss the national game, because this is about thinking (trying to know) and not about reacting.

So who, in the mass media, *is* going to talk football? The broadsheet newspapers will certainly, as will the proliferating fanzines, but most important by far in this context is television. The point about the virulently populist commentary on football, developed by the tabloid papers over the past two decades, is that it has increasingly set the agenda for the broadcasters. Television has become a terrain of struggle for football judgements. A number of points illustrate this.

In the coverage of the World Cup Finals of 1978, in Argentina, TV reporting on both BBC and ITV often framed the tournament in tabloid terms and colluded in the vilification by the tabloids of Alistair Macleod, the Scotland manager, when Scotland were eliminated (Wagg, 1986). England had not qualified for those finals, and they did modestly well in the finals of 1982 and 1986 but, by 1990, as we've seen, the popular press had created an unprecedented fog of patriotic indignation around the England manager and his team even before a ball had been kicked. Moreover it thickened with the early matches. The BBC's Desmond Lynam clearly wished, on occasion, to avail himself of this fog — for example, in an exchange with Liverpool manager Kenny Dalglish on the eve of England's match against Eire. What England team would Kenny pick? Dalglish is reluctant to comment. Whatever team England manager Bobby Robson picks, Dalglish tells Lynam, it'll be what Bobby thinks is the best team for this occasion. Why not commit yourself, asks Lynam, 'I'll commit myself,' replies Dalglish, 'but what I say won't have any substance.' 'But it's a punters game,' pleads Lynam. Dalglish agrees — when the game is taken away from the punter, it's lost. Nevertheless . . . Then, politely and with obvious misgiving, Dalglish concedes that his selection might differ from the one he expects Robson to make. In saying this, he knows he has helped to make possible another 'Bungler Bobby' story, if England do badly (BBC1, 9 June).

But the *Sun* football agenda is more manifest on ITV — an important consideration since, having bought exclusive rights to show League football in 1988, the commercial network now dominates the televising of the game in Britain. At the forefront of ITV's substantial football coverage are Ian St. John and Jimmy Greaves. Both ex-international footballers, they have become 'television personalities' — a kind of Little and Large for football — with their own football preview programme, 'Saint and Greavsie', on a Saturday lunchtime. St. John is measured and discursive; Greaves cheerily unanalytic. Greaves is a regular contributor to the *Sun*. He and St. John represent the twin possibilities: St. John wants to talk football; Greaves wants to Have a Laugh. St. John is therefore his straight man. Greaves, like another ITV regular Emlyn Hughes, is the channel's link to the culture of the six-pack and to the less reflective elements on the terraces.

During the World Cup of 1990, while the football people on BBC wore mostly suits, on ITV it was sports shirts. Greaves himself frequently had on a T-shirt bearing a slogan, in the manner of a *Sun* headline, which he recited to the camera. And, like the *Sun*, Greaves, Hughes and others strained towards the unpompous, and 'The Story'.

For example, on 11 June, with England due to play the Republic of Ireland, Bobby Robson talks to the ITV studio. Having found Robson courteously non-committal in response to leading questions about his team selection (still undisclosed) and his opinion of Scotland, the broadcasters settle for pleasantries. 'We're rooting for you,' offers Nick Owen. 'Wish ya everything y'wish y'self,' thunders Greaves. 'G'luck pal.' Later, after Scotland have lost to Costa Rica, Greaves concludes 'It was a Costa Rican voodoo hoodoo, this one was.' He re-emerges in the evening clad in a shirt which reads 'GO FOR GOAL KNOW WHAT I MEAN GARY' and confides that Scotland were dismal, although 'no disrespect to my Jocko friends'. Meanwhile, the England team has been announced and link-man Elton Welsby asks Robson's appointed successor, Graham Taylor, to comment on the inclusion of Paul Gascoigne. Bobby, he says, has picked the team he thought fit. Welsby persists: 'Graham Taylor, back in London [as the team list appears on the screen], is that the team you would have picked?' 'It doesn't matter what team I'd have picked . . .', replies Taylor patiently. He, too, wishes to avoid providing a pretext on which Robson, his fellow technocrat, can later be criticised.

Sometimes the contradiction between 'The Story' — British failure and managerial culpability — and football expertise comes out of the same mouth. For instance, Glasgow Celtic manager Billy McNeill, assisting in the ITV commentary on Scotland v. Costa Rica, agrees with commentator Alan Parry that Scottish supporters are rightfully angry with their team: 'I mean Costa Rica just came to this World Cup to enjoy themselves and take part.' Twelve days later on 23 June, during Cameroon v. Columbia, when his co-commentator suggests that Cameroon are 'no pushovers', he replies, as almost any contemporary football manager in private would, that there are 'no pushovers left in the world'.

Sometimes the contradiction is rancorous, as in the interview of England player John Barnes by Nick Owen and Emlyn Hughes (ITV, 25 June) Barnes had been persistently criticised in the tabloids for his performances. Does he feel 'under pressure', asks Owen. Barnes, unwilling to discuss media constructions, answers firmly, 'The manager hasn't put me under any pressure — only certain papers — people that don't matter.' 'John! Emlyn here!' Barnes responds with a muted hello. Hughes wants to know what Barnes thinks of the sweeper system. Barnes spots the trap: if he says he likes it and Robson abandons it, a rift between manager and players can be construed. Likewise, if he says he doesn't, and the manager keeps it. The sweeper system, explains Barnes, was for the Netherlands match; the manager will do what he thinks is required for the following day's match against Belgium. Does Barnes think there's a danger of underestimating Belgium? Not, asserts Barnes, on the part of the England team. Yet again, Robson is the subtext: if England lose might it not be because the manager underestimated the opposition?

Sometimes, too, the difference between the channels on this score can be quite vivid. For example, on 1 July, England play Cameroon in the quarter finals. On BBC1, where the game is understood and framed rather more in the technocratic tradition of the FA, commentator Barry Davies pays tribute to the progress of African Football. The Tunisian Under 16 side, he informs viewers, have won a tournament recently. The Cameroon FA only formed in 1959, and affiliated to FIFA in 1962. England, he acknowledges more than once, have enjoyed considerable good fortune in the match. On ITV, Jimmy Greaves agrees. Cameroon should be ahead. What they need, he tells Cameroon international Charlie Ntamark, a studio guest, is a witch doctor.

Graham Taylor: Hello, I must be going

Graham Taylor took over managership of the England football team in July 1990. By the following spring the team had played five games, lost none of them, and Taylor was discussing the end of his tenure.

On 1 May 1991, with England about to play Turkey in the Aegean port of Izmir, the *Sun* quoted him as saying 'MY NECK IS IN THE NOOSE'; 'Graham Taylor last night warned his England stars: I'll be strung up if you play a long-ball game'. The following day, with England having won the match, the *Sun* pronounced the rope 'loosened', but the *Daily Mirror* was not satisfied: 'WHAT A LOAD OF RUBBISH'. After the match, Taylor is interviewed by David Davies for BBC TV but the interview has to wait while a contingent of England supporters chanting 'F*** off Taylor' (*Daily Star*, 2 May 1991) are pacified. Davies probes him on the quality of England's performance and, taken in isolation, his questions are polite and reasonable. But Taylor, a very astute man, already sees himself being impaled on myths of England. 'We've *won*,' he reminds the interviewer tetchily, 'let's just recognise how difficult it is to win games of football at this level all over the world.'

That recognition may come but on recent evidence it will not be brought closer by the British popular press. In reality, England is a country like many others and the England football team is a football team like many others. Robson knew this, and Taylor knows it. But the *Sun*, a powerful definer, has created an atavistic fantasy in which it cannot be known, and merely to suggest it is contempt of court. That being so, it is unlikely that 'the tabloids' will in the foreseeable future find anyone who is good enough to manage the England football team. Any incumbent will instead bear the brunt of their oblique, post-imperial British racism which says: 'Our team *must* be gutless if it can't beat *that* lot.' All that has changed since the 1950s is the degree of virulence with which this is argued and the nature of the opposition against which the England team is measured: in this latter context, communist countries have been replaced by the Third World.

This, then, is another British disease: hunting the Guilty Men. There can be no ifs, no buts, no explanations, and no mitigating circumstances. For the football reporters who give it to you straight, there is no such thing as society, but seemingly, there will always be an England.

Bibliography

Chippindale, Peter and Chris Horrie (1990), *Stick It Up Your Punter: The Rise and Fall of the* Sun, London: Heinemann.

Clarkson, Wensley (1990), *Dog Eat Dog: Confessions of a Tabloid Journalist*, London: Fourth Estate.

Davies, Pete (1990), *All Played Out: The Full Story of Italia '90*, London: Heinemann.

Dunning, Eric, Patrick Murphy and John Williams (1988), *The Roots of Football Hooliganism: An Historical and Sociological Study*, London: Routledge and Kegan Paul.

Grose, Roslyn (1989), *The Sun-Sation: Behind the Scenes at Britain's Bestselling Daily Newspaper*, London: Angus and Robertson.

HMSO (1990), *The Hillsborough Stadium Disaster: Final Report*, Inquiry by the Rt. Hon. Lord Justice Taylor, Cmnd. 962.

Jenkins, Simon (1986), *The Market for Glory: Fleet Street Ownership in the Twentieth Century*, London: Faber and Faber.

Laing, R. D. and A. Esterson (1972), *Sanity, Madness and the Family: Families of Schizophrenics*, Harmondsworth, Penguin.

Lamb, Larry (1989), *Sunrise: The Remarkable Rise and Rise of the Best Selling Soaraway* Sun, London, Macmillan.

Overbeek, Henk (1990), *Global Capitalism and National Decline: The Thatcher Decade in Perspective*, London: Unwin Hyman.

Pursehouse, Mark (1987), 'Life's More Fun With Your Number One *Sun*: Interviews with some *Sun* Readers', stencilled occasional paper, Centre for Contemporary Cultural Studies, University of Birmingham.

Robson, Bobby with Bob Harris (1986), *So Near and Yet so Far: Bobby Robson's World Cup Diary 1982-86*, London, Willow Books.

Smith, A. C. H. (1975), *Paper Voices: Popular Press and Social Change 1935-65*, London: Chatto.

Tomlinson, Alan (1986), 'Going Global: The FIFA Story', in Alan Tomlinson and Garry Whannel (eds), *Off the Ball*, London: Pluto Press.

Wagg, Stephen (1984), *The Football World: A Contemporary Social History*, Brighton: Harvester.

Wagg, Stephen (1986), 'Naming the Guilty Men: Managers and the Media', in Tomlinson and Whannel (1986), op. cit.

13
It's not a knockout: English football and globalisation

Adrian Goldberg and Stephen Wagg

In this article we explore the relationship between English football and globalisation and, within this context, we examine two important convergences: the convergence in the interests of the economically powerful clubs, both within Britain and across Europe where a Super League is more and more confidently envisaged; and, secondly, allied to this, the convergence of the football world and the mass media to the point where, in the early 1990s, there is serious disquiet about the 'tail wagging the dog': the media running football. To preface our discussion we'd like to sketch in some brief historical background — on English clubs and European competition; on the relationship between football and television; and on globalisation itself, the rise of the transnational corporations and, in particular, the multi-media conglomerates.

Before the Second World War, both the major British football bodies — the Football Association and the Football League — were disdainful of foreign competition. At the FA this appears to have been born of high-handedness, inertia and a conviction, rooted in the amateur ethos, that lesser nations 'brought politics into sport'. According to the international situation of the moment, therefore, the FA were in or out of FIFA (Tomlinson, 1986) and England did not enter the World Cup competition until 1950, twenty years after its inception. At the League there was an often militant 'Little Englandism', rooted in the provincial lower middle classes who ran the League clubs and the League itself (see Tomlinson's article in this volume). In their roast-beef-and-Yorkshire-pudding philosophy, British clubs playing each other was what the game was about; what did they want to play foreigners for?

In the Europe of the post-war period, however, for political and economic reasons there were moves to establish European football competition. These resulted in the inauguration, in 1955, of the European Cup and the Inter-Cities Fairs Cup. The former was a competition for national club champions. The English League champions of 1955, Chelsea, wanted to enter but were forbidden to do so by the League. Manchester United, champions the following year, entered, in defiance of the League and they did so on the advice of

Stanley Rous, now developing a more expansive, outgoing policy at the FA.

Since that time, 'getting into Europe' has become the pinnacle of achievement for British clubs. Indeed, the importance of 'Europe' to the major clubs, to the TV companies, to sponsors and advertisers and, obliquely, to the nation's self-esteem, had by the mid-1980s become such that the banishment of British clubs following the Heysel stadium tragedy in 1985 created a major problem. The Prime Minister, a noted Little Englander herself and quite ignorant of football culture, expressed herself willing to see British football clubs go to the wall if they could not 'put their house in order'. She was rapidly persuaded to think again and despite her famed belief that there was 'no such thing as society', government ministries began funding teams of sociologists to investigate football hooliganism — the cause of England's exclusion from European competition.

Rous also encouraged the transmission of football on television, which, in Britain, had begun in 1938 with the broadcast of the England v. Scotland match and the FA Cup Final. The League, on the other hand, were more wary of broadcasters. Before the Second World War, the BBC was not permitted even to give the football results until 6.15 p.m. on Saturdays and the League were still opposed to televised football in the early 1950s (Barnett, 1990: p. 15). Commercial television, established in 1955, very soon pressed the League to be allowed to show 'live' football matches but the League demurred and, for the time being, conceded occasional recorded highlights only to the BBC, an institution whom, doubtless, it deemed less vulgar. Football did not appear on ITV until 1962.

Thereafter, the BBC and ITV effectively operated a cartel, which was undisturbed until the late 1970s, whereupon, in 1978, the ITV company London Weekend Television broke ranks with what became known as 'Snatch of the Day'. Here LWT reached an agreement whereby they would have exclusive rights to television coverage of football and distribute the recordings around the ITV network on their terms. LWT backed down from this gambit, following complaints to the Office of Fair Trading by the BBC and the other ITV companies, and for much of the 1980s, BBC and ITV alternated League football highlights programmes on Saturday evenings and Sunday afternoons. Live football on television in the UK, apart from the FA Cup Final and World Cup and other international matches, dates only from 1984 (Barnett, 1990: p. 61).

The balance of the relationship between football and television moved decisively in favour of the latter with the intervention of satellite broadcasters (Higham, 1989). In 1985, the newly established satellite-to-cable company, Screen Sport, owned by W. H. Smith, intervened in deadlocked talks between the terrestrial broadcasters and the football authorities with a bid of their own. It wasn't accepted but, significantly, they did set up a competition involving leading clubs. Then, in 1988, British Satellite Broadcasting, who were due to begin broadcasting the following year, proposed to the League a joint venture company to exploit football TV rights. BSB would pay the production costs of covering sixty matches and guarantee a minimum of £9 million revenue for the first year. Over ten years, however, BSB estimated that at least £200 million would accrue to the League and the FA from worldwide cable, satellite and video deals, plus 'live' and delayed broadcasts. The football authorities were attracted to the offer, believing it supported their belief that the broadcasters had hitherto had football 'on the cheap'. However, the other broadcasters countered the bid by stating that they would have no dealings with any company involving BSB if the bid was accepted. (Two ITV companies were BSB shareholders.) There now followed a joint bid by BSB and the BBC structured in a similar way to the limited BSB plan and guaranteeing £39 million over four years. ITV responded to this with a shot across the bows of the authorities: they offered £36 million over four years, but only to the top dozen clubs, *not* to the League (*Screen Digest*, August 1988). In the event ITV paid £44 million for four years' exclusive coverage of League football, while BSB and the BBC agreed £30 million with the FA for five years' rights to show the FA Cup Final and England internationals. We return to the implications of all this presently.

The inauguration of satellite TV in Britain, in 1989, is indicative of two important and interrelated trends: globalisation and, in the context of globalisation, the growth of the multinational media conglomerates (Golding and Murdock, 1986). Globalisation refers to the international diversification of production and consumption, assisted by the enactment of 'neo-liberal' policies by various first world governments — notably those of the United States, Japan, Britain and Germany. Central to this process have been the transnational corporations, whose shifting operations cover numerous countries at any given moment, and whose annual turnover will often exceed the gross national product of a whole nation in the Third World (Lash and Urry, 1987). Of course, many of these corporations are either wholly or substantially involved in the field of mass media and much academic and political discussion has focused on the implications of this. Some fear, and others welcome, the obliteration of national cultures and the rise of a more amorphous, unlocalised, 'postmodern' culture, led by an increasingly internationalised mass-media system (Sklair, 1991: ch. 5).

In the case of television, policies of 'deregulation' (in practice, commercialisation, with fewer 'public service' obligations) have been introduced in several countries, including the United States and most European countries, and there is a trend towards Pan-European TV (Negrine and Papathanassopoulos, 1990: p. 10). The British contributions to this trend were the Peacock Report (HMSO, 1986) and the subsequent Broadcasting Act. Peacock, a noted free-marked economist, stopped short of recommending the commercialisation of the BBC, but he did call for more commercial TV channels, the licensing of competitive satellite TV and, in general, for 'consumer sovereignty'. The Broadcasting Bill was based largely on his prescriptions, although within days of the bill becoming law the two competing satellite companies, BSB and Sky announced a merger.

Many doubt that these changes will make the consumer 'sovereign' at all. Indeed, critics have for twenty years been arguing that the growing concentration in the ownership and control of the mass media bestows on a few corporations and powerful individuals an unprecedented control over the flow of political and cultural information and imagery (Murdock and Golding, 1973). Within this broad concern, there is growing anxiety for sports such as football, which are increasingly dependent upon, and enriched by, revenue from the TV companies. Fears are growing of a slow 'Packerisation' of the sport — a reference to the Australian media entrepreneur Kerry Packer. When Packer failed in 1977 to secure broadcasting rights of the forthcoming Australia v. England Test cricket series for his Channel 9 TV station, he simply signed up most of the world's leading cricketers and held his own tournament (Blofeld, 1979). This demonstrates plainly the power of the new élites of impression management (Gouldner, 1972: p. 382) to dictate to sports administrators. For his own cricket competition, televised by his own channel, Packer amended the rules and conventions of the game much as he pleased. Packer's Channel 9 now shows Test Cricket in Australia. The one-day, limited overs tournaments, geared to television, which he introduced, are now well established in Australia and are shortly to be adopted in England. The financial power that he wielded is now being exercised more widely, as satellite and other media transnationals wave bigger and bigger cheques at sporting bodies. For example, in February 1989, Sky TV, then with only 20,000 subscribers but enormous financial resources, were able to show the Mike Tyson–Frank Bruno fight live on the Eurosport channel. Similarly, the Benson and Hedges Cricket Cup Final of July 1990 became the first major sporting event previously broadcast by the BBC, to be made available only to BSB subscribers. Moreover, the Broadcasting Act of 1990 'delists' major sporting events such as the FA Cup Final and the Derby, which were previously restricted to BBC and ITV on the grounds that they were of national importance. These developments in the media have, as we will now show, helped to accelerate the trends towards the cartelisation of British football (also discussed in this book by Tony Arnold).

Now we are five: the English football cartel and the Super League debate

The financial arrangements made by the Football League for its constituent clubs have, by tradition, been collectivist. For example, a 4 per cent levy was imposed on all gate receipts and the proceeds shared among League clubs. All clubs received equal financial benefits from TV deals. Also the structure of decision-making in the League was at least semi-democratic: clubs in Divisions One and Two had one vote each and the other clubs, as associate members, shared a further eight votes between them. This ensured that no one power group could dominate, although the bigger clubs were increasingly vocal in their objection to it. This objection, finally, in the season 1985–6, was expressed in a threat by the leading clubs to form their own 'super league'. Maurice Watkins, a director of Manchester United, said:

We are all committed here [at Manchester United] to retaining the Football League, but the feeling is that there has got to be a restructuring and there has got to be a change in the financial side . . . If these very modest proposals don't go through then there is a danger that some clubs will seek to form a breakaway. (*Off the Ball*, February/March 1986)

By this time, it was apparent that certain struggling clubs were not simply experiencing the temporary slumps in fortune that afflict any football clubs from time to time. Rather, given the deep-lying social, cultural and economic changes that had taken place — particularly the decline of extractive and 'smokestack' industries and the consequent effect on many northern towns — most of the ninety-two League clubs could no longer compete on equal terms. The élite clubs, centred on the large conurbations but transcending purely local affiliations (people all over the world support Manchester United, for example), were clearly in a class of their own. Moreover, against a background of generally declining attendances, the proportion watching games in Divisions Three and Four was falling quickest. This process was manifestly hastened by the decision of the League in 1983 to allow the retention of home gate receipts. This was clearly to the benefit of the major clubs, who had the largest home attendances. Between the late 1950s and the mid-1980s, gates in Division One fell by one-third, while income rose by 95 per cent in real terms; but in the same period, for clubs in the Fourth Division gates went down by two-thirds and income by one-third (Arnold and Benveniste, 1987).

Fissures between the bigger clubs and the rest were apparent throughout the 1980s and were exacerbated by the 'TV blackout' of the 1985–6 season. When the League demurred at the terms offered them for television coverage, the networks simply withdrew and no League football was seen on British TV that year. For the big clubs this experience confirmed what they already knew: that they needed TV (for sponsorship, perimeter and shirt advertising, and so on) more than TV needed them. Television, in a time of declining live attendances, was also thought to be an important source of promotion for football and, in any event, without television 'exposure', more leading British players would be inclined to move abroad. This situation was made worse by the banning of English clubs from European competition. The major clubs likely to qualify for European tournaments lost revenue — much of it media-related — and a number of leading players (including Liverpool's Rush, Everton's Lineker, Hughes of Manchester United and the Tottenham players Hoddle and Waddle) all moved to continental clubs.

Meanwhile, the smaller League clubs were failing to come to terms with their dependence on subsidy. For instance, Scarborough, after one season in the League and despite having both raised their prices by 50 per cent and doubled their attendances, were threatened by bankruptcy. Their chairman supported the idea of part-time players but, paradoxically, opted to expand his complement of full time professionals: 'It's the other clubs having the courage to do it as well. We can't be the odd ones out' (*Off the Ball*, Summer 1988).

But it was now clear that the top League clubs, led by the 'Big Five' of Arsenal, Tottenham Hotspur, Liverpool, Manchester United and Everton, were no longer prepared to bail out the Scarborough's and the rest. Threats of a breakaway super league were sufficient to bring significant changes to the distribution of power and wealth among League clubs: clubs in Division Two and associate members now no longer counted as equal partners in any TV deal, and the gate levy was cut by 25 per cent. A new voting structure gave First Division clubs 1.5 votes each from a twenty-club division (i.e. thirty votes), as against a combined total of thirty-two for the rest of the League. It was also resolved, however, that the Divison One would return to a twenty-two club format in the season 1991–2, giving it thirty-three votes in all, compared to thirty-two for the remainder of the League — the first time any one division will have had voting superiority.

There has thus been a change in the nature of the Football League: it is less a community of interests and more a vehicle for individual advancement by clubs. As Manchester City chairman Peter Swales reflected on the previous state of affairs 'It [was] like running a business and having to give part of your income to some other business. But who does that?' (*Off the Ball*, June/July 1987).

This economic liberalisation of the League was reflected in the subsequent negotiations with the broadcasters in 1988, talks which were once again characterised by threats of a super league. In this context, Everton's Philip Carter was voted out of the League presidency after holding clandestine discussions with ITV on behalf of the big clubs alone. But his work of securing a better deal for the League's larger clubs had, by then, already been done, aided by the arrival of the satellite networks which had jemmied the market open. In the ensuing contractual free-for-all, the league was able to close an unprecedentedly lucrative deal. The £44 million that they would be paid by ITV over four years (i.e. £11 million per year) compared to just £5 million the previous year. Put together with the BBC/BSB fee for the FA Cup Final, football was receiving £21 million for the season 1988–9 (*The Independent*, 19 February 1990). But, importantly, most of the benefits were now directed toward the élite clubs. Although the actual amount of TV money devolved to smaller clubs slightly increased, 75 per cent of the total TV revenue was channelled to the First Division, with the Big Five, as the most regularly featured clubs, emerging as the principal beneficiaries. Of the £11 million invested in the League game by ITV in 1988–9, around £3.5 million — just under a third — is believed to have gone to the Big Five, who were all shown regularly on 'The Match'. It's worth noting that the agreement struck with BBC and ITV governing edited highlights had at one time stipulated that a certain percentage of games shown each season should be from the lower divisions.

All this has, of course, created a *de facto* financial super league. The concentration of TV coverage on a small élite of clubs is justified on the basis of viewing figures, not League placing or geographical spread. For example, during 1988–9, the relative success of Coventry City and Derby County (sixth and seventh respectively in the First Division) was ignored by television, while Everton and Manchester United, who both finished in mid-table, were shown regularly. Executive Producer of 'The Match', Trevor East, commented:

No doubt the only way we're going to Coventry is if they're at home to one of the glamour clubs. No matter how well they're doing, they aren't going to fill the ground at home to Charlton or Crystal Palace. This is a major investment for us and we want to cover the big matches. We don't want to cover a game at a ground that's half empty. Our two lowest ratings last year were both matches involving Norwich City. And much as we all love Norwich . . . that just proves the point, I'm afraid. At the end of the day, we're a commercial station. It's not public service broadcasting. (*The Football Supporter*, November/December 1989, p. 8)

This is the familiar 'consumer sovereignty' argument. But who exactly was

'The Match' serving in the years after 1988? In addition to screening those matches likely to deliver the largest audiences, ITV seemed to be fulfilling certain obligations to the larger clubs: 'The Big Five can rest content in the thought that ITV have guaranteed each of them two home and two away games (or £390,000 in facility fees) when the live transmissions begin' (*Daily Telegraph*, 21 August 1988). An informal trading bloc thus appears to have been formed between ITV and the Big Five, which has had the practical effect of widening still further the gulf between the wealthy few League members and the rest.

Early in 1991 the Football Association, apparently recognising this situation as a *fait accompli*, issued proposals for a Premier League and waved away protests that such a League would mop up most of the game's extra curricular revenue. Nor was very much made of the argument that the FA was acting against the interests of its member clubs, since League clubs, like all English football clubs, come under FA jurisdiction. Indeed, a little bizarrely, the League's principal response to the FA proposal was to claim that they (the League) had had the idea first. One possible advantage of the proposed Premier League was, according to the FA, that it would improve the calibre of the England players. However, current England players John Barnes (at Watford), Lee Dixon (at Stoke), David Seaman (at Rotherham), David Platt and Geoff Thomas (at Crewe) all learned their trade in the lower divisions of the League.

Télévision sans frontières: parallel developments in Europe

English football has been one of the prime beneficiaries of the recent Broadcasting Act because networks have been forced to compete with the new broadcasters (principally satellite TV) to show attractive sports fixtures. This followed similar developments throughout the 1980s on the continent of Europe. In France, Spain, West Germany, Italy and a number of Scandinavian countries state-run or established commercial TV networks now faced the challenge of statellite and cable. The major football clubs moved swiftly to exploit this. In Spain Jesús Gil of Atlético Madrid threatened to bar cameras altogether if terms for his clubs did not improve; they did. In France, Claude Bez of Bordeaux disputed the convention of reciprocity, whereby local and national TV companies bought 'picture' rights for European games and effectively gave them to foreign networks, in return for free footage (paid for by the host network) in the return leg. Bez successfully argued that clubs were themselves entitled to sell 'pictures' to each network that broadcast the game, thus dramatically enhancing the revenues of clubs from European games. To illustrate the financial trend in Europe, the first TV football deal in France in 1977 brought the game the equivalent of £45,000; when all games of the 1987–8 season (including women's and youth games) were taken into account, income amounted to £20 million.

The European dimension is crucial because it is here that the big money is made and where clubs are, in many cases, freed from domestic league contracts and therefore able to negotiate their own deals. The arrival of cable and satellite TV meant a major injection of cash for European football but most of it, as in England, was diverted to the wealthiest and most successful clubs. Occasionally this brings an apparent conflict of interest between domestic commitment and European opportunity. An example was when, in the 1990-1 season, Aston Villa agreed to have their match against Inter Milan televised 'live' on a night of prearranged Football League fixtures. There were some moves to fine Villa, but they had not broken any League regulation or contract, and their game went ahead on ITV in competition with a number of simultaneous live League matches.

Also, manifestly, the developing relationship between television and the major clubs has begun to have ramifications for the organisation of football itself. The intertwining of interests is seen, for instance, in the decision to alter the format of the European Cup in 1992. From the quarter-final stage onwards, matches will be played on a group rather than a knockout basis, with the winners of each 'mini-league' meeting in the final. The motives for dispensing with the traditional two-legged tie system are primarily financial: having reached the last eight of the competition, each club will now be guaranteed three home fixtures instead of one, ensuring additional revenues from paying supporters and increasing the range of games that are likely to be attractive to a continent-wide television audience. If this 'round robin' format proves successful, it seems almost certain to be extended to the UEFA and Cup-Winners Cups, significantly reinforcing the playing and financial disparities between the clubs which regularly 'get into Europe' and those who are confined to domestic competition.

Indeed, this may be only the prelude to a more radical restructuring programme. For example, Silvio Berlusconi, media entrepreneur and president of AC Milan FC, is one of the main advocates of the new European Cup format (although, interestingly, it was originally proposed by Glasgow Rangers) and he has floated a number of similar innovations in recent years. He is believed to have been behind proposals for a self-selecting European competition, to be sanctioned by UEFA but featuring only those teams (including, in the British case, Liverpool, Glasgow Rangers and Arsenal) who would be attractive to international TV audiences (*Independent*, 19 December 1990). He has also been linked with a planned tournament exclusively for the past winners of the European Cup, and has lately argued that all of UEFA's three major cup competitions should be played on a seeded mini-league basis from the first round onwards. The underlying theme here, of course, is the removal of the uncertainty of commercial outcome. Berlusconi himself has said: 'In the champions cup you run the risk of many hazards: rain, refereeing, bad luck and the risk of first round elimination. It's not modern thinking' (Fynn, 1989: p. 165).

Though many of his suggestions have not come to fruition, the general principle of reducing previously accepted uncertainties does seem to have been adopted. Indeed, for the season 1991-2 seeding has been extended in the European Cup from the First to the Second Round, following the pairing of Glasgow Rangers and Bayern Munich in 1990. This has been paralleled by developments in England such as the introduction of seeding and two-legged ties in the Rumbelow's (League) Cup at the stage when the bigger clubs enter. This idea was presented publicly as a means of helping the finances of lower division clubs, but its practical effect is to ensure the progress of the major teams to the later stages and to exclude the 'minnows'.

Back on the continent, there has also been an informal cartelisation of entry: for the later stages of European competition, the requirement of an all-seated ground capacity of 40,000 in practice excludes — and at the very least handicaps — the great majority of potential competitors, and therefore benefits already established clubs. The most effective way of removing uncertainty of financial outcome for the likes of AC Milan would be to ensure that the clubs with the most drawing power — in terms of TV audiences and live crowd potential — played each other on a regular home and away basis in a formally constituted European League. But Berlusconi proposed this to UEFA in 1987, and they rejected the idea. Berlusconi's comments and suggestions are not simply those of an ordinary member of Italy's football hierarchy. Besides being president of AC Milan, Berlusconi is a major figure in European television. He has broadcasting interests in France, Spain and West Germany and is believed to control 40 per cent of the Italian market. More recently there have been rumours that Berlusconi is seeking to extend his already vast Fininvest media empire to Britain (*Sunday Correspondent*, 21 January 1990). This empire encompasses not only broadcast media but the newspaper *Il Giornale*, as well as Italy's largest supermarket chain. Perhaps inevitably he also harbours political aspirations which are said, less inevitably, to be socialist. Control of televised football would, as he sees it, give him the chance to integrate his wide range of business interests. For instance, one of his spokespeople, Giovanni Belingardi, has said: 'Clearly, with our resources in terms of television advertising, we will be in a position to give a tremendous boost to supermarket sales' (Fynn, 1989: p. 82). Indeed, it has become imperative, for business reasons to ensure all this. As another spokesperson, Giovanni Branchini, Berlusconi's director of TV Sports Promotions, put it:

The cost of bringing the best players to clubs like Milan is astronomical. It is difficult to justify such spending if it does not bring a successful season in Europe. This makes instant success necessary but such a thing cannot be guaranteed. We need to play to capacity crowds in every game and each match must be an event worthy of television. If Europe were arranged on a league basis, all the competing clubs could be guaranteed a basic number of home fixtures against top European opposition. (Fynn, 1983: p. 83)

Currently, Italian state broadcasting has the contract to show Italian League football, but competition from Berlusconi's Canale 5 brought significantly improved income to the League and, for Berlusconi, had the effect of reducing the financial competitiveness of a major rival in other areas. Berlusconi is now in a position to bid for the best European ties with the state channel.

Berlusconi is, of course, not the only international business person to have joint football, TV and other media interests. Robert Maxwell, for example, who is chairman of Derby County and has hovered in some capacity around other clubs such as Oxford, Reading, Tottenham Hotspur and Manchester United, owns the *Mirror*, the *Sunday People* and the *European*, as well as having shares in the French TV station Canal Plus and being financially involved in the unsuccessful launch of the satellite TV company BSB. Gianni Agnelli, president of Juventus and Fiat, the car company, also has an interest in TV Monte Carlo.

There has, furthermore, been a growth of 'made for TV' exhibition games as Berlusconi, in particular, explored ways to feature football outside of the traditional networks: for instance, AC Milan played Manchester United and Real Madrid at the tail-end of the 1987–8 season. Likewise, Zenith Data Systems provided backing for a match between Arsenal and Independiente at Joe Robbie Stadium in Miami in the autumn of 1989 and Makita International staged a pre-season tournament in Tokyo, in which Liverpool played the South American champions.

The staging of these games is informed by the recognition of football as a truly world game and hence a means by which powerful individuals can project their status and advertise their products to huge audiences worldwide. It is important, also, to note the growing convergence of football clubs and big business in this context. Some tie-ups, such as that between Juventus of Turin and Fiat, are long established but other links have been struck more recently. As well as the bankrolling by Berlusconi's Fininvest of AC Milan (believed to amount to more than £20 million in the first eighteen months, including initial investment), there is also Philips funding of PSV Eindhoven in the Netherlands and the sponsoring of the Football Association by British Aerospace (through which England international footballers can now actually be used to promote the sale of weapons). There is, incidentally, a further TV tie-in here because British Aerospace, whose chairman Roland Smith is a director of Manchester United, also owns the Sportscast TV channel, which did a deal for the GM Vauxhall Conference run-in at the end of the 1990–1 season and broadcast some of its closing games to a national network of pubs. (The Football League's Associate Members, in the lower divisions, are precluded from making such a deal by their involvement in the League's own TV contract.)

As well as big business, there is substantial local authority backing for clubs in Europe. For instance, a number of stadiums are owned by councils and there are grants for clubs, especially in France where football clubs are seen as regional representatives. Ironically, however, TV has a tighter grip on football in France than in many countries: the commercial station Canal Plus holds exclusive rights to screen French League football and they operate a subscription system. Their TV signal is scrambled as the match kicks off and cannot therefore be seen unless the viewer has a decoder and has paid a subscription fee (Boyle and Blain, 1991).

Tomorrow the world: football and globalisation

As we suggested at the beginning of this paper, developments in Europe must be seen in the context of the globalisation of the world economy, of mass communications and, indeed, of football itself. This latter development is reflected in the decision to award the venue of the World Cup Finals of 1994 to the United States. On the face of it, other countries had superior claims to the United States. For example, Morocco had successfully hosted the African

Nations Cup of 1988 and were an established football nation. The United States, by contrast, has no purpose-built football stadiums or national, outdoor eleven-a-side league. The decision to give the finals to them, therefore, underscores the pre-eminence now of TV and sponsors over and above the need for a guaranteed live audience. Commentary on this decision has drawn attention to the roles of the Brazilian Joao Havelange, President of FIFA since 1974, and his vice-president Guillermo Canedo. Both have been linked to television interests in South and North America (by, among others, ITVs 'World in Action' programme, broadcast July 1986).

Havelange has, naturally enough and with considerable justification, been accused of having conflicts of interest. But his activities, whatever their impropriety, are part of a wider pattern of commercial encroachments. For example, in Britain half-time breaks have been lengthened to accommodate more adverts during 'The Match' and cup draws and games have been arranged according to the convenience of TV companies rather than tradition. The power of television has, on occasion, transcended the traditional prestige of international matches: the made-for-TV 'friendly' between Berlusconi's AC Milan and Manchester United, for instance, deprived Scotland of the United players Gordon Strachan and Brian McClair for the Rous Cup game gainst Colombia, despite its importance in preparing the team for the World Cup qualifying matches. Similarly, 'The Match' rescheduled for TV on 5 February 1988 featured Tottenham Hotspur and Manchester United, both sides containing England players, just three days before the England World Cup qualifying game against Greece and on the actual day that England Manager Robson had planned to take his squad to Athens (*Daily Mirror*, 7 December 1988).

But these disturbances are minor compared to proposals emanating from the FIFA hierarchy in recent months. Early in 1990, Havelange was reported as suggesting that matches should be divided into four twenty-five minute spells so that TV networks could carry more adverts. This was before the World Cup Finals of 1990, although subsequent ruminations by FIFA about amending the rules have purportedly stemmed from that tournament's lack of goals (there was an average of 2.2 goals per game, the lowest ever). In December of 1990, FIFA's executive in Zurich decided it might be necessary to widen goals by a metre, reduce teams from eleven to ten players and ban defensive walls at free kicks. The Professional Footballers' Association's secretary, Gordon Taylor, commented: 'I don't buy this idea about the goals in Italy. There's no doubt it's American inspired. And if American (as distinct from Association) Football is any guide, then, more drastic commercial interventions can be anticipated'. The American National Football League is hugely profitable and is run entirely according to the dictates of TV: in one recent superbowl final lasting 3 hours and 38 minutes, the ball was in play for an estimated 7 per cent of the match (Barnett, 1990). Another important development here has been the growing role of international corporations in FIFA: Adidas, Coca Cola, Kodak and Mars were all involved in sponsoring Havelange's world expansion schemes for football and their main motivation for doing so was the prospect of privileged access to the massive World Cup TV audience, estimated at 31 billion spread over 137 countries. The evangelising of the game in the Third World, pioneered by people such as Rous for, as they saw it, the good of the game itself, now carries enormous commercial possibilities.

The future: pack some pyjamas?

This acquiescence by football administrators in such rampant commercialism opens the way to a complete 'Packerisation' of football, in that it could become a completely packaged, made-for-TV sport run by media barons (Goldberg, 1988: p. 3). Again, other sports are a possible guide. There is, first of all, cricket where the constant round of one-day games (not invented by Packer, but central to his tournaments) are said to have sapped traditional skills and where Packer's innovation of coloured clothing — 'pyjamarisation' to the purists — will be adopted in the English Refuge Assurance league in the 1991–2 season.

Then there is snooker. In January 1991, the Sky World Snooker tournament, held at Birmingham NEC was organised by the entrepreneur Barry Hearn, who has interests in satellite TV and who manages most of the top British snooker players. He is also an executive member of the sports governing body (the WPBSA) but his tournament, beamed throughout Europe on the Eurosport channel and offering bigger prize money, was effectively a competitor to the official snooker World Championship. Moreover, Hearn invited the wayward but popular Alex Higgins to take part in the Masters, despite the fact that Higgins was under suspension by the WPBSA (Higgins subsequently withdrew when other players objected). In golf, too, and tennis, organisations such as Mark McCormack's IMG, to which many of the leading players in both sports are signed, have arranged their own packaged tournaments featuring their own players. The multi-sport 'Superstars' programmes broadcast by the BBC are another example of this.

It seems plain that once the balance of power shifts away from traditional governing bodies towards TV companies and international business and marketing interests, football can be packaged in as many ways as TV viewers will take. Then, when its usefulness is past, it can be dumped as abruptly as darts and wrestling have been by Britain's independent TV network. This, of course, is a 'nightmare scenario' and many years may elapse before it is realised, if indeed it is realised at all. Nevertheless, the seeds have been sown by football's unthinking desertion of traditional principles in the cause of short-term enrichment. Clearly, though, vested interests such as UEFA and FIFA will want to preserve some of their traditional structure, if only to maintain its long-term value. In this respect, it is interesting to note the development of new trade barriers in European football.

A limit of four non-national players per sixteen-man squad is currently imposed by UEFA on all European clubs. From the season 1992–3 all clubs in Europe will be permitted to include up to five players from EC countries other than their own, but if a club has three foreign players from within the EC, the additional one or two must have been playing full-time in their own countries for at least five years, of which three must have been in youth teams. Players' organisations support such restrictions. The English PFA stated in 1990:

We are concerned about the implications of free movement. There is a strong feeling that football should be treated as a special case because of the nature of the job. The clubs are concerned because they envisage an exodus of the best players and an influx of inferior talent from the continent. We are making representations to the EC, but they insist everyone should be treated simply as workers. (*Daily Telegraph*, 21 May 1990)

Italian players delayed the kick-off of Italian League matches by 30 minutes one Saturday in 1988, and threatened a strike, in protest against proposals to allow Italian First Division clubs to sign three foreign players per season.

All this conflicts with political moves towards the free movement of labour within the EC. There is here a genuine desire to protect the competitive nature of existing European leagues, many of which could be decimated by a free football labour market, as the continent's major clubs seek to monopolise major playing talent. Another motive for attempting to restrict the free movement of labour may be to preserve the superiority of competition between national sides (and it is national FA representatives who sit on FIFA), but it would also be bad for the media, who thrive on the 'product differentiation' of club and national football.

This boils down, then, to the rights of capital to transfer across national boundaries while the movement of labour is restricted. The issue is complicated further by the threatened deluge of players from Eastern Europe, following liberalisation (see Vic Duke's essay in this book). UEFA claim not to be affected by EC regulations, since they are based in Switzerland, but tussles between the two bodies on these matters seem likely.

Just looking?

One group seldom addressed but always affected by these ongoing machinations is the supporters — whether it be those paying to sit in the stands or to stand on the terraces, those who subscribe to satellite channels, or those that simply like to watch football when it crops up on TV. In a football world increasingly organised according to the dictates of marketing people and advertisers, all these followers of the game are defined primarily as consumers. But they need not, and are not, always passive consumers.

Currently, there is no real supporter network in Europe to match those networks of football business and administration, but in many European countries, club presidents are at least accountable to supporters via club membership schemes. There is also the power of protest, as with the threatened boycott of the Italian club Fiorentina by their supporters after the popular player Roberto Baggio was sold to Juventus. In Spain, at Atlético Madrid, the president Jesús Guil has conducted at least one poll among supporters.

In Britain, we have seen the rise of the Football Supporters' Association. Its success suggests a potential role for an independent, Pan-European supporters' organisation that could mount consumer boycotts against major corporations like Coca Cola or Kodak if they were felt to be working against the game's best interests. Such a body could also try to organise a European supporters' charter, for adoption by UEFA, insisting that members accept certain conditions which could include supporter representation on the boards of clubs.

We must not forget the huge financial input to the game that football fans make, even in the television age — in England, for example, in 1987 £56 million was taken at the gate alone. Moreover, it is the supporters who make televised football worth watching; as ITVs Trevor East indicated to *The Football Supporter* magazine, games are simply not worth showing, if there's no 'atmosphere', i.e. not a large crowd.

So, supporters could yet exert some influence over the game and the major companies that now increasingly dominate it. Some small encouragement in this comes from the United States, where in 1990 the United Sports Fans of America claimed to have prevented the scrambling of televised National Football League games by mounting a boycott of Anheuser-Busch, one of US television's biggest advertisers on sports programmes.

We see, then, that the balance of power within the football world has changed, perhaps irrevocably. The economic and cultural power which the transnational media corporations can now bring to bear upon football administrations is formidable and it is they, and not the administrators, who increasingly seek to determine when, where and under what circumstances football will take place. However, football also has a massive, devoted and articulate following which will be difficult either to eliminate or to ignore. Football activism is growing — a European football supporters' association is currently being planned — and through the market and through the media (often their own) their views and their resistance will be expressed.

Acknowledgements

We'd like to acknowledge the help of Ralph Negrine, Liz Crolley, John Williams and Sally Cooper in the preparation of this chapter.

Bibliography

Arnold, T. and I. Benveniste (1987), 'Wealth and Poverty in the English Football League', *Accounting and Business Research*, **17** (67), pp. 195–203.

Barnett, S. (1990) *Games and Sets: The Changing Face of Sport on Television*, London: British Film Institute.

Blofeld, H. (1979) *The Packer Affair*, Newton Abbot: Readers Union.

Boyle, R. and N. Blain (1991), *Footprints on the Field: Televised Sport, Delivery Systems and National Culture in a Changing Europe*, paper presented to the Fourth International Television Studies Conference, July 1991.

Fynn, A. (1989), *The Secret Life of Football*, London: Queen Anne Press.

Goldberg, A. (1988), '1992: Games without Frontiers' *Off the Ball*, no. 15, Autumn p. 3.

Golding, P. and G. Murdock (1986), 'The New Communications Revolution', in James Curran *et al.* (eds), *Bending Reality*. London: Pluto Press.

Gouldner, A. W. (1972) *The Coming Crisis of Western Sociology*, London: Heinemann.

Higham, N. 'Game, Set and Cash' *The Listener*, 2 March 1989.

HMSO (1986), *Report of the Committee of Financing the B.B.C.* (Chair Professor A. Peacock), Cmnd 9824.

Lash, S. and J. Urry (1987), *Disorganised Capitalism*, Oxford: Polity Press.

Murdock, G. and P. Golding (1973), 'For a Political Economy of Mass Communications', in Ralph Miliband and John Saville (eds), *The Socialist Register 1973*, London: The Merlin Press.

Negrine, R. and S. Papathanassopoulos (1990), *The Internationalisation of Television*, London: Frances Pinter.

Sklair, L. (1991), *Sociology of the Global System*, Hemel Hempstead: Harvester Wheatsheaf.

Tomlinson, A. (1986), 'Going Global: The FIFA Story', in Alan Tomlinson and Garry Whannel (eds), *Off the Ball*, London: Pluto Press.

Index

Aberdeen FC 214
Aberfan 10
Absolute Game, The 152
AC Milan FC 190, 197, 204, 247
Acid House 155
Adidas 191
African Nations Cup 248–9
Agnelli. Gianni 18, 247–8
Alcock, Charles 26
Aldershot FC 25, 44–5, 117
Aldridge, J 9, 15, 79
Allen, Richard 146
Alison, Malcolm 225
Anderson, Viv 78
Anheuser-Busch 252
Anti Nazi League 147
Arsenal FC 40, 59, 67, 70, 176, 197
Aston Villa FC 34, 55, 69, 139, 171, 187, 246
Atletico Madrid FC 192, 245
Avant 155

Baggio, Roberto 251
Banik Ostrava FC 195
Banks, Gordon 77
Barcelona FC 201
Barclays Bank 199
Barnes, John 69, 77, 79, 171, 236
Barnsley FC 36
Basset, Annie 105
Bateman, Tracey 37
Bayern Munich FC 246
Beardsley, Peter 69, 79
Beat, The 147
Beauchampe, Steve 133
Benson, Gabriella (*The Manageress*) 87
Benson, Glenwyn 19
Bergman-Osterberg, Mme 89
Berlusconi, Silvio 18, 190, 204, 246–7
Best, George 76, 77
Bez, Claude 245

Birmingham City FC 43, 105
Blackburn Olympic FC 27
Blackburn Rovers FC 27, 30
Blanchflower, Danny 77
Blueprint for Football (FA) 14, 41
Bobroff, Paul 44
Boca Juniors FC 191
Bohemians Prague FC 196
Bolan, Marc 146
Bolton disaster (1947) 13, 163–4
Bolton Wanderers FC 94, 171
Book, Tony 7
Borstin, Daniel 78
Born Kicking 104, 180
Botham, Ian 76
Bowie, David 146–8
Boys Own 153–6
Bradford City fire 10, 11, 13, 40
Brake Clubs 113
Brentford FC 94, 104
Brighton High School 88
Bristol Rovers FC 134, 141
British Aerospace 248
British League 198
British Workers' Sports Federation 116
Broadcasting Act 245
Bruno, Frank 79
BSB (satellite TV) 199, 240–1
Buford, Bill 176
Bull, Steve 71
Burnley FC 30, 31, 32, 55
Burton, Frank 13
Burton, Pam 105

Calderdale Council 46
Callaghan, Ian 69
Canal Plus (TV channel) 248
Canedo, Guillermo 249
Carlen, Pat 13
Carling, Will 76

Case, Jimmy 69
Casuals FC 151-2
Centre for Football Research (Leicester
    University) 136, 176, 177-80
Channon, Mike 232
Charlton Athletic FC 133-4, 138, 197
Charlton, Bobby 77
Charlton, Jack 72, 77
Charnley, Tom 34-5
Chelsea FC 134, 171, 239
Chester City FC 131, 197
Chester Report 122, 244
Christie, Linford 80
City Gent 153
Clarke, Alan 178-80
Clegg, Charles 28-9, 33, 34, 43
Clyde FC 197, 202
Clydebank FC 214
Cohen, Phil 19
Corby Town FC 125
de Coubertin, Daron 8
Coventry City FC 118, 124
Coward, Ros 107
Cranford Institute of Technology 11
Croker, Ted 29, 97-8, 103
Crooks, Garth 78
Crystal Palace FC 138, 197
CSKA Sofia FC 195

Dalglish, Kenny 15, 67, 77
Dartford College of PE 89
Darwinism 88
Davies, Barry 237
Denning, Lord 98
Dent, David 40
Derby County FC 18, 43, 194, 244
Devonshire, Alan 226
Dick Kerr's Ladies 91-4
Dixey, Lady Florence 90
Dinamo Bucharest FC 196
Dnepr Dnepropetrovsk 193-4
Docherty, Tommy 75
Doncaster Belles 97
Donington School 27
Dukla Prague FC 195
Dumbarton FC 202
Dynamo Berlin FC 196

East, Trevor 244, 252
Eastham, George 38
Eastham v Newcastle United FC 53, 74
East Stirlingshire FC 202, 209-10
economics of football 48-60
Ecstacy (drug) 149, 153
End, The 150-4, 170
Elias, Norbert 177
English Ladies' FA 93
English Schools FA 99

Equal Opportunities Commission 99
European Commission 188
European Community 20, 188-90, 195, 197,
    251
European Cup Final (1977) 174, (1981) 174
European League 189, 192, 197-8, 204, 239
European Parliament 171
Everton FC 40, 59, 79, 171

fanzines 13-14
Face, The 149
Farm, The 149-50, 155, 175
Faulkner, Richard 102
FA Czechoslovakia 193
FA Netherlands 190
Ferencvaros FC 195, 198
Feyenoord FC 169
FIFA 28, 191, 198, 216, 239, 249, 251
Fininvest 248
Finney, Tom 77
Florentina FC 194
Fisac (Italian textile company) 195
Flag, The 171
Football Association 17, 26-31, 40-6, 52, 56,
    69, 72, 90, 92-3
Football in the Community Initiative 100,
    181-2
Football League 17, 25, 29-30, 31-46, 48-60,
    69, 72
Football Special 92
Football Spectators Act 157
Football Supporter, The 252
Football Supporters' Gazette 120
Football Supporters' Association 13, 14, 16,
    104, 153, 179, 181, 251
Football Trust 17, 102, 182
Follows, Denis 29
Ford, Glyn 145
Ford, Trevor 95
Forfar Athletic FC 202
Fox, Bill 40
Fulham FC 37, 134
Fynn, Alex 207

Gascoigne, Paul 67, 77, 78, 85, 160, 236
Genoa FC 197
Georges, Jacques 8, 9
Gerry and the Pacemakers 166
Gil, Jesus 245, 251
Glasgow 163, 204-5
Glasgow Celtic FC 202, 204
Glasgow Rangers FC 171, 197, 202, 204, 207-
    11, 246
Glitter, Gary 146
'Gooners' 176
Gorbachev, Mikhail 192
Greenwood, Ron 227
Grimsby Town FC 155
Gullit, Ruud 170

Hacienda club 155
Halifax Town FC 25, 44-6, 118, 182
Hamburg FC 76
Hampden Park 214
Hancock, Colin 45
Hansen, Alan 69
Happy Mondays 154
Hardaker, Alan 31, 35, 36, 38, 40, 44
Harford, Mick 71
Hateley, Mark 71
Havelange, Joao 249
Heart of Midlothian FC 134, 211-13
Helliwell, David 46
Herald of Free Enterprise 4, 10, 12
Heysel stadium disaster 9, 10, 19, 40, 68, 69,
    146, 153, 170, 180, 187, 240
Hibernian FC 134
Hill, Jimmy 37, 124, 227
Hillsborough 3, 4, 5-12, 15-17, 40, 101, 104,
    132, 140, 154, 180
Hoddle, Glenn 72, 86, 228, 230
Honeyball, Nettie 90
Hooligan (Thames TV documentary) 168,
    169
Hooton, Peter 149-50, 155
Hopcraft, Arthur 16
Houghton, Ray 69
Howarth, Fred 34-6
Huddersfield Atalanta 85
Hughes, Emlyn 69, 103, 227, 235
Hull City FC 197
Hummel UK 44

Ibrox Park 8, 13, 198, 214, 217-18 (disaster
    164)
Independent, The 41-2, 43
Inglis, Simon 6, 31, 33, 132
'Inter City Firm' 157, 166, 168, 175, 177
Inter Milan FC 197
Ipswich Town FC 69, 124-5
Italia '90 85, 145, 156, 167, 194

John, Barry 76
John, Elton 43
Johnson, David 69
Johnston, Craig 9
Johnston, Mo 204

Keegan, Kevin 69, 76, 77, 226
Kelly, Graham 30, 40, 46
Kettle, Martin 8
Kingaby case 34
Kings Cross fire 4, 10, 11
Knighton, Michael 11
Knoflicek, Ivo 194
Kubic, Lubos 194
Kumar brothers 171

Lansley, Stewart 19
Leasowe Ladies 101

Leeds United FC 78, 151, 171, 182
Leicester Fosse FC 113
Leicester University 161, 177-80
Leppings Lane (terracing at Hillsborough
    stadium) 3, 4, 7, 8, 9, 14, 15, 20
Leuven University 172, 177
Libertadores Cup 191
Lineker, Gary 43, 77, 78
Littlewoods Cup 37
Liverpool FC 3, 4, 8, 15, 20, 40, 59, 69, 70,
    132, 135, 165-6, 174, 197
Lofthouse, Nat 77
London University 176
London Weekend Television 240
London Zoo 25-6
Lopez, Sue 96
Lotteries Act (1956) 124
Lovejoy, Joe 43
LSD 149, 154
Luton Town FC 134, 140
Lynam, Desmond 235

Mackenzie, Kelvin 223
Madness 147
Madonna 77
Maidstone United FC 197
Major, John 162
Makita International 248
Manageress, The 87
Manchester City FC 59, 192
Manchester Corinthians FC 94
Manchester United FC 18, 37, 40, 43, 52, 67,
    135, 167, 187, 192, 239, 242
Matthews, Stanley 38, 77
Maxwell, Kevin 18
Maxwell, Robert 18, 43, 44, 118, 227, 247
maximum wage 53
McConnell sisters 91
McCormack, Mark 101, 250
McDermott, Terry 77
McDonalds (fast food chain) 46
McElhone Report 102-3
McGregor, William 30, 32, 43
McMahon, Steve 69
McNeil, Billy 236
Mee, Bertie 79
Mercer, Wallace 211-13, 216
Milichip, Bert 30, 230
Millwall FC 100, 182
Millwall Lionesses 100
Minolta Nitra 195
Monroe, Marilyn 77
MTK Budapest FC 196
Murdoch, Rupert 223
Murray, David 203-4, 216

Naples FC 201
National Federation of Football Supporters'
    Clubs 95, 111, 119-24

National Football Intelligence Unit 168
National Front 146, 170–2
National Women's League 102
National Workers' Sports Association 116
Nettleship, Rita 6
Newcastle United FC 76, 79, 89
New Musical Express 149
New Order 156
NFL (US League) 218, 252
Nicol, Steve 69
North East Women's League 91
Nottingham Forest FC 4, 69, 76, 157

Off The Ball 153
Old Etonians FC 27
Olympique Marseilles FC 190
On-U Sound 157
Owen, Syd 77
Oxford United FC 18, 43, 118, 139
Oyston, Vicki 105

Packer, Kerry 242, 250
Parker, Paul 80
Peacock Report 241
Pele 79
Pennant, Cass 160
perestroika 192–3
Phillips, Trevor 41
Piper Alpha disaster 10, 12
Plastica Nitra 195
Plymouth Argyle FC 118
Police and Criminal Evidence Bill 13
Popper, Dr Stefan 15
Popplewell Inquiry 13, 103, 164
Portsmouth FC 94
Port Vale FC 197
Powell, Jeff 41
Preston North End FC 182
Professional Footballers' Association 34, 40,
    181, 250–1
Pullein, Tony 122

Queens Park FC 27
Quixall, Albert 5

Raba Gyor 195
Raith Rovers FC 202
Ramsey, Alf 68, 225
Reading FC 18, 43
Real Madrid FC 174, 190–1
Red Star Belgrade FC 69, 195, 198
Reilly, Rose 98
Rhyl FC 117
Richards, Joe 36–8, 39, 40
Rimet, Jules 39
River Plate FC 191
Roberts, John 39
Robson, Bobby 70–1, 220, 225–37
Robson, Bryan 77

Rock Against Racism 147
Rodean (school) 88
Roeg, Nicholas 148
Rous, Stanley 27–8, 29, 38, 121, 221, 239–40
Rous Cup 249
Royal Engineers FC 28
Rush, Ian 9, 69, 77, 79
Rumbelows Cup 37, 199, 246

Sadler, John 228, 230, 234
Saint and Greavsie 103, 235
Sampdoria FC 197
Sampson, Kevin 153
Sandford, Arthur 44
Scarborough Town FC 243
Scholar, Irving 44
Scottish FA 203, 215
Scottish League 203
Scottish Office 216
Screen Sport 240
Scunthorpe United 76, 133, 141, 197
Seabrook, Jeremy 6
Searchlight 107–3
Selecter, The 147
Sex Discrimination Act (1975) 98
Sham '69 147
Shankly, Bill 154, 220
Sheffield United FC 113, 117
Sheffield Wednesday FC 4, 37, 95, 117, 132
Sherwood, Adrian 156–7
Shilton, Peter 77
Shipman, Len 39
Shoom club 155
Sky TV 241–2
Slavia Prague FC 194
Smith, Pat 105
Smith, Roland 248
Smiths, The 146
Socialist Workers Party 10
Sounds 149
Souness, Graeme 199, 207, 218, 220
Southall, Neville 77
Southampton FC 76, 117
Southend United FC 197
Southern League 52
Sparta Prague FC 195, 198
Specials, The 147
St. Helen's Ladies 92
St. Johnstone FC 141
St. Leonard's School 88
St. Pauli FC 194
Stas, Ivor 199
Steaua Bucharest FC 195
Stoke City FC 30
Storer, Harry 225
Strachan, Gordon 78, 249
Sun, The 9, 19, 76, 223–237
Sunderland FC 135
Super League 197

Sutcliffe, Charles 31–2, 33, 34, 38, 44
Swales, Peter 244

Tapie, Bernard 190
Taylor, Graham 71, 79, 237
Taylor, Gordon 249
Taylor, Mr. Justice (Taylor Report) 3, 4, 7, 13, 14, 16, 17, 20, 104, 116, 130, 197, 214–15, 222
Temporary Hoarding 147
Terrace Talk 153
Thatcher, Margaret 9, 78
Thomas, Russell 41
Thompson, Paul 6
Toshack, John 69
Tottenham Hotspur FC 18, 25, 40, 43–5, 52, 69, 169, 197
Transworld International 101
Trethewy, Spencer 45
Turner, Richard 157
Tyldesley, Clive 157

UEFA 97, 188–92, 198, 203, 214, 216, 246, 250–1, Cup Final 169
United! (BBC2 documentary) 87
United Sports Fans of America 252

Venables, Terry 45
Venglos, Jozef 199
Vigarello, Prof. George 8
Voice of the Valley 133
Volvo 191

Waddle, Chris 72
Wall, Sir Frederick 27–8, 29, 35, 121
Walker, Des 80
Wallsend Slipway Marine 91
Walsall FC 197
Walters, Mark 170
Wanderers FC 27
Wanderers Worldwide 153
Watford FC 18, 43, 79, 120
West Bromwich Albion FC 30
West Ham United FC 157, 167, 171
Westwood, Lord 39
WFA News 100
Wheatley Report (1972) 8
Whelan, Ronnie 69
When Saturday Comes 13, 104, 152
Whitehead, Linda 99
Williams, Raymond, 19
Wilson, Neil 44
Wimbledon FC 84
Wimbush, Doug 157
Winterbottom, Walter 221, 222, 233
Wogan, Terry 45
Wolverhampton Wanderers FC 30, 55
Women's FA 96–7, 99–100
Women's Hockey Association 90
World Cup Finals 1994 192
World Student Games 18
Wrexham FC 118

Yorkshire Post 171

Zavarov, Alexander 194